The Emergence of the Modern Middle East

Selected Readings

The Emergence of the Modern Middle East

Selected Readings

Robert G. Landen
University of South Carolina

VAN NOSTRAND REINHOLD COMPANY

New York   Cincinnati   Toronto   London   Melbourne

Van Nostrand Reinhold Company Regional Offices:
Cincinnati New York Chicago Millbrae Dallas

Van Nostrand Reinhold Company Foreign Offices:
London Toronto Melbourne

Manufactured in the United States of America

Published by Van Nostrand Reinhold Company
450 West 33rd Street, New York, N.Y. 10001

Published simultaneously in Canada by
D. Van Nostrand Company (Canada), Ltd.

10 9 8 7 6 5 4 3 2 1

To Tricia

PREFACE

This book provides a sampling of primary source materials illustrating the course of modernization in the Middle East and North Africa since the late eighteenth century. The work is designed particularly for students who are beginning their studies of modern Middle Eastern history and government. Included are materials that touch upon the recent history of the Arab West—North Africa—the Arab East, the Ottoman empire and its successor Republic of Turkey, and Iran.

The earliest document dates from 1785 and the latest appeared in 1968. The documents have been selected and their introductions prepared with a view to clarifying and exemplifying the reactions of various individuals, groups, and governments in the Middle East to the manifold challenges posed by the civilization of the modern world to the Middle East's peoples. The chapters, although generally arranged according to time sequence, also revolve around a major topical theme. Within some chapters a chronological order is followed while in others the introductions and selections reflect a topical order.

The anthology attempts to present issues from a Middle Eastern perspective. It is concerned only incidentally with treating the basic nature of modern civilization or of the imperial motivations of the various powers—European mainly—that carried aspects of modernism to the Middle East. Interpretive introductory analyses constitute a considerable part of the work; hopefully, these will provide a sense of the main trends of modern Middle Eastern history as well as indicate the chief significance of each individual document within the context of those trends. Finally, an effort was made to provide a fairly comprehensive historiographical "sampler" of the several varieties of source material available to the scholar who deals with the modern Middle East: indigenous and European chronicles, historical essays, newspaper editorials and stories, partisan tracts, official state papers, constitutions, speeches, decrees, travel accounts, memoirs, treaties, sociological studies, economic analyses, and political poetry are all represented.

Translations generally are by the editor unless otherwise noted or unless it is from an old publication which did not list the name of the translator. No attempt has been made to modify transliterations of Middle Eastern words as they appear in the original, although the editor has employed a consistent, simplified transliteration system in the introductions.

In any large compilation, an editor owes much to the prior labors and co-operation of many scholars, writers, and publishers as well as to the aid of various libraries and their staff. I wish to record my particular debt to Professor George Grassmuck, of the University of Michigan, who was going to be co-editor of this work until the mounting pressures of a vice-presidential post at Michigan forced his reluctant retirement from the project; as it stands, however, the compilation reflects many of Professor Grassmuck's ideas. Also, Professor Don Peretz, of the State University of New York at Binghamton, read the entire manuscript at one stage and offered a number of invaluable suggestions, which have been incorporated into the work. Special thanks to Dr. Alan W. Horton and the American Universities Field Staff for Document 56b. The patience and industry of Mrs. Carolyn Price Alls and Mrs. Becky Brown as well as the aid of Mrs. Malinda Burch, Mrs. Judy Jones, and Miss Patricia Williams in typing the manuscript is gratefully acknowledged. This work also reflects the criticisms of several generations of students at the University of Michigan, Dartmouth College, and Virginia Polytechnic Institute who contributed much to this volume. The University of Michigan Asia Studies Committee and the Research Division of Virginia Polytechnic Institute provided secretarial and other assistance to the editor at various stages in this book's maturation. Finally, I wish to thank the person to whom this book is dedicated—and her allies, Michael, Bobby, Jill and Amy—for allowing me to litter her home with bits and pieces of manuscript and assorted scholarly paraphernalia.

R.G.L.

Blacksburg, Virginia

CONTENTS

3

Defense Modernization: The Intellectual Phase   82

4

Imposed Modernization: Imperialism as a Vehicle for Change   144

PART TWO: Seeking a Reorganized Society

5

World War I and Political Reorientation   183

6

Assertions of National Identity   211

7

PART ONE:

An Awakening Awareness of Modern Civilization

1

The Intrusion of the Modern World Into the Middle East

By the late eighteenth century the Middle East was suffering from the effects of three centuries of decline. The deterioration of the region's once imposing civilization, a process still only imperfectly understood by scholars, appeared all the more striking when contrasted with the situation in Europe, which, during the centuries of Middle Eastern stagnation, invigorated itself through the combined influences of the Renaissance, the creation of maritime empires, the scientific revolution, and a rapid build-up in its economic, military, and political capabilities. In the late eighteenth century this modern, dynamic Europe began to expand into the Middle East in an explosive fashion.

The most formidable state in the Middle East during the late 1700's, the empire of the Ottoman Turks, was a sprawling crescent shaped mass enveloping the eastern Mediterranean region. The Ottoman Empire itself was divided into three parts: the predominant Slavic and Orthodox Christian Balkans; the Turkish Muslim heartland of the empire—Anatolia; and the Arab provinces in Syria, also Muslim for the most part. Legally part of the Ottoman realm but actually autonomous were Iraq, Egypt, and North Africa as far west as Morocco. The second major division in the Middle East, the Iranian plateau, was partitioned between Persia in the west and several tribal principalities in Afghanistan in the east; these countries often had shared some political unity in the past. A third main division in the region consisted of a huge triangle of loosely organized tribal territory in the Arabian peninsula and Syrian desert.

3

Although these several areas differed in many respects each was a variety of the same basic civilization. All Middle Easterners shared in a heritage of institutions and culture thousands of years old. The complex of traditions associated with the Islamic faith although variously interpreted, transcended all political frontiers. At the more mundane level the unity of the region was expressed by the fact that about eighty-five percent of the Middle East's people were supported directly by agriculture. While a fraction of the population consisted of nomadic herders and city dwellers, the average Middle Easterner of 1800 was a peasant toiling in an isolated, self-sufficient agricultural village. But, for the most part, agriculture was not prospering; most farming, based upon a technology essentially unchanged since Neolithic times, was subsistence activity. Meanwhile, large tracts of potential cropland lay uncultivated.

Cities, once ornaments of Middle Eastern civilization, were suffocating. Many erstwhile thriving centers had reached a point where they were little more than local market towns. This situation was one of the ultimate results of the opening in 1498 of direct sea communications between Europe, and South and East Asia via the around-Africa, Cape of Good Hope route, an event which diverted trade previously directed through the Middle East. Prior to 1500 the flow of long-distance commerce had strengthened the entire fabric of Middle Eastern civilization: governments derived revenue from taxing this commerce, the merchant community derived profit from distributing it, and artisans derived a living from processing it. But these groups, the area's cities, and the economy of the region in general suffered increasingly after 1500 as the flow of trade passing through the Middle East was choked off. By 1800 only a fluctuating, slackening regional trade was left. Artisans in cities like Cairo were relegated to serving a regional market after Middle Eastern goods lost their old place in world trade. Moreover, some old technological skills disappeared between 1500 and 1800. Nevertheless, the artisans' guilds retained their restrictive grip over handicraft occupations in the cities. The new technology pioneered in Europe was not used since it was expensive and there was a real psychological block against "infidel" European practices. Consequently, as economic depression spread, the Middle East fell back upon its basic, locally oriented, agrarian economy. Much of the cloth, hardware, and pottery used in the region was produced locally by villagers. Ties of economic interdependence were weak in the Middle East of 1800.

Accompanying these ills was financial chaos. Unlike Western Europe, the Middle East had not learned to cope with the financial revolution caused by the dumping of rich lodes of American gold and silver into the world economy during the sixteenth century. Inflation and an uncertain currency were still unsolved headaches for Middle Eastern merchants and government treasurers in 1800.

Spreading economic depression was accompanied by accelerating political breakdown. In the realm of international relations and in terms of political and military power the various Middle Eastern central governments were in a dangerous position by the late eighteenth century. They had retained essentially medieval military organizations and had not adopted many of the post-Renaissance advances in military science which had revolutionized Europe's armed forces. Thus the region was vulnerable to outside coercion.

Military weakness, however, only mirrored the generally debased capabilities— even when measured by pre-modern standards—of Middle Eastern central governments in 1800. Traditionally, Middle Eastern rulers had been concerned primarily with military and police matters, more specifically with raising the revenues and troops to sustain an effective military capability and with maintaining an orderly equilibrium among the several groups which composed society as a whole. As in medieval Europe, rulers felt little need to provide for their subjects' personal, social, or economic welfare. Since the eleventh century most Middle Eastern governments had been organized in a peculiar feudal pattern. Theoretically the various states in the region were the personal property of the ruler, who was assisted in governing this huge landed estate by military retainers and bureaucrats. On the local level the sovereign's writ was loosely enforced by a fief (*timar*) holder who derived his living by raising men and money for his own and for his ruler's use. Unlike medieval Europe, feudalism, as long as it was strong in the Middle East, effectively buttressed the area's central governments. But by 1800, the once efficient feudal system had decayed to the point where it produced more disorder than order, more corruption than revenue. The power of central rulers decreased as their armies and bureaucracies rusted. Offices once bestowed according to an individual's merit were sold to the highest bidder. In the absence of strong central and provincial rule by imperial authorities, the function of providing order and law increasingly devolved upon the remnants of the fief holder class and upon other masters of locally based power. More and more, decisions were made at the local level at the expense of centralized administration. Although sultans and shahs theoretically held sway over vast domains their empire actually were broken into a mosaic of semi-autonomous communities.

Consequently, localism, communalism, and family loyalties, which always had vied with the more universalistic tendencies in Middle Eastern civilizations, were particularly strong at the end of the eighteenth century. In many ways, the center of gravity in the region lay in the localities and the separate religious communities, not in the large empires. While it was true that the larger aspects of regional and imperial politics were the main concern of the small ruling elite, the important problems to most Middle Easterners of 1800 were local ones. The horizon of the average Middle Easterner was restricted to his family and local community, a small closely knit body which combined economic, political, social, and religious functions. Most Middle Easterners lived and died without leaving their birthplace. In the countryside the agricultural village, the nomadic tribe, or the family itself was the basic unit; in cities the primary units were again the family as well as the several occupational guilds. Tribes, villages, and guilds largely regulated their own immediate affairs, relying heavily upon local folk custom to guide their decisions. Except when they exchanged goods and services, the separate communities had little to do with one another. They existed in a situation of delicate, constantly shifting balance with each other. A headman served as community spokesman in dealings with the imperial or other outside authorities. It was he who was held responsible by the imperial ruling elite for his community's conduct and the delivery of taxes. Also, a point of contact between community and central authority was the local religious scholar who provided for spiritual and educational needs and who served as judge in questions of personal law.

Indeed, in the late eighteenth century it was religion which, in a parochial sense, and in the absence of strong central rule, provided the cement which held together the mosaic of localities which formed Middle Eastern society. Although Muslim, Christian, and Jewish communities were largely segregated from one another, religion did bind together scattered communities of similar faith. Religious dignitaries and their local representatives were responsible for administering the particular law of each faith among their co-religionists. Thus there were several religiously based legal systems regulating such things as marriage, inheritance, and divorce which existed side by side and which guided the various religious communities and Muslim personal law was not imposed upon Christians and Jews.

As long as loyalty, taxes, and an occasional fighting man were provided, the provincial and imperial authorities were content to leave the localities alone. In the final analysis, the effective allegiance of the average Middle Easterner was given to his family, local community, and religion rather than to the ruler or his provincial representative.

The deterioration of the economic, political, and social cohesion of medieval Middle Eastern civilization so apparent by the late eighteenth century was paralleled by a loss of vitality in the area's intellectual life which once was one of the most vital and innovative in the world. The pre-modern culture of the Middle East was permeated by religion and by superstitions often associated with religion. Although most Middle Easterners were Muslims, the practitioners of Islam were divided into many sects, as were the Christians and, to some extent, the Jewish minorities. The area's religious leaders were intellectual leaders as well. The religious-scholar class was small but influential. Unfortunately, by 1800 most in this group no longer displayed the dynamism and originality characteristic of their work in earlier times. But religion, although dominated by ritual and superstition, had a strong hold on all Middle Easterners whatever their creed. Intellectual activity usually consisted of things such as memorizing religious works like the Koran or of commenting uopn writings by authors long dead. Most of the savants of the time were deeply attached to their traditional culture and viewed innovation, particularly borrowings from the West, as suspect, scandalous or even sacrilegious. Most formal education was conducted in schools whose curriculum was weighted almost entirely toward religious study and virtually the only higher education available was conducted in theological seminaries. Although the writings of religious scholars were read by only a minuscule audience (even in towns it was very rare if ten percent of the population were literate), preaching and story-telling were effective means of reaching the masses.

There was a polarization in the area's cultural and religious traditions between a local orientation on one hand and an imperial or regional orientation on the other. For instance, although Islam was the religion of most Middle Easterners there was a real difference between the official state versions of Islam proclaimed by the rulers and the Islam practiced by the mass of the people. On the local level Islam often incorporated folk traditions peculiar to a community. If a village happened to be Christian, a Christian veneer was spread over local folk practices. Among Muslims, folk Islam was strengthened by widespread attachment to *sufi* orders. These orders combined religious functions with the social, and sometimes even the economic, functions of fraternities or social clubs. Their elaborate rituals, often institutionalized in a disguised fashion, localized folk beliefs. In 1800 the many local variations of Near Eastern culture and religion were flourishing and during the nineteenth and twentieth centuries these local cultural traditions were going to be especially resistant to change and modernization.

On the regional and imperial level, on the other hand, the tone of intellectual life deteriorated alarmingly during the eighteenth century. Superstition occupied the place once held by knowledge during the time of medieval Islam's greatness. Probably the most tragic part of the picture was the fact that few persons in the region, from sultans down to the meanest peasants, realized how sick their civilization was. Middle Easterners still were convinced that their civilization was and would continue to be superior to any other in the world.

When one turns to the several divisions which together form the Middle East, although details differ considerably, the essential similarity of their common plight is apparent:

The general decline of Middle Eastern medieval civilization did not spare the Ottoman Empire, one of the world's great powers until the eighteenth century. But by 1760 that once magnificent state presented a faded picture of its former glory. Certainly one major factor in the Ottoman decline was deterioration of the intellectual vitality of the empire's political and cultural leadership. Problems were avoided, or worse yet, not even recognized, rather than confronted as in the days before 1700. The sultan himself was, in too many respects, a prisoner of inaction, ceremony, seclusion, and unscrupulous or ignorant advisors. His writ did not count for much outside Istanbul, some agricultural areas near the capital, and a few provincial fortresses and urban centers. Much of the administrative apparatus from the sultanship down to obscure village judgeships was rusty from corruption, inefficiency, and neglect. Entire provinces were virtually autonomous, held by local dynasts, the *a'yan,* who were nominally vassals of the sultan. Thus, many of the pashaliks of Anatolia, Syria, and the Balkans, not to mention those in North Africa, delivered but token taxes and token obedience; Egypt and Iraq were dominated by near independent Mamluk oligarchies. Oftentimes an Ottoman governor seemed more the sultan's ambassador than his viceroy in an imperial province. In the largely Christian Balkan provinces of the Ottoman's separatist stirrings, stimulated in part by clerics, were abroad and destined to break out in open rebellion in Serbia and Greece in the first decades of the nineteenth century. The imperial standing army—the Janissaries and other units which had been the scourge of early modern Europe—was an unreliable pressure group, an ill-led, untrained rabble which collected its salaries but squandered money meant for munitions and spent its days in business and trade. The feudal militia—which supplied the bulk of the army in wartime—was more a threat to public order than a shield of the empire whenever a sultan was rash enough to order full mobilization. The once formidable navy consisted mainly of badly maintained, waterlogged ships unable in many instances to move from dockside. The advanced decay of Ottoman military power was partially obscured until the 1770's because the attention of most European powers was monopolized by challenges closer to home. Nevertheless, the 1700's witnessed some cautious, tentative borrowings by a small clique of Ottoman aristocrats from European fashions and from European military science. What is more, despite the gloomy prospects for the future, the Ottoman Empire still could count upon the basic intelligence and love of country of the best of its ruling class.

The picture was no more encouraging in the Arab-inhabited parts of the Middle East. Since the year 1250 A.D. Egypt's destinies had been ruled by a military aristocracy derived from the slave bodyguard of former rulers of the country. Until 1517 the slaves (Mamluks) maintained an independent regime in Egypt with one of their own number serving as sultan. The Mamluks were representative of the pre-modern military class in the Middle East as well as of those local magnates, who actually ruled much of the region in the late eighteenth century. To be a warrior required physical strength, years of training, and continued practice. The use of bows and swords as well as the control of war horses were not skills to be learned in a day or even a few months. Peasants, for instance, were relatively useless in pre-modern Eastern armies because they were unpracticed in the military arts. Armies throughout the area were manned in large part by members of a distinct military caste. Even in leisure, members of this caste spent their time hunting, riding, and perfecting their skill with various weapons. The Mamluk beys formed an awesome mounted force supported by their apprentices who operated on foot. Each bey was maintained by revenues derived from landed estates assigned to him. The individual bey normally had little interest in his estate outside of milking it for all it could provide and so he would delegate its management to an agent who was, in effect, the voice of the central authority in a given rural locality. In 1517 the last independent Mamluk sultan was defeated by the Ottomans and Egypt became a dependency of Istanbul. Although they suffered some tribulations during the initial stage of Ottoman occupation, it was not long until the Mamluks regained most of their old privileges. By the late eighteenth century the Ottoman hold was so loose that some of the great Mamluk beys (notably 'Ali Bey) openly asserted their independence. At that time an estimated 20,000 Mamluks shared the rule and the riches of Egypt. As a group they were divided into constantly shifting, constantly bickering factions who would cooperate *en masse* only to protect their position against outside intervention. The fact that these political and personal wrangles monopolized the attention of the ruling clique meant that the Egyptian people suffered not so much from anarchy as they did from the disinterest and static posture of their rulers.

Iraq, too, was dominated by a similar Mamluk regime in the eighteenth century. Meanwhile, political power in Syria was contested by a melange of locally oriented feudal lords including officers of Ottoman military units stationed in the area, sundry tribal magnates, and the *ashraf*—an urban Arab nobility descended from the Prophet. These contended with one another to dominate various of Syria's towns and districts. Once in power, the feudal lords were left alone by their nominal Ottoman overlords in return for token military support and tribute payments. Culturally and economically Syria shared the general decline experienced by the Ottoman empire after the sixteenth century. Population plummeted—especially so in rural areas: the French traveller, Volney, gave some indication of this when he estimated that of the roughly 3200 taxable villages in the vilayet of Aleppo at the start of Ottoman rule only 400 remained by the 1780's. And if cities such as Aleppo still retained some commerce in 1800, an increasing share of it flowed through the hands of those with close ties to European merchant houses. While the intellectual life of the region was not thriving, the wall of ignorance which shut off Syria from real knowledge of other civilizations, especially of Enlightenment Europe, was beginning to sustain some dents because of the activity of Catholic missionaries among Syria's large Christian minorities.

Doubtless, the most primitive part of the Arab Middle East was Arabia. Wresting a living from the harsh environment of the peninsula or from the waters of its surrounding seas was a task that left little surplus time or wealth to support activity in the arts or in learned speculation. The herding of camels and other livestock on the desert, the cultivation of date palms and grain in the oases, and the harvesting of fish, pearls, and trade profits on the seas were the mainstays of Arabia's people. Political power was wielded by a myriad of independent Bedouin tribes and confederations or by oasis and seaport city-states. The intense continual competition among the several towns and tribes stimulated a climate of constant disorder and warfare. One observer not inaccurately compared this situation to that which existed among the ancient Greek city-states. But out of this disorder emerged the beginnings of the political configuration which has characterized the Arabian peninsula since the eighteenth century. In the Hijaz, that part of western Arabia adjacent to the holy cities of Mecca and Medina, the Ottoman sultans retained sovereignty although the resident Sharifs of Mecca exercised de facto rule. Yemen, the relatively populous southwest corner of Arabia, remained under the sway of its ancient line of imams. Along eastern Arabia's shore a number of new political entities appeared. In 1749 the still reigning Al Bu Sa'id dynasty assumed power in Muscat and Oman. In the years following, other dynasties of Bedouin origin established a string of still-surviving maritime oriented city-states along Arabia's Persian Gulf shore from Kuwayt in the north to the Trucial States in the south. By all odds the most important of the new creations which appeared in Arabia during the eighteenth century was the so-called Wahhabi or Sa'udi state which sprang up in the central Arabian province of Najd. Based upon an alliance between a new puritanical reformist version of Islam as preached by the religious scholar Muhammad ibn 'Abd al-Wahhab (1703-1787) and the political strength controlled by the Sa'udi family, this state expanded rapidly. By 1800 it threatened to forcibly unify the entire Arabian peninsula and even to expand into Syria and Iraq. Indeed, some scholars argue that the appearance of Wahhabism, marked as it was by a determination to halt the decline of the Islamic world and to reform it from within, signals the beginning of modern Middle Eastern history.

North Africa, a mixed Arab-Berber area, had been something of a cultural backwater ever since Islam had been driven off the Iberian peninsula at the end of the fifteenth century. Indeed, both the Spanish and the Portuguese versions of the *Reconquista* spilled over into North Africa as the two kingdoms carved out territorial footholds for themselves on the African coast. For a time in the sixteenth and seventeenth centuries the Ottomans tried to rescue the region. A string of Ottoman military governorates commanded by officers who held the title "bey" were established in various North Africa's ports from Benghazi and Tripoli in Libya, Tunis in Tunisia, to Algiers and Oran in Algeria. But the North African beys by the eighteenth century were entirely autonomous of Istanbul. Nevertheless, the beys' rule never extended far into the countryside where the tribal factions held unruly sway. The beys continued the tradition of earlier North African Muslim rulers by waging a more or less constant war against the European Christian powers pressing in upon them. Ports such as Algiers and Tripoli sheltered fleets of privateers which preyed upon unwary European shipping. By the end of the eighteenth century, however, Western maritime states—among them the young United States—were maintaining powerful naval squadrons in North African waters to counter the North African seamen. The Ottomans never succeeded in establishing themselves in Morocco. During the eighteenth century something of a political revival occurred in that westernmost of Arab lands under the 'Alawi dynasty. This was stimulated by a powerful religious and political self-awareness. On one hand it was expressed by the integrating role played by the Sharifian monarchs of the 'Alawi family who were regarded as caliphs—"commanders of the faithful"—by their people and who became symbols of Moroccan particularism. In another way it was expressed in a political expansionism which extended Morocco's borders hundreds of miles southward to the Niger River. Still, internally Morocco's rulers had the constant task of trying to ease the tensions that existed within a population divided among tribal Berbers and settled Arabs. Thus, nowhere in the Middle East's western borderlands was there an environment of settled order.

One could make the same statement about the Middle East's eastern borderlands of Iran and Afghanistan. In Iran the establishment of the Qajar dynasty in 1794 arrested three quarters of a century of civil war, economic depression, and cultural decay. In 1722 the stagnant but once brilliant Safavid monarchy was toppled by an Afghan attack. Militarily astute but politically and culturally unsophisticated, the Afghans were unable to organize their new possession and Persia fell into anarchy, its wealth and resources wasted by a succession of would-be heirs to the Safavid imperial tradition. For a time it appeared that a military genius, Nadir Quli Khan (1732-1747) who proclaimed himself Nadir Shah in 1736, would restore Iran's greatness. A great conqueror in the tradition of Timurlane and Genghis Khan, Nadir temporarily restored Iran's unity and even sacked the cities of northern India. But after an assassin had ended Nadir's meteoric career it was obvious that he had been more a destroyer than a builder and had left Iran impoverished by his wars and in a far weaker state than he had found it. Numbers of quarrelsome local dynasties tried to fill the vacuum. The most promising of these dynasties was one founded by Karim Khan Zand (1750-1779) who, using Shiraz as his capital, subdued much of south and central Iran. Under Karim Khan a restoration of economic and cultural strength occurred but the weakness of the later Zand rulers signalled a return to instability.

Finally, the Qajars, a tribe of Turkoman descent long settled in northeast Iran, succeeded in conquering all Persia in the late eighteenth century. The first Qajar shah, the eunuch Aqa Muhammad (1794-1797), chose the small road-junction city of Teheran in north-central Iran as Persia's capital. Aqa Muhammad Shah, an energetic, stern monarch, was succeeded after his assassination by his nephew, Fath Ali Shah, (1797-1834) after having bequeathed an ideal for the new Qajar empire to realize: the reestablishment of a strong Iranian empire of a medieval variety. Politically the empire was organized on a feudal basis. Persia was treated as a huge personal estate by the shah; members of the royal family were invested as governors of the great provinces or as high officials of the state; other supporters of the dynasty were given estates from which they were to draw revenue and soldiers. The shahs also supported a revival of traditional Persian culture led by the Shi'ah muslim religious-scholar class. This policy, completely medieval in its outlook would have been a good one for the Iran of 1600. Indeed, in some ways the early Qajars were trying to recreate the Iran of 1600 in that they wished to restore the country to the levels it had reached at the height of the Safavid empire (1504-1722). Unfortunately for Iran the backward-looking policy of the early Qajars proved totally inadequate for the times. The policy failed once Iran became involved in the opening thrusts of European and Russian imperialism. But between 1794 and 1828 the Qajar monarchs refused to abandon the dreams on which their dynasty was founded.

This then was the Middle East at the end of the eighteenth century: weak, decaying, somnolent, but still ignorantly sure of itself. The great shock which awakened the region from the lethargy which gripped it was provided by a series of disastrous military defeats inflicted by Western European and Russian arms upon the Ottoman Turks, the leading powers of the Arab world, and the Persians between 1768 and 1844. Traditional Middle Eastern civilization, already rotten by internal decay, was struck from without by powerful armed forces, the heralds of a forthcoming invasion by European or European-inspired economic interests, politicians, as well as cultural and intellectual innovators. The defeats began to undermine the confidence of the Middle Eastern ruling classes in the established order. Indeed, in Egypt the ruling class was destroyed. Even before this period of invasion was over, the usefulness of certain institutions associated with the old order was being questioned and in some cases was undergoing actual alteration.

Twice the Ottoman army was mauled by foreign troops. Between 1768 and 1774 the Russians overwhelmed the Ottoman levies. Only a massive peasant rising in Russia and apprehensions concerning moves by her European rivals prompted Catherine the Great to call off her attack. Catherine struck again in 1787, to be joined the year following by the armies of Joseph II of Austria. A series of Austro-Russian victories conjured up an image of the imminent fall of the Ottoman Empire. The sultan was saved, however, by the outbreak of the French Revolution which diverted the two powers back to continental politics. Both of these wars clearly demonstrated the weakness of the antiquated Ottoman military-administrative system. One reason that the sultan survived the period was because of a deadlock among the European powers on how to partition his empire without disturbing the delicate European power balance. It was the continuation of this deadlock which enabled the Ottoman Empire to survive another century and a quarter.

Next, the Arab inhabited Middle East was awakened by the drums of Europe's armies. Between 1798 and 1801 Egypt and Palestine endured invasion and occupation by Napoleon's troops. The French occupation drew Egypt into the arena of modern world affairs and hopelessly shattered the established order. The forces of traditionalism, best represented by the Mamluks, were never able to restore their hegemony over the country. In other parts of the Arab world, the British neutralized the naval power of the several Arab principalities of the Persian Gulf and by 1820 they had strongly asserted their paramountcy in that area. A decade later, in 1830, the French toppled the autonomous Beylik of Algiers and then in 1844 crushed a combined Moroccan-Algerian army at Isli. France's 130-year period of colonial hegemony over al-Maghrib—the Arab West—had begun.

The Iranians did not escape the fate of their Ottoman and Arab neighbors. Between 1804 and 1812 the Persian cavalry armies were gradually ground down by Russian infantry and artillery. The fighting in Iran was restricted to Iran's northeast provinces in the Caucasus and in Azarbayjan. Yet with the Caucasus wall breached, Iran, after 1813, woke up to the fact that she would have to live with a hungry bear as a close neighbor. A romantic attempt to reverse the defeat of 1813 and recover the lost provinces was undertaken at the instigation of some of the Shah's backward-looking advisors in 1826. But Russian troops by 1828 completely smashed Iran's military power and her self-image of great power status.

Thus, the Middle East's introduction to modern civilization was a violent one. The implications of this have had a profound influence upon the course and nature of subsequent encounters of the Middle East with modernism.

1

Self-Delusions on the Eve of Disaster, a Persian Chronicler's View of Iran Under the Early Qajars *

The following selection is an example of the highly ornamented style of historiography typical of Islam's medieval period in the Middle East, a writing style which lasted well into the nineteenth century. Part **A.** of the selection describes the coronation of Fath Ali Shah (1797-1834), an event which occurred at a time when the Russians were beginning to probe into the Caucasus provinces of the Qajar Empire. The selection, however, betrays no sense of foreboding, only a generally self-satisfied if romantic view of Persia's relative place in terms of the realities of the world's international power situation in the late eighteenth century. Like its prose, the attitude expressed in the excerpt is permeated by essentially medieval concepts. Fath Ali Shah is presented as "the world-nourishing king," a monarch without an equal on earth. But like most Middle Eastern monarchs of pre-modern times, Fath Ali Shah was faced with the problem of asserting actual control over his kingdom once he was proclaimed its legal head. The account in part **B.** shows that as late as 1803, six years after his coronation, Fath Ali Shah had yet to establish his control over all Iran. The selec-

* 'Abd al-Razzaq ibn Najaf Quli Khan Dunbuli, *Ma'athir-i-Sultaniyah* (Tabriz, 1826), tr. by Sir H. Brydges, *The Dynasty of the Kajars* (London: J. Bahn, 1833), 41-43, 155-159.

tion is significant too, in its depiction of the military methods which prevailed among the Persians as late as the nineteenth century. Since ancient times, Persia's chief military reliance was its fine irregular cavalry largely supplied by tribal levies. The "armour-clad, mountain-strength, rock-cleaving, tiger-seizing" army of Fath Ali Shah also was this type of force.

A. THE CORONATION OF FATH ALI SHAH, 1797

In the spring of the year of the Crocodile, 1212 of the Hejira [A.D. 1797], when the world-illuminating sun proceeded in majesty from the dark chamber of Pisces to the portico of Aries, and delightful verdure budded forth from the river-bank like the musk-coloured locks of youths beautiful as the Moon; . . . then the mighty sovereign, dignified as Jamshid, whose court is elevated as the sky— (May the piebald courser of the sphere ever continue obedient! and may the desire of both worlds, entertained by his victorious majesty, be ever accomplished with the greatest rapidity!)—conferred ornament on the jewel-embossed crown, by placing it on his head, elevated as the constellation Ursa. The golden diadem of the Sun in the apex of the sky, on beholding this, flamed with envy, and thus exclaimed: "Would to Heaven that I could change place with that diadem! then might I have the honour to encircle the brows of the magnificent monarch; then might I cover the head of the world-nourishing king."—In the hour predestined, and when the fortunate conjunction arrived, this unequalled sovereign placed his hands on the throne of absolute dominion, rested his sublime foot on the seat of splendor, and reclined his head on the pillow of prosperity: and the Angel, the announcer of glad tidings, conveyed this news of security and safety to the ears of all, both young and old.

The haughty nobles of remote regions, and the rulers of the world, on beholding their bosoms and shoulders adorned with robes, splendid as the sun, from the wardrobe of the sovereign whose slave is Heaven, immediately placed on their necks the chains of submission with the collar of obedience, bore on their shoulders the yoke of devotedness and allegiance, and rubbed on their eyelashes the dust of the splendid vestibule. [i.e. Several nobles received robes of honor, ed.] With excelling sincerity, pure attachment, and devotedness, they exclaimed: "May this desirable accession be blessed and happy"! . . . The extent of the fortunate hall of audience witnessed the salutations and embraces of the princes of the various kingdoms. In front of the portico, sublime as the Seventh Heaven, were displayed strings of precious stones, taken from the custody of the imperial treasurer: one might suppose that the rubies of brilliant water were fixed stars and planets, torn from the stratum of the firmament: the numerous heaps of dirhams and dinars [coins of gold and silver, ed.], brought out from the exchequer of the world-possessing sovereign, one might imagine to be blossoms and leaves of flowers, which had been scattered on every side by the agitation of the vernal winds: the Ghoolams [court page boys, ed.], with sun-like cheeks, in presenting gold and jewels, seemed to empty the ocean and the mine, and filled the pockets and sleeves of those admitted to the royal audience: whilst those who kissed the ground of the royal court were, by the auspicious favour and smiles of the king, the asylum of the world, raised in glory to the zenith of the heavens."

B. FATH ALI SHAH ASSERTS HIS CONTROL OVER THE PROVINCE OF KHURASAN, 1803

At this period [1803] the friend-cherishing, enemy-consuming sovereign, like the great luminary on the throne of Aries, or the expanded rose on its emerald-coloured seat, reposed on his Jamshid-like throne: whilst the Princes, resembling full moons, with the arrangement of the Pleiades, and the highly dignified Ameers, in the order of the stars, stood around, in front of the celestial assembly; harvests of gold and silver, with munificent hands, were liberally poured over all; and from the wardrobe of the beneficent sovereign, splendid dresses, proportioned to their several ranks, were thrown over the breasts and shoulders of the nobles. For the purpose of arranging the important affairs of every part of the empire, the crescent-shaped falchion, the key to victory over the seven climates, adorned the king's waist; and with liberal hands, like the rain-pouring clouds, he conferred wealth on the triumphant armies. He then, with the determination of subduing the remainder of Khorasan [a northeastern province of Iran, ed.], displayed his energetic banner, powerful as the sun. In the first place, he ordered, previous to the march of the world-overpowering train, his uncle's son, Ibrahim Khan, dignified as Bahman, to proceed a few days in advance of the victorious troops, with 10,000 infantry and cavalry, all armour-clad, mountain-strength, rock-cleaving, tiger-seizing warriors, each a bastion of flint when halting, each an ocean billow when moving to chastise the rebels of Nishaboor. On the 17th of Muharram, the planet-attended sovereign, in an hour of blessed influence and auspicious omen, like that when lovers meet, placed his foot in the crescent-shaped stirrup, and with the determination of proceeding to Khorasan, the knot was untied from the waving tresses of the victorious standard. In order to muster his cavalry, he pitched the triumphant tents for a few days in the plain of Radakan: here Ishak Khan Karaby, and Jaaffer Khan Biyat, governor of Nishaboor, received honour and splendor from kissing the threshold of the royal tent. Allah Yar Khan also, with Ibrahim Khan Shad Lu governor of Asfarain, Ameer Guneh Khan, governor of Khabushan, and other nobles of Khorasan, in the discharge of the rules of devotedness and the performance of duty, stood under the shade of the banner powerful as the sun, and listened with respectful attention to the king's commands.

The prime minister, Suleiman Khan, was commended, along with Husain Khan Kuller Agasy, to reduce the Fort of Chenaran: the fortunate prince Muhammed Aly Mirza was detached, in conjunction with Ishak Khan Karaby Sardar, and a body of troops selected from the intrepid combatants in the field of battle, toward the Holy district [Meshed, ed.]. The world-subduing train, with a multitude of blood-shedding lions and ocean-like crocodiles, moved towards Meshed the Holy. On Monday, the 9th of Rabi-ul-Awwal, the exterior of Meshed was encompassed by the soldiers of the asylum of victory. Through the devastation and ravages committed by the intrepid Turks [Shah's troops, ed.], the bright world became enveloped with gloom in the sight of Nadir Mirza, and of those besieged within the fortifications of calamity and affliction: through the protracted blockade, the fire of scarcity and famine blazed on high, so that their state became desperate; and the most acute anguish pierced to the very marrow, when the sublimity of erudition, the intelligence of philosophy and jurisprudence, Mirza Muhammed Mehdy of Meshed, the lord of the learned, the practical theorist, turned his face to the threshold founded in justice, to intercede for the poor and helpless inhabitants of Meshed the Holy. In the sovereign's Paradise-resembling court he humbly presented a request for the liberation of the famished people from the misery of the blockade.... It was besides evident in his majesty's enlightened mind, that if the fort of the holy territory should be taken by storm, then the men and women of the district, now enjoying tranquility under the shadow of the Eighth Imam's protection, would become the prey of his blood-shedding warriors, or the sport of his intrepid Turks. Consequently, from the dictates of pure mercy, the king accepted the intercession of this pure sage; ... His majesty also conferred on Husayn Khan Kajar Kullar Agasy, the sardarship of Khorasan, in addition to the government of Nishaboor. The victorious standard was then put in motion, in the direction of Teheran, the capital, and during some days the king gave himself up to the pleasures of the chase in Chesmeh Aly.... His Highness, Prince Muhammed Aly Mirza gave delightful banquets, and presented suitable offerings to his majesty.

2

A European Account
of the Ottoman-Russian War
# of 1768-1774 *

Baron DeTott, a Hungarian-born artillery officer of French nationality, was one of a small group of Europeans who, during the eighteenth century, served as advisors to Ottoman officials. Unfortunately, neither the num-

* Baron DeTott, tr. from the French, *Memoirs of Baron DeTott containing the state of the Turkish Empire and the Crimea during the late war with Russia* (London: printed for G. G. J. and J. Robinson, 1785), II, part three, 4-6, 9-15, 23-29, 202-203.

ber of influential Ottoman officers sympathetic to borrowing from the West nor the number of European advisors was sufficient to bring any basic changes or to halt the drift and decay rampant in the sultan's domains. This was tragically reflected in the fact that the Ottomans threw into action an army still organized in the traditional medieval style to face the guns of Russia's modern military machine in the War of 1768-1774. In that conflict Catherine the Great's army and navy smashed one Ottoman force after another. The sad realities of the situation were further impressed upon the Ottoman leaders by the humiliating peace treaty they signed at Küçük Kaynarca in 1774. Not only Christian-inhabited lands in the Balkans, but also the Muslim-populated Crimea was given up. The Ottoman Forces described by DeTott represented in many ways other contemporary Middle Eastern military aggregations. They used methods and equipment strikingly similar to those used by the Muslim warriors who fought the Crusaders centuries earlier. The course of the Ottoman-Russian War of 1768-1774 was typical in its essentials of many other clashes fought between Middle Eastern and European troops during the succeeding decades. Brave charges were no match for modern weapons, training, and organization.

*   *   *

The Katty-Cherif (or Imperial Mandate) by which it [i.e., war, ed.] was proclaimed, conceived in the usual form, invited all True-believers, able to bear arms, to unite under the Standard of the Faith to combat its Enemies. This Kind of Convocation, by Arrier-ban, promised a numerous Army, but it was far from promising an army composed of good Troops. Ignorance and Avarice rather chose to assemble this Multitude of Volunteers, who were not to be provided for after the War, than to employ the Janissaries, whose pay and demands would be continually increasing. It may likewise be presumed, that the Grand Seignior [the Sultan, ed.], fearing to restore to this Corps the power of which his Father had been the Victim, wished only to make use of it as an addition to his Forces.

The most essential, though at the same time least expected, inconvenience, was the absolute want of foresight with regard to Provisions. It is the nature of Despotism continually to flatter itself, that Authority will supply the place of Prudence. The Grand Visir commanded the Army, all the Ministers accompanied him: even the Registers of the Chancery followed in his Train. No doubt was entertained either of Success or Plenty; and this blind Confidence was general....

Emin-Pacha, without any talents necessary for the Post, either of Visir or General, blinded by self-love, believed he could preserve the one without Danger, and fill the other with Glory, and finish the War before it was well begun. His Army, continually increased by the accession of Fanatick Mussulmen, soon became the most dangerous Enemy of the Empire. The want of Provisions, the disorder of this famished Multitude, the Pillage which attended distribution, and the Murder which followed, an authority always weak, and always despised when the administration is evidently vicious, mutually conspired to render an alteration necessary. The Grand Seignior, who, alone, really interested himself in the Success of his Army, dispatched, to the Visir, an order for some new Regulations. Emin-Pacha had the Audacity to disobey; his false Policy was mistaken, his Army defeated, and, soon after, an order, more punctually executed, placed his head on the Gate of the Seraglio, with this inscription: FOR NOT HAVING FOLLOWED THE PLAN OF OPERATIONS SENT HIM IMMEDIATELY FROM THE EMPEROR.

He was succeeded by Moldovangi. This new Visir proved more enterprising, though not more able; he was defeated in like manner; but he was fortunate enough, when deprived of the Visiriat, only to lose a Place no less dangerous than eminent, and which no one could properly fill.

To the haughty Ignorance of the Generals was added the stupid Presumption of the Subalterns; and the Turks, who took the field with a prodigious train of Artillery, but which consisted of Pieces ill mounted, and full as badly served, slaughtered in every Action by the Cannon of their Enemies, could only avenge themselves for their Disasters by accusing the Russians of cowardly Artifice. They overpower us, said they, by the Superiority of their Fire, which, in fact, it is impossible to approach; but let them leave their abominable Batteries, and encounter us like brave men hand to hand, and we shall soon see whether these Infidels can resist the slaughtering sabre of the True-Believers.

This Multitude of wretched Fanaticks even reproached the Russians for having attacked them during the holy Season of Ramazan....

Sultan Mustapha, whose first care, as we have already seen, was employed on his Finances, after having lavished enormous Sums, without Success, began to bargain with his Ministers concerning the new expences they proposed; and, while they reproached him with Avarice, he blamed himself for yielding too easily, which, he said, only served to enrich the Knaves about him. It certainly was not to be supposed, that this Prince could see, without concern, his Treasures squandered, his Army mouldering away, and those Enemies whom he imagined would be subdued in the first Campaign, already victorious on the Danube, and threatening him with an Invasion in the Archipelago [the Aegean Islands, ed.].

His activity caused him to discover new Abuses every moment. He complained of them to his Ministers, never without making them tremble, but always without effect; for, had they wished to re-establish good Order, it was scarcely in their power. The Recruits, who were to join the Army from the extremity of Asia, passed the Bosphorus, and stopt at Constantinople, not so much to solicit the Porte, as to force it to their Terms.

While the Officers were bargaining about their pay for the Campaign, these Asiatics, dispersed through the Capital, compleatly armed, and every night robbing every one they met, hastened the Negociation, by rendering it absolutely necessary to get rid of such a lawless Multitude. The Government, too weak to repress their Insolence, stipulated to no purpose, and ceded without shame....

While the feebleness of the Government made it connive at the excesses of a licentious Soldiery, the Ministers sought to conceal the War by Sea, with which the Empire was threatened. No Russian Ship had yet ever appeared at Constantinople; therefore, said they, the Russians have no Ships: or if, by chance, they have, that is nothing to the purpose, since there is no communication between the Baltic and the Archipelago. Neither the Danes nor Swedes, whose Flags were known to the Turks, could overthrow this favourite argument. Shewing them Maps had no better effect, and the Divan [Sultan's council of advisors, ed.] was not yet persuaded of the possibility of the fact, when news was brought of the Siege of Coron, the Invasion of the Morea [the Peloponnesus, ed.], and the appearance of twelve Russian Ships of the Line.

The uncertainty of the Ministry, however, did not prevent their preparing a Maritime Force. They hastened the fitting out of thirty Men of War, and expected, with such a decided Superiority, to make amends in the Archipelago, for the losses they had suffered on the Danube....

The land Army, though twice destroyed, was become more numerous than ever; and the Ottoman Empire, though powerfully attacked both by Sea and Land, defending itself, on every side, with forces triple to those of its Enemies, gave itself up to all the Pride of Success, of which it entertained no doubt.

The absence of the Troops restored tranquility to the Capital; and the presumptuous hopes of Victory kept the People in good humour. The Comte de Saint Priest [the French Ambassador, ed.] was willing to take advantage of this circumstance, to give an Entertainment, on account of the marriage of the King of France; and, to amuse the Turks, was desirous of adding to the Balls and Diversions, which could only suit the Taste of the Europeans, an Illumination, and some Fireworks, which I undertook to make. The Saloon we were obliged to build for the Ball was already finished, the Fireworks were prepared, and we were busy in arranging the Decorations, when the news of the destruction of an Army, and a Fleet arrived, spread a Consternation through the City, and rendered all our Preparations useless.

It was no longer possible to think of giving Entertainments. The Grand Seignior was in the greatest anxiety, his Ministers in despair, the People distracted, and the Capital filled with the dread of Famine and Invasion.

Such was then the Situation of an Empire, which, a month before, had believed itself so formidable; yet Ignorance, which is always ready to flatter the Pride that accompanies it, saw nothing in this double Catastrophe, but the impenetrable decrees of Providence, to which Mortals should submit with resignation. No one considered, that an undisciplined Multitude contributes more to its own destruction than all the efforts of its Enemies. But, though the want of Discipline, alone, sufficed to destroy the land Army, at Craool, the concurrence of the most extravagant stupidity, on the part of the Admiral and his Officers, was necessary to complete the destruction of the Fleet, at Tchesmai.

This Armament left the Strait of the Dardanelles to go in quest of the Russian Squadron; and, after passing by Chios, anchored on the coast of Asia, between the Continent and the Islands called Spalmadores, in front of the Port of Tchesmai. Some Frigates, newly built (for the Turks were ignorant of their use before this War) were stationed at the extremities of this long line, to give notice of the Enemy's approach; and had orders to let them get entangled in this Channel, where thirty Ships riding at convenient distances, and moored with four Anchors each, lay in wait.

This ingenious Ambuscade being thus prepared, the Russian Ships, better arranged, having doubled the Isle of Chios, and perceived the Turkish Vessels, penetrated quite to the center of their Line before the latter made any motion to get under Sail. The two Admirals, however, being laid side by side, the Russian, after having poured in his Broadside, closed with the Turk, in order to throw some Combustibles on board him, but blew up in the attempt. Hassan Pacha, then Captain of the Admiral-Ship, from whom I had this account, having disengaged himself from his Enemy, thought he was out of danger, when he perceived his Stern on fire, and his ships ready to undergo the same Fate. The Crew had already thrown themselves into the Sea; he soon followed; and was fortunate enough to lay hold of a Wreck of the Enemy's Ship, and escape the Explosion of his own; for the fire was not long before it reached the Powder-room.

It is easy to perceive, on a calculation of the real loss on each side, that of the Russians, being far the most considerable, justified them in resolving not to renew the Attack; but the Turks, whose military Knowledge scarcely extended to the effects of Saltpetre, terrified by those it had produced, thought of nothing but being blown up, if the Russians should engage them again. Tchesmai was the Asylum, whither all the Fleet retired in the greatest disorder, and some Cannon, landed in haste, and placed on the two Capes which shut in the Port, gave supposed Security to the Fugitives.

The Russians were, in the mean time, employed to watch the Motions of the Enemy; and the next day learned, no doubt with great astonishment, what had passed at Tchesmai. As they could only attribute this strange conduct of the Turks to a panic Terror, which will always justify attempts that otherwise would seem least likely to meet with Success, they appeared before the Harbour, with two Fireships, which they sent in. On the approach of the Russians, the Turks, still terrified with what had happened the preceding day, thought more of saving themselves on Shore, than defending their Ships; but the Sight of two small Vessels, sailing into the Port, awakened in them their ideas of Conquest; and, as they took them for Deserters, far from endeavouring to sink them, they were only anxious for their safe arrival: they resolved to lay the Crews in irons, and already enjoyed the pleasure of carrying them, in Triumph, to Constantinople.

But these supposed Deserters, entering without opposition, soon fastened down their rudders, threw out their graplings, and presently setting fire to their Vessels, the flames communicated to the whole Fleet. The Harbour of Tchesmai, encumbered with Ships, Powder, and Artillery, soon became a Volcano, which englutted the whole naval Force of the Turks.

Though this Misfortune humbled the Ottoman Pride, the Ministry were in danger from a still more important Calamity. The Capital was threatened with a Famine; for the destruction of the Turkish Fleet, by giving the Russians the command of the Archipelago, prevented Constantinople from being furnished with Provisions. The Enemy might even force the passage of the Straits, present themselves before the Seraglio, sack the City, and prescribe their own terms to the Grand Seignior. . . .

The Negociations for Peace, which had been begun a considerable Time, were only retarded by the personal Apprehensions of the Visir, who commanded the Army. The Porte pressed him to finish them, desirous, at all Events, to put an end to the War. But it was certain that all the Blame of a Dishonorable Peace must fall upon him, and his Life must pay for signing such a Treaty. He therefore required an Indemnification, which was refused, under the pretence that it was not necessary, but, in reality, for the same reason that it had been demanded. The Ministers, who thought of nothing but their own Security, treated the care which he took of his, as Pusillanimity; at length, his Wife, who was one of the Grand-Seignior's Sisters, put an end to the Contest. The Sultana wrote to her Husband, that he need not fear to conclude the Treaty; and the Visir, who was of a very advanced Age, died soon after he had signed the Peace and disbanded the Army.

Ised Pacha, who had before only possessed the Dignity of Caimakan, immediately received, with the Seals, that of Grand Visir; and the Turkish Government again concentered in the Capital, soon relapsed into its former Absurdities.

2

Defensive Modernization: The Military-Administrative Phase

The inward-looking, self-assured, but disintegrating Middle Eastern civilization of the late eighteenth century did not begin to change appreciably until after 1800. Essentially, the modernization of the Middle Eastern society began in response to outside attack. Between 1768 and 1844 the major powers in the Middle East—the Ottomans, the Egyptian Mamluks, the Algerians, the Moroccans and the Qajars of Iran—were defeated by various Western and Russian forces. In response to these beatings, a few Middle Eastern rulers determined to reestablish their society's political strength and social cohesion by jettisoning their discredited military organizations and substituting the obviously effective war-making methods of their Western adversaries in order to build military machines that could serve either as shields against further invasion and humiliation or as the means to overawe local Middle Eastern opposition to their ambitions.

Starting with Selim III's *Nizam-i Jadid* (*Nizam-i Cedid*) decrees in the Ottoman empire in 1792, followed by Muhammad'Ali in Egypt in 1805, 'Abbas Mirza in Iran in 1807, Mahmud II in the Ottoman Empire in 1826, and Ahmad Bey in Tunisia in 1837, serious efforts began in all parts of the Middle East to build up modern armies able to meet European troops on equal terms and local rivals on more than equal terms. Most of these leaders initiated the process of modernization within their domains in order to preserve and defend traditional Middle

Eastern civilization, its value system and its society against foreign attack. It is also true, however, that some leaders—notably Muhammad 'Ali—were at least as concerned with realizing their own, personal political ambitions as with defending traditional values against the foreigners. But, originally there was no desire among any Middle Easterners to introduce foreign "infidel" practices and institutions into their countries merely for their own sake. There was no wish to radically transform Middle Eastern society, its political system, or its ideology and value system as expressed in the Islamic faith. Indeed, the early Middle Eastern modernizers, such as Selim III and his supporters, defended their innovations against ultra-conservative objections by declaring that they were merely putting history back on its proper course by restoring forms and principles practiced in the earlier, greater days of Islam that had fallen into disuse after the region's strength began to decline. The prophet Muhammad himself was credited by some partisans of modernization with creating modern military science. It was not until the late 1850's that one could encounter numbers of individual Middle Easterners willing to embrace a self-consciously modern political and social order.

It was only with difficulty and harshness, if they succeeded at all, that Middle Eastern leaders were able to replace the basically medieval military methods of their armies with the modern techniques that clearly had demonstrated their superiority during the 1768-1844 wars. Some efforts to install new methods failed. Ottoman Sultan Selim III opened the door to change by initiating a modest program, the *Nizam-i Jadid* (*Nizam-i Cedid*), "the New Order," to modernize his army and the institutions that supported it in order to halt western and Russian encroachments on his empire. Unfortunately for Selim, he did not have enough internal support to counter the rise of an ultra-conservative coalition which determined to block any alterations in Ottoman political or military procedures because they feared that change might undermine the Islamic ideology upon which the empire had been founded. Selim, deposed in 1807, ultimately paid with his life for his partiality to innovation. Nevertheless, Selim's career showed that many among the Ottoman governing elite had been shocked into awareness of the empire's weakness by Ottoman defeats and were seeking ways to arrest growing weakness. Until 1826 the ultra-conservatives retained their grip upon the government and the empire continued to fail to meet the challenges which confronted it; this was notably demonstrated in the eventually successful revolts mounted by the Serbs and Greeks against the Ottomans, who had long regarded their Balkan subjects with disdain.

In Iran Crown Prince 'Abbas Mirza, his responsibility limited to the province of Azerbaijan, started some localized military-administrative modernization projects. But he was unable to overcome the disinterested apathy of his father, Fath Ali Shah (1797-1834), who failed to appreciate the need for change. The implications of this lack of realistic assessment of Iranian weakness resulted in the prosecution of the disastrous 1826-1828 war against Russia. Persia's pride was crushed by the peace treaty of Turkmanchai of 1828. Defeated, with some of her fairest provinces lost, the country's leaders reluctantly laid to rest dynastic dreams rooted in another age but no alternative vision was advanced. Iran after 1828 was one of a growing constellation of non-European states which lost initiative over their foreign policy and, to a large extent, even over their domestic affairs. Persia became a country that maintained her precarious sovereignty only by standing between rival great power ambitions—a state whose will could be disregarded with relative impunity. During the nineteenth century the schizophrenia so characteristic of modern Iran took root as the country, trying to be true to its tradition and its peculiar genius, was dragged one way and then another by competing foreign systems. Indeed, Iran almost disintegrated during the reign of Muhammad Shah (1834-1848). As in other parts of the Middle East, cheap Western machine-produced goods began to drive local craft manufactures off Iran's markets, a situation which threw most cities and towns into deep depression. Economic distress was reflected by growing social and political malaise as the country was convulsed by rebellion, the most serious of which coalesced around the occult *Bab* religious social protest movement. With the accession of Nasr al-Din Shah (1848-1896) the danger of total disintegration was eased by the energetic actions of the new chief minister, Mirza Taki Khan (the Amir Kabir), a centralizing modernizer who wished to institute in Iran programs similar to those being installed in the Ottoman Empire. But the Amir Kabir's strong-willed tactics earned him many enemies and eventually he was dismissed and executed. Although Nasr al-Din Shah was interested in innovation, his fascination was not shared by many of his countrymen. At the end of the century the conservative Muslim mullahs still enjoyed great influence among the masses; absentee landlords living in cities withdrew wealth from the countryside without putting anything back and dominated government. The shah's government, subject to immense foreign pressure and administratively and financially destitute, was only marginally effective. The towns remained locked in economic depression and only a tiny European influenced elite existed. In summary, Iran lost its way during the nineteenth century. The old order and old ideologies were largely discredited but in the absence of anything better most Persians countinued to give them apathetic loyalty. Yet if Iran seemed a tired and dusty country awaiting oblivion her traditional creativity was beginning to stir.

The most poignant failures of defensive modernization and disruption of the old ways took place in North Africa, particularly Algeria. There, although the cultural aspect of the impact of the modern world upon Middle Eastern society was strong, the other main element of this impact—the effects of Western imperial domination—was even more apparent. For 132 years after Algeria's conquest was initiated in 1830, a French colonial presence, alternatively repressive and paternalistic, was the central fact of life. Also, unlike other parts of the Middle East, al-Maghrib (North Africa) endured large-scale settlement by European colonists who, especially in Algeria, appropriated the best lands for themselves. While some Algerians undertook a stubborn guerrilla resistance, in Tunisia, a serious, sustained effort to keep the Europeans at bay was made through the institution of military and administrative reforms, a process that began under Ahmad Bey (1837-1855). This culminated in the promulgation of a European-style constitution in 1861 which, however, was soon curtailed and then suppressed entirely with the imposition of a French protectorate in 1881.

Nevertheless, defensive modernization in the Middle East also counted some tentative success and a great deal of permanent influence in establishing prerequisites for subsequent change. Muhammad 'Ali (1805-1848) in Egypt and Mahmud II (1808-1839) in the Ottoman Empire succeeded in assembling military machines that were effective by Middle Eastern standards although they could not really approach the power of European armed forces. Both of these monarchs, as well as most of their immediate successors, soon realized that a formidable limitation upon the progress of their military modernization programs was the absence of the institutional, administrative, economic, and especially the intellectual environment upon which the West's power was founded. The results of their efforts to cope with this situation constitute the chief legacy of the early defensive modernizers to the modern Middle Eastern situation. Because they saw that it was necessary to possess all the paraphernalia upon which modern military power rests—the factories, revenue systems, educational structures—innovations of profound import were imposed upon their realms. This reality posed a dilemma for the reformers because their original goal was to reconstruct only a military apparatus so that it could defend other existing institutions from destruction. This is why we can label this first variety of Middle Eastern modernization, "defense modernization." It is also important to note that after this decision regarding defensive modernization was taken, the military was to be a prime source of modernizing influence and questions of assuring a country's security have been given primacy when policy priorities have been allocated.

Still, as we have indicated, it was not possible to construct an efficient military machine without the functioning presence of other equally efficient supporting institutions. This fact was grasped quickly by leaders like Muhammad 'Ali and Mahmud II, and consequently they enlarged their original efforts and set out to build these other prerequisites of power. Both leaders started their years of effective supremacy by smashing the strength of the ultraconservatives who sought to block all change. Muhammad 'Ali did this in 1811 when he literally wiped out the Mamluks. Subsequently, in 1826 Mahmud II engineered what was, in effect, a successful coup d'etat ending ultraconservative supremacy by destroying the Janissary corps, scattering the remaining conservative factions, and taking actual control of an empire over which he had reigned but not ruled since 1808. The two rulers then spent the rest of their years instituting renovations which shattered irrevocably the established order and which guided the first stumbling steps of the modern system. Soon after routing their oppositions both men created European-style armed forces. Between 1815 and 1838 Muhammad 'Ali recruited some 150,000 soldiers and seamen. This host, led by a Turkish-Circassian-Albanian officer caste destined to retain influence in Egypt until the 1952 revolution, advised by ex-Napoleonic European officers, and served in the ranks by native Egyptian peasant conscripts (although the fellahin had not been extensively used as soldiers since pharaonic times) was, in its heyday, far and away the most efficient in the Middle East. Mahmud II's "Triumphant Soldiers of Muhammad," the direct descendant of Selim III's Nizam-i Jadid by the 1850's had grown into a 250,000-man Imperial Ottoman Army drilled and equipped in the Western fashion.

Because military innovation proved extremely expensive, the need to tap new sources of revenue necessitated extensive reconstruction of the existing administrative and financial apparatus. After 1811 in Egypt and during 1831 in the Ottoman Empire the feudal system—the basis of the medieval Middle East's administrative and economic system—was abolished. Thus, in order to clear the way for the construction of the new institutions needed to support a modern military establishment, old institutions were scrapped. By the 1830's much effort was being expended on erecting efficient centrally controlled bureaucracies, revenue services, legal codes, educational systems, and so forth. Indeed, this activity even more than strictly military innovation undermined the old order. Administratively Muhammad 'Ali and Mahmud II took steps to substitute a highly centralized administrative system staffed by a bureaucracy responsive to the sovereign's orders for the locally oriented feudal political mosaic over which they presided when they came to power. So successful were these moves that a tradition of administrative centralism was fastened upon the Middle East which continues to this day. To assist in administering their armies and governments a type of official new to the Middle East was trained, men versed in the techniques, if not always the philosophy, of the modern West. Foreign experts were employed but, in addition, numbers of locals were sent to Europe to learn of Western knowledge. These educational innovations were among the most significant innovations in terms of the Middle East's future. The first modern schools were military academies and ancillary institutions such as medical schools meant to serve military requirements; the first books translated from Western tongues were military manuals; the first foreign experts hired were military instructors. But once a young Egyptian learned French in order to read of Napoleon's tactics at Austerlitz, he could read also political philosophy. Yet educational reform quickly added another dimension— a capability of producing civil servants for the new bureaucracies. Since these efforts were continued by Muhammad 'Ali's and Mahmud II's successors, by the mid-nineteenth century an elite educated in Western fashion and at least conversant with modern civilization appeared, an elite destined to take over the modernizing leadership of the region. While most members of the new elite had ties with the traditional leadership it is also true that occasional individuals from groups that were traditionally barred from leadership roles began to move into the new elite on the basis of their modern training. Social mobility was also stimulated by tampering with other aspects of life in the Middle East.

The foundation for a new economic order was laid as a result of moves designed to enlarge the tax base and to supply manufactured goods. Middle Eastern agriculture was particularly changed by such activities. Irrigation and land resettlement projects increased the total of arable land, while new cash crops—notably cotton, sugar, and tobacco in Muhammad 'Ali's provinces of Egypt and Syria—oriented toward the world market were planted. Thanks to revised land tenure laws a new group of large private landowners not restricted as was the old feudal class by customary communal obligations to the mass of peasant cultivators was created. On the other hand, direction of the growing modern sector of the local economy was assumed by a commercial class dominated by Europeans and local minority groups which enjoyed relative immunity from local jurisdiction—a situation which frustrated the healthy growth of an indigenous Muslim middle class geared to manipulating modern economic enterprise. Eventually this led to the virtual monopoly by European concerns of large-scale modernizing projects such as railroad and canal building.

Much of this economic activity occurred after Muhammad 'Ali and Mahmud II had left the scene for the momentum of innovating activity touched off by these leaders survived their passing. In the Ottoman Empire the 1839 to 1871 period is known as the *Tanzimat*—the Reform. Commencing with a declaration of their goals, the *Hatt-i Sherif-i Gülhane* (Noble Rescript of the Rose Chamber), the reformers, often in high-handed fashion, proceeded to reconstruct the façade of Ottoman government. During the Tanzimat the ideal of a highly centralized, French style, administrative structure was fastened upon the consciousness of most Middle Eastern leaders who came after. The glorification of centralization did not contribute much to the growth of democratic institutions. Moreover, it was one thing to issue decrees in Istanbul and another to have them applied throughout the empire. In Syria, for instance, the 1840-1860 years were a time of spreading political, economic, and social chaos which finally led to peasant rebellions, the breakdown of the millet (religious communities) system, civil war, and finally, intervention by European troops. From this low point Lebanon was rescued by the establishment of an autonomous, European guaranteed government which proceeded to effect the province's rapid economic and educational development. The rest of Syria, too, after 1860 was reorganized and after a comparatively late start in its confrontation with the modern world, Syria was among the most advanced parts of the Middle East by the late nineteenth century. Iraq, however, was reintegrated into the empire during the 1830-1870 years. In Egypt, the accession of Sa'id (1854-1863) signalled a return to rapid modernization as the construction of the Suez canal was commenced. But the climax of Egypt's renewed modernization was reached in the reign of Isma'il (1863-1879). Under this khedive European fashions in dress, amusement, and architecture became a badge of modernity among the Egyptian elite and the richer parts of Cairo and Alexandria began to resemble Paris. Isma'il, attempting to organize this change, tried to reform Egypt's political apparatus but his efforts, often well meaning, also often were ineffective. A consultative assembly set up in 1866 to imitate European practice was repressed once it began displaying some legislative independence. Boom alternated with recession and great landlords emerged as land was practically given away by the government to a favored few. Although major public works were completed, their cost was too great for the country to bear and Isma'il fell deeply into debt as he availed himself of the high interest loans offered by European bankers. Beset by creditors, Isma'il was deposed in 1879. Three years later Egypt appeared to be right back where she was in 1798, unable to defend itself against an invading European army.

As the nineteenth century moved on, it became clear that refounding an ancient culture produced mixed blessings. The harsh imposition of laws directly copied from European models sometimes played havoc with the customary rights and the well-being of the lower and middle classes. The modernizing leaders were invariably authoritarian centralizers with more in common with enlightened despots than democratic reformers. Their goal was to create an efficient and centralized government headed by a sovereign who possessed the means to carry out his will. Also, the growing imitation of Western fashions and social practices by the ruling elite produced a profound split between the aspirations of the Middle Eastern masses and their leaders. Moreover, the adoption of modern aspirations by the new elite created frustration within their own ranks as the technological-economic gap between Europe and the various parts of the Middle East seemed to grow larger as the century progressed. Consequently, there was a constant need to update plans to modernize the area's military, administrative, and economic capabilities. In such an unstable environment it was difficult for any reform program to achieve much obvious progress.

Still, all of this was a by-product of change and without the program of selective reform initiated by the early defensive modernizers, Middle Eastern civilization might well have gone the same way as did that of the American Indian. Despite instances of the bizarre that accompanied the rather haphazard, certainly naive, modernizing activity of the earlier nineteenth century, ground was prepared and prerequisites were established for a subsequent, more viable, more sophisticated development of modern civilization in the Middle East.

3

Celebi Effendi's Defense of
Sultan Selim III's Nizam-i Jadid
(Nizam-i Cedid) *

After the Ottoman defeat by the Austrians and Russians in the war of 1787-1792 the young sultan Selim III determined to reorganize his armed forces and his government in order to discourage or repulse further attacks. After sifting through the recommendations of a fact-finding board of high Ottoman officials charged with studying the causes and possible remedies for the empire's weakness, Selim, in 1792 and 1793 issued a series of reform decrees collectively labeled the *Nizam-i Jadid* (*Nizam-i Cedid*)—the New Order. Although the decrees included directions to reform the empire's political and financial organization right down to the provincial level, the heart of the new regulations concerned the creation of a new body of troops which would be trained in the latest European military methods. Unfortunately, the presence of a most obvious and growing foreign influence among the sultan's closest advisors combined with the introduction of Western-inspired drill methods and uniforms into the Ottoman army was too much for the strongly entrenched supporters of ultraconservatism within the empire to stand. A good part of the Muslim religious-scholar class allied themselves with the traditional military elite, the Janissaries, to form a powerful reactionary coalition. Ultimately, Selim, unable to cope with reactionary-inspired riots in Istanbul and rebellions elsewhere, retreated to the point of ordering the *Nizam's* abolition. Not satisfied with this, the reactionaries, in May 1807, forced Selim's deposition, instigated his eventual murder, and placed upon the throne an ineffectual puppet, Mustafa IV.

*   *   *

It is said in the history which treats of the terms of peace concluded by the sublime person who has received the mercy of God [The Sultan Abdülhamid I, ed.], that those States which from carelessness did not take proper precautions to guard against the violence of strangers, have remained without either honour or reputation, and dependent upon others. Or even from the consequence of their

* Mustafa Reshid Čelebi Effendi, "An Explanation of the Nizam-y-Gedid by Tshelebi-Effendi," translation from Turkish in William Wilkinson, *An Account of the Principalities of Wallachia and Moldavia including various Political Observations relating to them.* (London: Longman, Hurst, Rees, Orme, and Brown, 1820), 217-218, 221-224, 227-228, 232-237, 266-268, 271-272.

negligence, having fallen entirely into the hands of foreigners, their kings have become subjects, and their rich men poor. It is a principle to be observed by those who rule governments, and are men of understanding and penetration, that, "even if your enemy is an ant, you should use every effort against him"; that conformably to this proverb, they may not suffer themselves to be brought into calamity, by the treacherous machinations of the neighbouring States, and other hostile nations. . . .

"This institution of the Nizam-y-Gedid has caused the established order of the world to be disturbed, and has given cause to the insolent conduct of the mountaineers in the country of Rumelia." [A reference to the uprising in Serbia which began in 1804, ed.] Such are the expressions employed by a set of contentious and ignorant men, incapable of learning reason. I have sometimes questioned such persons, saying as follows:—"Ho, friend! allow me in the first place to ask you a question. What is this institution against which you make such continual and senseless outcry? First know precisely what it is, and then continue to oppose it. If there be reason in what you say, I am open to conviction, and am ready to concede the point in dispute." On hearing this, all they could say was, that what they call the Nizam-y-Gedid is a body of troops trained and exercised; beyond which, and a mere profession of their aversion to it, they plainly showed that they knew nothing about the matter. Although I saw that an attempt to make this kind of rabble understand public affairs, is like trying to make a camel leap over a ditch, I proceeded to put some questions that occurred to me, as follows:—"Shall I give you some account of the troubles which occurred in the world before the Nizam-y-Gedid existed, during the reigns of their highnesses the former Ottoman Sultans, who have found mercy from God? Such as the disturbances raised in Anatolia by the Gellalli, and the insolence of Sarry Beÿ Oglou in the reign of Sultan Mahmoud, and especially the events which passed in Egypt, occasioned by Sacka-Yorghi Alli-Beÿ, the son of a glass-blower; and the affairs of Emir-Daher, of Abou-Vahib, all of which happened during the reign of Sultan Moustapha; and the calamities inflicted by the unemployed Levendis, who turned the province of Anatolia upside down; and the continued bad success which attended the arms of the followers of Islam, for the space of seven years, during the Muscovite war, which began in the year 1182; the defeats which our great armies suffered every year, with the loss of so many thousand tents, such abundance of camp equipage, treasure, artillery, bombs, and military stores, sufficient for the consumption of many years, and so great a loss of our troops, either taken, drowned, or killed, and the capture as well of our small forts and retrenched posts, as of our large fortresses, some of which were reduced by famine and others by force; and the impossibility of delivering so many thousand women and children whom they contained, and who, still remaining in captivity, pass their lives in tears. These are things, the bitter remembrance of which can never be erased from our hearts. Some of these calamitous events may be found in our annals, and some have happened in our days. Pray was the Nizam-y-Gedid the cause of all these disorders and disgraceful occurrences? It did not exist at that time, and yet you see that confusion was already introduced, and the regular order of things interrupted. Is then the Nizam-y-Gedid the only cause of revolution? ...

Be it known to men of understanding, that after the conclusion of peace with the Muscovite infidels, in the year 1206 [1792 A.D.], when ambassadors were passing to and fro, at the time that the prisoners were released, diligent enquiry was made of many persons who had been in the hands of the Russians, with regard to the power and condition of the enemies of our faith. ...

The Russian infidels having withal greatly improved the state of their dominions within the space of seventy or eighty years, and manifested their thirst of glory by their arrogant and insolent interference in the interior affairs of other States, and having annexed several foreign countries to their own dominions, especially the kingdom of Poland, we must not, by any means, consider ourselves secure from so treacherous and deceitful a nation. ...

That therefore, as it was a maxim established that in an urgent case, when some remedy must be sought, resources must be found in the whole body of those who are attached to government, without consulting the lower orders; there was no other method of dispelling and removing the danger we have spoken of above, but by keeping a body of troops on foot ready for service ..., and provided with requisite supply of artillery, ammunition, and military stores; and such troops as should not, like the rest of our forces, be composed of sellers of pastry, boatmen, fishermen, coffee-house keepers, baccals, and others who are engaged in the thirty-two trades, but of well disciplined men, who would take care to have their cannon and muskets ready for service, and on an urgent occasion, would be prepared in the space of half an hour to engage the troops and artillery of the enemy; to repulse them, and retaliate on them their own hostile devices. After these points had been taken into serious consideration, some men were in the first place dispatched to the corps of the Janissaries for the purpose of selecting from thence some young and chosen soldiers, whom they were to discipline and train to the use of arms. Upon this, our bravoes who are engaged in the thirty-two trades, considering that if they were obliged to attend punctually to the exercise of cannon and small arms, they would be occupied with that instead of their private affairs, and would be brought into trouble, no longer receiving their pay once in three months gratuitously, and without doing any thing for it, began to ponder the matter, stroaking their beards and mustachioes, and to vent their discontent by saying, "We are not made for this sort of work, and we will have nothing to do with it." Whatever pains were taken to enlighten their understandings, they obstinately persisted, addressing each other by these or similar terms, "Ho! Alli Sacka Baba, Oda Bashi, Bash Karakouloukgee! [The titles of some superior officers amongst the Janissaries, ed.] what say you to this business? the exercise of the Nizam-y-Gedid is now introduced; henceforth no pay is to be had without service, and what they call exercise is a very troublesome service; it is true that drawing up in a line makes a better show; but if they send us to war, we can fire our muskets, and then charging sword in hand, we can put the Russians to flight and storm their camp. May Heaven preserve from decay our corps and our chiefs! we shall then take our pay when it is issued, and pass our time agreeably." Such were their expressions, as though they could by frigid reasoning, and sense-less allusions, induce the Sublime Government to abandon this enterprise, when the experience of two wars had proved, beyond dispute, both the total ineffi-ciency of their services, and the feeble condition of the Mahometan community.

With respect to the apprehensions entertained of . . . [an attack on Istanbul] . . . by the Russian infidels, the first step which was taken for the purpose of pro-curing speedy and effectual means of guarding against so devilish a piece of treachery, consisted in an ordinance for levying a body of Bostangees [literally "gardeners," actually a royal guard, ed.], who were to be quartered at the Levend-Chifflick, a military post newly established at no great distance from the reservoirs, in order that in an urgent crisis when we fly for refuge to Divine protection, they might be ready for service in a very short space of time. But the most important point is this: that the new levied troops, instead of engaging in trade, should remain day and night in their quarters, applying themselves daily to mili-tary exercises, and keeping their arms, cannon, muskets, and warlike imple-ments of every description necessary for immediate service; thus practising a disci-pline suitable to their appellation of soldiers of the new regulation. To complete all, every Orta [regiment] . . . [had] an *Imam* attached to it for the due per-formance of religious worship, that nothing requisite might be omitted. . . .

The advantages of the new corps, and their superiority over the old are in-finite; were we to write them all down, we should fill several volumes. In order, however, to make the people comprehend well, we will point out to them another of these advantages. The soldiers of our ancient corps, are not at all clothed alike; from this diversity of garment, the following bad effect results: if, in time of war, any of them should desert from the army, as there are no marks by which we can distinguish whether the deserters belong to the troops, or whether they are tradesmen, or servants, they have thereby the opportunities of escaping without being known. Whereas the new troops have a particular uniform of their own, so that the stragglers would be soon discovered. Hence it results, that in a large camp of the new troops, every man will be forced to remain fixed in his company, and steady in the performance of his duty, whether he would or no, since it is impossible to desert without greatly incurring the danger of punishment.

Another of their advantages is this: our old forces, when in presence of the enemy, do not remain drawn up in a line, but stand confusedly and promiscuously like a crowd in a place of diversion. Some load their muskets, and fire once, some twice, or oftener, just as they think proper, whilst others being at their wits' end, and not knowing what they are about turn from side to side like fabulous story-tellers [i.e., sufi dervishes, ed.]. If in consequence of any movement which they perceive on the side of the enemy, the officers endeavour to make the troops fall back a little, some will obey them, others will not, every one does just as he likes. If they wish to retire a little; the soldiers make that a pretence for flying to the distance of some days' journey.

But the new troops remain drawn up in line as though they were at prayers, the rear ranks being exactly parallel with the front, and consisting of the same number of companies, neither more nor less, so that, when it is necessary, they turn with as much precision as a watch. The whole body, consisting of many thousand men, observe attentively the signals given them by the two fuglemen who explain by signs the commands of the officers, and not one dares so much as to turn his head. . . .

Although many similar stratagems have been employed at various times, by holy warriors, . . . and although the great Prophet hath given full permission and authority to do any thing which may conduce to the defeat of the infidels, yet an ignorant rabble keep chattering like parrots, some of whom do not approve of the dresses of the new troops, while others say that their exercise belongs specially to the Kiafers [i.e., "infidels," the Europeans], and does not become Mussulmans.

4

Mahmud II's Firman Abolishing the Janissary Corps, 17 June 1826 *

Mahmud II was the lone surviving prince in the direct royal line when he began his reign in 1808. He realized that he had to break the power of the reactionaries who had destroyed Selim III before he could attempt to attack his empire's maladies. Moving very cautiously, he extended his influence within the palace, the government at large, and the military. Finally in May of 1826 Mahmud felt strong enough to decree the establishment of a new military unit. He spoke of this force—actually a restoration of Selim III's *Nizam*—as a restoration of the military organization utilized by Sulayman the Magnificent in the sixteenth century. At this point an event known to Ottoman historians as "the auspicious incident," occurred. The Janissaries, knowing an innovation when they

* Translation from the Turkish in Howard A. Reed, "The Destruction of the Janissaries in 1826; how Sultan Mahmud II Abolished the Corps" (Princeton University, typescript of Ph.D. dissertation, 1951), 242-249.

saw it, rejected Mahmud's verbiage and raised the banners of revolt. After bloody fighting in the capital in which the population supported the sultan, the Janissaries were forced back to their barracks where they made their last stand. The destruction of the Janissaries was followed by the firman appearing below which officially abolished the ancient military order that was so closely identified with the great days of the Ottoman state. Mahmud was free to assert his will over an empire he had previously governed only in name. Thus, the abolition firman of 1826 was the first of a series of edicts by which the Ottoman empire began to embrace the modern world.

*   *   *

As all Muslim people know, the Ottoman state owes its creation and its later conquest of the East and the West solely to the powerful influence of Islamic religious spirit, Muslim law, the sword of *jihad* ["striving" to spread Islam, ed.] and the *gazi* ["warrior for Islam," ed.] spirit. It had always been necessary for the Ottoman state to maintain brave and numerous Muslim soldiers to fight as *gazis* against the enemies of the faith. The Janissary corps was first organized in a regular way for this purpose and rendered valuable services to the Ottoman state, may it endure forever. Thanks to the abandon with which they presented their bosoms to the enemy in *jihad* and *gazi* warfare, to their undaunted valor in battle, and their discipline, they were responsible for many victories.

However, as time went on, their discipline began to break down, evil men entered their ranks, and they began to be involved in criminal movements. Their obedience changed to insubordination. For the past century, on all the campaigns they have participated in, they have spread all sorts of baseless rumors against their commanders and have refused to obey their orders. They have shamefully deserted and abandoned our fortresses and our provinces to enemy infidels, by their lack of discipline and cowardice. On account of this, our enemies have been emboldened by these signs of our weakness and have taken advantage of this situation. From day to day they have invented countless insolent pretexts and demands upon us. They have encircled us on all sides with a belt of dangers and have threatened the very core of Islam.

Finally, this situation aroused the Muslim zeal. We longed to avenge all these defeats and sought to find the reasons for them and a means of avoiding them. It appears clear that the infidels' apparently easy victories were the result of a knowledge of military tactics and a trained soldiery. Therefore, after the campaign of the year [1202 A.H. 1788, second war with Catherine the Great of Russia], and again on two other occasions [not specified, but apparently a reference to the attempt of Selim III, 1789-1807, to reform the army and the abortive attempt of Mahmud II and his first Grand Vizir, Bayrakdar Mustafa Pasha, to undertake military reform in 1808], there were attempts made to organize disciplined troops. However, although they themselves were no longer competent or able to fight successfully, the Janissaries rioted three times against the formation of these troops which they did not want. They were the cause of the failure and abolition of the useful new formations, which were beginning to take shape.

Even several sultans, who were to the universe what the spirit is for the body, became the victims of the Janissaries and lost their lives in the disasters brought about by their insubordinate sedition.

In this situation, nothing was said against the Janissaries because they were such an ancient body. There had been no thought of destroying them, but rather, in spite of everything, they had been allowed to do as they pleased, to obey when the spirit moved them and to mutiny if they felt like it. The result of this forbearance was that the enemies of our religion were not idle. No sooner did they observe our condition than they seized the opportunity to advance against us. They threaten us, press us on all sides and work for our total destruction. God forbid it but they have almost attained their objective.

In view of this situation, these matters were considered at a recent general council held in the mufti's residence with all the *vizirs, ulema, rijals* and again before all the officers of the Janissary corps when everything was explained. The ulema gave their sanction and issued a *fetva* in support of the plan and the sacred oath to support it which was prepared, signed, and sealed by all those present. In accordance with these decisions, and with the firm conviction that today Muslim troops cannot accomplish their religious duty of combating and overcoming the infidel maneuvers without discipline and instruction in military science, it was unanimously decided to institute the *eshkenji* corps. This paid, standing army would not in any way infringe upon the ancient customs and regulations of the Janissaries, but each mess would supply only 150 men to the new formation.

The government, moreover, did not wish to evade its fiscal responsibility and the treasury would bear the burden of the additional expenses involved, for the establishment and maintenance of the new troops. At the same time the treasury guaranteed to honor all the extant Janissary pay tickets.

The recruiting began, and a proclamation, issued in accordance with a *fetva,* declared that any person who spoke or acted in opposition to the new law, would be severely punished. This statement was circulated to all quarters of Istanbul. Finally, last week, uniforms and weapons were issued to the new recruits and their drills were held.

Nevertheless, the Janissaries, deaf to the call of religion and to the reiterated councils of the *ulema,* broke into revolt Thursday evening, the 9th of Zilkade. First, they attacked the residence of the Janissary *agha* [commander], then that of the grand vizir. They also sacked and fired on other houses. They committed all sorts of sacrilegious crimes and infamous horrors, and even went so far as to cut with knives pages of the Koran which fell into their hands.

They shouted, "We don't want any drill," and, in spite of the holy sanctions, the proclamation, their sworn allegiance, and the sacred *fetvas,* they turned the weapons given them by the state against the government of the Muslim people and broke out in rebellion against their legitimate sultan.

As this behavior was beyond the bounds of religion and decency, the grand vizir, *mufti, vizirs, ulema, rijals,* other high officials, and a host of faithful servants of the sultan who were incensed against the Janissaries, assembled at the imperial palace. They held a meeting there and received the glorious Banner of the Sultan of the Prophets and proceeded to hoist it in the Sultan Ahmed mosque where they all foregathered. From there they dispatched criers to all the quarters to inform the loyal Muslim people to rally to the defense of their faith and the Prophet's Standard. In response, the faithful Muslims, risking their heads and lives, hastened eagerly to the rendezvous.

In spite of the general anger they had aroused against themselves by their notorious deeds contrary to religion and the Ottoman state, the Janissaries persisted in their rebellion. Entrenched in the square which was the center of their plots, they resisted the sultan and the law. They dared to start a civil war in which many faithful Muslims were to perish. The sacred law has abandoned them to public retribution. Their barracks have been burned and the hand of Allah has thrown them before the sword of justice where they found their just desserts.

A group of the rebels had died fighting, but their accomplices and those who began the rebellion were also to share their fate. Careful search was made for all of these by means of their names and descriptions, and many were seized. Some, already convicted of participation in the rebellion, have been punished. The others cannot escape the punishment they richly deserve.

Thus, after so many insurrections and calamities instigated by the Janissaries, it is clear that their corps, far from fulfilling the object of its establishment, is, today, nothing more than a useless and insubordinate body which has become the asylum of the spirit of unrest and sedition in which the number of evil men have outgrown the number of good ones. The Janissary name and insignia have become synonyms for disorder and rebellion. Even infidels have managed to infiltrate themselves. Among those who have just been executed were found some Janissaries who bore, tattooed on their arm along with the insignia of the 75th mess, the cross of the *ghiaurs* [Christians]. This simply proves that infidel traitors parading in the disguise of Muslims have for a long time been using the Janissary corps to further their own nefarious ends by spreading false rumors. Their officers and former aghas have not kept a careful check on new recruits so that they remained ignorant of the undersirable elements in their midst who fomented disorder and trouble. It is an irrefutable truth that, even if one should wish to preserve the Janissary corps in the future, there is no practicable means which might be adopted to correct these abuses which would succeed.

Therefore, the *mufti,* the grand vizir, all the great officials and *ulema* and all the zealous supporters of the state, assembled together in the Sultan Ahmed

Mosque beneath the sacred Banner of the Prophet, taking cognizance of the aforementioned facts, have, in consequence, today unanimously agreed and decided that, in accordance with sacred law and for the preservation of the state, the ensign and name of the Janissaries shall be abolished. The Janissary corps is hereby annulled and in its place there is to be organized a trained body of troops bearing the name "Triumphant Soldiers of Muhammad." These new troops will be useful to Islam and the state and capable of giving an answer to the enemy in *gazi* and *jihad* warfare.

It is further resolved that the supreme command of these "Triumphant Soldiers of Muhammad" is conferred upon my daring vizir, the present governor of the provinces of Brusa and Kojaeli and the commander of the Rumeli [European] shore of the strait of the Black Sea, Huseyin Pasha. He will establish himself in the residence of the [Janissary] agha, which henceforth is to be called the residence of the *Serasker Pasha* [Commander-in-Chief of the Army]. The barracks and orderly rooms which will shortly be built are to house the new troops. Moreover, the titles of Janissary agha, *Katar* agha, and *Bölük* agha, and all titles and ranks of the Janissary corps are likewise hereby abolished.

The present Janissary commander, Mehmed [Jelaleddin, who had refused an offer to command the new troops] is hereby granted the rank of one of my grand equerries and chief gatekeeper; the lieutenant-general, Hasan, is promoted to the rank of *Mirmiran* [District Commander] and attached to the staff of the Serasker Pasha [that is, the above-mentioned Hüseyin]. The other general officers, the *Zagharji Bashi, Seksonju Bashi,* and *Sekban Bashi* are hereby appointed chief gatekeepers, while the other loyal company commanders are granted the rank of equerry of the sultan. Each will also receive, in addition, grants in order of rank. The former senior officers will retain their military fiefs which are transformed into *Ziamet* fiefs and will remain in the sultan's service. Furthermore, the owners of Janissary pay tickets will, as heretofore, receive the exact amount due to them for as long as they live, by presenting these tickets at the appointed time and place. It is my imperial desire that no one should suffer any loss or difficulty on this account.

Hence, let all the congregation of Muslim people, and the small and great officials of Islam and the *ulema,* and members of other military formations, and all the common folk be as one body. Let them look upon each other as brethren in faith. Let there be no differences and contrariness between you. Let the great ones among you look with a merciful and compassionate eye upon the little ones, and let the minor ones, moreover, in every instance be obedient and submissive to their superiors. And may you all strive together towards the ultimate goal to exalt the blessed word of Allah, the preservation and exposition of the religion and holy law of the Lord of the Prophets. And Allah grant that your union, established and persevering for this noble aim of beneficent reform may continue and endure for ages and ages to come. And let no one allow himself to utter any word or do any deed in opposition to the general desire and welfare. If he should do so he will at once, by the grace of Allah, be struck on the neck by the sword of the holy law.

Such is the decision of the general council. Steps to put into execution these resolutions were immediately begun and my imperial commands have been sent to all my royal provinces in Remeli and Anatolia. They are addressed to you, my viziers and generals and commanders and judges and magistrates and administrative representatives and all my aforementioned officials, you, who are to abolish the Janissary name and everything associated with it such as the rank of master of the barriers and master of the cranes and the Janissary officers and commanders in the provinces, and the Janissary unit messes all their insignia are to be completely wiped out.

You, chief judge of Istanbul, who will assemble at your tribunal and in your presence the *imams* of all the quarters of Istanbul. You will communicate this *firman* to them and give them copies which they are to read in the mosques. The *imams* are to inform the faithful Muslims of these matters and are to explain to them the precious advantages they embody. They are to tell them that it is the duty of the true believers to thank the state for its beneficent intentions on this occasion, and that they are to live quietly and contentedly in the shadow of the power of the sultan. They must have no other thought but to beseech Allah to preserve their gracious ruler. You, yourself make certain that the *imams* fulfill this duty with care, and continue to display your zeal and care to encourage to observation of the decrees of our holy law.

5

The Hatt-i Sherif (Hatt-i Şerif) of Gülhane, 3 November 1839 *

Mahmud II died in 1839 in the midst of a war with Muhammad 'Ali of Egypt. Partly as a device to show his attachment to the innovations instituted by his father, and partly to attract European, particularly British, support in a critical wartime situation, the new sultan, Abdulmejid (Abdülmecid), issued in the *Gülhane* or Rose Chamber of his palace the famous *Hatt-i Sherif* or Noble Rescript of 1839 which initiated the *Tanzimat* (Reform) period of 1839-1871. The *Hatt-i Sherif* was largely drafted by Reshid Pasha, the new foreign minister, and perhaps the leading figure in the first stage of the *Tanzimat*. The

* J. C. Hurewitz, *Diplomacy in the Near and Middle East, a documentary record: 1535-1914* (Princeton: D. Van Nostrand, 1956), Vol. I, 113-116.

document served as a declaration of goals which the Ottoman modernizers hoped ultimately to achieve. Whereas Mahmud II had designated his innovation merely as restorations of past practices, the *Hatt-i Sherif*, although it claimed to be a continuation of great Ottoman traditions, pointed to "new institutions" and "new laws" which were to be established to halt the decline of the empire. In its reference to the "council of justice" the rescript made shadowy illusions to new legislative functions that the council would assume. Couched in very general terms, the document foresaw the creation of a modern political and social apparatus to carry out its principles. In a sense it also was a "bill of rights" which guaranteed certain civil liberties to all Ottoman subjects no matter what their creed, a matter which received further attention in the Hatt-i Humayun of February 1856. In summary, the *Hatt-i Sherif-i Gülhane* stands as an imposing landmark in the history of the Middle East's modernization.

*   *   *

All the world knows that in the first days of the Ottoman monarchy, the glorious precepts of the Koran and the laws of the empire were always honored.

The empire in consequence increased in strength and greatness, and all its subjects, without exception, had risen in the highest degree to ease and prosperity. In the last one hundred and fifty years a succession of accidents and divers causes have arisen which have brought about a disregard for the sacred code of laws and the regulations flowing therefrom, and the former strength and prosperity have changed into weakness and poverty; an empire in fact loses all its stability so soon as it ceases to observe its laws.

These considerations are ever present to our mind, and ever since the day of our advent to the throne the thought of the public weal, of the improvement of the state of the provinces, and of relief to the [subject] peoples, has not ceased to engage it. If, therefore, the geographical position of the Ottoman provinces, the fertility of the soil, the aptitude and intelligence of the inhabitants, are considered, the conviction will remain that by striving to find efficacious means, the result, which by the help of God we hope to attain, can be obtained within a few years. Full of confidence, therefore, in the help of the Most High, and certain of the support of our Prophet, we deem it right to seek by new institutions to give to the provinces composing the Ottoman Empire the benefit of a good administration.

These institutions must be principally carried out under three heads, which are:

1. The guarantees insuring to our subjects perfect security for life, honor, and fortune.

2. A regular system of assessing and levying taxes.

3. An equally regular system for the levying of troops and the duration of their service.

And, in fact, are not life and honor the most precious gifts to mankind? What man however much his character may be against violence, can prevent himself from having recourse to it, and thereby injure the government and the country, if his life and honor are endangered? If, on the contrary, he enjoys in that respect perfect security, he will not depart from the ways of loyalty, and all his actions will contribute to the good of the government and of his brothers.

If there is an absence of security as to one's fortune, everyone remains insensible to the voice of the Prince and the country; no one interests himself in the progress of public good, absorbed as he is in his own troubles. If, on the contrary, the citizen keeps possession in all confidence of all his goods, then, full of ardor in his affairs, which he seeks to enlarge in order to increase his comforts, he feels daily growing and doubling in his heart not only his love for the Prince and country, but also his devotion to his native land.

These feelings become in him the source of the most praiseworthy actions.

As to the regular and fixed assessment of the taxes, it is very important that it be regulated; for the state which is forced to incur many expenses for the defense of its territory cannot obtain the money necessary for its armies and other services except by means of contributions levied on its subjects. Although, thanks be to God, our empire has for some time past been delivered from the scourge of monopolies, falsely considered in times of war as a source of revenue, a fatal custom still exists, although it can only have disastrous consequences; it is that of venal concessions, known under the name of "Iltizam."

Under that name the civil and financial administration of a locality is delivered over to the passions of a single man; that is to say, sometimes to the iron grasp of the most violent and avaricious passions, for if that contractor is not a good man, he will only look to his own advantage.

It is therefore necessary that henceforth each member of Ottoman society should be taxed for a quota of a fixed tax according to his fortune and means, and that it should be impossible that anything more could be exacted from him. It is also necessary that special laws should fix and limit the expenses of our land and sea forces.

Although, as we have said, the defense of the country is an important matter, and that it is the duty of all the inhabitants to furnish soldiers for that object, it has become necessary to establish laws to regulate the contingent to be furnished by each locality according to the necessity of the time, and to reduce the term of military service to four or five years. For it is at the same time doing an injustice and giving a mortal blow to agriculture and to industry to take, without consideration to the respective population of the localities, in the one more, in the other less, men than they can furnish; it is also reducing the soldiers to despair and contributing to the depopulation of the country by keeping them all their lives in the service.

In short, without the several laws, the necessity for which has just been described, there can be neither strength, nor riches, nor happiness, nor tranquility for the empire; it must, on the contrary, look for them in the existence of these new laws.

From henceforth, therefore, the cause of every accused person shall be publicly judged, as the divine law requires, after inquiry and examination, and so long as a regular judgment shall not have been pronounced, no one can secretly or publicly put another to death by poison or in any other manner.

No one shall be allowed to attack the honor of any other person whatever.

Each one shall possess his property of every kind, and shall dispose of it in all freedom, without let or hindrance from any person whatever; thus, for example, the innocent heirs of a criminal shall not be deprived of their legal rights, and the property of the criminal shall not be confiscated. These imperial concessions shall extend to all our subjects, of whatever religion or sect they may be; they shall enjoy them without exception. We therefore grant perfect security to the inhabitants of our empire in their lives, their honor, and their fortunes, as they are secured to them by the sacred text of the law.

As for the other points, as they must be settled with the assistance of enlightened opinions, our council of justice (increased by new members as shall be found necessary), to whom shall be joined, on certain days which we shall determine, our ministers and the notabilities of the empire, shall assemble in order to frame laws regulating the security of life and fortune and the assessment of the taxes. Each one in those assemblies shall freely express his ideas and give his advice.

The laws regulating the military service shall be discussed by a military council holding its sittings at the palace of Seraskia. As soon as a law shall be passed, in order to be forever valid, it shall be presented to us; we shall give it our approval, which we will write with our imperial sign-manual.

As the object of these institutions is solely to revivify religion, government, the nation, and the empire, we engage not to do anything which is contrary thereto.

In testimony of our promise we will, after having deposited these presents in the hall containing the glorious mantle of the prophet, in the presence of all the ulemas and the grandees of the empire, make oath thereto in the name of God, and shall afterwards cause the oath to be taken by the ulemas and the grandees of the empire.

After that, those from among the ulemas or the grandees of the empire, or any other persons whatsoever who shall infringe these institutions, shall undergo, without respect of rank, position, and influence, the punishment corresponding to his crime, after having been well authenticated.

A penal code shall be compiled to that effect. As all the public servants of the empire receive a suitable salary, and as the salaries of those whose duties have not up to the present time been sufficiently remunerated are to be fixed, a rigorous law shall be passed against the traffic of favoritism and bribery (richvet), which the Divine law reprobates, and which is one of the principal causes of the decay of the empire.

The above dispositions being a thorough alteration and renewal of ancient customs this imperial rescript shall be published at Constantinople and in all places of our empire, and shall be officially communicated to all the ambassadors of the friendly powers resident at Constantinople, that they may be witnesses to the granting of these institutions, which, should it please God, shall last forever. Wherein may the Most High have us in His holy keeping. May those who shall commit an act contrary to the present regulations be the object of Divine malediction, and be deprived forever of every kind of [protection] happiness.

6

Selections from the Ottoman Land Code, 21 April 1858 *

Following the proclamation of the *Hatti-i Sherif-i Gülhane* in 1839, the Ottoman government issued a series of revolutionary decrees designed to shift the basis of the Ottoman government onto a more modern foundation. Administrative, legal, financial, educational, and military reforms followed each other in rapid succession. By the 1860's the facade of a modern style central government had been erected. Typical in form, spirit, and ultimate applicability, of most pieces of Tanzimat "reform" legislation was the Land Code of April 1858. Imitating Western legal codes, such legislation was instituted upon the naive assumption that the application of western legal concepts would quickly lead the Middle East to modernity. The Land Code was a logical step in the process started by Mahmud II when he abolished feudal rights to land and started pensioning off fief holders. Officially, it was instituted in order to replace the older melange of communal ownership and customary agrarian rights and relationships with a new system based upon western principles of individual ownership of parcels of land. A new wealthy landowning class emerged through manipulation of the Land Code. Possessing full title, including the right to sell land, and no longer restricted by the traditional communal rights and individual usages enjoyed by the actual cultivators of the land, a new "feudal" class of landowners appeared. Nevertheless, the law was one more step in the reduction of the rural population's status and independence. Laws similar to the Code of 1858 were promulgated in other Middle Eastern states.

* Stanley Fisher, *Ottoman Land Laws* ... (London: Oxford University Press-Humphrey Milford, 1919), 1-7, 11; F. Ongley, *The Ottoman Land Code* (London: William Clowes and Sons, 1892).

OTTOMAN LAND CODE (7 RAMAZAN 1274—
21 APRIL 1858)

Preface

Art. 1.—Land in the Ottoman Empire is divided into classes as follows:—

    (i.) "Mulk [Arazi Memlukē]" land, that is, land possessed in full ownership;

    (ii.) "Miriē [Arazi Miriē]" land;

    (iii.) "Mevqufē [Arazi Mevqufē]" land;

    (iv.) "Metroukē [Arazi Metroukē]" land;

    (v.) "Mevat [Arazi Mevat]" land.

Art. 2.—Mulk land is of four kinds:

    (i.) Sites (for houses) within towns or villages, and pieces of land of an extent not exceeding half a donum situated on the confines of towns and villages which can be considered as appurtenant to dwelling-houses.

    (ii.) Land separated from state land and made mulk in a valid way to be possessed in the different ways of absolute ownership according to the Sacred Law.

    (iii.) Tithe-paying land [Arazi Ushriē] which was distributed at the time of conquest among the victors, and given to them in full ownership.

    (iv.) Tribute-paying land [Arazi Kharajie] which (at the same period) was left and confirmed in the possession of the non-Moslem inhabitants. The tribute imposed on these lands is of two kinds:—

        (a.) "Kharaj-i-moukassemē" which is proportional and is levied to the amount of from one-tenth to one-half of the crop, according to the yield of the soil.

        (b.) "Kharaj-i-mouvazzef" which is fixed and appropriated to the land.

The owner of Mulk land has the legal ownership. It devolves by inheritance like movable property, and all the provisions of the Law, such as those with regard to dedication pledge or mortgage, gift, pre-emption, are applicable to it.

Both tithe-paying land and tribute-paying land become State land when the owner dies without issue, and the land becomes vested in the Treasury [Biet-ul-Mal].

The provisions and enactments which are applicable to the four kinds of mulk land are stated in the books of the Sacred Law, and will not therefore be dealt with in this Code.

Art. 3.—State land [Arazi Miriē], the legal ownership of which is vested in the Treasury, comprises arable fields, meadows, summer and winter pasturing grounds, woodlands and the like, the enjoyment of which is granted by the Government.

Possession of such land was formerly acquired, in case of sale or of being left vacant by permission of or grant by feudatories (sipahis) of "timars [small fiefs]" and "ziamets [large fiefs]" as lords of the soil, and later through the "multezims [tax farmers]" and "muhassils [tax collectors]."

This system was abolished and possession of this kind of unmovable property will henceforward be acquired by leave of and grant by the agent of the government appointed for the purpose. Those who acquire possession will receive a title-deed bearing the Imperial Cypher.

The sum paid in advance [muajele] for the right of possession which is paid to the proper official for the account of the State, is called the tapon fee.

Art. 4.—Mevqufē, dedicated, land is of two kinds:—

(i.) That which having been true mulk originally was dedicated in accordance with the formalities prescribed by the Sacred Law. The legal ownership and all the rights of possession over this land belong to the Ministry of Evqaf [Muslim religious and charitable foundations]. It is not regulated by civil law, but solely by the conditions laid down by the founder. This Code therefore does not apply to this kind of Mevqufē land.

(ii.) Land which being separated from State land has been dedicated by the Sultans, or by others with the Imperial sanction. The dedication of this land consists in the fact that some of the State imposts, such as the tithe and other taxes on the land so separated have been appropriated by the Government for the benefit of some object. Mevqufē land of this kind is not true vaqf. Most of the Mevqufē land in the Ottoman Empire is of this kind. The legal ownership of land which has been so dedicated (of the takhisat [special appropriations of revenue] category) belongs as in the case of purely State land to the Treasury, and the provisions and enactments hereinafter contained apply to it in their entirety. Provided that, whereas in the case of purely State land the fees of transfer, succession and the price for acquiring vacant land are paid into the Public Treasury, for this kind of mevqufē land such fees shall be paid to the vaqf concerned.

The provisions hereinafter contained with regard to State land are also applicable to mevqufē land, therefore whenever in this Code reference is made to mevqufē land this land which has been so dedicated is to be understood as being referred to.

But there is another kind of such dedicated land of which the legal ownership is vested in the Treasury (Beit-ul-Mal) and the tithes and taxes thereon belong to the State and of which only the right of possession have been appropriated for the benefit of some object.

To such dedicated land the provisions of the civil law with regard to transfer and succession do not apply; it is cultivated and occupied by the Evqaf Authorities, directly or by letting it and the income is spent according to the dedicator.

Art. 5.—Land left for the use of the public (metroukē) is of two kinds:—

(i.) That which is left for the general use of the public, like a public highway for example;

(ii.) That which is assigned for the inhabitants generally of a village or town, or of several villages or towns grouped together, as for example pastures (meras).

Art. 6.—Dead land (mevat) is land which is occupied by no one and has not been left for the use of the public. It is such as lies at such a distance from a village or town from which a loud human voice cannot make itself heard at the nearest point where there are inhabited places, that is a mile and a half, or about half an hour's distance from such.

Art. 7.—This Code is divided into three Books:

Book I.—State Land. "Arazi Miriē."

Book II.—Land which has been left for the public, "Arazi Metroukē," and "Arazi Mevat." In this Book jebali moubaha [unowned mountain land] will also be dealt with.

Book III.—Miscellaneous kinds of land not classified in the preceding categories.

Concerning the Nature of Possession

Art. 8.—The whole land of a village or of a town cannot be granted in its entirety to all of the inhabitants, nor to one or two persons chosen from amongst them. Separate pieces are granted to each inhabitant and a title deed is given to each showing his right of possession.

Art. 9.—State land may be sown with all kinds of crops such as wheat, barley, rice, madder (boia), and other cereals. It may be let on lease or loaned for the purpose of being sown but it must not be left uncultivated, except for sound and duly established reasons set out in the chapter headed Escheat of State Land.

Art. 10.—Meadow land the crop of which is harvested by *ab antiquo* usage, and on the produce of which tithe is taken is reckoned as cultivated land. Possession of it is given by title-deed. The possessor alone can profit from the herbage which grows there, and can prevent all others from making use of it. It can be broken up and put under cultivation by leave of the official.

Art. 11.—The possessor by title-deed of an arable field which is left fallow in accordance with its needs can alone derive profit from the herb called "kilimba" which grows there. He can also refuse admission to the field to anyone wishing to pasture cattle there. . . .

Art. 13.—Every possessor of land by title-deed can prevent another from passing over it, but if the latter has an *ab antiquo* right of way he cannot prevent him. . . .

Art. 24.—Places which have been used as winter (kishlak) and summer (yaylak) pasturing grounds *ab antiquo,* other than those that are appropriated to the common use of one or several villages, differ in nothing from cultivable land when they are possessed by title-deed by one person exclusively or by several persons jointly. All enactments hereinafter applicable to State land, are equally applicable to such pasturing grounds. From the owners of both kinds of pasturing grounds (whether those of communities or private persons) are taken dues called "yaylakie" and "kishlakie" in proportion to the yield.

7

Smashing Traditional Institutions, Muhammad 'Ali's Destruction of the Mamluks, March 1811 *

Muhammad 'Ali's rise to supremacy over Egypt began in 1803 when he emerged from the obscurity of a subordinate command in a contingent of Albanian troops originally sent to Egypt to support a restoration of Ottoman authority after the French evacuation in September 1801. By 1805 the wily Muhammad 'Ali maneuvered his recognition as governor by judiciously throwing the support of his troops behind one or another of the factions contesting the supremacy of Egypt and by gaining support from the local ulema who were growing weary of the prevailing unrest. By 1807 only the Mamluks stood between Muhammad 'Ali and complete control over Egypt. Finally, in 1811 in order to free himself to answer a plea from the Porte to contain the Wahhabis in Arabia, Muhammad 'Ali decided to end the Mamluk threat once and for all. Accordingly, he invited all the leading Mamluks to a parley in the Cairo Citadel for the sup-

---

* 'Abd al-Raḥmān ibn Ḥasan al-Jabarti, *'Ajā'ib al-Āthār fi al-Tarājim wa al-Akhbār* (Cairo, 1322/1904), Vol. IV, 136-138.

posed purpose of settling all outstanding differences. As the selection below rather gruesomely illustrates, the parley was not held although the outstanding differences were settled permanently. After the Citadel massacre the Mamluks hiding in the countryside were hunted down. By destroying the old governing and landholding military aristocracy which had dominated Egypt since the thirteenth century Muhammad 'Ali smashed the barriers blocking change.

*   *   *

. . . Conforming to the old practice used to announce important processions, on Thursday the 4th * [of the month of Saffar, 1226 A.H./August 1811] a military officer circulated through the market places. He wore full dress, rode a large donkey, and was preceded by an officer carrying a long baton; around and about him were soldiers calling out the announcement. In this fashion they paraded through the different quarters of the city, including those of the high military officers, the notables, the Egyptian Mamluk amirs of the Alfiyyah and other factions, and invited them to come to the Citadel early the next morning so that they could all ride together in their finery at the head of a procession.

And with the dawning of Friday the 6th the group rode up to the Citadel; it included the Egyptian Mamluks together with their personal mamluks, their servants, and their soldiers. The Mamluk amirs went up to the pasha [Muhammad 'Ali], greeted him, and remained with him for some time drinking coffee while the pasha joked with them.

Then the procession began to march according to the order which the pasha had set down. In front was the Dalat corps [Muhammad 'Ali's elite corps of Turkish and Syrian troops] and their commander, named Azun Ali; following them came the governor, and the prefect, the agha, the Wajaqiliyyah corps, and the soldiers of the Egyptian Mamluks, accompanied by retainers; these were followed by infantry troops, cavalry, high military officers, high officials, and then by Ibahim Agha, Agha of the Porte. Sulayman Bey al-Bawab moved back and forth keeping order in the procession. But meanwhile, that morning the pasha had revealed to Hassan Pasha, Salih Quj and the katkhuda [the pasha's lieutenant] his plan to betray the Mamluks and to kill them. Also, that morning he told Ibrahim Agha, Agha of the Porte, of the plot.

After the Dalat corps, the Wajaqiliyyah and the Mamluk troops passed through the Citadel's al-Azab gate, Salih Quj ordered the gate to be closed and then told his troops of the scheme. These turned on the Mamluks who were bunched up in a narrow passage cut through the rock adjacent to the al-Azab gate which led out of the Citadel. Realizing that they were blocked, the Mamluks tried to turn back but they were unable to do so for on one side their horses blocked the passage and on the other side soldiers who had been stationed high on the walls

---

* Note: The Arabic text seemed to be in error and the proper date should be the 5th of the month, ed.

started firing when they learned of their orders. Then the Mamluks, realizing their situation and seeing that many were being killed, dismounted from their horses. Shahin Bey [a leading Mamluk amir], Sulayman Bey al-Bawab, and a number of others, accompanied by a number of their Mamluks, tried to get up the passage in spite of the bullets which were raining down on them from every side. Then, after having thrown off their heavy furs and robes and with their swords drawn, they were able to reach the central courtyard in front of the hall of pillars. But already many of them had fallen and Shahin Bey, too, was hit and fell to the ground. The soldiers cut off his head and hurried back to the pasha with it in order to get a reward. When the procession began the pasha had ridden from the courtyard of the palace and returned to the house where the harem lived, that is to Ismail Effendi's house—the mint.

As for Sulayman Bey al-Bawab, he escaped to climb up the wall of the Great Tower but they continued to fire at him until he fell; then they cut off his head. A number of (other Mamluks) fled to Tusun Pasha's [Muhammad 'Ali's son] palace believing that they would find asylum there but they were killed too. The soldiers exceeded all bounds in butchering the Mamluks, stealing their clothes, giving mercy to nobody, and showing their deep hatred for them, their followers, and those who accompanied them in the procession. These latter were crying and screaming and denying that they were soldiers or Mamluks or members of their party. But the soldiers turned a deaf ear to all of them and pursued those who tried to escape around and inside the Citadel, as well as those who fled into houses and other places. They seized all who were not killed as well as those (Mamluks) who had not appeared in the parade such as Ahmad Bey al-Kilarji, Yahya Bey al-Alfi, and Ali Kashif al-Kabir who were sitting with the Katkhuda. Next, their clothes were taken and they were imprisoned under Katkhuda Bey's council chamber. Then they were killed one after another; this went on from noon until night. The courtyard was full of dead bodies. The headless bodies of the high-ranking people killed in the Citadel were dragged to be piled up with the rest. Even Shahin Bey's hands and feet were tied and his body dragged on the ground like a dead donkey to the courtyard. This is what went on at the Citadel.

Meanwhile, when the gate of the Citadel was (first) shut, those in the center of the city at Al-Ramilah heard the sound of gun-fire. As confusion spread among them, the soldiers and people who were waiting for the parade ran away. In the market quarter too, people became frightened. Those who were waiting by the shops to see the procession fled and the merchants closed their shops; nobody knew what was going on. But when the soldiers discovered what had happened and learned of the killing of the Mamluk amirs they spread like locusts to the houses of the amirs and their neighbors to rob and loot. Quickly they invaded these houses and began taking anything that they could lay their hands upon, disgracing the women and servants, and stealing whatever jewels and clothing were at hand. With nobody to oppose them (Muhammad 'Ali's) soldiers revealed what was hidden in their hearts. Some of them, when they were unable to remove a bracelet easily, would cut off a woman's wrist. The terror, fear, and horror that spread that day is beyond description. . . .

Many houses of well-known persons who were not Mamluk amirs, but who were in the service of the pasha, were looted including those of Zulfiqar Kat-khudah, overseer of the pasha's gardens in Shubra, Amir Uthman Agha al-Wardani, Mustafa Kashif al-Murali, as well as government clerks, and others.

As Saturday dawned the looting and killing continued. People were pointing out or informing about the hiding places of some of those who were in hiding. But at noon the pasha rode down from the Citadel with his high-ranking commanders walking around him wearing full dress, decorations, and ornaments. The pasha was the only one riding and a large number of his court walked in front and behind him. You could see pleasure and happiness in their faces because of the killing and looting of the Mamluks. Whenever the pasha passed soldiers, officers would stop and blame them for the stealing and for not preventing others from doing it when in fact they were the ones who started looting while others followed their example. . . .

That day, Tusun, the pasha's son, rode down town at the same time his father came down and killed one of the looters too and then the plunder subsided. However, had it not been for the coming of the pasha and his son that morning the soldiers would have pillaged the rest of the city and much misfortune would have occurred.

8

Creating New Institutions,
Clot Bey's Organization of Egypt's
First Modern Medical Establishment,
1827-1837 *

In order to support and staff the modernized military and administrative apparatus he constructed in Egypt, Muhammad 'Ali had to recruit

* Clot Bey, "Historico-Statistical Account of the Present State of Medicine in Egypt," contained in John Bowering, "Report on Egypt and Candia, A Report addressed to the Right Hon. Lord Viscount Palmerston and presented to both Houses of Parliament," *House of Lords, Sessional Papers 1840*, Vol. XXXV, 139-142. This report appears in *House of Commons, Sessional Papers*, Vol. XXI.

a large group of men educated in a broad spectrum of subjects. Always relying heavily upon foreign experts, the pasha also undertook a program of educating his subjects in modern knowledge. Many students were sent to Europe; others were trained in a hastily improvised educational enterprise which tried to convert religious schools into elementary schools which could feed students into a state system of secondary and higher education. The attempt to coordinate religious and secular education was not successful and the subsequent existence of separate religious and secular educational system did much to doom the early development of an effective Egyptian consensus on how to confront the modern world. The first schools established were military academies designed to provide the armed forces with officers conversant with modern military science. A government press and a bureau charged with translating European works into local languages was established to facilitate the spread of those kinds of Western knowledge—science and technology, but not philosophy—considered useful by the government. In some cases education had to be provided in subjects entirely foreign to Egyptians. Such was the case of modern medical education. The educational efforts of Muhammad 'Ali were of fundamental importance in inoculating Middle Eastern society with the germs of modernism.

*   *   *

Organization of the Service.

"In Egypt, as in other parts of the East, all the sciences were buried under the ruins of the empire of the caliphs; hardly have some disfigured and badly understood manuscripts transmitted to us a dim reflection of that era of glory and intelligence.

"Medicine was given up to the achievements of empiricism; surgery passed into the hands of the barbers; pharmacy, to the traffic of the merchant. But when more friendly political relations between Christian Europe and Turkey rendered communication more easy and more frequent, the East was over-run with physicians, who easily established their superiority over ignorant pretenders. Since that time the Orientals have attributed to Europeans a general medical reputation; and even in our day, the public credulity is but too often practised upon by men whose foreign extraction is the only scientific title they possess.

"In commencing the great work of reformations that he determined upon, Mahomet Ali made offers to European officers of every rank and department; a general military organization was introduced, and then, as a matter of course, a medical service was created for the preservation of the Egyptian forces.

"Clot Bey, engaged as physician and surgeon-in-chief to the new army, arrived in Egypt, followed by a number of medical officers, who were immediately appointed to the different regiments and hospitals then in progress of establishment. Thus began a regular service.

"The surgeon, the physician, and the apothecary constituted the general council of health, placed under the immediate authority of the minister of war, and having under its authority secondary councils for the land and sea forces established upon all the possessions of his highness.

"The medical service is almost exclusively organized according to the spirit of the French regulations.

"The foreign physicians and apothecaries employed among the troops and in military hospitals belong to the different nations of Europe, and appear on the medical list in the following proportions:—

Italians	105
French	32
English	6
Germans	5
Poles	4
Spaniards	2
	154

"The title of 'doctor of medicine' from one of the faculties of Europe is required to obtain the rank of major.

"The general council of health, at present, is composed as follows:—

MM. Clot Bey, inspector-general—president.

Gaetani Bey, private physician to his highness—honorary member.

Delsignore, inspector physician—incumbent member.

Destouches, inspector apothecary—incumbent member.

"The salary given to the different ranks was fixed as follows:—

	Francs.
Inspector-general of the land forces and the marine; president of the general council of health	30,000
Inspectors and members of the council general of health	10,000
Inspectors of the army	8,500
Principals	5,000
Majors	3,400
Assistant-majors	2,200
Under-assistants	1,500

Formation of the Hospital and Medical School at Abouzabel.

"The opening of the hospital at Abouzabel dates from the year 1825. The camp of instruction, situated in the vicinity of this establishment, and composed of the infantry of the army, the staff, and artillery schools (in all 25,000 men) provide it on an average with about 1,500 or 2,000 sick.

"The dearth of native physicians and the existence of materials proper for the formation of a school suggested to Clot Bey the idea of establishing within the hospital itself a medical class, destined to furnish surgeons and apothecaries for the service of the army. His views were approved of; and in 1827, young men, chosen from the schools of the mosques, were the first initiated in the science of the Avicennas and the Albucazars.

"The programme of the studies comprised the following subjects:—

1. Anatomy and physiology.
2. Pathology and external clinique.
3. Pathology and internal clinique.
4. Materia medica and therapeutics.
5. Hygiene and forensic medicine.
6. Physics and chemistry.
7. Botany.

"Clot Bey was appointed director of the school and professor of pathology and of external clinique. This school has produced, in the ten years since its formation, 420 medical officers, incorporated in the army and navy, with the rank of under-assistants, assistants, and majors.

"Twelve young Arabians were brought in 1833 to Paris, by Clot Bey, for the completion of their medical studies; and six of them have been employed since their return to Egypt as assistant professors in the national school of Abouzabel, where they had received, as pupils, insructions in the art they practise. The six others, still in Paris, will be forthwith restored to their country, where they will turn to good account, like their predecessors, the knowledge they have acquired.

Creation of the Second Schools at Alexandria and Aleppo.

"In 1837, two secondary medical schools were created, one at Alexandria and the other at Aleppo, for the improvement of the practical instruction of the pupils who leave the school at Abouzabel. They were instructed in descriptive anatomy, pathology, internal and external clinique, and practical pharmacy. The instruction devolved upon the physicians, surgeons, apothecaries (en chef) of the army and navy.

Removal of the Hospital and Medical School from Abouzabel to Cairo.

"In consequence of the suppression of the camp, which had given rise to the creation of the hospital and the school of Abouzabel, the sick-ward received none but individuals labouring under chronic affections. From that time the usefulness and the success of the two establishments ceased; and their removal to a more convenient place for the sick, and for instruction, became an absolute necessity. The vast edifice of Kasr-el-ein, occupied by a preparatory school, was destined to receive the sick, and the pupils from Abouzabel, and *vice versa*. It was an exchange profitable both to science and humanity.

"The edifice of Kasr-el-ein is situated on the eastern bank of the Nile, and about a quarter of a league from Cairo, and upon the site of the summer farm of Ibrahim Bey, where the French, at the time of their conquest, established their military hospitals.

"It is formed by four ranges of buildings, in a square; 64 spacious apartments, of 40 beds each, composed of two stories; a separate building for the pharmacy, the chemical laboratory, the museum of physics and natural history, for the amphitheatre, baths, kitchens, &c.

"Since the creation of the medical school, works on the following subjects have been translated into Arabic:—

1. Anatomy.
2. Surgical pathology.
3. Physiology.
4. Physics.
5. Chemistry.
6. Botany.
7. Materia medica.
8. Toxicology.
9. Hygiene.
10. Midwifery and diseases of women and children.
11. Treatise on general anatomy.
12. Treatment of asphyxia.
13. Guide to military surgery.
14. Treatise on bandages.
15. Diseases of the skin.
16. Rules of military hospitals.

"The duration of medical studies is five years.

"The renewal of the students takes place by fifths every year. The pupils wear a uniform, and are subject to military rule; fed, dressed, lodged at the expense of the government; and receive, besides, pay, which varies according to the class to which they belong. Thus, the pupils of the first year receive 40 piastres a-month (10 francs), those of the second year 50 piastres, and thus progressing to the fifth year.

"The lectureships are given by cæncæms, or in some cases to those whose services have sufficiently deserved the reward.

"The salary of the professors is 5,000 francs a-year; that of the directors of the school, 7,000 francs.

"The following is a list of the professors and the courses of study:—

M.M. Duvigneau, director—pathology and internal clinique.
Scisson—pathology and external clinique.
Fischer—anatomy and physiology.

Perron—medicine and chemistry.

Figari—botany and materia medica.

Pacthod—pharmacy.

Pruner, chief physician to the military hospital—ophthalmology.

"Each European professor is assisted by an Arabian professor, who understands French.

Formation of a Lying-in Establishment.

"The importance of a maternity was sensibly felt in Egypt, where lying-in women were entrusted to the care of the most ignorant and superstitious midwives.

"In 1832 Clot Bey proposed and obtained the establishment of a school for midwives; 20 negresses and Abyssinians were collected in a place for this purpose, under the direction of a midwife of the *maternity* at Paris, an Arabian physician, who had graduated in France, and an 'ulema,' to instruct in religion and literature. The pupils read and write Arabic and learn the theory and practice of midwifery. This school of obstetricity daily acquires importance; the number of pupils now amounts to 50, and their instruction is confided to the five most skilful among them, under the direction and surveillance of the principal midwife physician and ulema.

Formation of the Hospital.

"The removal of the hospital from Abouzabel to Kasr-el-Ein caused the suppression of that of Cairo, situated in the great Esbekieh-square, which has just been converted into a civil hospital, divided into five departments—a hospital for men, a hospital for women, a maternity, a lying-in hospital, and a lunatic establishment: it is capable of accommodating 500 sick.

"The Civil Hospital at Cairo was the first erected in the Ottoman empire since the Caliphs, and although they had in the height of their power erected some, they never were so complete as the Asylum of Piety, which Mahomet Ali has opened for human sufferings.

"Thus in the regeneration of Egypt, medicine has been, as it ought to be, one of the most powerful instruments.

"The ascendancy which its ministers exercise throughout the whole of society by their mission of philanthropy, has rendered the union of the people of two religions essentially different, more intimate, exacted gratitude on the one side, created devotedness on the other, and has broken down the barrier which had been erected between the worshippers of Christ and those of the prophet by a superstitious but popular hatred.

"The devotedness of the European physicians, their heroic struggles against the most fatal disorders, their praiseworthy and entire disregard of their own lives, have produced invaluable and incalculable results; but it was especially the formation of the school at Abouzabel which gave a new era to medicine in Egypt—a glorious epoch for a humane and imperishable sovereign.

"Initiated in the different sciences which belong to the art of medicine, and which constitute the well-informed man, the medical pupils are become so many apostles destined to spread the light of knowledge in the midst of a people still enslaved by prejudice and ignorance.

"Henceforward to apply the dissecting knife to a dead body, is not a sacrilege worthy of damnation. The wonders of medicine and chemistry are no longer supposed to be brought forth by magic, or by the devil.

"The ulema himself has progressed—has applauded the acquirements of the young girls, knowing the Arabic language equally with those who study in the mosques. They are able to give an account of the structure of the organs, to explain the phenomena of conception, the principal functions of life, the sublime discovery of Harvey, the chemical decomposition of air, the geometrical proportions of the pelvis, parturition, both natural and unnatural, and have quoted, by turns, the names of Semlié and Baudeloque.

"Mother of all the schools established in Egypt—their model by its regular organization, its order and discipline, by the professorships given at the annual public examinations, or in recompense of distinguished merit, worthy the patronage which presides over its destinies and of the gratitude of the country, by the numerous scientific treatises which are, in some degree, naturalized by translation—the school of medicine has given the first impulse to the regenerative movement, and has not stopped one single instant, continuing, with success, the humane and intellectual task it has thus auspiciously undertaken.

"December 27, 1837."

9

Economic Change, Muhammad 'Ali's Development Schemes in Egypt and Syria, 1834 and 1837 *

Muhammad 'Ali's need to pay for his expensive military modernization program prompted him to introduce a comprehensive develop-

* a. John Bowering, "Report on the Commercial Statistics of Syria," *House of Lords, Sessional Papers, 1840,* Vol. XXXV, 9-10.

  b. James A. St. John, *Egypt and Muhammad 'Ali* (London: Longman, Reese, Orme, Brown, Green, and Longman, 1834), Vol. II, 408-414, 417, 423-425.

ment program which brought sweeping change to the economies of Egypt and Syria. His reordering of agriculture smashed the Mamluk land tenure system, asserted Cairo's control over the rural economy, increased the cultivated area through the construction of irrigation works in Egypt and reestablishing abandoned villages in Syria, and encouraged market crops such as cotton, sugar cane and tobacco. More spectacular, although of less fundamental importance, were the pasha's attempts to build a new industrial-commercial system. Factories, many of whose machines were powered by animal-driven treadmills, were thrown up in the cities and in the countryside as well. The new factories were state-owned and by 1837 were supervised by a central Ministry of Industry but most of them were abandoned in the austerity program initiated in 1841. Commercially, there was an immense quickening of activity as Egypt became closely enmeshed with the European dominated modern international economy. Besides controlling production the government undertook the sale and distribution of goods through the state agencies; members of the old craft guilds, masters and workers alike, as well as laborers hired by the new factories all became state employees. So the major legacy of the pasha's industrial drive was to complete the destruction of the medieval corporate economy. Since foreign experts and businessmen played a large role in all these projects, foreign participation in Egypt's economic life became a feature of the period and of later years as well.

A. THE AWAKENING OF RURAL SYRIA

The agricultural produce of Syria is far less than might be expected from the extensive tracts of fertile lands and the favourable character of the climate. In the districts where hands are found to cultivate the fields, production is large and the return for capital is considerable; but the want of population for the purposes of cultivation is most deplorable. Regions of the highest fertility remain fallow, and the traveller passes over continuous leagues of the richest soil which is wholly unproductive to man. Nay, towns surrounded by lands capable of the most successful cultivation are often compelled to import corn for the daily consumption; as is the case at Antioch, in whose immediate neighbourhood the fine lands on the borders of the Orontes might furnish food for hundreds of thousands of inhabitants. But men crowd into towns for protection and security, and leave the rural districts without labourers to sow or to reap the harvest.

Agricultural knowledge is generally in a backward state; the old Roman plough, drawn by bullocks, is almost universally employed. In Mount Lebanon, however, where the scantiness of appropriate soil requires a succession of terraces for cultivation, spade husbandry is much used, the space being too narrow for the plough. . . .

To these more important articles of export may be added wheat, barley, maize, millet, lentils, sesame-seed, and other produce, consumed principally by the inhabitants. The production of which the increased cultivation is most obvious is the mulberry tree, for the use of the silkworm, which may be attributed to the demand for silk in every part of manufacturing Europe; but a considerable increase has also taken place in the cultivation of the vine, and plantations have also been made for the extension of the growth of the olive-tree, principally in the districts of Tripoli and Latakia, the localities adapted to their developments.

At Suediah, in the vale of Antioch, Latakia, Tripoli, and many other places, the cultivation of tobacco is one of the first importance, and is on the increase; and there is scarcely any place in Syria where it is not now grown, but the qualities are very various.

Mr. Werry thinks there is no agricultural produce whose cultivation has decreased, but that, on the contrary, grain and pulse of every kind, as well as produce for exportation, are produced to a much larger extent than formerly from one end of Syria to the other. Great exertions have been made on the part of the government to effect this object by obliging all the chief officers and the most wealthy inhabitants to take upon themselves the restoring of ruined villages, and the cultivation of the lands belonging to these villages; but it is very doubtful whether in the mode of cultivation there is any improvement.

The following is the extension given to the agriculture in the Aleppo district from 1836 to 1838.—Villages and lands belonging to the town of Aleppo:

329	Villages	Old
238	Parcels of land	
74	Villages or Hamlets	New
445	Parcels of land	
1086	Belonging to Aleppo District	Baylan [Beilan]
410	Villages and land	Antioch
206	Villages and land	Aintab
36	Villages and land	Baylan [Beilan]
397	Old Villages	
149	Lands	Killis
27	New Villages	
2311	In all	

And similar extension has taken place in the Damascus district.

Last year (1837) Ibrahim Pacha forced an increased cultivation throughout Syria and the inhabitants of the different towns were obliged to take upon themselves the agricultural charge of every spot of land susceptible to improvement. He himself set the example, and embarked a large sum in such enterprises. The officers of the army, down to the majors, were forced also to adventure in similar undertakings. The result was, however, extremely unfortunate, from the want of the usual periodical rains, which caused the failing of the crops generally in Syria, and in most cases a total loss of capital ensued. Mr. Werry says, a considerable extension of the plantation of the mulberry and olive-tree, and vines, took place at Tripoli, Latakia, and to the south, and in fact in every place susceptible to their culture. It was the intention of his highness Ibrahim Pacha, and of the government in Egypt, by the increased cultivation, principally of wheat and barley, to render Syria independent of supplies from without, and, if possible, to obtain a superabundance to become an article of export. In the time of abundant crops Syria generally produced, chiefly in the south, sufficient for its own consumption; and the north, when in want, usually received supplies from the country surrounding Orfa, across the Euphrates. The productive plains of the Adana district also supplied Syria, and where the measures undertaken by the government persevered in, there is no reason to doubt that they would in every respect become highly beneficial to the population of Syria generally, and render it independent of import from any other quarter.

The chief observation to be made on these measures is, that there is no want of land generally in Syria, nor is there a want of capital for such an object, but there is want of agricultural population and of livestock....

B. MUHAMMAD 'ALI'S ATTEMPT TO MAKE EGYPT A MANUFACTURING COUNTRY

Not content with imparting to his people a knowledge of the sciences, and the arts of war, Mohammed Ali, in 1819, was led by the advice of Europeans to attempt the introduction of the manufacturing system. In this undertaking he was deluded by fallacious calculations. Being persuaded that, with the aid of certain French and Swiss adventurers, it was possible to render Cairo a second Manchester, he commenced operations with his usual rapidity. French, Italian, Maltese, and Savoyard manufacturers and artisans were employed. Kromfish, a district of miserable houses and narrow streets, in the centre of the metropolis, infamous for murders and every other horrid crime, was cleared of its inhabitants, and the whole den of thieves and cut-throats converted, with very trifling alterations, into factories. No expense was spared in procuring every description of machinery from Europe. Magazines were formed; mills, worked by bullocks, constructed; and the machinery was erected by the principal French and Italian mechanics. This establishment was directed by M. Morel of Chamberi; and another large factory, erected at Boolak, was placed under the superintendence of M. Jumel, a Frenchman. The number of natives employed in this new species of industry amounted to eight hundred.

At Kromfish an attempt was made to produce velvets equal to those of Genoa, and muslins not inferior to those of England; but, after a short trial, the destruction of the machinery, which could not be repaired, and the extremely inferior quality of the articles manufactured, induced the Pasha,—perhaps before the experiment had been fairly tried,—wholly to abandon this portion of the scheme. Kromfish was not, however, entirely forsaken. Mohammed 'Ali was still desirous of rendering Egypt a manufacturing country; a failure in one experiment not being sufficient to deter him from attempting others. The cultivation of the cotton-plant already promised to become a fertile source of revenue. He now, therefore, determined to manufacture from the raw material, and Kromfish became a cotton-mill.

On the first introduction of European manufactories into Egypt, the Turks in office, and even the people in general, openly evinced their disapprobation in their mutual discourse; and the former were often bold enough to represent to the Pasha, in open Divan, the impolicy of his conduct. But courtiers in all countries are too much the slaves of habit, too timid in their apprehensions, and too ignorant of whatever concerns the public good, to be competent judges in an untried line of internal policy. The Pasha, therefore, despised their representations, which arose out of no superior degree of foresight, but from a puerile aversion to every thing new; and his will necessarily prevailed. Encouraged by the first samples produced at Kromfish, he now caused cotton-mills to be erected at Mehalet-el-Kebir, at Mansourah, and in the southern parts of the metropolis. At first, no persons were employed in the factories but black slaves from Darfour and Kordofan, who displayed great intelligence, and quickly acquired a competent knowledge of the business; but so great a change of life, co-operating with the peculiar unhealthiness of the occupation, gradually thinned their ranks, so that the Pasha was shortly compelled to have recourse to the Fellahs.

It must be observed that, with the exception of a few machines adapted to each manipulation, brought out from Europe as models, no cotton-spinning apparatus has been imported into the country. The store-houses were furnished with tools; lathes, screw-tapping lathes, instruments for fluting rollers, and cutting the teeth of wheels, with other preparatory instruments,—all purchased in England and France at an enormous cost; and upon these models preparatory instruments were soon multiplied by the carpenters, smiths, filers, turners, &c. formed under the tuition of the French and Italian artisans; who, under the superintendence of M. Jumel,—a professional spinner and mechanic,—constructed all the spinning machinery which now fills the numerous cotton-factories throughout Egypt.

The Pasha regards his manufactories in so important a light, that, to promote emulation, and confer a superior degree of respectability on the professors of the useful arts, he honours their directors with a seat in the Mashwarrah (or council), and further distinguishes them by diamond decorations, which they wear on the breast. All the operative Nazirs, one of whom is placed over every mill, have likewise their badges of honour. The officers engaged in the factories deem their employment peculiarly honourable; but their conduct is too frequently directly the reverse; for though in the receipt of handsome salaries, they sordidly avail themselves of the mal-organisation of the establishments to commit dishonesty, and plunder their master and their inferiors. Being entrusted with the regulation of the expenses, and the paying of the workmen, they accept bribes to favour an indifferent artisan at the expense of the government, and commit innumerable other frauds difficult of detection. Thus it is that commissioners from the treasury are perpetually engaged in examining accounts and detecting imposition.

The fellahs employed in the various manipulations have an extreme dislike to the business; being pressed into the mills, they labour only because they are compelled. Though they generally arrive at the factories in good health, the insalubrious nature of the employment, imprisonment, their scanty wages, the insufficiency of their food, and the odious vices which, by the example of their superiors, they quickly learn to commit, in a short time render them diseased and despicable. They seldom see their wives and children, nor are they allowed the requisite time for meals, ablutions, or religious duties. Inattention or mismanagement is followed by immediate chastisement; the directing Nazirs being regularly accompanied by their executioners, who flog the delinquents with the Koorbash. From two hundred to five hundred blows are not unusual; so that a cotton-spinner in Egypt is no less brutally punished than a West India negro; while, in the Pasha's navy, fifty blows are considered a sufficient punishment for ordinary offences. Such being their treatment, it is not at all surprising that the operatives eagerly avail themselves of the first opportunity which presents itself of making their escape; or, where this is impracticable, of revenging their wrongs in a more serious manner. Of the twenty-three or twenty-four cotton-mills existing in Egypt, there is not one which has not, at various periods, been accidentally or designedly set on fire. The factory at Siout, which employed about six hundred hands, was purposely burned to the ground; and, towards the close of December, 1832, the power-loom weaving mill of Khand-el-Merood was likewise designedly destroyed by fire. In the latter establishment the loss was estimated at 35,000*l.* On the day preceding this accident, a fellah, who had been dragged against his inclination into the rope-walk, stabbed himself in three places, and, after a short struggle, expired.

In the provincial mills the raw material is beaten, carded, and spun by men and boys; and the yarn, when taken off the reefs, is put loosely into large bags, and transported to Cairo on camels. But, in some of the factories, a small portion is retained and woven into cloth, part of which being sent to the capital, the remainder is appropriated to the payment of the operatives. For this purpose they make use of hand-looms, built after French models. At present not one of the mills keeps its full complement of machinery at work, and there are several where not one half is employed; in some cases because the machines are actually worn out; in others from the scarcity of hands. Through the ignorance and carelessness of the directors and their operatives, about fifty per cent of the raw material is wasted; ...

The traveller, on his way to the upper country, is astonished at the vastness of the cotton-mills, which, though differing in dimensions, are all built on the same plan. They are constructed with rubble and mortar, and covered externally with stucco. For the small number of machines they contain, they are much more spacious than necessary. The apartments, which are flagged with stone, are extremely lofty, and the doors and windows proportionably large. All the bullock-mills, along the front of the buildings, are enclosed in large towers, adorned with bow windows, balconies, and balustrades. Spacious flights of stone steps ascend to the second story, and the entrance is generally shaded by a light wooden trellis-work. All these buildings are erected in the finest situations. At Minieh, for example, the mill is situated on the edge of the Nile, and surrounded by a grove of orange and date trees, which give it a picturesque appearance. The expense of building one of the smaller mills amounts to about 7,000*l.* sterling; ...

I subjoin a list of the factories of different kinds now existing in Egypt:—

1. Sugar and rum manufactory at Er Raramoun.
2. Powder manufactory at Rhouda.
3. Saltpetre refinery at Rhouda.
4. Chemical works, at Masr el Atikeh (*Old Cairo*).
5. Tannery, *Old Cairo.*
6. Founderies for brass guns and carriages in the citadel.
7. Copper-mills.

CITADEL.

8. Pyrotechnic school: fire works, carcasses, stink-pots, signal rockets, &c.

CAIRO.

9. Cotton-mills.
10. Weaving, silk and cotton.
11. Rope walks, for Alexandria.
12. Musket manufactory: here they repair monthly 1600 old muskets, and manufacture 400 new ones, under the direction of Ali Aga, a French renegade, with the rank of Colonel.
13. Cloth manufactory.
14. Calico printing works.
15. Bleaching fields.
16. Iron foundery: to appearance the finest in the world. By Galloway.
17. Power-loom weaving factory. By Galloway.
18. Dying works.

ROSETTA.

19. Rice-mills. By Galloway.
20. Tannery.

21. Corn-mills: there now exist about forty; but it is contemplated to increase the number to two hundred.

22. Glass-house.

23. At Malta-Fabrick, four hundred forges, employed for the fleet and army.

24. At Gallioop, one hundred and fifty forges set up, but not worked.

25. Paper mill; recently established near Cairo.

26. Manufactory of Tarbooshes, at Fouah. Directed by Tunisians.

10

The Collapse of the Old Order, Anti-Feudalism and Peasant Revolts in Lebanon, 1859 *

The traditional way of life in Syria and Lebanon was vigorously attacked and weakened during the eight years of Egyptian rule between 1832 and 1840. With the defeat and evacuation of the Egyptian army from Syria the region was turned back to the Ottomans. Never really able to reestablish themselves, the Ottoman task was complicated by British-French rivalry, dislocation of the economy in the wake of penetration of local markets by European exports, growing communal unrest, and the failure of the established aristocracy and established precedents to come to grips with the new situation. By the 1850's large areas of Lebanon and Syria were fast approaching a breakdown in established social and political relationships. Fundamentally, this breakdown was caused by the disintegration of traditional patterns of life in the face of encroachments by the modern world. More specifically the breakdown was reflected in a struggle between the old feudal elite who tried to collect their traditional revenues, exercise their traditional police and judicial functions, and enjoy their traditional privileges, and the rural masses who were discontented with the way their aristocratic leaders were coping with a new age. Further complicating an involved situation was the rise of religious tension among Syria's and Lebanon's many sects. The following selection contains a petition sent in 1859 to the anti-aristocratic, pro-

* Anṭūn Dāhir al-'Aqīqi, *Thawrah wa Fitnah fi Lubnān: Ṣafḥa Majhūla min Tārikh al-Jabal min 1841 ila 1873,* tr. by Malcolm H. Kerr included in, *Lebanon in the Last Years of Feudalism,* 1840-1868 (Beirut: American University of Beirut Faculty of Arts and Letters, 1959), American University of Beirut Faculty of Arts and Letters Oriental Series, No. 33, 96-99.

gressive Maronite Patriarch Bûlus Mas'ad (1854-1890) outlining the demands of the anti-feudal faction.

*   *   *

(Letter from certain villages to Patriarch Bûlus Mas'ad)

To the most holy Father, may God prolong his reign!

After kissing the places where your sacred feet have trod, and seeking your Apostolic blessing forever, we submit to you the following petition:

The disturbances that have taken place in this district are no secret to Your Beatitude. Because of them we have been robbed of our peace, an account of the presence of ignorant people. Whereas on this date your son our brother Shaikh Saj'ân al-'Uḍaimî came to us on behalf of the people living in the region of al-Zûq, asking of us to unite with them in order to bring peace to all us, we, your children the people of the villages whose names are recorded at the end of this petition, therefore met in the village of Dlibtâ on the 12th of this month. After deliberation with the representatives (wakîls) of all our people, we came to an agreement. Since Your Beatitude is considered to be a spiritual father to us, we present to Your Beatitude this petition, which we beg you to examine with a generous eye, with an explanation of the headings listed above, so that by force of your superior wisdom you will be obliged in conscience to secure the return of our rights to us, not only for the present but for always. Since your children who are presenting this are unable to secure for themselves the foregoing and Your Beatitude will feel obliged to inquire about that, we therefore repeat our plea, knocking at the gates of your paternal justice and compassion, saying: Look at our weakness and save us from our oppressor. As for the question of the office of ma'mûr, this we entrust to the command and the wish of Your Beatitude. Whomever you consider suitable to deal with our situation and able to restore the general peace, we shall recognize his orders. Whereas not everything is explained in our petition, at this time the bearers of this petition who were appointed to present it to you will lay the matter before you more adequately. All depends on what your commands call for. May God prolong your reign!

Again we kiss the places where our feet have trod.

Your Beatitude's children,
The people of

Al-Judaida, Shnan'îr, Dlibtâ, 'Aramûn, Ghûsṭâ, Baṭḥâ.
December 17, 1859.

(The demands of the people, referred to in the preceding letter, No. II)

Statement of the items requested by which peace may be secured for us and for Their Excellencies the Shaikhs.

First: that the collection of the [mîri] tax money be in accordance with principles, and likewise the head tax, falling on the great and the small according to the register instituted by His Grace Shakîb Pasha, so that even the Shaikhs shall be obliged to pay what is apportioned to them in the collective and head taxes, without the people having to bear an excessive head tax.

Second: Whereas oppressions, wrongdoings, exaction of extras from travelers and servants, and the money transfers (ḥawâlât) taken from the people by the dissimulations of Their Excellencies the Shaikhs, are contrary to the laws of the Sublime State and the benevolent decrees, when these deeds are ascertained by whatever body is designated, whether the present [judicial] council or another, the doer of these offenses and of violations of the law, after confirmation, must return and repay what he has taken in its entirety.

Third: the presents and marriage taxes currently paid to Their Excellencies the Shaikhs in certain places, or the presents to the Shaikhs attached to the sale of their goods to the people, must be discontinued and removed in their entirety.

Fourth: As for the question of the office of ma'mûr, which is of the greatest importance, having to do with governing the people and removing grievances and violations, the ma'mûr must govern in accordance with justice and law so that there shall be no further disputes between us and Their Excellencies the Shaikhs. Whoever is appointed to deal with our affairs, we pray that he will be deserving of this position and worthy of it, and possessing all the conditions suited to the authority and activities of ma'mûrs. Similarly it is incumbent on all the people to render their due obedience and consideration to the ma'mûr, he being distinct from the mass of the people, and there must be great efforts made to keep his commands. For every village one or two representatives (wakîls) should be instituted, according to the large or small size of the village, so as to achieve peace and facilitate the ma'mûr's orders and to facilitate his work and interests without hindrance.

Fifth: Whereas the Sublime State—may the Lord of Creation preserve it!—has granted us universal equality and complete freedom, so that there should be no distinctions or degradations in addressing persons, and so that all the old principles should be changed in regard to the registers, and whereas new taxes have been levied on all, we pray that all this may be kept in mind by Your Beatitude.

Sixth: The submission of the question of ma'mûrs in Kisrawân to the decision of Your Beatitude is done on condition that the authority of the ma'mûr be effective on everyone without exception in accordance with the reform measures taken, so that from now on no one will be set apart and distinguished from the general public except for the ma'mûr himself. As for those remaining of Their Excellencies the Shaikhs, if any offenses on their part occur against the people, they shall be punished in accordance with the laws upon confirmation by the council, as it shall be done also to offenders from among the people.

11

Tension Between Aspirations and Capabilities, Khedive Isma'il's Speech to the Egyptian Assembly of Delegates, January 1869 *

The following selection illustrates the aspirations of one second-generation modernizer, Khedive Isma'il (1863-1879) whose ambitions, although seemingly thwarted in the short run, produced immense and permanent alterations in Egypt. Agricultural changes included the move to perennial irrigation, and an increase in crop yields—particularly cotton whose export value quadrupled in the decade 1860-1870; the Suez Canal, modern port facilities, a railway, road and telegraph net, and the first major modern urban development projects in the Middle East were constructed. Social changes included a cultural flowering that involved the reopening of schools closed during Muhammad 'Ali's declining years, and the growth of a cadre of intellectuals conversant with the modern world. Also, the erosion of rural Egypt's isolation intensified while increasing opportunities became available to those native Egyptians who were able to obtain a modern education. Politically, there was a temporary revival of Egypt's military strength. Even more significant was the growth of the governmental bureaucracy which continued the process begun by Muhammad 'Ali of centralizing political power in Cairo. Isma'il relied more and more upon foreign loans raised in Europe and, too, encouraged foreign investment adventuring in his country. The Khedive, despite the glib references concerning state solvency in the speech below, did not understand finance. He squandered huge sums on palaces, foreign wars, and a grandiose prestige-oriented foreign policy. Invariably, he paid too much to finance his legitimate schemes. By 1876 Egypt was bankrupt, unable to service its £100,000,000 debt. A joint Anglo-French Debt Commission took over the country's economy. The political implications of this imposition of foreign control were immense and they contributed to Isma'il's deposition in 1879 and to Egypt's falling under British "protection" in 1882.

*   *   *

It has been one year since our last meeting so I am happy to assure you that Egypt is prosperous and that the questions submitted for your consideration dur-

* Translated from a French version of the speech quoted in G. Douin, *Histoire du Regne du Khedive Ismàil* (Rome: Royal Geographic Society of Egypt, 1934), II, 128-136.

ing your last session have been settled in accordance with your advice and to the great advantage of the country.

The condition of our finances is excellent; they have been administered in such a way that we have been able to repay some large obligations without embarrassment to the government and without unusual sacrifices by the people.

Unfortunately, it is also true that this year the Nile did not attain its usual level and so, along a considerable length of its banks, the fields lacked the precious ingredient of water. Still, thanks to the measures taken by your government we have been able to arrange for the normal irrigation of the provinces of lower Egypt. Although the same measures were undertaken in upper Egypt, I must say with regret that our efforts were not crowned with equal success along the upper Nile and a rather large number of fields in upper Egypt were not irrigated because of their overly high elevation.

In this situation I was quick to come to the aid of the farmers struck by an unforeseen disaster by remitting taxes and tithes on non-irrigated fields. Also, I remitted their salt tax so that salt was delivered to them without charge, and I gave orders that they should be furnished with enough grain to sow their fields for planting. Finally, I exempted them from labor on public works. These measures cost the government a sum in excess of 80,000 purses ... [app. $1,770,000] but contrary to what used to be done in such circumstances, we sustained the sacrifice without incurring debts that would have to be paid in the future.

Independently of these extraordinary measures taken to deal with specific circumstances, also, I was able to come to the aid of each and every one of the people of upper Egypt thanks to the prosperous condition of our finances. I remitted the payment of the tax which was levied by the Chamber last year and I granted new terms for the payment of the salt tax. Encouraged by these moves, the peasants of upper Egypt are working courageously. Some of the unflooded fields have been irrigated by using irrigation methods traditional in the region or from newly excavated wells. A supplementary harvest consisting chiefly of corn, has rewarded these efforts, and just as I expected, this interesting segment of the populace once again has justified its ancient reputation for skill in the practice of agriculture.

I can only thank Providence for these good results and you will be happy, as I am, to know that an important part of Egypt has escaped from a disaster which could have brought fatal circumstances. The famine which menaced those districts has been averted, the needy have found their bread each day, and no trace of want remains today in the country.

We are confident that with the aid of divine protection these exceptional circumstances will not reappear for a long time and that this year the normal flood of the Nile will bring us its usual benefits. Nevertheless, since man often tries to augment the masterworks of Providence with his own personal efforts I wanted to prepare a proper program that would ensure the flooding of upper Egypt's fields under all circumstances. After conferring with our principal engineers about the best way to realize this goal, I named a commission that went to upper Egypt; after an on-the-spot study of the scientific measures needed to assure the irrigation of the most elevated fields no matter what the level of the Nile flood might be, they proceeded immediately to put these measures into operation. Thus I hope that those kinds of dangers will be averted in the future.

To return to our financial situation, previously I stated to you that, in spite of the many sacrifices enumerated above taken to relieve the population of upper Egypt, our finances are in a very prosperous state.

The government has been able to bear some extraordinary expenses because of the resources that it has amassed through sage reductions in certain services as well as by the conclusion of the last loan. The debts contracted by Sa'id Pasha [Viceroy of Egypt, 1854-1863] totaled twenty-two million pounds as you were told in the report which was presented to you in the meeting of 12 Moharrem 1285 [1868] and which was based upon an inventory of the accounts of the Ministry of Finance conducted by a commission emanating from your body. A large part of this debt has been retired and our debt has been reduced today to approximately seventeen million pounds including the new loan. As for the sums borrowed by my government, they have been, as you have been informed, contracted in large part for public works and for expenses undertaken for the general well-being and progress of the country. Above these amounts, eight million pounds have been paid to the Suez Canal Company. It is true that from the start some of the charges of the construction of the Suez Canal have been borne by our people but I expect that soon the country will find compensation for these charges. In effect, according to solemn promises, the canal will open during the month of October next year, which corresponds to the month of Redjeb 1286 [1870]. The government possesses almost half of the stock shares of the company and will have the right to 15% of the profits resulting from its operations; so soon we will have, in the exploitation of the canal, a new source of revenue.

In order to justify the large size of our debt I need only enumerate the important projects which have been completed recently. I can cite in the first place the new 850 mile long railroad line. The results which this new means of communications has produced in the benefit of the country's prosperity are too apparent for me to have to dwell on them. As for the expenses occasioned by these works, the Ministry of Finance has taken them over by agreeing to redeem the railroad loan which amounts to four million pounds and, using some funds from the last loan, by redeeming the bonds issued by the railroad administration for a sum of three million pounds. I can cite, moreover, 4 draw bridges built, one over the Owady [al-Wadi] Canal and three others over the right-of-way of the upper Egypt railway, 100 ordinary bridges of which 40 are in lower Egypt and 60 are in upper Egypt, 2 movable bridges over the Mahmudiyah Canal near the Alexandria railroad station; the Suez dry-dock, the passenger dock and the enlargement of the port of Suez, and finally a great number of buildings and works of other types none-the-less useful—built in upper and lower Egypt, in the cities of Cairo and Alexandria and in other cities of Egypt.

Following this listing, I believe it would be useful if I placed before you a table of the works constructed in the several provinces in the interests of agriculture—especially for irrigation.

Qalyubiyah: 19 bridges, 2 canals, 1 aqueduct
Sharqiyah: 71 bridges, 2 canals, 3 aqueducts and siphons, 2 canal locks, 2 flood gates
Daqahliyah: 32 bridges, 6 diversion canals, 2 aqueducts
Minufiyah: 17 bridges, 5 diversion canals, 2 aqueducts, 2 flood gates
Isma'iliyah Canal: 1 canal, 2 bridges near Cairo
Gharbiyah: 20 bridges, 8 diversion canals
Bahayrah: 18 bridges, 9 drainage overflow canals, 1 floating bridge, 2 aqueducts, 24 flood gates
Gizah: 2 canals, 1 stone dock
Bani Suwayf: 1 stone dock
Asyut: 10 bridges, 3 vaulted conduits, 2 canals, 2 canal locks
Qinah and Isnah: 15 bridges, 1 canal
Minya and Bani Mazar: 1 bridge, 1 canal lock, 6 vaulted conduit aqueducts
Girgah: 2 bridges and aqueducts, 6 siphon sluices, 2 stone docks
Ibrahimiyah Canal: 1 canal

Summary:

207 bridges
 40 diversion, drainage overflow, run-off canals
 25 aqueducts, siphons, vaulted conduits, sluices
  5 canal locks
 30 flood gates
  1 floating bridge
  4 stone docks

TOTAL 312

From the financial point of view, which occupies me at the moment, you will find in the establishment or in the reorganizing of many civil or military schools and in the organization of our land and sea military forces the justification for large expenses. At the time of my accession to the throne the army's strength was no more than 3,000 men; the number of sailors was scarcely 600, and the navy was composed of three or four vessels. The troops were completely disorganized and our military equipment was in such a state that all of it was not sufficient to arm 15,000 or 20,000 men in an emergency. Since my accession our military establishment has been completely reformed and modernized; a large quantity of new model guns has been ordered. The execution of this order is being supervised by a high official of the War Ministry and the resulting expenses are being carried on this year's budget which will be placed before you. Factories for the manufacture of uniforms and military material have been established, warships and transports such as steam frigates, armored corvettes, and 22 various sailing ships have been built or purchased and are at our disposition, some in the Mediterranean, some in the Red Sea. Today, thanks to God, our army and our navy are on a regular and respectable footing and we are completely able to provide for the country's security.

Given the preceding information, it is clear that the size of the debt is insignificant in relation to the projects completed and to the expenses incurred in the interest of the country. Still, it is well to observe that if the government had accepted the propositions which have been presented to it by diverse parties for the purchase of the railroad then the public debt would have been all but paid off. The sums suggested for the purchase of the railroad certainly would have covered, in large part, the repayment of debt.

I have to thank Providence that I have been able to realize in large part the ideas for increasing Egypt's prosperity which It inspired in me at the time of my accession to power. In my remarks addressed on that occasion to the consuls representing the several foreign powers, I emphasized five points which I pointed out would be guides for my government.

The first point relative to the suppression of the "corvée" [forced labor required of peasants] happily is no longer a question today. I have not avoided any sacrifice in order to gain its suppression and today, thanks to your helpful assistance, it is an accomplished fact of great satisfaction and great benefit to our people.

In the second point of my remarks, I called for the development of agriculture and commerce. Have I any need to remind you of what I have done to encourage this development? As for agriculture, it will suffice if I remind you that the works already listed have increased cultivated land by 327,485 feddans. Evidence of this will be furnished to you in detail by the inspector general for the provinces. As for commerce, it has profited greatly—predictably enough—thanks to the extension of the railroads and the creation of facilities which have grown up because of them. The best demonstration which I am able to give you is furnished by the summary of customs revenues which show, when comparing this year with the one preceding, an increase in receipts from import duties. Thus you see my expectations realized and agriculture, commerce, and the country's prosperity progressing together.

These remarkable improvements have been accomplished despite the several calamities which the country has suffered in recent years, such as the epidemic, the great Nile flood which devastated most of our cultivated fields over a four year period, and lastly, the insufficient rise of the Nile. What progress would the country have made without these disasters! I pray God to keep them from us in the future and to aid me in realizing my plans for the prosperity of Egypt.

I should add that my attention has turned also toward the provinces of the Sudan. I have exerted myself to improve the state of that vast country. Today, telegraph lines are being built to Khartoum, capital of the Sudanese provinces, and also to Suwakin; these lines are almost finished. Also, it is planned to link Massawa to Suwakin by another line and to construct secondary branch lines wherever they will be useful. Moreover, I have introduced into the government of those up to now neglected provinces, reforms and improvements which already have begun to bear fruit to the point where the revenue which the government collects there has doubled. A short time ago the Ministry of Finance used to furnish a subsidy of 30,000 purses [app. $665,000] to the Sudanese provinces, but today it receives from there 15,000 purses [app. $333,000] per year extra for expenses and for the salaries of civil and military officers.

In the third point of my discourse I stated that public education was the foundation of the civilization of a country. You have been shown what I have done in this matter and you know the many schools which I have founded as well as the results I have obtained. You should consult carefully the attached table which indicates the variety of these schools and the number of their students.

Schools of Cairo

	Students
Primary school	388
Preparatory school	400
Polytechnic and architecture school	63
School of administration and languages	39
School of surveying and accounting	55
School of arts and crafts	82
Design class	11
TOTAL	1038

Schools of Alexandria

Primary school	108
Preparatory school	133
School of seamanship	31
TOTAL	272

Provincial Schools

School of Tantah	193
School of Asyut	95
TOTAL	288

Schools Supported by the Ministry of War

Artillery school	100
Cavalry school	70
Infantry school	217
Staff school	28
Veterinary school	21
School of fencing	24
School of accounting	32
School of agriculture	38
School of ordnance	26
School of arts and crafts	22
TOTAL	578

TOTAL: Schools, 22   TOTAL: Students, 2176

In a fourth point I promised to draw up a civil list for my personal expenses. You know with what care I have carried out that engagement for several years.

Finally, the fifth point of my remarks declared that a well-organized judicial structure was necessary to ease and strengthen relations between Europeans and locals. Since my accession to power to this day I have not forgotten for an instant this important question and constantly I am preoccupied with finding a way to bring the issue to a successful conclusion. Knowing your ardent desire to see reforms accomplished so that all this country's people can enjoy their advantages without distinction of nationality, I have the satisfaction of announcing to you that I have obtained the adherence of most of the great powers to the principle of judicial reform. I can only thank those governments which have promised their support and soon I hope to obtain the agreement of the French government which always has shown itself to be most sympathetic to the progress of our country. Also, I hope that a special commission will be organized shortly to outline the organization of the new jurisdiction and to define its structure to the mutual advantage of the interested parties.

You see, gentlemen, that the prosperity of the country has been and is still my constant preoccupation. Moreover, I am happy to recognize that in the labors of your first two sessions you too have never ceased to keep the public interest in mind. Therefore, I have a well-founded expectation that in all your efforts during the course of the session now beginning you will seek to contribute to the improvement of the condition of our people, and to the wealth and progress of the country.

12

Urbanization and the Diffusion of Modern Fashion, the Creation of Modern Cairo*

By the 1870's a remarkable Europeanization of the tastes of upper-class Egyptians was being displayed in countless ways. French rather than Arabic was usually spoken in the plush furnished salons of wealthy pashas. European styles of dress were adopted by men and women alike. Even the city of Cairo began to resemble a European city, not only in the Opera House and the broad paved boulevards which appeared, but also in the water pipes and gas lines which were buried below the ground level. The city became a primary point where modern influences filtered into the Middle East, the place where modernism in all its aspects most dramatically confronted traditionalism. Nevertheless, it is important to remember that most of these changes initially affected only the more fashionable parts of the city and that the mass of Egyptians still retained their faith in their ancient beliefs and still lived in a traditional environment. By the 1870's a split had appeared in Egyptian society separating the aspirations of a modernist minority—most noticeably represented in the 1870's by the European imitating upper-class elite—and the traditionalist majority. This split seriously weakened Egypt's ability to resist outright European domination. The selection below illustrates how dramatically and how early the pressures of urbanization forced themselves upon the consciousness of Middle Eastern leaders and planners. Indeed, the parallel between the rebuilding efforts in Cairo that are described below and those that are going on today in cities such as Kuwayt, while not exact, are striking.

*   *   *

But it is on approaching the Cairo station that the great improvement of that city and its suburbs, becomes perceptible to the visitor who has been absent for several years. He rubs his eyes, and almost distrusts his vision; for, looking up

* Edwin De Leon, *The Khedive's Egypt* (London: Sampson Low, Marston, Searle and Rivington, 1877), 49-51, 55-59, 137-139.

the Shoubra road which leads into Cairo, as well as outside the former limits of the city, where formerly stretched for miles fields under cultivation, he now sees, far as his eyes can reach, in every direction well-built and even palatial residences, surrounded by gardens, adding on new cities, for several miles. The old Cairo was formerly surrounded by high and massive walls, and entered by a wide gate, both of which have disappeared, while broad boulevards open an easy way into the city and out to the desert. Passing over where wall and gate used to stand, new surprises await the returning visitor. The old has given place to the new; and blocks of high buildings have replaced the picturesque old tumble-down erections of mud and wood, four stories high, with jealously latticed windows jutting out into the street.

But when you descend at Shepheard's Hotel, your astonishment reaches its climax, and you rub your eyes as hard as Rip Van Winkle; for the great characteristic feature of the Cairo of old, the Ezbekieh—the pride, the glory of the city and people—has utterly vanished! Where once waved the branches of the stately sycamores planted by Mehemet Ali, are now to be seen only solid blocks of stone houses, with arcades in imitation of those of the Rue de Rivoli at Paris. Over three-fourths of the space formerly occupied by that primitive garden-wilderness, so dear to the memory of its old *habitués* who used to sit every evening and night under its grand trees, sipping coffee and smoking nargilehs, on those Cairene nights brighter than Western days, while an endless procession of natives and Levantines passed under its leafy arcades, are imitation European houses and shops. The garden has vanished like a dream. The same change has swept over the aspect of all four sides of the square which surrounded that great park, or garden, whose disappearance I have lamented. The quaint old Eastern buildings, with their latticed windows, and entrances beneath by a small door pierced, in a thick wall, through which you passed into an inner open court in which was tethered a donkey, passing up a flight of break-neck, narrow winding stone steps to enter the house—all these, too, have followed the Ezbekieh, and their fronts at least are now on European models: square, formal, uniform, hideous-looking imitations of the ugliest architecutre in the world, replacing the most picturesque, if not the most comfortable or convenient. A small portion of the old Ezbekieh has been saved from the building mania, but so "translated" that its oldest friend scarce recognizes it as an acquaintance; for, originally the least wooded and most unattractive portion of the old open space, it has been converted into a French or German tea-garden, under the auspices of a French ornamental gardener, partly on the trim Versailles model, partly in imitation of the Bois de Boulogne, with even its little artificial lake with swans in it, and small mock-steamers for sailing over three feet of water....

All is now decorous, dull and European in the prim gardens, which usurp a portion of that vanished pleasure-ground, which, picturesque as it was, must be confessed to have been a public nuisance in many respects, however "sentimental travellers" may bewail the substitution of cleanliness and order for dirt and disorder, savoury for unsavoury smells... in a sanitary and progressive point of view, no sensible man or woman, however sentimental, can deny the improvement and growth of Cairo, under the demolishing tendencies of the Khedive. The change in the modes of conveyance, however, may merit regret; for now, instead of "mounting barbed steeds," the pachas and beys, and other native gentlemen, who used to be seen prancing by in all their bravery, loll lazily back in open victorias or barouches, drawn by sorry jades, and driven by very dirty Arab charioteers, smoking strong cigars of German origin, and habited in Frank dress, with only the red fez cap to mark their nationality....

In the outdoor life, the only touch of the Orient left is afforded by the constant apparition, or rather flitting by the hareems, whose fair representatives very freely take the air, and pass and repass constantly in front of the great hotels, wherein the travellers do congregate, in their well-guarded carriages—one of the last relics of the old system visible to the eye. Yet their habits, too, have undergone a great change. No longer are they ambulating or equestrian balloons of black silk perched on donkeys, or concealed in closed carriages; although the inevitable and irremovable black guards still "guide their steps and guard their rest," as in the days when Byron sung of them. Standing in the front of your hotel, you see the veiled fair ones of the hareem slowly borne past, at morning and eventide, in the neatest Parisian or English *coupés*, drawn by the finest English horses, and dressed in the latest Parisian modes—all except the face, which, half-hidden, half revealed, is covered with a gossamer veil, which also drapes the bosom. This veil, of the most cobweb lace, does not prevent their seeing and even saluting occasionally the passing stranger, to the great disgust of their sable guards; and the intensity with which they regard the outer world from the windows of their carriages, augurs well for their thirst for information. All the follies of European fashion have been, I am told, transferred to the East; for European costume is now the rage in the hareems, and Lyons silks of brightest colours, and French boots with impracticable heels, have succeeded the flowing draperies and shuffling slippers and baggy breeches of the Eastern fair ones. Frank women who have visited freely in the hareems for the last two winters, deprecate this change, fully as much as any of our sterner sex can do: and declare that it not only robs the hareem of all its romance, but most decidedly diminishes the peculiar beauty of its inmates.

The Ismaïlieh quarter of Cairo is entirely a new creation within the last six or seven years, and is one of the prettiest portions of the city. In order to encourage the erection of good houses for the European and Europeanized residents, and to attract new ones from abroad, the Khedive offered to give building lots, of the value of £2000 and upwards, to every person who would build thereon a house of a fixed value; rising in proportion to the estimated worth of the gift. The bait took, and the lots mapped out in the rear of the great hotels, where there were no buildings, on the outskirts of the city, in the direction of Boulak—the old port of Cairo—were soon snatched up; and a new town of several thousands of houses soon occupied the site. Most of these are good substantial houses, in imitation of Swiss *chalets* or English houses, and some are very fine, costing as much as £20,000. Almost all have gardens surrounding them, some very spacious ones; for reserved lots were purchased by enterprising natives in the vicinity. These latter are chiefly the native or Levantine bankers, who are the richest class in the community; and some of the pachas have also built large houses on the Eastern plan, hareem accommodation included. . . .

Formerly the route to the citadel was one of the most winding and tortuous in all Cairo, corkscrewing through the bazaars and the narrow streets leading out of the Mooskie, or quarter of European shops, and compelling a *détour* as picturesque as it was provoking to people pressed for time. But the spirit of Haussmann has seemingly descended on the Khedive, who, possessing the power as well as the inclination, has on a smaller scale followed in the footsteps of the French leveller. For not only here, but in other quarters of the old city, broad open boulevards, as wide as the French, have been cut straight through the old houses, with a most ruthless disregard for the prejudices or the prayers of the old householders, who loathe light, air, and sunshine, as well as publicity, as much as they do "plague, pestilence, and famine"; even although indemnity is given or promised them for all demolition or damage to their premises. Nor are they entirely without reasonable excuse for grumbling at this arbitrary and compulsory change in their "ancient ways," narrow, damp, dirty, and gloomy as they seemed to the stranger. For here, where the sun gives more than enough of heat and glare from his rise to his setting, shade and coolness, alone attainable in narrow streets with but a small slit of sky visible between the projecting housetops above, are the chief wants of the residents, and it is questionable whether what is a real improvement at Paris, may ultimately prove so at Grand Cairo. . . .

The broad open road, leading in a straight line to the massive pile of citadel buildings which crown the hill, back of which towers the frowning and rugged chain of the Mokattam Hills, on the desert edge, is finished and in tolerably good condition. But with the usual careless way of doing things in the East, the demolitions on each side of the roadway have been but partially completed, or never repaired, in most cases, by the erection of new outer walls. So you pass through what looks like a city that has recently been shelled—houses in all stages of dilapidation, though still inhabited, giving most odd views of domestic interiors, frowning down upon you; while not even a screen, much less a wall, has been placed between the dilapidation and the street.

13

Spreading Malaise, Mirza Husayn-i-Hamdani's Protest Against the Influence of Iran's Religious Establishment *

Much of the discontent and intellectual malaise that characterized Iran during the nineteenth century was expressed through the vehicle of
religious protest. Some of the disenchanted even joined the *Babis,* a new sect that
drew much of its appeal by capitalizing on Iran's post-1828 troubles by preaching
the coming of a millennium that would initiate a reign of justice in the world.
The *Bab,* Mirza 'Ali Muhammad, claimed that he was a prophet sent to establish
a new faith that would combine the truth found in all existing religions and
enable its followers to surmount their current difficulties. Originally, the *Babis* directed most of their criticism at the obscurantist Persian Muslim scholar-clerics,
the mullas, but later, even the shah was included in their attacks. Major uprisings
swept Iran in 1848 and 1852 which caused the government to retaliate with sav-
age persecution and the use of troops, actions which broke the immediate political
threat posed by the *Babis.* Still, the Babists did articulate much of the discontent
and general unease felt by Iranians of all levels. Thus, the following selection can
be interpreted in a broader context than simply as a piece of *Babi* propaganda,
for it voices many of the frustrations, and self-reproaching doubts shared by most
Persians regarding their fall from greatness.

*   *   *

. . . Such is the influence which the [Persian Shi'ah] clergy enjoy, and so great
is their power in every department of the state, that they have nullified the
sovereign's authority in exactly the same way as they have destroyed all but the
name of religion and law. . . . The King cannot issue any command or take any
step opposed to their views, and they imagine that he exists but to maintain their
authority and to give effect to their decisions. Thus should any governor or minister, however powerful, issue any order or take any steps to secure the well-being
of those subject to him, or to promote the national prosperity, without first con-

* Mīrzā Husayn-i-Hamdānī, *Tārīkh-i-Jadīd,* translated by E. G. Browne in, *The Tārīkh-i-Jadīd
or the New History of Mirza 'Ali Muḥammad, the Bab* (Cambridge: Cambridge University Press,
1895), 180-185.

sulting them, they will, by a mere hint, incite the people of his province or city to harass, vex, and thwart him till they have driven him out ... at no previous time have any clergy possessed such power as is now wielded by the *mullās* of Persia, who regard themselves as the representatives of the Imāms, and call their kings "dogs of the Imāms' threshold." ... On the return of His Majesty the King [Nasr al-Din Shāh] from Europe [in 1873] they not only clamoured for the dismissal of the Prime Minister, circulating false reports of his atheism, but also prevented the introduction of railways, which would have greatly conduced to the prosperity of the country and the freedom of the people. . . .

Did not the territory of this same Persia once extend eastwards to Transoxanis and the mountains of Thibet [*sic*] and China, westwards to the river Euphrates, southwards to the Gulf of Oman, and northwards to the Aral Mountains? ... All the kings of the earth rendered homage to the monarchs of the Achaemenian dynasty [559-330 B.C.] and were as naught beside them, just as at the present day Persia is as naught beside the nations of Europe, but is like a dismissed governor or a cancelled edict, heeded by none. This abasement is the outcome of the learning of these divines, these upholders of religion and law, and the result of their undue power and influence. By the troubles which they have stirred up Persia has been made desolate and reduced to a few empoverished and deserted provinces, the total revenue derived from which at the present day only amounts to seven crores (of *tūmāns*) [between a million and a million and a half pounds sterling in 1890], and even of this, were the taxes fairly levied, not half would come into the royal treasury.

Shame on the people of Persia for their lack of spirit! By God, they have not a spark of patriotic or manly feeling; they have grown habituated to cowardice, falsehood, and flattery; they acquiesce in tyranny and oppression, and, relinquishing the position of free agents, have become mere passive instruments in the hands of the clergy! Do they forget that in days of yore their glory and honour, their wealth and prosperity, were the envy of all peoples? Do they not ask themselves why they have now become a byword amongst the nations for abject misery, meanness, and baseness? Moreover did they not once excel all mankind in every art, trade, and handicraft? ... Do they never reflect why it is that their science is now restricted to such things as purifications, washing the orifices of the body, dyeing the beard, clipping the moustache, disputing about payment of tithes and alms, atonement for wrongs, Imām's money, and the like, for the determination of which things even it does not suffice? Yet so heedless are they that they do not perceive that most of these divines originally spring from the rustic population or the scum of the towns. They enter our cities and colleges with a smock and a staff, and feet full of sores encased in coarse socks and canvas shoes. There, by the alms and votive offerings of the people, by begging from this one and that one, by prayers and fastings paid for at the rate of two *tūmāns* a year, by reading through the whole Kurān for a *ḳrān,* and by fees obtained for the performance of devotions, they manage to live in extreme wretchedness and poverty. After reading a few books, learning Arabic, filling their minds with all manner of doubts, hesitations, and vain scruples, and developing their obsolete superstitions and prejudices, they leave college, take their seats in the chair of the Law and the Imàmate, and forthwith become the absolute arbiters and lawgivers of the nation, the controllers of all men's lands and possessions, the owners of horses, mules, gold, and silver. They then think themselves entitled to set their feet on the necks of all mankind, to lord it over the noble, to maintain troops of horses and retinues of servants, to claim to be the (vice-regents) of the Imām, to receive his tithes, and to make atonements for wrong. They account themselves the most noble amongst all creatures and the most perfect, the generality of men as "like cattle," and the common folk as "even more astray." They become dead men's heirs, consumers of endowments, and collectors of tithes and "thirds," and usurp the station of "the One, the Dominant" "to whom belongeth dominion." . . .

Most people, however, have not sufficient sense to perceive from what sources all these luxuries, powers, shops, villages, lands, aqueducts, possessions, and moneys which the clergy possess are derived. Have they skill in working mines? No. Do they traffic in the merchandise of India, China, America, or Europe? No. Do they traverse land and sea, or cultivate fields which lie waste? No. Have they amassed their wealth by the discovery of new arts? No . . . Such being the case, what folly it is to take as guides men so notoriously evil and hypocritical, to follow their opinions, to be governed by their decisions, to cringe to them, flatter them, beseech their favour, and reckon them, forsooth, as the repositories of learning!

14

The West Through the Eyes of a Ruler, Nasr al-Din Shah's First Trip to Europe, 1872 *

Nasr al-Din Shah's questioning, alert mind, his sense of humor, and also his knack for diplomacy are well illustrated in those excerpts taken from the diary of his first trip to Europe. This diary, published and distributed in Persia, served to educate the Shah's subjects about the wonders of

* Nasr al-Din Shah, *The Diary of H. M. The Shah of Persia During His Tour Through Europe in A.D. 1873,* translated by J. W. Redhouse (London: John Murray, 1874), 96-97, 140-142, 183, 229-230, 236-237.

modern civilization. Like most other nineteenth century Middle Eastern travellers in Europe, the Shah was greatly impressed by the material wealth of Europe. The Shah's diary is notable, however, in its omission of speculation concerning political philosophy. All in all, Nasr al-Din's attitudes were those of the centralizing authoritarian defensive modernizer who was more impressed by Krupp's steam hammers than in the workings of Parliament.

*   *   *

[Germany]

...At an hour to sunset we arrived at the works of M. Krupp, who came himself to the railway (to meet us). He is a tall, thin old man. He has himself, in a certain space of time, created the whole of these works. The cannon of every government does he furnish from hence. Guns of every description, such as large cannon for forts, cannon for ships, and cannon for field use in campaigns, are all manufactured here. His plant and workshops, of which steam is the motive power, resemble a mighty city. He employs 15,000 workmen, for the whole of whom he has erected houses and lodgings, paying them salaries and wages. After deducting his expenditure, his own yearly income amounts to 800,000 tūmāns (320,000 £).

We went to the shop of the steam hammers. They are singular hammers, like mountains; and, worked by steam, fulfill the office of forging cannons. They make these of any pattern they desire. When the hammer strikes the gun, the earth floor of the workshop emits a sound and trembles. It was a marvelous thing. We went all over the works, and they turned out some large and some small cannon. We then went to a house which he had prepared, and there we dined. He gave us an excellent dinner. In the conservatory of this house we saw a tree, the leaves of which were two ells (seven feet) long, and half an ell (twenty-one inches) wide. The steam-hammers, in spite of their great distance from this room, made the earth shake here as though in an earthquake. M. Krupp made us a present of a most magnificent breech loading six-pounder cannon, with all its appliances.

[Britain]

...We returned to our train, and took our seat in a carriage with the self same personages. We started. Everywhere we passed over the bosoms of mountains and across valleys, traversing numerous tunnels ("holes in the mountain"), of which two were about a quarter of a league in length, very dark and suffocating.

The country of England has no resemblance to that in other territories. It has much forest, large trees, population without interval, and cultivation enormous. The wealth of the English is famous throughout the world; there is no need to describe it (here).

We passed by the town and outlying districts of Chiselhurst, the abode of Napoleon III, and where he died. His tomb is also there. The train travelled at so furious a rate that it was impossible for one to distinguish any place. From the rapidity of our motion fire came out of the wheels, and one carriage caught fire. It wanted but little for all to be burnt. They stopped the train, got down, and extinguished the fire. All was right, and again we went on until we reached the beginning of the city of London. Again it is impossible to describe the prosperity, the populousness, the extent of the city, the numbers of lines of railway over which incessantly the trains come and go in every direction, the smoke of manufactories, and the like. We travelled over the exteriors of the roofs of the houses; and thus we reached the station and stopped . . . The population of the city city is said to be over eight crores (four millions) of souls. It has most lovely women. The nobleness, the greatness, the gravity and sedateness of the women and men shine out from their countenances. One sees and comprehends that they are a great people, and that the Lord of the Universe has bestowed upon them power and might, sense and wisdom, and enlightenment. Thus it is that they have conquered a country like India, and hold important possessions in America and elsewhere in the world. Their soldiers are strong of frame and beautifully attired; their armour wearing household cavalry are very strong and handsome young men, exquisitely dressed, like the cavalry of Russia. Their horses are very fine and strong, but their number is few. They are but four regiments, each of four hundred men. . . .

The city of Manchester, by reason of its exceeding number of manufactories, has its houses, doors, and walls, black as coal. So much so, that the complexions, visages, and dresses of the people are all black. The whole of the ladies of that place at most times wear black clothing, because, no sooner do they put on white or coloured dresses, then lo! they are suddenly black.

[France]

. . . We and the Marshal [MacMahon, President of France] took seats in a carriage, went into the gardens of Versailles, and drove about. They have many basins and fountains of water, the source of which, like that of the fountains at the Crystal Palace of London, is derived from a steam-engine. They had opened the sources and let the water on in the fountains. There was a lake below the basins and fountains, very beautiful and spacious avenues, forest trees, the heads of which were all intertwined so as to form a kind of roof, with every here and there a circular open space of grass with trees around, having in the centre a large basin with a fountain of great altitude. It is a very charming place.

One spot was formed into a kind of artificial mountain, with a cascade falling from the mountain. Several marble statues were placed behind the cascade,— one, a group named Apollo, who was the specific deity of manly beauty, of light, and of poetry. He is adorning (himself), the others round him are holding a mirror, flowers, or implements of the toilet. It was so beautiful a piece of statuary that one could not even imagine it. I formed the desire to go up near to these statues under the cascade. The Marshal and General Arture said it would be very difficult to go there, as the path was altogether precipitous, of rocks and steep. I said I would go; I alighted from the carriage, and went up. It is true that the way was disagreeable; but to us, who had seen and traversed much worse paths in the hunting grounds of Persia it offered no difficulty. When we had arrived near the statues, General Arture came (also); but, meeting with a fall, all his clothes were bemired, and his sword was either bent or broken. The Marshal likewise came up; but with great difficulty, and with the assistance of several persons. But this manner of getting up there by a Marshal and a general of France is in no way derogatory to their firmness and courage. Well; the statues were very beautiful, though somewhat soiled, and covered with cobwebs. . . .

The celebrated Rothschild, a Jew also, who is exceedingly rich, came to an audience, and we conversed with him. He greatly advocated the cause of the Jews, mentioned the Jews of Persia, and claimed tranquility for them. I said to him: "I have heard that you, brothers, possess a thousand crores of money. I consider the best thing to do would be that you should pay fifty crores to some large or small State, and buy a territory in which you could collect all the Jews of the whole world, you becoming their chiefs, and leading them on their way in peace, so that you should no longer be thus scattered and dispersed." We laughed heartily, and he made no reply. I gave him an assurance that I do protect every alien nationality that is in Persia.

M. Lesseps, so well known, who has joined the Mediterranean to the Red Sea, —i.e., a large company having been formed, has, through the exertions of this personage, opened that road, and by this means shortened for commerce the passage to India, Persia, China, etc. and, from Europe, by about two thousand leagues,—came to an audience, together with his son, a youth. He has now a fresh scheme in his head,—that of making a railway from the town of Orenburg in Russia to the city of Samarqand, and thence on to Peshawur in British India. But this is a notion very remote (from reason) and distant (from practicability).

3

Defensive Modernization: The Intellectual Phase

           If the first response to the intrusion of modernity into the Middle East was an attempt by authoritarian leaders to adopt those practical techniques such as centralized political administrations or hardware items such as modern arms that obviously contributed to Western power, the second response reflected a deepening awareness that the secret of the West's world ascendancy involved more than a mere mastery of cannon and steamships. Particularly after the mid-nineteenth century, growing numbers of the elite came to realize that Western strength derived from political, social, and intellectual concepts too.

    As early as the 1820's intellectuals such as the Egyptian Rifa'ah al-Tahtawi (1801-1873) began visiting Europe, learning Western languages—particularly French—and transmitting information about the modern world through their teaching and their translations of Western works into Middle Eastern idioms. Essentially, the response of these men was to assert the superiority of the Islamic value system while at the same time urging the selective adoption of Western material advances.

    By the 1860's modernly oriented intellectuals began to wrestle with problems more complex than the mere transmission of information and impressions of the West. In particular, the disturbing pressures of modernism upon the values of the Muslim Middle East began to perplex various thinkers. How much could an Islamic society borrow from the West without losing its cultural, and above all, its ideological identity? Thus, efforts to accommodate Western practices to the indigenous Islamic ideology began to appear in the writings of various reformist thinkers. Evidently the environmental touchstone of late nineteenth century reformism throughout the Middle East was the fact that the traditional order's disintegration was proceeding at an ever-accelerating rate under the combined effects of local defensive and Western-imposed modernization. Consequently, by the 1860's several thinkers were articulating the need for a new social and political order and began advancing suggestions on how that new order should be designed. The post-1870 generation of Muslim Middle Eastern intellectuals, although still asserting the validity, indeed the superiority, of Muslim values, increasingly emphasized the moral rather than the social or political aspect of the local value system. Most of the reformists were willing to admit that Western political and social institutions might well be adopted in the Middle East. It was argued that while Middle Eastern civilization might be backward, this was the result of the failure of Muslims to live up to the eternal ideals of their faith or to distinguish its moral essentials from cultural accretions which had become associated with Islam in past centuries.

It was during the 1850's, after the Crimean War, that young intellectuals—many of them bureaucrats—in various parts of the Middle East began to wrestle seriously with the problem of creating a new political and social order albeit one that would preserve the basic values of Islam. One such group emerged in Tunis, an amalgamation of savants at the Zaytunah University and young civil servants. The most illustrious of the Tunisian reformists was Khayr al-Din al-Tunisi (1810-1889) who was instrumental in convincing Muhammad Bey (1855-1859) to issue the *'Ahd al-Aman* (Fundamental Pact) in 1857, a statement of reformist goals. This was followed by a European-style constitution, the first in the Middle East, which was in effect from 1861 until it was suspended in 1881 with the imposition of the French protectorate over Tunisia. Khayr al-Din later served as chief minister of Tunisia from 1873 to 1877 when he resigned, went to Istanbul, and ultimately became grand vizier of the Ottoman empire in 1878-79.

Khayr al-Din enjoyed close contacts with the Istanbul based group of reformists known collectively as the Young Ottomans. Obviously deriving much of their approach from the study of Western liberal political philosophy, Young Ottoman writers such as Namik Kemal, nevertheless, anchored their theories in loyalty to the concept of a multinational, Islamic, Ottoman state. They saw no contradiction in borrowing much of Europe's civilization in order to restore health to an idealized Islamic society which they romantically believed to exist in the past. Reaching the height of their influence between 1865 and 1878, the permanent influence of the Young Ottomans was in their making the study of things modern fully respectable for an intellectual, in popularizing modern education as a means to master the latest political and economic techniques, and in advancing precepts such as "patriotism" and "progress" which were later incorporated into the corpus of secular Turkish nationalism.

Much of the actual political agitation undertaken by the Young Ottomans, because they were liberals who opposed the concept of a centralized autocracy favored by the major *Tanzimat* leaders, was directed against the unlimited power of the sultan to enforce his will upon his subjects. However, it was the inefficiency of the despotism of Sultan Abdülaziz (1861-1876) that provided the environment and stimulus for the rise of constitutionalism in the Ottoman Empire. This, rather than Young Ottoman editorials, prompted a coalition of high ranking Ottoman civil servants led by Midhat Pasha, himself an administrative centralist, to grasp the concept of constitutional monarchy as a means to control an incompetent monarch and thus to save the *Tanzimat*. Nevertheless, the Ottoman Constitution of 1876 was promulgated in a time of emergency, it was an artificial creation which did not reflect Ottoman realities, and its supporters were unable to defend it against Sultan Abdülhamid II's reorganized autocracy which was firmly rooted in the Ottoman tradition. Although Abdülhamid II suspended the constitution in 1878 and ruled on as absolute monarch until the Young Turk revolution of 1908, he was a fairly energetic innovator, especially in educational and communications development.

The other major center of reformist thought was Cairo. During the 1860's and 1870's Al-Tahtawi and later, Jamal Al-Din al-Afghani (1839-1897), attracted many young Egyptians in the reformist camp. Al-Afghani particularly influenced the small but influential group of modernly oriented intellectuals in Egypt. Al-Afghani preached a reformist message especially notable for its pan-islamic content. He believed that religious solidarity was potentially the strongest bond available to a Muslim society if it were properly interpreted in a reformist spirit and was free of traditionalist accretions. Consequently Al-Afghani championed the ideal of a pan-islamic union of Muslim states united against Western imperialism and vitalized through the activities of a reformist, constitutional regime. However, it was the activist attitude—the method—advocated by Al-Afghani rather than the exact content of his message which was his most enduring legacy and it was in this sense that he can be counted a precursor of Arab as well as other Middle Eastern nationalisms. The immediate political result of Al-Afghani's preaching was to give intellectual content and justification to the rise of the first Egyptian constitutional movement which, by 1881, fell under the domination of native Egyptian military officers led by Colonel Ahmad al-'Arabi Pasha. The movement opposed the supremacy of Khedive Tawfiq (1879-1892) who seemed to be turning the country over to foreign control and it called for constitutional limitations on the monarch's power. Its real appeal lay in the fact that it organized the general discontents caused by the dislocations attending the breakdown of the traditional order; its ideological basis was but a veneer covering specific grievances such as peasant discontent with high taxes or the resistance of the military to the curtailment of military modernization and the consequent freeze on promotions. With the British occupation of Egypt in 1882 the Egyptian Constitution of 1881 was suppressed.

It is obvious that "constitutionalism" became a major element in the late nineteenth century reformist platform. Apparently, there were two elements to this appeal. First, as is well expressed in the writings of men like Khayr al-Din and Namik Kemal, constitutionalism was part of the theoretical tool kit of the reformists. It was seized upon as something of a methodological panacea that would lead inevitably to a new political order and halt the disintegration of society. Secondly it was adopted by practical men of affairs such as Midhat Pasha or 'Arabi Pasha as a defensive device to take exclusive direction of their country's affairs out of the hands of monarchs who at best appeared politically and financially inept and at worst seemed to be handing over control of their realms to foreigners. At any rate, in every case the hopes of the constitutionalists were frustrated by a combination of the strength of local authoritarianism, general apathy and lack of understanding of the rationale behind the constitutional movement, and finally foreign opposition which led to outright armed suppression of the regimes in Tunisia in 1881 and Egypt in 1882.

Until the 1870's the main centers of the Middle Eastern intellectual response to modernism were Cairo, Tunis, and Istanbul and most of the figures involved were Muslim. By the 1880's Christian Arabs in Syria, Lebanon, and to some extent, Egypt, began to play a role in the process, too. At the same time, certain Iranian intellectuals, some of whom were living or studying abroad in Europe, Russia, India, and the Ottoman empire began to coalesce into an Iranian reformist movement. However, it was not until reformism became associated with the rise of various nationalisms in the Middle East that Christian and Iranian thinkers became significant participants in the several modernist intellectual movements.

The evolution of an exclusive, secular oriented Turkish nationalism out of the multinational Islamic "Ottomanism" championed by the Young Ottomans was a thirty-year process. It was natural that nationalism should develop among the Ottoman empire's subject nationalities, particularly those of the Christian Balkans, before it appeared among the dominant race in a multinational state. So it was with the Ottoman Turks. In the 1870's Western orientalists and turkologists began treating the Turks as a separate language group with a unique history and, at the same time, Ottoman historians first began to regard the Turks as a separate component within the Muslim world. In his writings, Namik Kemal occasionally and rather tentatively utilized the term "Turk." The movement received particular encouragement from the expatriate Ottoman intellectual community gathered in Paris in the 1890's as a consequence of Sultan Abdülhamid II's repressive thought-control policies which often resulted in exile for anyone who tried to express a nonorthodox opinion. The content of the new Turkish nationalism was secular, patriotic, and progressive. It, along with constitutionalism, was adopted by the anti-Hamidian Young Turk coalition of intellectuals and army officers and suddenly, in 1908 after the successful Young Turk revolution, it became the official ideology of the Ottoman state. Once in power, the Young Turks proceeded to undermine the unity of the empire by antagonizing the non-Turkish Muslims by enforcing a strict turkification program in the schools, the army, and the government which was combined with a renewed drive toward centralized administration.

The creation of an exclusive Arab nationalism, then, was in part the consequence of an Arab revulsion against the exclusiveness of a Turkish nationalism that tended to treat the Arabs as an inferior subject people unedr Ottoman Turkish protection. Yet Arab nationalism began as a multiheaded organism that sprang up in many centers and was influenced by many stimuli. In Egypt after 1882 the Islamic reformist school inspired by Al-Afghani combined with growing frustration with the British protectorate to produce a movement that was destined to become Egyptian nationalism. Early Egyptian nationalism, however, hardly was a unified movement. One group, formed by Muhammad Abduh (1849-1905), a disciple of Al-Afghani, and ultimately headed by Rashid Rida (1886-1935), retained its Islamic reformist orientation. Others, more secular and militantly political in outlook coalesced into a number of nationalist parties in the first decade of the twentieth century. The most popular of these was the *Hizb al-Watani* (National Party) organized by the lawyer-journalist Mustafa Kamil (1874-1908). These parties all favored the restoration of a constitutional regime, and generally, an end to British occupation. Still another school adopted Western liebralism as their intellectual stance but tended to shun active politics for philosophical debates; in particular, writers such as Ahmad Lutfi al-Sayyid (1872-1964) and Taha Husayn emphasized the pharaonic and Mediterranean as opposed to the Arab and Middle Eastern aspects of the Egyptian heritage. Thus, Egypt at this stage was progressing along the path of defining its own peculiar identity and concerning itself with its own problems rather than participating in developing a pan-Arab nationalism. A similar process took place a few decades later in North Africa.

Pan-Arabism received its first articulation in Syria mainly among Christians who were repelled by the strong Islamic revivalism displayed by so much late nineteenth-century reformist thinking in the Middle East. However, when Turkish nationalism began to assert its exclusive claims, Muslim Arabs in Syria and Iraq began to discover the virtues of pan-Arabism, too. Between 1908 and World War I pan-Arabism's aims, however, remained tied to the past, in that usually its adherents called for little more than Arab autonomy within the Ottoman Empire.

Iranian reformism, constitutionalism, and nationalism matured as a unified process between 1880 and 1910 as a reaction against foreign meddling and the shahs' inability to halt this interference. The grant of the Tobacco Concession by Nasr al-Din Shah in 1890 to British interests galvanized the hitherto unorganized proto-reformist-constitutionalist-nationalist sentiment into an identifiable movement which is very interesting because it embraced such a large spectrum of the populace with the major exception of the peasantry. Conservative divines strongly supported by merchant and artisan groups who were threatened by foreign competition and landholding nobles who feared the shahs' centralizing tendencies joined with the small, progressive wing of Western inspired intellectuals. This unlikely coalition which united those opposed to change with the progressives who wanted much more change held together long enough to force the weak Muzaffar al-Din Shah (1896-1907) to promulgate a constitution in 1906-1907. Although the constitutional coalition was able to counter absolutist inspired counterrevolution between 1908 and 1911, the constitution did not prove very effective initially. Foreign interference—particularly after the Anglo-Russian Accord of 1907 which partitioned Iran into spheres of influence—grew to such intensity that Iran never enjoyed the breathing spell necessary to institute orderly political procedures until the 1920's. Nevertheless, while no consensus was forged on how best to attack the problems of the nation's backwardness at least a constitution—still in effect today—was produced.

A major complicating factor in the process of reformulating the basis of Middle Eastern society was the quickening of foreign influence and interference in the region coincident with the spread of imperialist fervor in Europe. After 1870 the success, the immensity, the pervasiveness, and the ruthlessness of Western and Russian political, economic, and cultural efforts, in the Middle East produced a situation where the brilliance and power of the modern world stimulated both a desire to share in certain aspects of Western culture along with a revulsion, indeed a hostility, toward Western actions. One result of this confrontation was the evolution of reformism into nationalism. The various Middle Eastern nationalisms retained reformism's positive modernizing bias toward revitalizing society but the actual or implied threat of a foreign take-over gave them an even greater immediate concern with asserting and preserving a people's identity.

Until World War I, reformism as well as its various nationalist offsprings, was a movement restricted largely to the modernly educated upper- and middle-class elite. It was actively resisted by traditionalists whose most powerful citadel was the Islamic clerical establishment despite the fact that some of the most important reformists—men like Al-Afghani and Abduh—were products of the religious institution. Moreover, the attitudes of the average Middle Easterner, the peasant cultivator, had yet to be influenced in any significant way by reformist ideas despite the fact that his life was being changed significantly by the breakdown of the old order under the impact of modernizing pressures.

15

Early Reformism in the Arab World, the 'Ahd al-Aman (Fundamental Pact) of Tunisia, 10 September 1857 *

The Tunisian Fundamental Pact was issued by Muhammad Bey: (1) in order to placate the resident European consuls who were not satisfied with the state of religious freedom among minorities in Tunisia, (2) at the urging of the Tunisian reformists who wished to have their government bound by a statement of reformist goals, and (3) because the ruler was a Turkophile who wished to imitate the great Ottoman reform decrees of 1839 and 1856. Certainly, the Pact incorporates features of the Ottoman documents but it is more significant as an example of the reformists' preoccupation with trying to accommodate European political philosophy with basic Muslim precepts. It reflects to a large degree the liberal constitutionalism of Khayr al-Din al-Tunisi who was most instrumental in drawing up the document. The Pact's promulgation was followed by the creation of several bodies to implement its principles including an advisory Grand Council of 60 members whose first presiding officer was Khayr al-Din. In 1861 Muhammad al-Sadiq Bey issued an Organic Law which, combined with the Pact, gave Tunisia the first European style constitution in the Middle East. In the Organic Law the ruler's responsibilities were clarified and he was required to swear loyalty to the Fundamental Pact at the time of his accession. In practice neither the Pact nor the 1861 constitution functioned very well as the resident European community disliked the threat they posed to their separate consular courts while Tunisians disliked the provisions concerning religious equality. By 1864, riots caused in large part by spreading financial difficulty, slowed the application of the Pact's provisions and in 1881 the French protectorate suppressed the constitutional regime altogether.

*　　　*　　　*

In the Name of God the compassionate the merciful.

Praise to God, who has shown the way to justice, who has sent down wisdom

---

* Translated from a French version in Elie Fitoussi and Aristide Benazet, *L'Etat Tunisien et le Protectorat Français, Histoire et Organisation 1525 à 1931* (Paris: Librairie Arthur Rousseau, 1931), Annexe III.

to guarantee the preservation of order in this world, who has provided knowledge of the law for man's benefit, who has promised a reward to the just and a punishment to the oppressor. Nothing is so true as the word of God.

Blessings upon our lord, Muhammad, whom God has honored with humane and compassionate words in His Book (the Koran) which was sent down together with knowledge of the correct path. This the prophet revealed and explained to us, just as God had ordered him to do, according to the principles of the sacred law which upholds the just and brings down the unjust, in such a way that the word of God has been the object neither of change nor of false interpretation. Honor and blessings upon his family and his companions, who have themselves demonstrated the truth and have converted through their knowledge, and who knew both the word and the meaning of the law, and who have left us as clear proof of its validity their exemplary conduct, their justice, and their wisdom.

I ask you, Oh God, to lend me your mighty aid to achieve deeds that will please you, to aid me in fulfilling my princely duties, a task which is the heaviest burden a man can carry. I put all my confidence and all my hope in You: What greater aid is there than that of the Almighty?

The mission which God has given to us in our charge of governing His creatures in this quarter of the world imposes lordly duties and religious obligations upon us which we are able to carry out only with His assistance. Without this help who could perform his duties toward God and toward men satisfactorily?

Convinced that it is necessary to follow God's precepts in everything that concerns His creatures, I have decided that neither injustice nor scorn will be borne by those under my care. I will neglect nothing in order to assure them full possession of their rights.

Can one fail, be it in his actions or in his intentions, in his responsibilities when one knows that God will not permit the least injustice and that He will reject those who oppress His creatures?

God has said to His well loved prophet: "Oh David, I have made you my viceroy over the land; judge men according to the ways of justice, do not let yourself be guided by passion, for it will detour you from the path of God, and those who separate themselves from the ways of the Lord are destined for the most frightening torments for they have forgotten the day of judgment."

God is witness to the fact that I accept His high precepts in order to prove that I prefer the happiness of my country to my personal advantage. I have consecrated my time, my strength, and my reason to ensure this happiness. I have started already, as is known, to lighten those taxes which bear heavily upon my subjects. God has permitted this reform to be a source of good, and these happy results have given our people hope for new improvements.

Since then the hand of the unfaithful official has been stayed.

In order to gain these improvements it is necessary first to set down general principles. To try to attain them without establishing these principles would be to create for oneself insurmountable difficulties.

We are convinced that most of the people of our country do not have complete confidence in the things which we have done with but the best of intentions. It is a law of nature that man achieves prosperity only in so far as his liberty is guaranteed, only so far as he is certain to find a defense against oppression behind the ramparts of justice and sees that his rights will be respected up to the point where his guilt is irrefutably demonstrated, and only so far as he is sure that this guilt will not be established by unsupported testimony.

The guilty man who has seen himself judged by many can not hesitate, if he retains a glimmer of reason, to recognize his crime and ought to say to himself: "Whoever passes beyond the boundaries set by the Lord condemns himself."

We have seen the ruler of Islam [the Ottoman sultan] as well as the leaders of the great powers, who have been placed by their wise policies at the head of nations, give their subjects the most complete guarantees for their liberty; they have understood that this was one of their primary duties dictated by reason and by nature itself. If its advantages are to be realized, the Shari'ah [Islamic law] ought to be so consecrated itself, for the Shari'ah has been instituted by God in order to defend man against evil desires. Whoever subjects himself to justice and law in so doing unites himself with godliness.

The heart of the man who has faith in his liberty is reassured and strengthened.

A short time ago we informed our religious leaders and other high officials of our intention to establish courts staffed by men well known for their knowledge of crimes and misdemeanors, and of the disputes which cause strife in commerce —that source of prosperity in states. We have established the sacred principles of our law as the basis for the organization of these courts.

The decisions emanating from the Shari'ah Courts will continue to have their full effect. Please God to perpetuate up to the day of the last judgment the respect which this court inspires.

An administrative and judicial code must be drawn up and adopted to the circumstances of our country. We hope that God who exists in our heart will give us the grace to establish these reforms in the best interests of our government and that they will not deviate at all from the principles which have given the glories of Islam to us. And we, humble and poor servants of the Almighty, will strive to conform to Islam's precepts and to reassure the people. Nothing, in this code will be contrary to its holy prescriptions.

Its provisions are as follows:

I

Complete security is formally guaranteed to all our subjects and to all inhabitants of our realm whatever might be their religion, their nationality, or their race. This security will extend to their respective persons, to their religious rights, and to their personal reputations.

Exceptions to this guarantee will be made only in legal cases which will be submitted to the courts; then the case will be submitted to us and it will be our duty to order the execution of the sentence, or to commute the punishment, or to issue a new instruction.

II

All our subjects are subject to the taxes now in effect—or which will be established later—proportionately and according to an individual's wealth so that the great will not be exempt from the law because of their high position while the humble will be no more exempt because of their weakness. This article will be explained later in a clear and detailed manner.

III

Muslims and other inhabitants of the country will be equal before the law for the law applies by nature to all men whatever may be their situation.

Throughout the land justice is a balance which should guarantee good against injustice and the weak against the strong.

IV

Our Jewish subjects need not submit to any pressure to change their religion, and they should not be harassed in the exercise of their religion; their synagogues will be respected and protected from all insult.

V

Whereas the army is a guarantee for the security of all, and the advantages which result accrue to the public benefit, and considering also that man needs to dedicate part of his time to his self-protection and to the needs of his family, we declare that we will enroll soldiers, strictly in accordance to law, by means of conscription. A soldier will remain in service for a limited time which will be determined by a military code.

VI

When the criminal court is going to pronounce sentence upon a Jewish subject Jewish judges will join the court. Moreover, religious law requires them to give merciful recommendations.

VII

We will establish a commercial court composed of a president, a clerk of court, and several members chosen from among the Muslims and the subjects of friendly powers. This court which will judge commercial cases will begin to function after we reach agreement with the great foreign powers, our friends, concerning the procedures to be followed so that their subjects can be accountable to this court. The rules of this institution will be drawn up in detail in order to prevent any conflict or misunderstanding.

VIII

All our subjects, Muslim and otherwise, will be equally subject to the rules and procedures in effect in the country; no single one of them will enjoy any special privileges over any other.

IX

Freedom of commerce for all, special privileges for none. The government will not participate in any type of commerce and it will not impede anyone from engaging in it. Commerce, in general, will be the object of a protective solicitude and anything that hinders it will be suppressed.

X

Foreigners who wish to establish themselves in our realm may engage in any industry or any profession provided that they, like all inhabitants of the country, submit themselves to existing regulations and to those that will be established later. Nobody in this regard may enjoy any special privileges.

Foreigners will gain this right after we have reached agreement with their governments concerning its application, the details of which will be explained and developed.

XI

Foreigners, subjects of their several governments, who wish to establish themselves in our realm are permitted to purchase all types of property such as houses, gardens, and land in the same manner as any inhabitant of the country on condition that they conform to existing regulations as well as to those which might be established without attempting to avoid them.

There will be no difference of treatment in respect to foreigners regarding the country's regulations. We will publicize also residency regulations so that proprietors will know them in detail and be able to observe them.

We swear by God and by the holy covenant that we will put into practice in the manner indicated the great principles which we are presenting and that we will follow them up with the necessary explanations.

We promise, not only in our name, but in the name of our successors: each of us can reign only after having promised to observe these liberal institutions, the result of our solicitude and our efforts; we take as witness to this, before God, this illustrious assembly composed of representatives of friendly great powers and high officials of our government.

God knows that the goal which I have set forth and which I come to explain to those who surround me, has been anchored by Him deep inside my heart. God knows that my most ardent desire is to put into effect immediately the principles and the consequences of these new institutions. One can demand only the possible of man.

Those who have sworn by God must fulfill their oath.

Justice is the most valuable blessing.

The life to come alone endures.

We welcome the oath of the great personages and of the high officials of our government by which they engage themselves to unite their intentions and their actions to ours in executing the reforms that we have come to describe. We say to them: Guard against breaking the oath which you come to make before God, for God knows your most secret intentions and acts.

Oh God! Sustain those who have helped to contribute to the well being of your creatures; give them the nectar of your grace to drink.

Oh God! Grant us your aid, your assistance, and your mercy; let this work produce its fruits. We ask of you your support for this task and offer you thanks for the mission which you have confided to us. Happy is the one who you have chosen in order to guide him upon the path of truth! Good is in that which you decree.

After having taken various advice, we, poor servants of God, have promulgated this act, which we have perceived will be advantageous to the country's prosperity, with the benediction of the Koran and the mysteries of its opening prayer.

Greetings from the servant of God, the viceroy, Muhammad Pasha-Bey, ruler of the kingdom of Tunis, the 20th of Muharram 1274 (10 September 1857).

16

The Young Ottomans,
Namik Kemal's "Progress," 1872 *

Born in 1840 into an old Ottoman official family, Namik Kemal (d. 1888) entered the bureaucracy at the age of seventeen with a post in the Translation Bureau. He soon drifted into the Young Ottoman circle, became one the group's major literary spokesmen and increasingly an embarrassment to the government. For Kemal, a man at home with symbols and abstractions, the three ideas of "progress," "liberty," and "the fatherland" were central to his philosophy. Although he had great faith in reason, and believed that the deliberations of a representative assembly would halt the disintegration of the Ottoman Empire, his influence can be traced in large part to the emotional appeal in his writings which glorified ancient Ottoman greatness. His writing was free of much of the Arabic and Persian phraseology still used by his contemporaries. Thus he was a pioneer in developing the modern Turkish idiom and he is still read with appreciation by Turks. Today his influence rests largely upon his popular reputation as a founder of Turkish nationalism; it would be more accurate, however, to describe him as a proto-nationalist, a transitional figure whose consciousness was inspired more by a multinational Ottoman patriotism and by reformist Muslim ideals than it was by the more exclusive ideals of secular Turkish nationalism.

TERAKKI (PROGRESS)

What necessity is there to travel through all civilized countries? If one only visits London with observant eyes, the wonders one will see will amaze one. If all the improvements in the world were photographed in a picture, the whole civilized world could only show as much as London. It is no exaggeration to say that London is a type of the world. Therefore we have chosen it as a sample (of the civilized world).

This city is generally enveloped in a black mist, like the happiness of mankind is involved in clouds of doubt and uncertainty, and its houses are as deeply covered with blacks as its very stones and trees are affected by the habits of civilization. But if we look behind that dark veil, the beauty of civilization is

---

* "Terakki" (Progress), editorial in *Ibret*, Istanbul, No. 45, November 1872, translated in Charles Wells, *The Literature of the Turks, a Turkish Chrestomathy* (London: Bernard Quaritch, 1891) 156-161.

revealed to us in such splendour and majesty that an intelligent man must be smitten by it.

If anyone who is in London wish to see the principles of justice in full play, before all things, there is that gigantic House of Parliament, which was the cradle of many of the constitutions (rules of politics) which we see in the world. If one looks at its construction, it seems as if the power and resistance of public opinion with regard to the administration had been embodied, and that that tremendous body had been turned to stone, to show as it were, that it is protected from destruction by any shock. If one enters it, he sees three or four hundred representatives, the most distinguished men of a nation (composed of one hundred and eighty millions of members) which, if not the first of all civilized nations, is one of the first, every one of whom explains, with extraordinary eloquence, the wishes of the people and the wants of the future, and displays all possible skill in expounding the principles of justice and the secrets of progress.

This distinguished body has, as its basis and support, political assemblies, each one as extensive as a town, which consists of forty or fifty, or sometimes, a hundred, or a hundred and fifty thousand people, who have all agreed about a common object. When they meet, not only is there no disorder or turmoil, but very often, except the polite discussions which are going on, not even a cough is to be heard. So many men meet together in one place; some of them speak, and their defects are listened to in silence and then, at once, they go candidly and politely to their government, and explain what they need. Ninety out of a hundred of their demands are granted, as they are consistent with right and support by overwhelming force.

Judges in the Court of Justice, appointed in accordance with the principles laid down by the Parliament, are to be seen, whom all parties trust even more than the indulgence of their own fathers. These judges are helped and controlled by a body called the "jury," who swear to do their utmost to investigate the truth, and who are themselves the friends and neighbours of the two litigants. There are lawyers to state clearly both sides of the question in the presence of the Jury, who (some of whom) would prefer gaining a deserving case than a lap of full gold.

Behold, this is the state justice is in, but education is still more perfect. If you go into any school, children ten or twelve years of age are accustomed to order and education only to be found amongst men of twenty and thirty (elsewhere). There are higher schools where the pupils study three or four languages, and know six or seven sciences.

Twenty, or five-and-twenty-children, ten or twelve years of age, will go to a garden (park). Either they have a newspaper in their hand and try to make themselves acquainted with what is going on in the world, or they sit in a corner and enjoy the pleasantness of the air, and freshness of the trees, which they survey with an intelligent glance. In their ships, crews are to be found who study the most abstruse mathematical questions, like the laws of gravitation. In the shops clerks are to be found who will discuss the ideas of the *savans* of Germany about the philosophy of rights.

There is a Zoological Garden. When all the animals in the cages pass before one's eyes, one by one, one fancies that Noah's Ark has just arrived there saved from the Flood, and all in it just landed.

If you enter their libraries, there are two or three millions of books, in all languages, and hundreds of librarians, who deserve to be called "Universal Geniuses," to help you find them. There are never less than eight hundred readers, and, amongst them, there are professors ninety years of age, and girls eighteen.

Well! in the Museum Library, if any one want a printed book, in no matter how outlandish a language, they must give it to him, or if they have not got it, they must send for it as quickly as possible.

There is a library in the House of Parliament to which one lord alone bequeathed thirty thousand volumes.

If one goes to a "refined place of amusement," he can see experiments in difficult matters connected with chemistry and natural philosophy which, if they were made in China, would be considered miracles.

If one sees the jewels and precious things in the shops, one thinks that the hidden treasure of nature, and the wealth of the world, have been plundered and brought there.

The traffic is such, that in every street the rapid and continual circulation is like a whirlpool of men, which flows from one end to another without cessation.

In the town, besides more than forty thousand private carriages, there are more than thirty-five thousand hired vehicles, and more than fifteen thousand omnibuses. At the centre of the railways of the town, for fourteen hours every day there is a train with sixty carriages every two minutes. Nevertheless, it often happens to any one that he has to wait his turn to get into a train or an omnibus, and sometimes, in a crowded part of the town, he can find no vehicle.

There is one place in the town where three trains run one above the other by means of bridges; and there is a park, in which, at promenade times, fifty or sixty thousand carriages circulate.

When one goes to the warehouses on the banks of the River Thames, and looks at the exports and imports every day, he thinks that the tide, which causes the river to rise and fall every day, casts all the productions of the world here, and that all the manufactures made by man go from here to be distributed.

If one goes to the factories here, his hair stands on end! He thinks the thing at work is not a machine, but an iron monster as big as a piece of a mountain, who spouts forth fire from his mouth, and every member of whom, when it moves gives out a terrible cry, and that he is continually working without repose, day and night, to carry out the orders of "King Intellect," who has made him his prisoner.

There are printing-machines, which print in one hour two hundred and fifty thousand copies of a newspaper eight times as large as the *Ibret* (an Ottoman newspaper). In one printing office fifty thousand workmen are employed, and in one beer brewery they have fifteen thousand cart horses.

There are hotels one mass of gilding, ornamented in a way to make palaces envious, where three thousand people can sleep, and four thousand persons can dine at their tables. There is a tailoring establishment where sufficient cloths are to be seen to dress all the people in our town of Scutari, from seven to seventy years of age; and there are seven to eight hundred shopmen, and five or six hundred shopwomen, to show the goods to customers.

There are regular markets under the river, and splendid bridges up in the air!!!

There is a place of amusement called the "Mirror Palace" (Crystal Palace), which owing to all the colours of the rainbow sparkling on it from the reflection of the light, on a skyblue ground, looks, from a distance, like a mountain of diamonds.

In the daytime the water from the fountains forms steeples of light! In the evening, when the gardens are flooded with gas (light) and moonlight one thinks it is day, and one can see from one end of them to the other. These gardens are such that it is doubtful whether anyone who was capable of visiting Paradise could produce any better imitation of it in this world of affliction.

To see the military strength of their government, it is sufficient to go down to the banks of the river, or to the old castle of the town (the Tower). There are ironclad vessels to be seen which are like a big city made of iron.

If you wish to know what the people can do, you need only look at the lists of subscriptions in the newspaper.

One widow lady presents three hundred thousand pounds to an orphan asylum!

A blacking manufacturer, in his will, leaves twenty thousand pounds to the poor!

It is very wonderful that one sees no other signs of such a powerful government in public but the police, who are employed only in preserving public order.

As regards the police, their work consists in the daytime of such things as seeing that carriages do not collide, and stopping the greatest people of quality with a sign, if they wish to go out of their turn before some ordinary individual: and at night, in quelling a few drunken squabbles, examining the doors of shops and houses to see if they are closed, and windows to see if they are fastened, and such like things connected with order and justice.

Although the people are so opulent, the greatest millionaire will go to his shop when he is eighty, and work till evening, like a shopman.

By continual effort and knowledge they have produced a world of opulence, compared to which, all the golden palaces and jewelled castles, and splendid flower gardens which the imagination of the Persian poets described in the most exaggerated way in India and China, are as nothing.

Well, we know it is impossible in a few years to make [Istanbul] * like London, or Roumelia like France. But, as Europe has got into this condition in two centuries, and they had to discover the means of progress, whereas we find those means ready to our hands, if the work be properly taken in hand, there is no doubt that in two centuries, at any rate, we shall be able to get into a condition to be counted one of the most civilized nations. And as regards two centuries, are they more than a twinkling of an eye in the life of a community?

17

The First Ottoman Constitutional Regime, The Constitution of December 1876, Selected Articles †

The First Ottoman Constitution was the product of several converging pressures: (1) the pragmatic considerations of senior civil servants such as Midhat Pasha who wished to continue the *Tanzimat* aimed at creating an efficient, Western style, centralized government and who abandoned their one-time support for the principle of an absolute monarchy when Sultan Abdülaziz proved himself an incompetent spendthrift; (2) the demand of liberal Muslim reformists such as the Young Ottomans who, motivated more by ideological attraction than by pragmatic concerns, favored a constitutional limitation of the autocracy as a means to guarantee the regeneration, progress, and liberty of all Ottomans; (3) the pressure of the European powers who, impatient with the Ottoman government's failure to protect minority rights and anxious to protect their considerable financial investments, badgered the Porte to set its house in order. When civil war engulfed much of the Balkans after the outbreak of insurrection in the province of Herzegovina in 1875 the separate pressures fused. By May 1876 Sultan Abdülaziz was deposed (to be followed a few weeks later by his mentally unstable successor, Murad V) ultimately to be succeeded by Abdülhamid II. These events cleared the way for a radical reordering of the government which the wily Abdülhamid II initially supported although he was looking

---

* "Istanbul" is the term used in the original Turkish text although the translator used the name "Constantinople."

† Translation based on the full French text in *British and Foreign State Papers* (London: W. Ridgeway, 1883). Vol. LXVII, 683-698. Most articles follow the wording used in the partial English translation that appears in Sir Edward Hertslet, *The Map of Europe by Treaty* (London: H.M.S.O., 1891), Vol. IV, 2532-2540.

toward rebuilding the absolute power of his office. The Constitution of 1876 was drafted by a commission representing diverse elements in the constitutional coalition. As a result of disagreements over the final form of the document, the sultan was able to retain important powers. When promulgated, the principle of limited monarchy was established in the constitution although it has more in common with Prussian than with British procedures. The final document was a mélange of articles—some too specific, some too vague—incorporating bits and pieces of various European models. But the constitution's greatest weakness was the fact that it had to operate in an inhospitable environment. Its existence was not due to the evolution of wide support in favor of limited monarchy as much as it was the result of emergency pressures and the political maneuverings of a small clique of government officials. Thus, when Abdülhamid II suspended the constitution's operation during the exigencies of the Ottoman-Russian War of 1877-1878 and then failed to call parliament back into session until the Young Turk revolution of 1908, few voices were raised in defense of the principle of parliamentary government.

CONSTITUTION OF THE OTTOMAN EMPIRE
11/23 DECEMBER 1876

The Ottoman Empire

Art. I.   The Ottoman empire comprises present territory and possessions, and semi-dependent provinces. It forms an indivisible whole, from which no portion can be detached under any pretext whatever.

Art. II.   Istanbul is the capital of the Ottoman empire. This city possesses no privilege or immunity peculiar to itself over the other towns of the empire.

Sultan, "Supreme Caliph"

Art. III.   The Ottoman sovereignty, which includes in the person of the sovereign the supreme caliphate of Islam, belongs to the oldest prince of the House of Osman, in accordance with traditional practice.

Art. IV.   His Majesty the Sultan, under the title of "Supreme Caliph," is the protector of the Muslim religion. He is the sovereign and padishah (emperor) of all the Ottomans.

Art. V.   His Majesty the Sultan is irresponsible; his person is sacred.

Art. VI.   The liberty of the members of the Imperial Ottoman Dynasty, their property, real and personal, and their civil list during their lifetime, are under the guarantee of all.

Sovereign Rights of the Sultan

Art. VII.   Among the sovereign rights of His Majesty the Sultan are the following prerogatives:—He makes and cancels the appointments of ministers; he confers the grades, functions and insignia of his orders, and confers investiture on the chiefs of the privileged provinces, according to forms determined by the privileges granted them; he has the coining of money; his name is pronounced in the mosques during public prayer; he concludes treaties with the powers; he declares war and makes peace; he commands both land and sea forces; he directs military movements; he carries out the provisions of the Shari'ah (the sacred law), and of the other laws; he sees to the administration of public measures; he respites or commutes sentences pronounced by the criminal courts; he summons and prorogues the General Assembly; he dissolves, if he deems it necessary, the Chamber of Deputies, provided he directs the election of new members.

PUBLIC LAW OF THE OTTOMANS'
PERSONAL LIBERTY

Art. VIII.   All subjects of the empire are called Ottomans, without distinction, whatever faith they profess; the status of an Ottoman is acquired and lost according to conditions specified by law.

Art. IX.   Every Ottoman enjoys personal liberty on condition of not interfering with the liberty of others.

Art. X.   Personal liberty is wholly inviolable. No one can suffer punishment, under any pretext whatsoever, except in cases determined by law, and according to the forms prescribed by it.

RELIGION

Art. XI.   Islam is the state religion.

THE PRESS

Art. XII.   The press is free, within limits imposed by law.

RIGHT OF PETITION

Art. XIV.   One or more persons of Ottoman nationality have the right of presenting petitions in the proper quarter relating to the breaking of law and regulation, done either to their own or public detriment, and may likewise present in protest signed petitions to the General Ottoman Assembly, complaining of the conduct of state servants and functionaries.

EDUCATION

Art. XV.   Education is free. Every Ottoman can attend public or private instructions on condition of conforming to the law.

SCHOOLS

Art. XVI.   All schools are under state supervision. Proper means will be devised for harmonizing and regulating the instruction given to all the Ottomans, but without interfering with the religious education in the various districts.

Equality before the Law. Public Offices

Art. XVII.   All Ottomans are equal in the eyes of the law. They have the same rights and owe the same duties towards their country, without prejudice to religion.

Art. XVIII.   Eligibility to public office is conditional on a knowledge of Turkish, which is the official language of the State.

Art. XIX.   All Ottomans are admitted to public offices, according to their fitness, merit, and ability.

Taxes

Art. XX.   The assessment and distribution of the taxes are to be in proportion to the fortune of each taxpayer, in conformity with the laws and special regulations.

Property

Art. XXI.   Property, real and personal, of lawful title, is guaranteed. There can be no dispossession, except on good public cause shown, and subject to the previous payment, according to law of the value of the property in question.

Inviolability of Domicile

Art. XXII.   The domicile is inviolable. The authorities cannot break into any dwelling except in cases prescribed by law.

Tribunals

Art. XXIII.   No one is bound to appear before any other than a competent tribunal, according to statutory form of procedure.

Property. Forced Labour. Contributions in Time of War

Art. XXIV.   Confiscation of property, forced labour ("corvée"), and taking temporary possession of property are prohibited. Nevertheless, contributions lawfully levied in time of war, and measures rendered necessary by the exigencies of war, are exempt from this provision.

Taxes and Imposts

Art. XXV.   No sum of money can be exacted under the name of a tax or impost, or under any other title whatever, except by virtue of law.

Torture and Inquisition

Art. XXVI.   Torture and inquisition, under any form, are wholly and absolutely forbidden. . . .

Ministers of the Crown

Art. XXVIII. The Council of Ministers shall meet under the presidency of the Grand Vizier.

The functions of the Council of Ministers comprise all the important business, domestic or foreign, of the State. . . .

Art. XXX. The ministers are responsible for decisions or acts under their management. . . .

Public Functionaries

Art. XXXIX. All appointments to various public functions shall be made in conformity with the regulations which shall determine the conditions of merit and capacity required for admission to employment under the state. No functionary appointed under these conditions can be dismissed or transferred; unless it can be proved that his conduct legally justified such removal; unless he shall have resigned, or unless his retirement is considered indispensable by the government. . . .

Art. XLI. Every functionary is bound to pay respect to his superior, but obedience is only due orders given within the limits defined by the law. In respect of acts contrary to law, the fact of having obeyed a superior will not relieve the official who has carried them out from responsibility.

The General Assembly

Art. XLII. The General Assembly is composed of two chambers: the Chamber of Notables or Senate, and the Chamber of Deputies.

Art. XLIII. The two chambers will meet on the 1st of November of each year, the opening to take place by imperial iradé [decree], the closing, fixed for the following 1st of March, also to take place following an imperial iradé. Neither of the two chambers can meet while the other chamber is not sitting. . . .

Art. LIV. Bills prepared by the Council of State are submitted in the first place to the Chamber of Deputies, and in second place to the Senate. These bills do not have the force of law unless, after having been adopted by the two chambers, they are sanctioned by imperial iradé. All bills finally rejected by one of the two chambers cannot be resubmitted for deliberation in the course of the same session. . . .

Art. LVIII. The deliberations of the chambers are carried out in the Turkish language. . . .

The Senate

Art. LX. The president and members of the Senate are directly named by His Majesty the Sultan. The number of senators shall not exceed one third of the number of the Chamber of Deputies. . . .

Art. LXII.   Senators are named for life....

Art. LXIV.   The Senate examines the bills or the budget transmitted by the Chamber of Deputies. If in the course of an examination of a bill the Senate finds a disposition contrary to the sovereign rights of His Majesty the Sultan, to liberty, to the constitution, to the territorial integrity of the empire to the internal security of the country, to the interests of national defense, or to good morals, it rejects it finally by a vote showing its reasons for so doing, or it returns it finally by a vote showing its reasons for so doing, or it returns it, accompanied by its observations, to the Chamber of Deputies, with the demand that it be amended or modified in the sense of its observations. The bills it accepts it shall confirm and transmit to the grand vizier. The Senate shall examine the petitions which are presented to it; it will transmit these to the grand vizier, if it thinks it necessary, accompanied by its observations.

THE CHAMBER OF DEPUTIES

Art. LXV.   The number of deputies is fixed at one deputy for every 50,000 male Ottoman subjects....

Art. LXIX.   The general elections for the Chamber of Deputies shall take place every four years. The mandate for each deputy is for four years only; but he may be re-elected....

Art. LXXI.   Every member of the Chamber of Deputies is the representative not exclusively of the constituency which has elected him but of all Ottomans.

Art. LXXII.   Electors are bound to choose their deputies from among the inhabitants of the province to which they belong....

Art. LXXX.   The Chamber of Deputies discusses the bills which are submitted.

It adopts, amends, or rejects dispositions concerning finances or the constitution.

It examines in detail, the general expenditures of the state included in the budget law, and it fixes the amount with the ministers. It also determines, in accord with the ministers, the nature, the amount, and the means of distribution and of levying the revenues destined to meet expenses.

THE LAW COURTS

Art. LXXXI.   The judges nominated in conformity with the special law on this subject and furnished with the patent of investiture are irremovable, but they can resign....

Art. LXXXII.   The sittings of all tribunals are public. The publication of judgments is authorized. Nevertheless, in cases specified by law, the tribunal may sit with closed doors....

Art. XC.   No judge can combine his functions with other functions paid by the state....

High Court of Justice

Art. XCII. The High Court is formed of thirty members, of whom ten are senators, ten councillors of state, and ten chosen among the presidents and members of the Court of Cassation and the Court of Appeal.

All members are nominated by lot.

The High Court is convoked, when necessary, by imperial iradé, and assembles in the senate building.

Its functions consist in trying the ministers, the president, and the members of the Court of Cassation, and all other persons accused of treason or attempts against the safety of the State.

Art. XCIII. The High Court is composed of two chambers—the Chamber of Accusation and the Chamber of Judgment....

Provincial Administration. Councils

Art. CVIII. The administration of provinces shall be based on the principle of decentralization. The details of this organization shall be fixed by law.

Art. CIX. A special law will settle on wider bases the election of the administrative councils of provinces ("vilayets"), districts ("sandjaks"), and cantons ("cazas"), as also of the Council-General, which meets annually in the chief town of each province.

Art. CX. The functions of the Provincial Council-General shall be fixed by the same special law, and shall comprise:—The right of deliberating on matters of public utility, such as the establishment of means of communication, the organization of agricultural credit banks, the development of manufacturers, commerce, and agriculture, and the diffusion of education....

Art. CXI. There shall be in every canton a council appertaining to each of the different (religious) confessions. This council will be charged with controlling—

1. The administration of the revenues of the real property of pious foundations ("vakoufs"), the special destination of which is fixed by the express provisions of the founders or by custom.
2. The employment of funds or properties assigned by testamentary provision to acts of charity or beneficence.
3. The administration of funds for orphans, in conformity with the special regulation covering the matter.

Each council shall be composed of members elected by the community it represents, conformably to special rules to be established. Those councils will be subordinated to the local authorities and the councils-general of provinces.

Art. CXII. Municipal business will be administered at Constantinople and in the provinces by elected Municipal Councils....

Various Provisions

State of Siege

Art. CXIII.   In the case of the perpetration of acts, or the appearance of indications of a nature to presage disturbance at any point on the territory of the empire, the imperial government has the right to proclaim a state of siege there.

The state of siege consists in the temporary suspension of the civil laws.

The mode of administering localities under a state of siege will be regulated by a special law.

Expulsion of Persons Dangerous to the State

His Majesty the Sultan has the exclusive right of expelling from the territory of the empire those who, in consequence of trustworthy information obtained by the police, are recognized as dangerous to the safety of the state.

Primary Education

Art. CXIV.   Primary education will be obligatory on all Ottomans. The details of application will be fixed by a special law.

Execution of Constitution

Art. CXV.   No provision of the constitution can, under any pretext whatsoever, be suspended or neglected.

Modifications in Constitutions on Certain Conditions

Art. CXVI.   In case of duly proved necessity, the constitution may be modified in some of its provisions. This modification is subordinated to the following conditions:—

Every proposal of modification, whether presented by the minister or by either of the two chambers, must be, in the first instance, submitted to the deliberations of the Chamber of Deputies.

If the proposition is approved by two-thirds of the members of the chamber it shall be forwarded to the Senate.

In case the Senate also adopts the proposed modification by a two-thirds majority, it shall be submitted for the sanction of His Majesty the Sultan.

If it is sanctioned by imperial iradé it shall have force of law.

Articles of the constitution, which it is proposed to modify, remain in force until the modification, after having been voted by the chambers, shall have been sanctioned by imperial iradé.

Interpretation of Laws

Art. CXVII.   The Court of Cassation will interpret the civil and penal laws; the Council of State administrative laws; and the Senate the articles of the constitution.

Art. CXVIII. All the provisions of the laws, regulations, usages, and customs now in force shall continue to be applied so long as they shall not have been modified or abrogated by other laws or regulations. . . .

18

Islamic Reformism, Jamal al-Din al-Afghani on Religious Solidarity as a Basis for Political Organization, March 1884 *

Al-Afghani (1839-1897), one of the great figures of Islamic reformism, and a man whose message and personality attracted many disciples, lived and influenced the course of events in the Arabic, Persian, and Turkish speaking parts of the Middle East. His appeal was broad enough that often he is listed among the precursors of several modern movements that are considered to be theoretically distant from one another: thus, he is claimed as an antecedent of secular Arab nationalism on one hand, and the multinational Muslim Brotherhood on the other. In any event, he preached an Islamic reformist message calling for a regeneration of the Islamic world in both thought and deed that eventually could lead all Muslim nations into a constitutionally organized political union strong enough to repulse Western interference in their affairs. It was during Al-Afghani's Paris stay of 1883-1886 that he edited, in conjunction with his Egyptian disciple, Muhammad Abduh, the weekly journal *Al-'Urwah al-Wuthqā* during 1884. This was the organ of a pan-Islamic society of identical name dedicated to the revival of Islamic nations and opposition to British imperialism in the Middle East and India. The article which appears below is typical of Al-Afghani in the spirit of militant activism which pervades it. The activist attitude popularized by Al-Afghani was one of his major legacies and it outlived several of the intellectual ideals he advocated during his lifetime.

*   *   *

A study of the particular identity which characterizes some nations and an examination of their beliefs proves to anyone blessed with a clear and accurate sense of observation that in most nations there is a spirit of ethnic solidarity which

* Jamal al-Din al-Afghani, "Jinsīyah wa al-Dīn al-Islāmīyah" (Nationality and the Muslim Religion), *Al-'Urwah al-Wuthqā* (The Indissoluble Bond) No. 2, 20 March 1884, 2. There is a French translation by Marcel Colombe, "La Nationalité (Djinsiya) et la Religion Musulmane," in *Orient,* Paris, Vol. 6, No. 22, 125-130.

in turn produces a sense of pride. Those whom this spirit animates are proud of the glorious deeds of their ethnic brothers. They become angry with any misfortune which touches them to the point where, in order to combat it, they kill without thinking about the reasons or the causes of the sentiment which pushes them to act. This is why many who are seeking for truth have come to the conclusion that a strong feeling of ethnic identity must be counted as integral to human nature. Yet their opinion is not correct as we can ascertain by the behavior of a child who, born in one country subsequently is taken before he reaches the age of conscious thinking into the territories of another nation; if he grows up and reaches the age of reason in that place, he will not mention his birthplace nor display any natural partiality for it. He will have no idea about his birthplace. Indeed, perhaps he will be more attached to the place where he grew up. Yet, that which is truly natural does not change.

Therefore, we do not think that such a feeling is natural to man, but rather that it is composed of a number of accidental attributes which necessity stamps upon the feelings. Actually, wherever he is, the human being has many wants. Individuals have a tendency to set themselves apart and to seek profit for themselves when they have not been properly taught. Also, they have a tendency to have numerous selfish desires which, when united with power, gives them an aggressive character. That is why some men find themselves struggling against the aggression of others. After fighting troubles for long years they were constrained to band together according to their parentage and in various ways until they formed ethnic units. That is how they became divided into nations such as the Indians, the Russians, the Turkomans, etc. Each of these groups, thanks to the combined strength of its members, was able to preserve its interests and to safeguard its rights from any encroachment by another group. Moreover, they have gone even farther than necessary as is common in the evolution of man: they have reached the point where each group is bitter if it falls under the rule of another. It believes that domination will be oppressive even if it is just....

However, if necessity has created this sort of individualistic racial solidarity, there is no doubt that such solidarity can disappear just as it can arise. Such can take place when an arbiter is accepted and the contending forces are brought together.... This arbiter is the Prince of all things, the Conqueror of heaven and earth.... When men recognize the existence of the Supreme Judge ... they will leave it entirely to the possessor of sacred power to safeguard good and repel evil. No longer will they have any need for an ethnic sentiment which has lost its purpose and whose memory has been erased from their souls; judgment belongs to Allah, the Sublime, the Magnificent.

That is the secret of the aversion which Muslims have for manifestations of ethnic origin in every country where they live. That is why they reject all clan loyalty with the exception of Islamic sentiment and religious solidarity. The believers in Islam are preoccupied neither with their ethnic origins nor with the people of which they are a part because they are loyal to their faith; they have given up a narrow bond in favor of a universal bond: the bond of faith.

Actually, the principles of the Islamic religion are not restricted to calling man to the truth or to considering the soul only in a spiritual context which is concerned with the relationship between this world and the one to come.... There is more besides: Islamic principles are concerned with relationships among the believers, they explain the law in general and in detail, they define the executive power which administers the law, they determine sentences and limit their conditions; also, they are concerned with the unique goal that the holder of power ought to be the most submissive of men to the rules regulating that power which he gains neither by heritage, nor inheritance, nor by virtue of his race, tribe, material strength, or wealth. On the contrary, he acquires it only if he submits to the stipulations of the sacred law, if he has the strength to apply it, and if he judges with the concurrence of the community. Thus, in truth, the ruler of the Muslims will be their religious, holy, and divine law which makes no distinction among peoples. This will also be the summary of the ideas of the nation. A Muslim ruler has no other privilege than that of being the most ardent of all in safeguarding the sacred law and defending it.

In safeguarding the rights and the protection of people, of property, and of reputations, the lawgiver has not taken any account of lineage, nor of ancestral privilege. Moreover, any bond, with the exception of the bond of Islamic law, was disapproved by Him. Whoever relies upon such bonds is subject to blame and whoever advocates them deserves criticism. The Prophet said, in this matter: "Tribal solidarity should not exist among us; it does not exist among those of us who are bound by religion; it does not exist among those of us who die believers." The *hadith* (traditions) of the Prophet all agree upon this point. In summary, whoever surpasses all men in piety, that is to say, in the practice of Islamic law, will be distinguished by the respect and veneration accorded to him: *The noblest among you in the eyes of God, is the most pious* (Koran, XLIX, 13). It has followed, down through many ages, and in spite of the differences in generations, that power has been wielded by men who are not noble in their race, nor especially privileged in their tribe; who do not hold sovereignty because of hereditary royalty, or do not claim it by virtue of their noble descent or highborn antecedents; they are raised to power only because of their obedience to the law and to the intense zeal they display in observing it.

The amount of power given to Muslim rulers is a product of their observance of divine regulations, of the way in which they follow the good directions which these prescribe, and of the absence of all personal ambition in them. Each time a ruler tries to distinguish himself by surpassing all others in luxury or the magnificence of his mode of life, or each time that he tries to assume a greater dignity than his people, then the people return to their tribal loyalties, differences arise, and the ruler's power declines.

Such is the lesson which one can learn from the history of the Muslims from the day their religion was revealed up to our own time. They set little value on either ethnic ties or racial sentiment but take only religious ties into consideration. That is why one can say that an Arab has no aversion to domination by Turks, why the Persian accepts the sovereignty of the Arab, and why the Indian obeys the laws of the Afghan without any bitterness or hesitancy among them. That is why one also can assert that the Muslim does not revolt or protest against either the regimes which impose themselves over him or against the transfer of power from one tribe to another so long as the possessor of authority maintains religious law and follows its precepts. But if these regimes stray in their conduct and unjustly deviate from the laws' teachings and attempt to execute that which is not right, then the hearts of the Muslims are detached from them and they become the object of disaffection, and even if they are a Muslim people's own blood brothers, they will appear more odious than foreigners in the people's eyes.

One can also say that Muslims are different than the adherents to other religions because of the emotion and regret they feel if one piece of Muslim territory is cut off from an Islamic government whatever may be the ethnic origin of the inhabitants of this territory or the group which has taken it over.

If among the Muslims one found a minor ruler of whatever racial origin, who followed the divine commandments, was zealous in applying them, compelled the people to apply the punishments which they ordain, obeyed the law himself like his subjects, and gave up trying to distinguish himself through vain pomp, it would be possible for this ruler to enjoy widespread power and great influence. He could assume great authority in Muslim-inhabited countries. He would not encounter great difficulty in doing this for he would not have to spend money, or build up his army, or conclude alliances with the great powers, or seek the assistance of partisans of civilization and freedom.... He could accomplish all this by following the example of the orthodox caliphs [the early caliphs of Islam in the seventh century A.D., ed.] and by returning to the original sources of Islamic religious law. His conduct would bring a revival of strength and a renewal of the prerequisites of power.

Let me repeat for you, reader, one more time, that unlike other religions, Islam is concerned not only with the life to come. Islam is more: it is concerned with its believers' interests in the world here below and with allowing them to realize success in this life as well as peace in the next life. It seeks "good fortune in two worlds." In its teachings it decrees equality among different peoples and nations.

The times have been so cruel and life so hard and confusing that some Muslims—they are rare—have lost patience and assert with difficulty that Islamic principles are their oppressors and they give up using religious principles of justice in their actions. They resort, even, to the protection of a foreign power but are filled with regret at the things that result from that course of action.... Actually the schisms and divisions which have occurred in Muslim states originate only from the failure of rulers who deviate from the solid principles upon which the Islamic faith is built and stray from the road followed by their early ancestors. Certainly, opposition to solidly based precepts and wandering away from customary ways are the very actions that are most damaging to power. When those who rule Islam return to the rules of their law and model their conduct upon that practiced by early generations of Muslims it will not be long before God gives them extensive power and bestows strength upon them comparable to that wielded by the orthodox caliphs, who were leaders of the faith. God give us the will to act with justice and lead us upon the road to integrity.

19

The Culmination of Early Egyptian Nationalism, Mustafa Kamil's Aims, October 1907 *

By the early twentieth century, nationalism had replaced traditional Islam as the creed of most of the modernly educated groups in Egyptian society and was being propagated actively by the professional elite. Its appeal derived not only from anti-British grievances but even more from its promise to provide a modernizing ideology that would enable Egypt to enjoy the potentials of modern civilization once full freedom was achieved. Although early Egyptian nationalism was divided into many wings, among the most influential was a middle-class group, the *Hizb al-Watani* (National Party) which coalesced around the skillful orator-journalist Mustafa Kamil (1874-1908), a graduate of the Egyptian Law School. His goal was to achieve political independence for Egypt. His ideas, never too precisely defined, contained portions of Western secular constitutional—indeed *laissez-faire*—liberalism, a dash of European left wing economically oriented anti-imperialism, and a large measure of fairly traditional Islamic social theory. Although his early career was spent largely in seeking European—particularly French—support, after the forging of the Anglo-French Entente in 1904 such an approach seemed futile and he shifted his emphasis to the themes that Egyptians would have to gain independence through their own efforts and that they were fully worthy and capable of this. Yet Mustafa Kamil's main influence was not as a thinker but as a propagandist for the nationalist cause. The speech,

* Mustafa Kamil, *What the National Party Wants, Speech Delivered on 22nd October 1907 at the Zizinia Theatre at Alexandria* (Cairo: The Evening Standard, 1907), 4-11, 17-18, 20-21, 28-29.

appearing in part below, delivered to 6000 people during a time of nationalist upheaval, summarizes the aims and some of the emotional fervor of early Egyptian nationalism.

*   *   *

GENTLEMEN,

Egypt, during the last three years, has progressed with great strides in the path of nationalism and has made her voice heard by nations and powers which were not accustomed to hear it.

English diplomatists had thought that by allying themselves with France on the Egyptian question they would throw this important matter into the shadow of oblivion. They believed that by this *entente* all voices would be silenced, every hope would die, and despair replacing hope, that the Egyptian people would become a mere antiquity, to be gazed at, like other antiquities, by the tourists who come here every year.…

They were deceived, because the isolation in which we found ourselves enabled us to discover a new soul and made us understand this truth without which no people can live, namely that nations can only be upraised, can only reconquer their independence by their own efforts, and that people like an individual cannot be at peace if it be not strong, and ready to defend its honor, its fortune and its life.…

You say, enemies of Egypt, that this country has lived long enfeebled and under the foreign yoke. And you ask us how she can be noble and independent. You forget that her dark past only further justifies our right to a brilliant and resplendent future. You forget that long suffering entitles us to a spell of happiness equally long, and that a people which has passed weary centuries in which its forces were not spent for the benefit of the fatherland, will be the strongest amongst the peoples of the earth the day on which it can direct its energies towards a sublime purpose.

Enemies of Egypt, you say that if success is possible at all, we can gain our independence only after a long time. We reply that even if what you say were true, we should not for one instant neglect our work. We do not work on our own behalf, but on behalf of our country. It remains, while we pass away.

Of what account are days and years in the life of Egypt which assisted at the birth of all nations and which has endowed the entire human race with its civilization?…

The ignorant and poor in sentiment say that I am overardent in my love of Egypt. Can an Egyptian ever be overardent in the love of his country? He may love it to the best of his power; he will never succeed in loving it as much as its beauty, its history, its majesty and its grandeur make it worthy of being loved.

Let those who criticise me visit Egypt and see it as it really is; let them read its past and ask those who come to visit it from every quarter of the world, has

God created a country more noble, more lofty, with a nature more beautiful, memories more majestic, soil more fertile, a sky more pure, water more sweet, a country more worthy of love and praise than this land of Egypt?

Ask the entire world, and the unanimous reply will be that Egypt is the paradise of the world, and, that the people which inhabits and inherits it must be the best in the world so long as it preserves it, and that on the contrary the people would commit a crime against the country and against itself, if it yielded its rights and allowed the stranger to subjugate it.

If I had not been born an Egyptian I would have desired to be an Egyptian. Some ignorant and small-minded people think that to belong to an oppressed people like the Egyptian people is unworthy of a man. But what greater honor can a man yearn for than to work for the renaissance of a nation which knew the sciences, civilisation, and literature before all other nations?

What greater source of pride can there be for a man of noble instincts than the honor of contributing to the redemption of a nation which has been the master of the human race and the educator of the world? What greater glory can generous souls desire to comtemplate than that of bringing forth the Egyptian people from darkness into light, and giving it the first place among those other countries which were sunk in black obscurity when our country was the fountain of all knowledge?

What pleasure, what happiness, and what recompense can an Egyptian patriot demand greater than his participation in this colossal work, the greatest which the twentieth century will be called upon to behold? The moral gain of the Egyptian patriot is greater, much greater than his endeavors and his fatigue....

Some of those who are ignorant of the truth, or who are paid to serve the English, call us extremists and divide the nation into groups and coteries. They do not know that in a country which has lost its independence and is under the dominion of the foreigner there should exist but one Party alone: The Party of the Nation, the Party of Freedom, the Party of Independence.

They forget or feign to forget that a country occupied by the foreigner can have only one policy, that of demanding independence, and that every word and every action which consists in weakening the national soul and destroying all or even a portion of the confidence of the nation in itself and in its future is the greatest evil that can be inflicted on a country....

We are called extremists. And why? Because we claim the rights and the independence of Egypt. Because we remind England of her honor, her promises, and her pledges. Because we tell her clearly and with strong conviction that the future guarantees independence to Egypt and that it is more advantageous to England not to withstand fate and not to seek to kill a nation which the Almighty has destined for life and action.

Extremists! Because we proclaim our unshakeable confidence in the future of our country. Because we say in the morning and at evening to this nation: today misfortune, tomorrow good fortune; today slavery, tomorrow glory; today the occupation, tomorrow independence; today misery and suffering, tomorrow happiness and joy.

Extremists! Because we say to the nation: Act and preserve peace and tranquillity. Keep away from disturbances. They can only serve our enemies and are ruinous to the country. Flee from divisions, they are the cause of misery and of all disasters. Flee religious hatreds, they are the worst of all calamities and the source of all misfortunes. Do nothing calculated to make yourself suspected by the civilised world. Civilisation renders people strong, and woe to the people which walks against it.

Extremists! Because we say to the nation: Educate yourselves as much as possible, arm yourselves with the arms of science, fill the Valley of the Nile with its beneficent light, and give to the poor their share in education.

Extremists! Because we reply to the accusations of the enemy, because we proclaim to the whole world that we are civilised beings, that fanaticism does not exist in our midst, and that Islam is a powerful factor of development and progress and civilization.

Extremists! Because we have indignantly protested against the horrors of Denshawai, and resisted the pretentions of the British, armed as we are with the right and with frankness and sustained by our daring.

Extremists! Because we show to other nations Egypt living and strong, rising up and devoting herself to noble ends, refusing to endure humiliation and ignorant lies and flattery.

Extremists! Because we do not seek to conquer the territory of others, and to enslave another people, but are contented with demanding the independence of our country.

If we are called extremists because we have done all that and because that is our attitude, let extremism be welcome and let us proclaim our pride in being called extremists.

Who amongst you would not then feel honored by being extremists, and who amongst you in that case would not wish to see all the Egyptians extremists? . . .

We are called extremists because we demand the independence of our country by the most noble means and because we have no desire to trespass on the rights of anyone, whereas the English have not been at all satisfied with the independence of their country. They have subjugated other races, have spread themselves out by colonisation, have taken possession of the sea, and most of them continue still to cry out; more conquests!

Are they to be called sages and organizers, because they are English, while we are termed extremists?

The patriotism which is good in that country and arouses admiration, is it in Egypt of a nature to arouse displeasure?

Is Egypt less beautiful than England, that the love of the Egyptians for their country should be limited, whereas the love of the English for England has no limits?

No, ten thousand times no! Egypt deserves to be loved with all our strength, all our feeling, our entire soul and our entire life. . . .

You are not unaware that the Egyptian National Movement has frightened the English Imperialists. By Denshawai, by increasing the Army of Occupation, and by the accusation of religious fanaticism they have made war on it.

But they have miserably failed, and the whole world has scoffed at their tactics. Today they attack us by means of traitors and intriguers after relying in vain for a long time upon the intruders.

This new policy will also fail. In vain do they create armies, and enemies of the national movement, this movement will rise up before them, stronger, more capable of resistance and always more daring.

Let them ruin the system of education to the best of their ability. Let them war as they will against our young men; the men of tomorrow will only be Egyptian patriots, full of love for their country and anxious to bestow on it the maximum of happiness and pride possessed by the other nations.

Let them scatter their money broadcast, to buy venal consciences and vile souls. For every one they win, ten will step out from the ranks of the patriots to destroy their work.

A nation patriotic and anxious to achieve its independence never dies. All the thunders of politicians cannot prevent a single soul from remaining attached to the fatherland. . . .

Those who ask us not to clamor for independence desire to kill the national soul of Egypt, in other words, to bury the Egyptian nation herself. For the life of this nation and its future depend upon the degree of strength of the patriotic sentiment.

Some ask how it is possible for them to reconquer their independence. The history of the human race indicates the means.

The means consists in creating and fortifying the national sentiment, courage and daring, in raising the level of the nation, in teaching it the love of glory and the desire of emulating the advanced nations and in always placing independence as the supreme ideal towards which it should march.

These sentiments win over every Egyptian; they mean the opening everywhere of scientific, industrial and commercial schools, the striking demonstration in everything and everywhere of energy and union; complete harmony amongst the members of the nation in the end which they pursue; the augmentation of the national patrimony in the domain of money, science, patriotism, and harmony; the condemnation of all the factors of division and quarrel. On that day the nation will be effectively one of the strongest. England herself will be obliged to come to an understanding with her on the question of evacuation and independence, finding it her interest to cultivate her friendship rather than her hate.

For a people which attains this degree of strength will not fail to exploit events, and to achieve its independence in spite of all opposition.

The call to independence and the development of the national sentiment are thus the two methods by which the wishes of the Egyptian nation will be realised. Let the Egyptians be assured of this truth that the salvation of Egypt depends upon us and our efforts, and that our progress will be measured by our output of energy. . . .

To introduce the sentiment of nationalism into the souls of the Egyptians, to unite the people round the idea of fatherland and to demand that it be great and independent is the noblest of actions. He who contradicts this truth would merely be making no account of religions and their effects, of history and its judgments and of the forces at work in every nation. . . .

What Egyptian can recall the Sudan treaty and thank the Occupants? How can we thank them who obliged a government which was under their control to sign this act which is opposed to the imperial firmans and juridically null? ·

Who can praise this policy of force and arbitrariness, which has effectively repudiated the rights of Egypt in the Sudan after we had watered it with our blood and expended therein colossal sums of money?

PROGRAM OF THE NATIONAL PARTY

GENTLEMEN,

The program of the National Party, which has been working for several years to redeem the country and improve it, is not difficult to understand. We have made outspokenness the basis of our policy, we have never employed ruse, subtlety or mystery.

The ends which we pursue and which we wish the entire nation to pursue in harmony with us are the following:

1.—The autonomy of Egypt (or her internal independence) as established in 1840 by the treaty of London and guaranteed by imperial firmans. (This autonomy guarantees the throne of Egypt to the descendants of Mohamed Ali and the internal independence of the country; it comprises all the countries given to Egypt by the Imperial firmans.) This autonomy England has officially promised to respect.

2.—The institution of representative government, so that the governing authority may be responsible to a Parliament possessing authority like that of European parliaments.

3.—The respect of treaties and financial conventions which bind the Egyptian government to pay its debts and to accept a financial control like the Anglo-French condominium, so long as Egypt remains the debtor of Europe and Europe demands this control.

4.—The outspoken criticism of all ill courses and actions, the recognition and encouragement of the good, and the demonstration to the Government of the interests of the nation, of its desires and the reforms of which it stands in need.

5.—The furtherance and spreading of education throughout the entire country on a strongly national basis, so that the poor may have the largest share; war against errors and stupidities; the propagation of sound religious principles which inculcate progress; and the incitement of the rich and influential to aid education by founding universities, by sending missions to Europe and by creating night-schools for the working classes.

6.—The development of agriculture, industry, commerce, and all the branches of social life, in order to enable the nation to win scientific and economic independence.

7.—The enlightenment of the minds of the Egyptians regarding the present situation, the propagation of the national spirit, the inculcation of union and harmony between the two elements of the nation, the Mussulmans and the Copts, the indication of the duties incumbent on all towards their country and the accomplishment of these duties while taking care to assure peace and security in every nook and corner of Egypt.

8.—The encouragement and assistance of every useful project and the amelioration of the sanitary conditions now prevailing, so that the inhabitants may increase in numbers and in that manner augment the strength of the nation.

9.—The development of the bonds of union and friendship between Egyptians and the foreign colonists, the effacement of all misunderstanding, and the judging of foreign criminals by the Mixed Courts.

10.—The strengthening of the ties of friendship and of attachment between Egypt and the Ottoman Empire, the development of the relations of friendship and confidence between Egypt and the European Powers, the refutation of all accusations framed against Egypt, and the winning over to the national cause of partisans everywhere so that they may constitute a superior moral force, helping the nation to gain recognition by others of its legitimate rights and to foil the attempts made against its interests to hide the truth.

20

The Young Turk Revolution, The Second (1909) Constitution of the Ottoman Empire, Selected Articles *

The young Turk Revolution of 1908 culminated the rise of an anti-Hamidian coalition. As early as the 1880's opposition to Abdülhamid II's despotism which rose in the schools and among the educated elite led to the formation of conspiratorial cells both within the empire and among the growing Ottoman exile community centered in Paris. In 1895 Ahmed Riza Bey (1859-1930) founded the "Union and Progress" group in Paris. Later a body favoring a liberal, federal Ottoman state was formed by Prince Sabaheddin (1877-1948). Increasingly "Union and Progress" identified itself with the new creed of Turkish nationalism. Until 1905 the anti-Hamidian movement was dominated by exiled intellectuals but after that date young officers in the Ottoman army, worried about the slow pace of military modernization joined the group and soon controlled it. The young officers were supporters of efficient, centralized government, and Namik Kemal's concept of "vatan"—the fatherland. By 1907 a formal coalition of the various anti-Hamidian aggregations, united in their common adherence to the principle of restoring the 1876 Constitution, was organized and after their successful putsch of July 1908 Abdülhamid II agreed to return to constitutional rule. However, the sultan was deposed in April 1909 after backing a counter-revolution. The Young Turk leaders, convinced that the 1876 Constitution had left too much power in the hands of the monarch, promulgated a revised Constitution in August of 1909. This converted the sultan into a ceremonial head of state without much political influence. Nevertheless, by 1913 the Young Turk government, buffeted by foreign wars, had itself become an authoritarian military regime.

*   *   *

3. The Imperial Ottoman sovereignty, which carries with it the Supreme Caliphate of Islam, falls to the eldest Prince of the House of Osman, according to the rule established *ab antiquo*. On his accession the Sultan shall swear before Parliament, or if Parliament is not sitting, at its first meeting, to respect the pro-

* *British and Foreign State Papers, 1908-1909* (London: H.M.S.O., 1913), Vol. CII, 819-820, 822, 824-825, 833.

visions of the Sheri (canon law) and the Constitution, and to be loyal to the country and the nation....

7. Among the sacred prerogatives of the Sultan are the following:—

The mention of his name in prayers; the minting of money; the granting of high public offices and titles, according to the law *ad hoc;* the conferring of orders; the selection and appointment of the Grand Vizier and the Sheikh-ul-Islam; the confirmation in their offices of the members of the Cabinet formed and proposed by the Grand Vizier, and, if need arise, the dismissal and replacement of Ministers according to established practice; the approval and putting into force of general laws; the drawing up of regulations concerning the workings of Government departments and the method of administering the laws; the initiative in all kinds of legislation; the maintenance and execution of the canon and civil laws; the appointment of persons to the privileged provinces according to the terms of their privileges; the command of the military and naval forces; the declaration of war and the making of peace; the reduction and remission of sentences passed by penal Courts; the granting of a general amnesty with the approval of Parliament; the opening and closing of the parliamentary sessions; the summoning of Parliament before its time in extraordinary circumstances; the dissolution of the Chamber of Deputies if necessary, with the consent of the Senate, on condition that elections take place and the Chamber assembles within three months; and the conclusion of Treaties in general. Only, the consent of Parliament is required for the conclusion of Treaties which concern peace, commerce, the abandonment or annexation of territory, or the fundamental or personal rights of Ottoman subjects, or which involve expenditure on the part of the State. In case of a change of Cabinet while Parliament is not sitting, the responsibility arising out of the change rests upon the new Cabinet....

27. Just as His Imperial Majesty the Sultan entrusts the posts of Grand Vizier and Sheikh-ul-Islam to men in whom he has confidence, so the other Ministers, who are approved and proposed by the Grand Vizier entrusted with the formation of the Cabinet, are confirmed in their offices by Imperial Iradé.

28. The Council of Ministers shall meet under the presidency of the Grand Vizier. It shall deal with affairs of importance, both home and foreign. Such of its decisions as need the Imperial assent shall be put into force by Imperial Iradé....

30. Ministers shall be responsible to the Chamber of Deputies collectively for the general policy of the Government and personally for the affairs of their respective departments. Decisions which need the Imperial sanction shall only become valid if signed by the Grand Vizier and the Minister concerned, who thus accept responsibility, and countersigned by the Sultan. Decisions arrived at by the Council of Ministers shall bear the signatures of all the Ministers, and in cases where the Imperial assent is necessary, these signatures shall be headed by that of His Imperial Majesty the Sultan....

43. Both houses of Parliament shall meet without being summoned on the 1st (14th) November of every year. . . .

44. If need arises His Imperial Majesty the Sultan may open Parliament before the specified time, either on his own initiative or on application from an absolute majority of the members. He may also prolong the session either in virtue of a decision of Parliament or on his own initiative. . . .

54. Bills become law after being examined and accepted by the Chamber of Deputies and the Senate, and sanctioned by Imperial Iradé. Bills submitted for the Imperial sanction must either receive that sanction within two months or be returned for re-examination. If a bill sent back to be discussed again is to be accepted, it must be voted by a two-thirds majority. Bills which are voted urgent must either be sanctioned or be returned within ten days. . . .

120. Ottomans enjoy the right of assembly, on the condition that they obey the law on the subject.

The societies are forbidden which aim at injuring the territorial integrity of the Ottoman Empire, changing the form of the Constitution or of the government, acting contrary to the provisions of the Constitution, or bringing about a separation between the various Ottoman elements, or which are contrary to public morals.

The formation of secret societies in general is also forbidden. . . .

21

The Rise of Turkish Nationalism, from Mehmed Emin to Ziya Gökalp, 1897-1913 *

The concept of Turkish nationalism developed rapidly in the first decade of the twentieth century. In 1897 the youthful poet Mehmed Emin (Yurdakul) wrote "Cenge Giderken," a verse inspired by the 1897 Ottoman-Greek War. In this poem, familiar to most Turkish school children, Emin gloried in calling himself not an "Ottoman" but a "Turk," a term hitherto used to refer

* a. Mehmed Emin, "Cenge Giderken" (Going to Battle), in *Türkçe Şiirlar* (Poems in Turkish) 1897, translated by Nancy C. Dorian from the Turkish text in P. Witteck, *Turkish Reader* (London: Lund Humphries, 1956), 49-50.

b. Ziya Gökalp, "Üç Cereyan" (Three Currents of Thought), *Türk Yurdu,* Istanbul, 1913, Vol. III, No. 35, translated by Niyaki Berkes, *Turkish Nationalism and Western Civilization* (New York: Columbia University Press, and London: George Allen and Unwin, 1959), 71-76.

to the farmers and herders of the Anatolian countryside. Moreover, Emin utilized a folk Turkish vocabulary and meter in composing his poetry. Within a few years of Emin's poem, powerful arguments against the concept of a multinational, pan-Islamic Ottoman empire were being advanced including a 1904 appeal by Yusuf Akçura (Akçoraoğlu) for a secular, linguistic-cultural Turkish national state. Because the Young Turks adopted Turkish nationalism as their ideology, the movement made rapid strides after 1908. By 1911 Ziya Gökalp (1876-1924) had become the major prophet of Turkish nationalism. His theories, broadcast in essays based in large part on Durkheim's sociology appeared in many Istanbul journals between 1912 and 1919 and stressed that Turkey should consciously be· come part of Western civilization. With Gökalp the question of how should the Ottoman empire modernize itself was left behind because he was concerned with Turks rather than Ottomans. The ideology of modern Turkish nationalism has borrowed heavily from the attitudes if not always the exact language pioneered by Gökalp.

A. GOING TO BATTLE (Cenge Giderken)

I am a Turk, my religion, my race are great,
My breast, my soul are filled with fire.
He who is a man is the servant of his fatherland
The Turkish child does not stay at home—I go.

I do not allow the book of Muhammad to be abolished,
I do not suffer the flag of Osman to be taken away,
I do not permit the enemy to attack my fatherland
The House of God will not be destroyed—I go.

This earth is the home of my ancestors;
My house, my village are a corner of all this place.
Here is the homeland, here is the lap of God.
The fatherland needs sons—I go.

My God is witness that I will keep my word,
All my love for my country deep in my heart,
In my eyes nothing but my fatherland.
The enemy shall not take my native soil—I go.

I wipe my tears with a white shirt,
I whet my knife with a black stone.
I desire grandeur for my fatherland;
No one stays in this world forever—I go.

B. THREE CURRENTS OF THOUGHT

In our country there are three currents of thought. When we study their history we see that in the beginning our thinkers realized the need for modernization. The current of thought in that direction, which originated during the reign of Selim III [1789-1807], was followed later by another—the movement towards Islamization. The third, the movement of Turkism, has come forth only recently.

Because the idea of modernization has always been a main theme, it has no particular exponent. Every journal or paper has been an exponent of it in one way or another. Of the doctrine of Islamization, the chief organ is *Sirat-i Müstakim* ([later] *Sebil-ür Reşat*); and of the school of Turkism, *Türk Yurdu*. We can easily see that all of these trends have been the expression of certain real needs.

Gabriel Tarde tells us that the idea of nationalism has been the product of the newspaper, and gives the following explanation: the newspaper has given a common consciousness to those who speak the same language by uniting them into a 'public.' In addition to this influence, which has been made rather unconsciously and unwillingly, the newspaper which has spurred the feelings of honour and sacrifice in the masses, merely to increase its circulation, has consequently aroused a consciousness of national traditions and of cherished ideals. The sentiment of nationality once it arises amongst the masses spreads easily over neighbouring peoples. Once awakened, it leads to revivals in moral life, in language, in literature, and in economic and political life by reinforcing the feelings of solidarity, sacrifice, and struggle among its supporters. Naturally the idea of nationality spreads quickly when emulated by neighbouring peoples, especially if they also have the press appealing to the masses in the vernacular.

The ideal of nationalism appeared [in the Ottoman Empire] first among the non-Muslims, then among the Albanians and Arabs, and finally among the Turks. The fact that it appeared last among the Turks was not accidental: the Ottoman state was formed by the Turks themselves. The state is a nation already established (*nation de fait*), whereas the ideal of nationalism meant the nucleus of a nationality based on will (*nation de volonté*). With intuitive cautiousness, the Turks were reluctant, in the beginning, to endanger a reality for the sake of an ideal. Thus, Turkish thinkers believed not in Turkism but in Ottomanism.

When the movement of modernization started, the supporters of the *Tanzimat* reforms believed that it would be possible to create a nation based on will out of an existing 'nation' composed of several nationalities and religions; and they thus attempted to give a new meaning, devoid of any colour of nationality, to the older term 'Ottoman,' which had a certain historical meaning. Painful experiences proved that this new meaning of 'Ottoman' had been welcomed by no one save the originators of the term. Inventing this new conception was not only useless but also detrimental, for it gave rise to harmful consequences for the state and the nationalities—and especially for the Turks themselves.

Today the West as well as the East shows unmistakably that our age is the Age of Nations. The most powerful force over the mind of this age is the ideal of nationalism. States, which have to govern on the basis of national consciousness, are doomed to failure if they ignore the existence of this important social factor. If our statesmen and party leaders do not hold this ideal, they cannot establish a spiritual leadership over the communities and the peoples constituting the Ottoman state. The experiences of the last four years have shown that the Turks who, in order to maintain understanding between the nationalities [under the Ottoman rule], denied Turkism and proclaimed Ottomanism have, at last, realized bitterly what kind of a conciliation the nationalities would accept. A people moved by the sentiment of nationality can be ruled only by men who have the idea of nationalism in themselves.

The Turks' avoidance of the idea of nationalism was not only harmful for the state and irritating to the diverse nationalities, but it was fatal for the Turks themselves. When the Turks identified the nation and the state with the already existing nation and state, they failed to see that their social and economic existence was deteriorating. When economic and social ascendancy passed into the hands of the [non-Muslim] communities, the Turks did not realize that they were losing everything. They believed that they were the only class constituting the Ottoman nation, and did not pay attention to the fact that they were excluded from certain classes, especially from those that constituted the most important strata of their age. They were not bothered by seeing the existence of economic and occupational classes of which they were not a part, from which they were excluded. As a consequence, they ceased to constitute the masses of people even in Anatolia. They were merely government officials and farmers. Farmers and animal breeders live only on the creative powers of nature, and are not themselves creative powers. Government officials also are not actively productive. The growth and development of the mental faculties, of will and character, are the products of active occupations as in industry and manufacturing, and of practical arts like trade and the liberal professions. It is because of this that it is almost impossible to create a national organization out of a people composed solely of farmers and civil servants. Our incompetence in administration, our difficulties in strategy and logistics, which led to the Balkan disaster, are all due to this state of affairs. The non-existence of efficient government in our country is mainly due to the non-existence of economic [commercial and industrial] classes among the Turks. Wherever the government is based on economic classes, there an efficient government exists. Business men, artisans, and traders want an efficient government for their own interests. Wherever the government is based on the class of state functionaries, it is always inefficient because those who are dismissed from government service always have their eye on government jobs, and those who are in the administration always have an eye on higher posts, and both are for ever discontent with the existing government.

As the non-existence of the ideal of nationalism among the Turks resulted in the lack of any national economy, so the same factor has been an obstacle to the development of a national language and to the appearance of national patterns in fine arts. And, again, because the ideal of nationalism was not present. Turkish morality remained only a personal and familial morality. The notions of solidarity, patriotism, and heroism did not transcend the confines of the family, the village, and the town. As the ideal of *ümmet* [religion] was too large and the ideal of the family too narrow, the Turkish soul remained a stranger to the sort of life and to the intensive moral feelings that should be the bases of sacrifice and altruism. The disintegration seen in our economic, religious, and political institutions is the consequence of this state of affairs.

Turkish nationalism is not contrary to the interests of the Ottoman state; in fact, it is its most important support. As in all young movements, there are some extremists among those who uphold Turkish nationalism, mainly among a portion of the youth, who have caused certain misunderstandings to arise. In fact, Turkism is the real support of Islam and of the Ottoman state, and is against cosmopolitanism.

Tarde had also shown that the idea of internationalism is a product of the book. Since the newspaper appeals to the sentiments of the masses, it uses the vernacular, the living language. Books, on the other hand, appeal to the abstract thinking of the scholar and the scientist, and are dependent upon neologisms rather than the living word. Scientific and philosophical terms, as a rule, do not grow out of the vernacular of the people, which is natural and living, but are artificial constructs, lifeless words. The natural words of the vernacular carry vital and emotional meanings, and as such are not suited to abstract and conceptual usage. For this reason, every nation has borrowed its neologisms from its religious language. European nations have derived their scientific terminology from the Greek in which the Gospels were written and, as Latin bcame auxiliary to Greek in the Church, the Germanic and Slavonic languages also inherited much from the Latin. Islamic peoples derived their neologisms mainly from Arabic and, secondarily, from Persian. Even today, when we translate contemporary scientific works [of the West] into our language, we coin Arabic and Persian words for the Greek and Latin terms [therein]. The earliest books were the Scriptures. As ethics, law, literature, science, and philosophy were developed out of religion as separate branches, books bgan to be written about them as well.

It follows, then, that as the newspaper helped the rise of the ideal of nationalism by expressing the social and local sentiments of the masses in a colourful way, so the book has been instrumental in the creation of the idea of internationalism, or those aspects of life commonly shared by various nations, by formulating, in an abstract and exact style, the principles, rules, and formulae of civilization whose foundation of knowledge and science originated in religion.

It is not true that the sentiment of internationalism prevailed among men during the earlier stages of history. It is true, however, that there was a sentiment of internationalism during the European Middle Ages. But if we analyse this sentiment, we see that the international love and solidarity of that period was confined only to Christian peoples, and international law likewise pertained only to the rights of the Christian states. The Balkan wars demonstrated to us that even today the European conscience is nothing but a Christian conscience. If we analyse the conscience of the Turk, we shall see that he agrees, for instance, to wed his daughter to an Arab, to an Albanian, to a Kurd, or to a Circassian, but not to a Finn or to a Hungarian. He will not wed her to a Buddhist Mongolian or a Shammanist Tunguz unless he embraces Islam. During the Tripolitanian and Balkan war, those who shared the griefs of the Turks and gave freely of their moral support were not Hungarians, Mongols, or Manchurians, but Muslims of China, of India, of Java, and of the Sudan, whose names we do not even know. It is because of this that the Turks regard themselves as one of the Muslim nations, although they belong to the Ural-Altai group from the linguistic point of view.

Anthropologically, human beings of the same anatomical types constitute a race, but sociologically the nations that belong to the same civilization constitute an 'internationality.' When the Turks, as an ethnic people, joined Islamic civilization, the Turkish language assumed an Islamic character with the introduction of the Arab script and terms.

Thus, the factor that creates the spirit of internationality, and hence civilization, is the book. Consequently, there is no incompatibility between Turkish nationalism and Islam, since one is nationality and the other is internationality. When Turkish thinkers entertained the idea of Ottoman nationality composed of different religious communities, they did not feel the necessity of Islamization, but as soon as the ideal of Turkism arose, the need for Islamization made itself felt.

However, as nationality is the creation of the newspaper and internationality the creation of the book, modernity is the product of technology. Those peoples are 'contemporary' who make and use all those machines made and used by the peoples most advanced in the techniques of the age. For us today modernization [being contemporary with modern civilization] means to make and use the battleships, cars, and aeroplanes that the Europeans are making and using. But this does not mean being like them only in form and in living. When we see ourselves no longer in need of importing manufactured goods and buying knowledge from Europe, then we can speak of being contemporary with it.

As there is no contradiction between the ideals of Turkism and Islamism, there is none between these and the ideal of modernism. The idea of modernity necessitates only the acceptance of the theoretical and practical sciences and techniques from Europe. There are certain moral needs which will be sought in religion and nationality, as there were in Europe, but these cannot be imported from the West as if they were machines and techniques.

It seems, therefore, that we should accept the three ideals at the same time by determining the respective fields of operation of each. To put it in a better way, we have to create 'an up-to-date Muslim Turkism,' realizing that each of the three ideals is an aspect of the same need taken from a different angle.

Contemporary civilization, which has been coming into existence for some time through the development of modern machines and techniques, is in the process of creating a new internationality. A true internationality based on science is taking the place of the internationality based on religion. The participation of Japan, on the one hand, and of Turkey, on the other, in Western civilization is giving a secular character to European internationality, as we shall show later; and thus the area of the *ümmet* is differentiating itself from the area of internationality increasingly.

In short, the Turkish nation today belongs to the Ural-Altai group of peoples, to the Islamic *ümmet,* and to Western internationality.

22

An Arab Reaction to the Rise of Turkish Nationalism, Program of Al-'Ahd (Covenant Party), 28 October 1913 *

While pan-Islamic thinking had been in vogue since the 1870's among Arab intellectuals, the assertions of a secular Turkish nationalism by the Young Turk regime which took control of the Ottoman Empire after 1908 eroded the confidence of many Arab thinkers in the desirability of remaining under Ottoman rule. The enforced Turkification program which went so far as to suppress instruction in Arabic in favor of teaching Turkish in schools within Arab provinces of the Ottoman empire was particularly disturbing. Educated Arabs—particularly those from the Ottoman provinces in Syria and Iraq—turned

* Program of Al-'Ahd translated from Arabic copy in Amīn Sa'īd, *Al-Thawrah al-'Arabīyah al-Kubra* (Cairo: Al-Haliby, 1935), 46-47.

to some of the pan-Arab attitudes first formulated by Christian Arabs in the late nineteenth century and countered the Young Turks' downgrading of Arab culture by advancing schemes ranging from a decentralized Ottoman state to complete Arab independence. Al-'Ahd, a secret society of about 300 members composed mainly of Iraqi and Syrian officers serving in the Ottoman army, was among the most important of the groups which pressed for the recognition of Arab rights within the Ottoman system. Al-'Ahd represented a fusion of many protest groups and advanced a romantic plan to convert the Ottoman Empire into a dual Turkish-Arab monarchy patterned after the Austro-Hungarian empire. Outlawed by the Ottoman authorities, its program was never considered seriously, but several of its members, notably the Iraqi, Nuri al-Sa'id, were to play important roles in the post-World War I Arab world. Moreover, although the major efforts to unite the various sub-strains of Arab nationalism did not begin until the 1930's, al-'Ahd's activities were an early example of pan-Arab sensibilities and cooperation.

*   *   *

1. The Al-'Ahd (The Covenant) Society is a secret organization established in Istanbul with the object of gaining internal autonomy for the Arab countries in which they would remain unified to the Istanbul government in a system of government similar to the Union of Hungary and Austria.

2. Al-'Ahd believes in the need to retain the Islamic caliphate as a holy trust in the hands of the Ottoman family.

3. The society believes Istanbul to be the head of the (Middle) East and if it is cut off by a foreign state, the (Middle) East will not live. Consequently, the society believes in protecting Istanbul from any peril.

4. Since the Turks have been the defenders of the border fortresses of the (Middle) East against the forces of the West for six hundred years, the Arabs must train to be the reserve forces for the border fortresses.

5. The members of al-'Ahd must endeavor to act with integrity, for countries cannot preserve their national political existence except with upright actions.

23

The Emergence of Iranian Reformism, Hassan Taqizadeh's Reminiscences on the Rise of the Constitutional Movement in Azerbaijan *

This remarkable memoir by Hassan Taqizadeh (b. 1878), scholar, statesman, diplomat, and a member of Iran's Senate from 1949 until his retirement in 1960, summarizes the growth of modernist thought in the Iranian province of Azerbaijan up to the time of the creation of the Iranian Constitution in 1906. The document details the vital role played by Iranian expatriates in nurturing reformism. This process seemed to develop in three stages: (1) a period of preparation dominated by Iranians residing in Istanbul, Russia, Europe, and India; probably the most symbolic figure of this stage was Malkam Khan (1833-1908), Nasr al-Din Shah's ambassador in London from 1872 to 1889 and later a leading advocate of constitutionalism; (2) a period of intense opposition to foreign interference in Iranian life that began with stubborn resistance to the Tobacco Concession of 1890 granted to British interests and culminated with the assassination of Nasr al-Din Shah in 1896; Jamal al-Din al-Afghani's Islamic reformist message was particularly influential during these years; (3) a period of propagandizing and discussion of various schemes for limiting the Shah's absolutism; between 1896 and 1906 much of this activity took place within the confines of secret societies.

*   *   *

A short time ago I delivered a talk in Teheran about the events of the first period of the Iranian constitutional revolution, from its beginning in 1906 to 1909. This was really a series of reminiscences of things which I had witnessed myself. In that talk I spoke briefly also of the early stages of the awakening of the Iranians; their learning of political conditions in the West, of the form and principles of government in civilized countries; and the reflection of this knowl-

* Sayyid Hassan Taqizadeh, "Tahiyyeye Moqaddamāte mushrutiyyat dar Azerbaijan," *Nashriyyeye Ketābkhaneye Melliye Tabriz,* Vol. I, 18-25; translated by Nikki R. Keddie as "The Background of the Constitutional Movement in Azerbaijan," *Middle East Journal* (Washington: Middle East Institute, 1960), Vol. 14, No. 4, 456-465.

edge in the thought of enlightened Iranians. Since Azerbaijan and especially Tabriz were to a degree the centers of modern thought in the period before the constitution and had an important share in beginning the reform movement, now that I have the pleasure to revisit my native city, Tabriz, several friends have asked me to speak briefly from my own memories and knowledge about the first intellectual stirrings and the origins of modern ideas here. I accepted these kind friends' request, and will say a few words, which of course are extremely summary. They will be a description of the first periods when the seeds of Western ideas and opinions were diffused.

The story must begin with the government of Abbās Mirzā *Nāib os Saltaneh*, the wars between Iran and Russia, and the internal measures of that enlightened prince. Fath 'Ali Shah, whose reign must be considered the period of rehabilitation of the central government in Iran in recent centuries, was himself a tribal man, ignorant of the world. He was able, however, to capitalize on his uncle and predecessor's strength, ruthlessness, and foundation of order to stabilize in Iran a center of power, order, and security (as they were understood at that time). His great miserliness filled the treasury. His extraordinary sensuality brought about the birth of over 160 princes, among whom were some able governors and military commanders. The best of these was Abbās Mirzā, who lived and ruled in Tabriz. This prince, due to his innate talents, and perhaps to his proximity to Russia and the Ottoman Empire and to the stay of some Europeans in Tabriz, was aware of Western conditions and wanted to achieve some of the features of Western civilization. He also wanted to acquire modern military science and arms for defense preparations against the Russians, who, with their great military power, were constantly progressing, through successive attacks, to the East and into the northwest provinces of Iran and Ottoman territory. He engaged a group of English military officers to train the Iranian army and prepare the instruments of war, and also hired some Europeans to found other institutions. Among his measures was the sending of some students from Tabriz to England to learn new techniques. One of them, Hājj Mohammad 'Ali Chakmāqsāz (The Flintmaker), was assigned to learn gunsmithing, two others medicine, another engineering, and one painting. The story of these students is long and fascinating, but there is not time to recount it here. Preliminary steps to acquire some Western accomplishments began in Tabriz in the time of Abbās Mirzā. One important thing which helped progress on the road of civilization was that, because of the presence in Tabriz of Abbās Mirzā and his vizir, Qāim Maqām Farāhāni, who was a very intelligent man, this city became the exclusive center of Iranian foreign relations. Foreign ambassadors usually came here and Iranian envoys abroad, with few exceptions, went out from Tabriz. As far as I know, in the hundred years up to the middle of the reign of Mozaffer ed Din Shah, almost nine-tenths of Iranian representatives abroad were Tabrizis or Azerbaijanis.

In later periods also many of the leaders of modern civilization were from this province. Modern civilization came to Azerbaijan primarily from two sources: through knowledge of the Turkish language there were intellectual ties (which were close to the other parts of Iran), first with Istanbul and Ottoman territories, and second with Russian territories, especially Transcaucasia and to a degree Haji Tarkhān (Astrakhan) and Ashqābad.

Āqā Mohammad Tāher, the founder and owner of the newspaper *Akhtar* in Istanbul, which for a time was the only modern-style newspaper in Persia, was a Tabrizi. So were two editors of that newspaper, Hājj Mirzā Mehdi, and Mirzā Mehdi, later called *Za'īm od Dowleh*. The latter afterwards went to Egypt and founded the Persian newspaper *Hekmat* in Cairo, which lasted almost until the beginning of the constitutional movement, and whose articles were very influential. Of course other Persian newspapers abroad like *Sorayyā* and *Parvaresh* in Egypt and *Habl ol Matin* in Calcutta were also influential in the preparation of ideas. Hājj Zein ol 'Ābedin Taqiyef, a well-known, progressive, benevolent, and wealthy man of Baku, paid for a large number of subscriptions to *Habl ol Matin* and had them sent free to the religious students at Najaf, an act which had no small influence.

One of the sowers of the seeds of progress in Iran was Mirzā Yussef Khān *Mostashār od Dowleh* Tabrizi, whose books—entitled *Yek Kalema* (One Word: discussing the agreement of the French legal code with Islam), *Ganje Dānesh* (The Treasury of Wisdom), and *Tabaqāt ol Arz* (The Strata of the Earth: about geology), and others—were good for his time. There were several other Iranians of Azerbaijan origin in Istanbul and the Ottoman provinces whose efforts to awaken the Iranians had important effects, such as Hājj Zein ol 'Ābedin Maraghe'i, the author of *Siyāhatnāmeye Ebrahim Bey* (The Travelbook of Ibrahim Bey), and Hājj Mirzā Hassan Khān *Khabir ol Molk,* who was for a time Iranian consul in Syria. The latter finally became a follower of Seyyed Jamāl ed Din Afghāni, and was executed along with two friends in Tabriz. The two friends were Mirzā Āqā Khān Kermāni and Sheikh Ahmad Ruhi, and were likewise residents of Istanbul who strove for the political and cultural development of Iran in that early period.

Najar Qoli Khān, who was a son or grandson of Hājj Mirzā Abdollah Khoi'i, was Iranian consul in Trebizond and the author of the famous book, *Mirzān ol Mavāzin* (The Scale of Scales: a polemic against Christianity).

In Istanbul there were also several men who wrote in Turkish who were originally from Azerbaijan, such as Feizi Effendi, a poet and writer who came from Tabriz. Ramzi, the well-known Turkish poet, was apparently also originally from Azerbaijan. Hossein Khān Dānesh also, whose father was originally from Esfahan, grew up in Istanbul and there became a well-known writer in both Turkish and Persian. The above men were educated in Istanbul, and a number of them came under the influence of Seyyed Jamāl ed Din Afghani and became enthusiastic reformers and progressives.

Some of the leaders of the next period and of the early constitutional movement were also influenced by the Ottomans, or had their eyes opened in Istanbul. Among them were Āqā Seyyed Mohammad Shabestari (later known as Abuz-Zia, an editor of the outstanding newspaper of the second period of the Revolution, *Irane Now*), Hājji Rasul Sadaqiāni, and Mo'tamad ot Tojjār. Others could be added to this group, whose hearts were aroused by Turkish books and articles such as the writings of Nāmeq Kemāl, the famous freedom-loving Turkish writer and poet, and later the writings of Ahmad Reza in the newspaper *Shourāye Ummat,* published in Paris. I remember well that *Shourāye Ummat* reached the late Hājj Mirzā Āqā Farshi in Tabriz, and in my youth I always used to read that newspaper and other similar things in Turkish and Persian in his home.

The late Hājj Mirzā Āqā Farshi was an initiator and a leader of the freedom lovers and enlightened men of Tabriz. As early as about twenty years before the constitutional movement he felt patriotic fervor and had modern ideas. He was my companion for years, and was especially a booklover, having made a collection of writings favoring liberty. (He also later accompanied me from Iran to London when I had to flee, in 1908, after Mohammad 'Ali Shah bombarded and closed the *Majles*.) At his home we read pamphlets and articles by Mirzā Malkam Khān, which of course were kept hidden. Among them was one treatise about the advantages of constitutional principles, and we used to repeat many of its sentences in this fashion: "If the people had a representative," or "If national representatives were supervising matters," such and such a governor or landowner could not do so and so. Almost all the writings of Malkam without exception were there, and I also had them all, having copied them with my own hand, and having often acquired them from the complete collection of Mashhadi Qorbān 'Ali Sharifzādeh of Nakhjevān (in Russian Transcaucasia), who will be mentioned later. I lacked, however, the treatise on the benefits of national representatives, about which I have found no information in the past sixty years, and however much I hunted for it I could not find it. Only at the home of the late Farshi have I seen it.

*   *   *

After this description of the light which came from Istanbul to Iran, and especially Tabriz, and gradually influenced the awakening of minds and the political revolution, I must also give a brief account of the intellectual relations of enlightened Azerbaijanis with Russia, particularly with the Caucasus and Daghestan.

Printing presses originally came from Russia to Tabriz. The lines of the Indo-European Telegraph Company also went from Odessa and Tiflis and Jolfa to Tabriz, and this linked Tabriz with Europe. After the installation of telegraph lines in Iran, in 1868 several men were sent from Tabriz to Tiflis to learn to be telegraph operators. After their training they returned here. Apparently one of them was *Sa'ad od Dowleh* Mirzā Javad Khān, who was later a well-known deputy in the first *Majles*.

Among the men educated in Transcaucasia whose civic activities were influential in Azerbaijan was Mirzā Fath 'Ali Akhundof, from Shakki (originally from Khāmena, near Tabriz), who was one of the first pioneers of modern civilization among the Moslems of the Caucasus. In addition to his excellent Turkish plays, he wrote many things in Persian, such as criticism of *Rouzat os Safa,* Persian poetry, and on the need to change the Persian script. Mirzā Kāzem Darbandi, who lived in St. Petersburg, was also a well-known scholar whose concordance for the Qorān is famous.

One of the oldest Turkish newspapers which was published in Transcaucasia was *Aḳinchi* (The Cultivator). Better known than it was the newspaper *Tarjomān* published in the Crimea by Esma'il Gāsperinsky, which continued for years. Later the very famous daily newspaper *Sharqe Russ* began publication, about 1903 or earlier. It was published by Mohammad Āqā Shāhtakhtinski, a landlord and notable of Shahtakhti, in the area of Nakhjevān. It flourished greatly and was the first large daily newspaper for Transcaucasian Moslems. This paper had a wide circulation during the Russo-Japanese War. Its writers were Mirzā Jalil Mohammad Qolizādeh Nakhjevāni (who later published the outstanding humorous newspaper *Molla Nasr ed Din* in Tiflis); Rashid Beig Esma'ilof (who later was a political agent for the Russian Bank in Tehran); Fā'eq Effendi No'mānzāde and others. Mohammad Āqā, the publisher, was one of the best-educated men of the modern period, having been educated in France and Germany, and in my opinion was the most learned man in politics in the Middle East. Later Mirzā Jalil and Fā'eq Effendi founded the paper *Molla Nasr ed Din,* which was one of the best publications of the Islamic world and very influential, and was much in demand in Tabriz.

In the early twentieth century there was a rapid development of thought and political activity among the Moslems of the Caucasus. The Russo-Japanese War, the subsequent First Russian Revolution and the creation of the Duma, and fighting between Armenians and Moslems increased the agitation among Caucasian Moslems. Baku, the real center of Caucasian Moslems, had become very wealthy and flourishing due to its oil production and there arose Moslem millionaires. The most famous, beneficent, and nationalistic was Hājj Zein ol 'Ābedin Taqiyof (mentioned above as paying for subscriptions to *Habl ol Matin*). He was widely known for his aid to Moslems, founding of schools, and other activities. The Turkish language newspaper *Hayāt* was established with his assistance. Its editor was, I believe, named Hāshemof.

Later Ahmand Āqāof, the well-known nationalist extremist from Qarābāq, founded the daily newspaper *Ershād,* which had many incendiary articles and was much in demand. Then he published another *Ershād* in Persian, written by the late Seyyed Mohammad Sādeq *'Abid ol Mamālek* Farāhāni, who had gone to Baku. It was under the same management as the Turkish *Ershād* but published separately. A literary magazine in Turkish named *Foyuzāt,* which was very pro-

Ottoman, was written and published by 'Ali Bey Hosseinzādeh. In the same period Mirzā 'Ali Mohammad Khān Oveisi, who is still alive and who was then the Iranian vice-consul in Baku, published a Persian magazine called *Haqāyeq* in Baku which was pro-Iranian, as against the Turks. It was the subject of heavy attacks by *Foyuzāt*. I remember at that time I was in transit in Tiflis and later in Baku, and I got to meet all these writers and talked with them, especially Shāh-takhtinski, Mirzā, Jalil, and Āqāyof.

One of the witty writers of *Molla Nasr ed Din* was 'Ali Qoli Najafof Nakhje-vāni, who wrote good poetry in Turkish. The best of its writers was *Sāber*, known as Hop Hop, who later became very famous and whose statue was erected in Baku.

Parenthetically, I should say that after the bombardment of the *Majles* and our exile, I came to Baku and, with the help of Heidar Khān Tārivirdiyof, known as Cherāque Barqi and later as Amu Oqli, and Ahmad Bey Āqāof, set out and went to the Baku millionaires one by one, requesting money and arms to help Sattār Khān and the other revolutionaries in Tabriz. None of them agreed except Mortaza Mokhtārof, who had a summer palace several miles from Baku, where we three went. He refused cash assistance but promised arms, including 800 Mausers. I do not know, however, whether this promise was fulfilled.

Since I have brought up the name of Heidar Khān I should say a few words about him. He was the son of Mashhadi 'Ali Akbar Tārivirdiyof from Gomri (Alexandropol-Leninakan), which was almost an Armenian town. It had only a few Moslem families, of whom the most important were the Tārivirdiyofs, con-sisting of the family head, Hājj Molla 'Ali; his two brothers, Mashhadi 'Ali Akbar and Mashhadi 'Ali Ashraf, and their children. I stayed in their home for a few days in 1908 when Heidar Khān was not there but in Khoi. Mashhadi 'Ali Akbar, the father of Heidar Khān, despite his old age, after Mohammad 'Ali Shah's bom-bardment of the *Majles,* went to Tehran to find the late Āqā Seyyed Mohammad Rezā Shirazi (better known under the name of his newspaper, *Mosāvāt*). Later the late Mirzā Mohsen Najmābādi found him and accompanied him to the Cau-casus and from there he came to Tabriz. The same Mashhadi 'Ali Akbar in 1908, when I crossed from Russia in disguise and came to Tabriz, took me from Alex-andropol to Jolfa.

Later the scope of political and cultural activities among the Moslems of Baku became wider and a group of young socialists arose, one of whose leaders was Mohammad Amin Rasulzādeh, the founder of the newspaper *Takāmol*. There were many Moslem socialists in Ganje (Elizavetpol), Baku, and Tiflis, and in Baku they took the name "Ejtemā'iyyun Āmiyyun," which is a translation of "So-cial Democrats."

At that time there was no great difference between the Moslems of the Cau-casus and Iranians, and Caucasians considered themselves quite as Iranians and sympathized with them, since both were Moslems, and since Ottoman influence had not yet advanced into areas of Shi'a population. The people were constantly going to Mashhad and Karbala; and enlightened Caucasians sometimes came to Tabriz and some of them were influential in Azerbaijan.

Mashhadi Taqi Sedqi Ordubādi was a modern and progressive Caucasian who opened a modern primary school in Ordubad, in Russian Transcaucasia. He attracted the attention of the higher authorities and was invited to Nakhjevān. There he began a good secondary school and succeeded in propagating modern ideas. He wrote Persian works as well as articles and treatises in Turkish, one of which was on the occasion of Pushkin's centenary. One of his articles, entitled "Söz" (Discourse), we published in Tabriz as a pamphlet. Other enlightened Caucasians were Mashhadi Nasrollah Sheikhov Nakhjevāni Vāmirof, a relative of the living Āqāye Nakhjevāni, and Bakhsh'ali Āqā Shāhtakhtinski, a brother of the above-mentioned Mohammad Āqā, who was an employee of the customs in Russian Jolfa. (The Shāhtakhtinskis were three brothers, Mohammad Āqā, Jehāngir Āqā and Bakhsh'ali Āqā.) Another very noble man named Mashhadi Qorbān 'Ali Sharifzādeh was in Nakhjevān, and he may be considered the best man of this group. He was a great proponent of modern civilization and progress. He gathered, copied and bound the books and articles of Mirzā Malkam Khān.

There was another man named Mashhadi 'Ali Asqar of Ordubad, about whom perhaps many of the older men here remember that he acted with unlimited Iranian patriotism and with extraordinary civic favor in Tabriz and became well known finally as "Mellat." He was a common man, scarcely literate, but he devoted himself enthusiastically to the cause of enlightenment and gave copies of *Habl ol Matin* free to this person and that person. He can be considered one of the pioneers of the new movement in Tabriz. Some of his Tabrizi friends, such as Āqā Mohammad 'Ali Javāheri and others worked on the same path.

It is worth knowing that in that period the reading and writing of the Persian language was just as common in Transcaucasia as in Tabriz, and it was read in the elementary schools under the mollas, and people wrote their correspondence in Persian. I myself in about 1897-98 crossed over to the Caucasus, and in Russian Jolfa Bakhsh'ali Āqā and Sheikhof, who lived there, received me very well. I went to a village named Vanand, where my ancestors had lived and where my uncles were living, and stayed there two or three weeks. This village had about a hundred families, and near it on neighboring hills was another small village named Valāvar. The people of Vanand used to recite a poem in the Persian language, as follows:

> Vanand and Valāvar, behold o my brother,
> Their land is paradise and their men are devils!

Mirzā Shafi', a schoolmaster in Tiflis, from whom the well-known German poet Bodensted learned Persian, was a writer of poetry in Persian. He gave his *Divan* of poems to Bodensted, who translated them into German under the name of

Mirza Shafi, and published them in Germany. The book was well received and for a time no one knew its author's identity, until, in the preface of the fiftieth printing of the book, Bodensted revealed that he was the translator and who the real author was.

To show the Iranian nationalism of the Caucasian Moslems, and especially the Shi'ites there, there could be no better example than the following: When, in 1897 or 1898, I went from Tabriz to the Caucasus, reaching Jolfa in three days, I spent the night in the village of Sujā near the Jolfa crossing in order to reach and cross the Araxes River the next morning. There, from one of the villagers who were gathered in the coffeehouse, I heard this story: He said he had gone one day to a nearby village on the Russian side of the Araxes named Yāji, and there, in the square in front of the mosque where the old men of the village used to sit and talk, they had planted plane trees and would watch and water them every day. He said to the old men, "Uncles, you who are so old, what benefit will you get from spending your time on plane tree saplings which require so many years to reach maturity?" When he said this the old men wept and said, "The only desire in our lives is that these trees should grow and this territory become Iranian again and the Iranian tax collectors should come here to collect taxes and we should not be able to pay the taxes and that they should tie us to these trees and beat us!"

Travel back and forth between Azerbaijan and Russia was one of the important factors in the progress of civilization in Azerbaijan. Russian commercial and oil wealth attracted the people of Iran. In Baku in the winter there were eighty thousand Iranian workers and in the summer fifty thousand. They naturally brought back money chiefly, but also some knowledge.

In the first period of the movement for reform in Tabriz it happened that the late Mirzā Seyyed Hossein Khān (later well-known as Adālat) went in his youth to Russia and stayed for a while with his cousin, Mirzā Ja'far Khān, who was the Iranian consul in Haji Tarkhān (Astrakhan). He later went to St. Petersburg and learned Russian and became acquainted with European civilization. In St. Petersburg he became for nearly two years a companion and associate of Seyyed Jamāl ed Din Afghāni, whose personality had an extraordinary influence on him. Upon his return to Tabriz he became an official of the passport department in Iranian Jolfa, where he was a friend and associate of the aforementioned Bakhsh'ali Āqā Shāhtakhtinski from the opposite side of the river. Later, in about 1896, he returned to Tabriz with fervent modernizing ideas. Here he found the late Āqā Seyyed Mohammad Shabesteri (as mentioned before, later known as Abuz-Zia), and since he had the same ideas, they became friends and associates. Later these two found me and the late Mirzā Mohammad 'Ali Khān Tarbiyat, who was my schoolmate and companion, and we four formed the nucleus for modern ideas in Tabriz.

Mirzā Seyyed Hossein Khān founded in 1897-98 a newspaper named *Al Hadid,* whose first number contained excellent verses by the late Lāli. After the publication of two or three numbers, however, the Russian consulate in Tabriz invited Mirzā Seyyed Hossein Khān into their service and entrusted the passport work of the consulate to him. We continued to work together, however, for nearly ten years, until the dawning of the constitutional movement. An account of the history of our activities would be very lengthy. Among them was our founding of a bookstore of a modern type, called Tarbiyat, and bringing in foreign books and distributing them. We three—that is, Mirzā Seyyed Hossein Khān and Mirzā Mohammad 'Ali Khān and I—with the addition of Mirzā Yussef Khān Āshtiyani E'tesāme Daftar (later E'tesām ol Molk, publisher of the magazine Bahār and head of the Majles Library), published a scientific and cultural magazine called Ganjineye Fonun which flourished and lasted from 1903 to 1904. We four above-named companions founded a large secondary school named Tarbiyat, which was rendered abortive by the uproar of preachers, especially Hājji Seyyed Mohammad Yazdi Tāleb ol Haq.

A man named Mirzā Hossein, who was later known as Kamāl, also founded a modern type of secondary school named Kamāl in the Leilābād quarter in 1898, which played a great role in modern education.

Another educated, modern and enlightened man of the period was Mirzā Seyyed Ne'matollah Khān, who was later known as Jāvid. He was a fellow student of mine and of Mirzā Mohammad 'Ali Khān Tarbiyat, and we studied the French language and natural science together. His father was from Esfahan, living in Tabriz, and was of the "Zahabi" Sufi order.

At that time and before then there were no newspapers in Tabriz, except for one named Azerbaijan which was published about a hundred years ago in Tabriz and of which no copy could be found in our time. I found one or two pages of it in the Royal Library in Berlin. There was also the semi-official Nāsseri newspaper which had started publication in 1893-94 and continued for years in Tabriz, whose publisher was Nadim Bāshi or Nadim os Soltan, and later was managed for a time by Safā ol Molk, the son of 'Adl ol Molk. In the same despotic period several years before the constitution, another newspaper named Ehtiyāj was started in Tabriz, whose writer was 'Ali Qoli Khān, known as Safār'of. This newspaper was suspended by Hassan 'Ali Khān Amir Nezām Garrusi, the governor of Tabriz, who bastinadoed 'Ali Qoli Khān because of an article he had written in it. The article was about a china factory in Tabriz and the lack of industry in Iran. This beating was the cause of the victim's entry into the court of the Crown Prince, Mohammad 'Ali Mirzā, where he became head of the secret service. Later this same man started the newspaper Eqbāl. In the same period 'Abid ol Mamālek came to Tabriz, gained the favor of Amir Nezām, and started the newspaper Abad.

Later the Loqmāniyye secondary school was founded through the efforts of Loqmān of Mamālek, the head physician of the crown prince and father of Dr.

A'lām ol Molk, the present Senator, and of the late Loqmān od Dowleh. This school was very modern and I used to teach there. Before all these private schools (Kamāl, Tarbiyat, and Loqmāniyye) the Dar ol Fonun Mozaffari school was founded in Tabriz. It was similar to the Dar ol Fonun in Tehran and was known as the mo'allemkhāneh. The children of notables and of the court staff were educated there. I myself also studied mathematics and other things there for a time, and later taught physics and other subjects there. Naturally this school had great influence in the spreading of civilization.

Another of the awakening and modern people of the autocratic period was Mirzā 'Ali Khān Lā'li Shams ol Hokamā (the uncle of Āqāye Nakhjevāni), whose Divan of poetry is very famous. Another very learned and enlightened man of Tabriz was the late Hājj Mohammad Āqā Iravāni, and everyone who has seen him knows what a patriotic and progressive man he was. His son, Mirzā 'Ali Akbar Khān, was also a good, educated man. The Kalāntari brothers of Bāqmishe, and especially the youngest brother, Mo'azzaz od Dowleh, were also progressive. Mo'azzaz od Dowleh established a reading room near "Qāri Kurpisi" and built a guest house which were very useful.

Several learned persons in that period came to Tabriz from whose presence the young generation benefited very much. Among them were 'Al Khān Nāzem ol Olūm, whose physics and mathematics book is well known, and Dr. Mohammad Kermanshāhi, known as Kofri (the unbeliever), who came as Amir Nezām Garrusi's physician. Dr. Mohammad Kermanshāhi's scientific position is too high to be discussed briefly, and, as some of you may have noted, I recently wrote an article about him entitled "Memories of a Learned Man" in the journal Yaghmā. I was his student for several years.

Among the very important factors leading Azerbaijan to modern civilization were the American schools in Tabriz and Ormiya, which had an extraordinary and admirable educational influence. I myself studied some English in the Tabriz school, although I was not enrolled there as a regular student. Similarly the French Roman Catholic school to a certain extent and the Russian Suzanof school in Tabriz for teaching Russian and other things, had a beneficial influence. In the final period of the autocracy some other private schools were founded, such as Ma'refat, Roshdiyye and others. In reality Hājj Akhund and his brother Hājj Mirzā Hassan of Roshdiyye laid the foundations for modern methods of teaching. The coming of Amīn od Dowleh as governor of Tabriz, although he did not stay long, also had some effect, and he promoted and encouraged the Roshdiyye.

Among the most influential things in education and awakening, as I have said, were Turkish books from Istanbul and, especially, Arabic books from Egypt and the magazine Al Hilāl and books such as Tabāye' ol Esteodād by Seyyed 'Abd ol Rahman Kavākebi.

Since we have arrived near to the time of the constitution, I must note some very important factors, among them the books in Persian by Tālibof, such as

Ketābe Ahmad (Ahmad's Book), *Masālek ol Mohsēnin* (Paths of the Benevolent) and *Masā'el ol Hayāt* (Problems of Life); also the *Siyāhatnāmeye Ebrāhim Bey* by Hājj Zein ol Ābedin Marāghe'i; and the secret jellygraphed sheets such as *Hammāme Jenniyān* and the *Shabnāmeh* which we and others circulated.

At the dawn of the constitutional movement a group of intellectual young men appeared among whom the late Seyyed Hassan Sharifzādeh, who was my pupil, and his friend Hakkābāshi (the son of the former calligrapher and engraver Hakkākbāshi), and especially Hājj Mirzā Āqā Farshi, and some others, are worthy of mention and praise. A man who had extraordinary influence in the constitutional revolution in Azerbaijan and was, in my opinion, perhaps its foremost agent and popular speaker, was the late Āqā Mirzā Hossein Vā'ez (later Hājj Mirzā Hossein). Afterwards his colleagues were the late Sheikh Salim and Mirzā 'Ali Veijuye'i and also His Noble Presence Mirzā 'Ali Āqā *Seqat ol Eslām,* the martyr, who was a very enlightened man of the top rank of the *olema.* These last three were hanged by the Russians in 1912.

The famous orators of the constitutional revolution in Tehran, Āqā, Seyyed Jamāl ed Din Esfahani and Hājj Mirzā Nasrollah Beheshti (later called *Malek ol Motakallemin*), also came two or three times in different years during Moharram to Tabriz, where the effect of the personality of Seyyed Jamāl ed Din Esfahani was very great. Also influential was the Tabriz *Majles* deputy Mirzā Sādeq Khān *Mostashār od Dowleh,* who had been educated in the Soltāniyeh school in Istanbul, and who was the nephew of Sheikh Mohsen Khān *Moshir od Dowleh,* the Iranian ambassador in Istanbul.

This talk has dealt with the origins of the constitutional movement in Azerbaijan from a hundred years before that happy event until the beginning of the auspicious revolution in 1906. This account has been miscellaneous, incomplete, and disconnected, like memoirs. I know that my listeners are tired and to explain things more fully would have required at least two talks. I am also afraid that I omitted some important subjects and names of some people who were worthy of mention. In that case, since the neglect was unintentional, I hope for forgiveness. I have just remembered that I forgot to mention Mirzā Hossein Khān Kāzemzādeh (now Irānshahr), who was a student in the Kamāl school, and his bookstore in Tabriz, and his instructive magazine.

24

The Creation of the Iranian Constitution; Selections from the Fundamental Laws, 30 December 1906 and 8 October 1907 *

By 1906 both the conservative and modernizing opposition to the inefficient absolutism of the Shah's government had been frustrated to the point where they combined into a constitutional coalition. While the large conservative bloc of small merchants and craftsmen led by religious mullas (teacher-preachers) provided mass, emotional support, the small modernly oriented body of intellectuals provided much of the philosophical content for the constitutional movement. In their secret societies these latter groups articulated demands calling for equitable administration of justice, taxation and finances, military reforms, encouragement of local business, and limitation of the shah's absolutism. Following serious rioting and strikes in Teheran during the summer of 1906 Muzaffar al-Din Shah (1896-1907) capitulated to the pressure and called for a National Consultative Assembly to consider a constitution. The document was issued in two parts which dealt respectively with the composition and functions of the National Consultative Assembly and with the rights of the people and the powers of the state. While the document's language copied Belgian and French models, it dealt directly with the matters which disturbed the constitutionalists. Provision against the uncontrolled issuing of economic concessions recalled Persia's recent experiences with such practices. The progressives' familiarity with Montesquieu inspired an article ordaining a clear functional separation of state powers. Meanwhile, there are numerous articles of conservative inspiration including one (that has remained largely ignored since the 1920's) stating that the Majlis (Assembly) cannot pass laws contrary to Islam as decided by a panel of religious leaders. Thus a certain tension between progressive and conservative goals is built into the document. Although the Iranian Constitution remains valid to this day it has not yet been fully implemented (the Senate, for instance, did not hold its first meeting until 1950). Thus, like many other documents of modern Middle

* *British and Foreign State Papers, 1907-1908* (London: H.M.S.O., 1912), Vol. CI, the "Fundamental Law" (Persian Constitution) of 30 December 1906, 527-534; the "Supplementary Fundamental Law" (Persian Constitutional Law) of 8 October 1907, 534-542.

Eastern history the Iranian Constitution of 1906-1907 was as much a declaration of intention as it was a guide for practical administration.

THE PERSIAN CONSTITUTION. DECEMBER 30, 1906

In the name of God the all-Merciful!

WHEREAS by our Firman of the 5th August, 1906, we commanded the constitution of a National Assembly for the progress and welfare of the State and nation, the strengthening of the foundations of the kingdom, and the carrying out of the laws of Islam; and whereas, in accordance with the clause by which it is provided that, as each individual member of the State has a right to take part in the superintendence and decision of public affairs, we therefore have permitted the election and appointment of Deputies on behalf of the nation; and whereas the National Assembly has been opened through our gracious benevolence, we have decreed the following Articles of constitutional Regulations for the National Assembly, including the duties and business of the Assembly and its limitations and relations towards Government Departments. . . .

2. The National Assembly is the representative of the whole Persian nation, which shares in political and domestic affairs. . . .

11. As soon as members of the National Assembly join they must take the following oath and sign it: . . .

"We who have signed below invite God to be our witness, and we take oath by the Koran that, so long as the rights of the Assembly and the members of the Assembly are protected and carried out in accordance with these Regulations, we will carry out the duties entrusted to us, as well as possible, with the greatest sincerity and straightforwardness, and to our best ability, and we will be true and faithful to our just Sovereign, and will not be traitors to the foundations of sovereignty or the rights of the nation, and we will have no other object but the advantage and the interests of the Government and nation of Persia."

12. No person will, by any excuse whatever, have the right to proceed against any member of the Assembly. Should by chance one of the members be guilty of a public offence or crime, and should he be caught in the act of committing the offence, the carrying out of punishment must still be with the knowledge of the Assembly.

13. In order that the result of the discussions of the National Assembly should be carried out, their proceedings must be public. Newspaper reporters and the public have the right to be present and to hear, in accordance with the internal Regulations, but without the right of speaking. The newspapers may print all the debates of the Assembly without altering their meaning, . . .

15. The National Assembly has the right to discuss truthfully and sincerely all matters it considers to be desirable in the interests of the State and nation to in-

vestigate; and, subject to the approval of a majority, to submit them, in the enjoyment of the utmost safety and confidence, with the approval of the Senate, to His Imperial Majesty the Shah, through the first person of the Government, for His Majesty's signature, and to be then put into execution.

16. In general all laws necessary for the strengthening of the Government and kingdom, and the regulation of State affairs, and for the constitution of Ministries, must receive the sanction of the National Assembly.

17. The necessary Bills for making new laws, or for the alteration, amplification, or cancellation of existing laws, will, when desirable, be prepared by the National Assembly to be submitted to His Imperial Majesty the Shah for signature with the approval of the Senate, and to be then put into execution.

18. The regulation of financial matters, the modification of the Budget, the alteration of the arrangement of taxation, the refusal or acceptance of impositions, as well as the inspections which will be undertaken by the Government, will be done with the approval of the Assembly....

22. Whenever a part of the revenue or property of the Government or State is to be sold, or a change of frontier or border becomes necessary, it will be done with the approval of the National Assembly.

23. Without the approval of the National Assembly no concession whatever for the formation of Companies or Associations shall be granted by the Government.

24. Treaties, Conventions, the granting of concessions, monopolies, either commercial, industrial, or agricultural, whether the other party be a native or a foreigner, can only be done with the approval of the National Assembly. Treaties which it may be in the interests of the Government or nation to keep secret are excepted.

25. All Government loans of any nature whatsoever, whether internal or foreign, will be made with the knowledge and approval of the National Assembly.

26. The construction of railways or roads, whether the cost be defrayed by the Government, by Associations or Companies, whether native or foreign, can only be undertaken with the approval of the National Assembly....

PERSIAN [SUPPLEMENTAL] CONSTITUTIONAL LAW
as passed by the National Assembly and signed by the Shah.—Teheran, October 8, 1907.

Preamble.

In the name of God the Merciful, the Compassionate.

THE following are the Articles which, in order to complete the fundamental laws of the Constitution of Persia, have been added to the Constitutional Law signed by His Imperial Majesty the late Muzaffer-ed-Din Shah Kajar on the 14th of Zilkade-ul-Haram, 1324 (30th December, 1906):—

ART. 1. The official religion of Persia is the branch of the Twelve Imams of the Shia Sect of Islam. The Sovereign of Persia must be of, and contribute to the spread of, this religion.

2. The National Assembly has been founded by the help of the Twelfth Imam, the bounty of His Islamic Majesty, the watchfulness of the Mujteheds and the common people. The laws passed by it must never to all ages be contrary to the sacred precepts of Islam and the laws laid down by the Prophet. It is obvious that the decision as to whether the laws passed by the Assembly are in opposition to the precepts of Islam rests with the Ulema. It is therefore officially decreed that for all ages a Committee composed of five persons, who shall be Mujteheds and religious doctors, and who also must be acquainted with the requirements of the times, shall be elected in the following manner: The Ulema and doctors of Islam who are recognized by the Shias as the centre of imitation shall make known to the National Assembly the names of twenty of the Ulema possessing the above-mentioned qualities. The National Assembly shall, by agreement on casting of lots, elect five of them or more, according to the requirements of the age, and admit them as members. This Committee shall discuss and thoroughly investigate the Bills brought in by the National Assembly, and reject every one of these Bills which is contrary to the sacred precepts of Islam, in order that it may not become law. The decision of this Committee is final.

This Article will not be liable to change until the advent of the Twelfth Imam. . . .

6. The life and property of foreigners resident in Persia are secured and guaranteed except in those cases in which the laws of the realm make exceptions.

7. The Constitution, in part or in entirety, is not liable to interruption.

8. The people of Persia enjoy equality of rights before the civil law.

9. The life, property, domicile, and honour of every individual is secured and guaranteed from every kind of injury. No one can be disturbed except by order of, and in the manner defined by, the laws of the land.

10. Except when found *in flagrante delicto* committing crimes, misdemeanours, or important offences, no one can be immediately arrested except by a written order of the President of the Tribunal of Justice in accordance with law. Even then the offence of the accused must be made known to him at once, or at the latest within twenty-four hours.

11. No one can be prevented from appearing before the Court which should decide his case, and be forced to refer the matter to another Court.

12. No punishment shall be decreed or executed except by law.

13. The dwelling-place and house of every individual is inviolable. In no dwelling-place can forcible entry be made, except by order of, and in the manner defined by, law.

14. No Persian can be exiled or prevented from residing in any place, or forced to reside in any place, except in cases defined by law.

15. No owner can be deprived of his land except by sanction of the Sheri, and then even only after the fixing and payment of a just price....

18. The study or teaching of arts, letters, and sciences are free, except in so far as they are forbidden by the Sheri....

26. The powers of the realm spring from the people. The Constitutional Law defines the method of using those powers.

27. The powers of the realm are divided into three parts:—

Firstly, legislative power, whose province it is to make and amend laws. This power emanates from His Imperial Majesty the Shah, the National Assembly, and the Senate. Each one of these three sources possesses the right of originating laws; but their passing is conditional on their not being contrary to the laws of the Sheri, and to the approval of the two Assemblies, and to their receiving the Imperial signature. But the making and approval of laws relating to the revenue and expenditure of the realm belong to the National Assembly alone.

The interpretation and commentary of laws is the peculiar duty of the National Assembly.

Secondly, the judicial power, which consists in the distinguishing of rights. This power belongs to the Sheri Tribunals in matters appertaining to the Sheri, and to the Courts of Justice in matters appertaining to the civil law ("urf").

Thirdly, the executive power, which rests with the Sovereign. That is to say, the Laws and Decrees will be executed by the Ministers and Government officials in the name of His Imperial Majesty in the manner defined by law.

28. The three above-mentioned powers shall always be differentiated and separated from one another....

35. The sovereignty of Persia is a trust which, by the grace of God, has been conferred on the person of the Sovereign by the people....

39. No Sovereign can ascend the throne unless, before his coronation, he appear before the National Assembly, and in the presence of the members of the National Assembly and the Senate and the Cabinet of Ministers swear the following oath:—

"I take the Lord Most High to witness, and I swear by the Holy word of God and by all that is sacred before God, that I will devote all my energy to preserving the independence of Persia, guarding and protecting the limits of the realm and the rights of the people. I will be the guardian of the fundamental law of the Constitution of Persia, and will rule in accordance with it and the laws which have been decreed. I will strive zealously to propagate the sect of the Twelve Imams of the Shia religion. Deeming God Almighty a witness to my every act and deed, I will have no other object in view save the greatness and happiness of the State and people of Persia. I pray for the grace of God to serve the progress of Persia, and I ask help in my task of the pure souls of the saints of Islam."

40. In like manner the person who has been elected to the Regency cannot take charge of affairs unless he has sworn the above oath....

43. The Sovereign cannot, without the approval and sanction of the National Assembly and the Senate, interfere in the affairs of another country.

44. The Sovereign is absolved from all responsibility. The Ministers of State are responsible in all matters.

45. All the Decrees and Rescripts of the Sovereign shall only be put into execution when they have been signed by the responsible Minister, who is responsible for the accuracy of the contents of the Firman or Rescript. . . .

48. The Sovereign has the right, with the approval of the responsible Minister, to choose the important officials of the Government Departments, either at home or abroad, except in cases excepted by law. But the appointment of the other officials does not concern the Sovereign, except in cases defined by law.

49. The issuing of Firmans for the execution of laws is one of the rights of the Sovereign, but he may not delay or suspend the execution of those laws.

50. The supreme command of the military and naval forces is vested in the person of the Sovereign.

51. The declaration of war and the conclusion of peace rests with the Sovereign. . . .

4

Imposed Modernization: Imperialism as a Vehicle for Change

Change in the modern Middle East has been a multidimensional process involving a continual interaction between indigenous and European cultures. While much of this process has involved a more or less voluntary transformation of Middle Eastern institutions, other aspects of modern civilization were imposed upon the region by the Europeans usually under the aegis of some sort of colonial relationship. But even here, European intentions as expressed in documents of the colonial regimes outlining various kinds of development schemes, seldom were implemented without important modifications resulting from the actual contacts between the two cultures. Even if elements of modern civilization were injected into a Middle Eastern country with the full backing of a colonial government, the diffusion of the idea or institution into the body of a Middle Eastern society was more likely to produce a mutation than a reproduction of the original model. Thus, the story of Western and Russian imperialism in the Middle East is seriously distorted if it treats imperialism as a strictly controlled European phenomenon with the several Middle Eastern states passively serving as so many pawns bing manipulated by the diplomatic chess players in the great capitals of the modern world. Certainly, it is true that there was a European-oriented aspect of imperialism: the development of the separate aims and policies of the various imperial states, the clash of conflicting interests, and the progress of the Middle Eastern rivalries of the great powers. This aspect is dealt with in an immense literature that outlines the intricacies of the "Eastern Question" and the contribution of various domestic forces in Britain, Russia, France, Austria, Germany, Italy, and the United States to its movement. But the implications of the attempts of various representatives of the modern world to instigate change in the Middle East's political, economic, or social and intellectual order is an even more important aspect of imperialist influence in the Middle East. Historians of the future probably will agree that the primary importance of modern imperialism was that it provided a vehicle through which many facets of modern civilization were carried to and in some cases, forced upon less-developed civilizations.

It is possible to isolate three major subvarieties of imperial regime in the Middle East according to the degree of control exercised by the paramount power. Extensive areas became the scene of attempts to colonize a large resident European population in the midst of the indigenous populace and to assimilate a country culturally with the ultimate view of totally absorbing it into the mother country. Looser forms of control characterized the various protectorates or formally declared "spheres of influence" where the paramount power ruled more or less indirectly by associating the local political elite with the imperial governmental structure. In other Middle Eastern states that retained actual sovereignty imperial powers were content to exercise considerable, albeit indirect, influence through extraterritorial privileges or behind the scenes diplomatic and economic pressure.

The most extreme forms of assimilationist colonialism were practiced by the Russians. So successful was Russia's absorption of large Muslim-inhabited tracts in the Crimea, the Caucasus, and Central Asia that often we forget that those areas once were considered adjuncts of the Middle Eastern political, social, and cultural order. North Africa, too, was the center of several repressive assimilationist colonial experiments none of which, however, were destined to achieve the permanence of the Russian creations. After 1830, the French in Algeria pursued a program of expropriation of local land as part of a policy of facilitating large-scale European settlements. This was coupled with an attempt to encourage the spread of French culture among the local population at the expense of Islamic learning. By the 1890's the European colons, a group with little respect for indigenous culture, exercised decisive influence on France's Algeria policy and had gained the concession that only those Algerians who were willing to live under French law—in effect to give up living as Muslims—could participate in Algerian political life alongside the European colonial community. By that time, too, the fiction that Algeria was actually part of metropolitan France was legalized. But the mass of Muslim Algerians tried to remain true to their heritage and loyalty to the Islamic faith became particularly important to their sense of self-identification as the traditional social order crumbled under the impact of France's expropriation of productive land. European settlement under French aegis also was imposed upon Tunisia after 1881 and Morocco after 1912 with some of the same results that occurred in Algeria. Still, the fact that Tunisia and Morocco were both officially protectorates rather than colonies mitigated the harshness of colonial rule somewhat. In all her North African colonies France emphasized the differences between Berber and Arab and between rural and urban cultures as well as the superiority of their own culture. This had the result of substituting French for Arabic as the language of learning. By the time of World War I France welcomed local recruits into her armed forces and, although locals seldom advanced beyond non-commissioned or junior officer rank, the army became a principal vehicle whereby North African Muslims learned of modern civilization; this military experience, also, was to become a key to North Africa's eventual escape from French control in the 1950's and 1960's. The Italian regime in Libya that was set up in 1911 was similar in its essentials to that established in Algeria; pacification was followed, in the 1930's, by large-scale settlement by Italian peasants on land wrested from Arab tribes.

A looser form of imperial political control over Middle Eastern countries was the "protectorate" system. Protectorates took many forms; some were legally constituted, others were "unofficial." Nevertheless, in all of them the paramount power held the final right to make decisions concerning its vital interests in the protectorate even if local rulers were left in nominal charge of affairs. The key to an imperial state's control over a protected state was the actual presence of its land or sea forces upon the scene. Britain's imperium in the Middle East was exercised with the exception of crown colonies in Aden (and Cyprus after 1914) through various forms of protectorates the first of which were established in the Persian Gulf in 1820. Britain's main interests in the Middle East were strategic—protecting her imperial life line to India and the East—so she was concerned chiefly with keeping order rather than with promoting rapid modernization. Thus, she tried to exercise control with a minimum of direct interference. The local ruling group was kept in power and traditional institutions were left largely intact in return for the protectorate's cooperation. The specific relationship between the British and the indigenous governing classes varied from one protectorate to another and it was not based entirely on formal engagements. It was founded, too, on a constantly changing body of practices, procedures, and unofficial usages not sanctioned by treaty but nevertheless considered binding by local ruling groups. This system saved the British much administrative and financial grief for they faced problems enough trying to govern a world-straddling empire with only limited economic and military resources. Nevertheless, by the twentieth century indirect rule through protectorates increasingly proved to be a limited method of administration suitable mainly for preserving a status quo. It came to stand neither for traditionalism nor for change and more and more often was challenged by partisans of both positions.

A far more pervasive technique for assuring imperial interests, particularly the interests of individuals, was the nearly universal availability of devices suitable for applying indirect pressure on Middle Eastern governments—even those, such as the Ottoman Empire, Iran or Afghanistan which retained titular sovereignty. Europeans residing in the Middle East were regulated until World War I and after by commercial capitulatory treaties which gave the foreigners exemption from local jurisdiction and allowed them to live under their own laws as administered by the various resident European consuls. Originally granted by late medieval Middle Eastern monarchs as a means to escape the trouble of regulating resident foreigners, the capitulations, after the political decline of the Muslim world, became a shield behind which the foreigners could ignore or manipulate local laws and procedures with legal impunity and to their own advantage. In the mid-nineteenth century Middle Eastern governments tried to reform the situation by instituting Western-style legal practices, but the powers cooperated with these efforts only to the extent that they were willing to submit cases to "mixed-courts" staffed by panels of Europeans and local jurists. Still, the mixed-courts became a vehicle whereby modern legal practices filtered into the Middle East. Extraterritorial privileges were often claimed, too, for Middle Eastern employees, agents, and clients of European firms and individuals resident in the area. In a nation such as Egypt where most merchants were either foreigners or enjoyed close ties with foreigners practically the entire commercial class enjoyed various immunities from local legal jurisdiction. Other sources of indirect pressure rose from claims of certain powers to represent the interests of the many Christian sects indigenous to the Middle East: the Russians claimed to represent all Orthodox Christians, the French all Uniate Christians in communion with the Papacy. Moreover, Western and Russian interests often dictated that they champion the separatist independence drives of the various Balkan nationalities.

In retrospect the political apparatus used by imperialist powers to assert their ambitions directly influenced the modernizing process in the Middle East. The capitulatory regime encouraged an entrepreneurial environment which placed at least the modern sector of the business community under foreign protection and discouraged the rise of local modernly-oriented commercial middle classes, particularly among Muslims. Some training was provided, however, to local officials in the techniques of administering a modern governmental and military structure. Most important, the mere presence of imperial regimes in the Middle East was a prime stimulant to the rise of nationalist movements dedicated not only to ejecting the foreigner, but also to internal political, social, and economic modernization.

At least as strong as the West's direct political influence was its direct economic and social impact upon the Middle East. Between 1800 and the 1950's those parts of the Middle Eastern economy which were touched by modernization came largely under some sort of Western direction. There were several stages in this process. First came the capture of Middle Eastern markets by cheap factory produced manufactors carried in dependable steamships. As early as the 1830's established local industries, especially textiles, were undermined, while new industries founded by modernizers such as Mohammad 'Ali proved unable to meet the competition of Western imports. The destructive effects of this intrusion reduced the Middle East to more dependence than ever upon its still largely traditional agricultural economy. Nevertheless, the nineteenth century also saw the first large-scale modernization of Middle Eastern agriculture. The initiation of irrigation works, large plantations sowed with cash crops such as cotton, a legal re-ordering of land holding practices which stimulated the rise of a wealthy new land-owning class and the simultaneous reduction in the independence and status of peasant cultivators all were features of the period. Despite many unfortunate aspects of the agricultural innovations, at least most rural wealth, except in areas of European settlement such as Algeria, remained under local control. But everywhere Westerners took over direction of most other components within the modern sector of the economy. Large-scale commerce fell under the control of Westerners or their agents. Moreover, because of lack of indigenous capital and technical ability Middle Eastern rulers increasingly accepted the seemingly attractive offers of European bankers to provide loans to pay for modernizing schemes and they granted concessions to European combines to undertake the actual construction of large development projects. The reliance upon loans, started in the 1850's, reached the point, as early as the 1870's in Tunisia, Egypt, and the Ottoman Empire and by the 1890's in Iran and Morocco, that local governments, unable to pay the interest much less the principal on their debts, approached bankruptcy. This situation, predictably, stimulated the intervention of various imperialist states in favor of their bondholders. Often, European-controlled debt administrations were forced upon defaulting Middle Eastern governments to ensure repayment of loans. These debt administrations, however, took control not only of finance, but of economic affairs in general and so, of many aspects of the modernization process and the political apparatus in general. Concessions played a large part initially in creating a modern communications and transport net in the Middle East. In the 1850's and 1860's the Suez Canal, telegraph lines, railroads, and river steamer lines were all started by European concessionaires who undertook to reap profits from the enterprises they built in return for the very modest royalties they paid to local governments. Concessions for the exploitation of Middle Eastern mineral resources were first granted in the 1870's although it was not until the twentieth century that the great oil concessions were granted, the prototype of which was the D'Arcy concession of 1901 for Iranian oil rights. By the post World War I period the oil business became the major attraction for Western business activity in the Middle East.

By 1914 two economies existed more or less side by side in the Middle East. One, the traditional, still basically locally oriented agricultural economy of the peasant masses; the other a modern world-oriented economy of the market-crop plantations of the large landowners and the Western-dominated commercial, financial, communications, and mineral exploiting enterprises. This configuration was also present in the social structure of the region where old and new coexisted in an increasingly unstable symbiosis. Most of the modernization of Middle Eastern social standards had its source in undirected, inadvertent Western influence which inspired voluntary moves by Middle Easterners to copy and adopt modern practices. Changes in clothing, furniture, eating, or architectural tastes seldom had to be forced upon the Middle East's elite after the 1830's. Western tastes were observed and described enviously by local visitors to Europe. Such modes also were directly observed, especially in cities, by many who came into contact with Westerners residing in the Middle East. When foreign residents erected French-style town houses in Cairo many pashas were quick to build their own imitations. Other alterations flowed from the unforeseen consequences of things such as the increasing reliance upon Western-produced consumer products. For various reasons, then, modern fashions and practices were copied extensively and gradually brought important variations in traditional habits in their wake.

Other changes were sometimes grudgingly adopted after the application of foreign pressure. Policies such as those enshrined in the Tunisian *'Ahd al-Aman* of 1857 were designed to assure legal equality and reflected the values championed by diplomats of many modern nations. Diplomatic protection and material aid was extended by Western countries and Russia in favor of various missionary activities, particularly in the fields of education and health. Direct interference with established Middle Eastern social practices was generally but not always avoided. Russian and French undercutting of Islamic social institutions in their colonies were part of a general policy of asserting their own cultural superiority. The attack led by Britain upon slave trading and ownership is another example of a policy which resulted when Western social and moral convictions were so strong that little compromise was possible with traditional Middle Eastern attitudes, beliefs, and practices. Armed force was used in some areas to impose Western standards in the slavery question. By 1914 a facade of Western-model social practices had arisen in the region although the rural masses were still little affected by the new standards. A gap in social practices and aspirations had opened between those among the local elite who nominally represented Middle Eastern opinion and those loyal to the old ways.

The tempo of imposed modernization reached its peak in the years prior to World War I. After that conflict, Europe's fading confidence in its own superiority plus the rise of energetic Middle Eastern nationalist movements contributed to a gradual decrease in all sorts of controls and the effectiveness of unofficial restraints.

25

The Creation of Colonies, First French Land Confiscation Decree in Algeria, 8 September 1830 *

When Husayn Bey surrendered Algiers to the victorious army of King Charles X of France in July 1830 it marked the beginning of the imposition of a European colony of settlement into the midst of a Middle Eastern population. North Africa was the only part of the Arab Middle East that had to endure this particular type of Western imperial presence. The French conquest of Algeria occurred in a series of stages: from 1830 to 1837 the major coastal cities were taken; from 1839 to 1847 the high plains where the Arab tribes dwelled were annexed; from 1851 to 1871 the Kabylie mountain tribes were reduced; and from 1870 to 1900 the Sahara Desert was penetrated in force and its tribes pacified. This expansion encountered bitter resistance especially between 1839 and 1847 when the Arabs found a resourceful leader in 'Abd al-Qadir (1808-1883). These wars resembled the Indian Wars in the American West and, like them, decimated the indigenous population which was reduced by almost a third between 1830 and 1871. Moreover, the Algerians lost more than the war—they lost their best land as well. The first of a long series of land expropriation decrees important for the precedents and procedures it embodied is reproduced below. By 1851 some 150,000 Europeans, many of them veterans of France's Algeria army, lived in the towns and in large agricultural enclaves. The colonists were energetic workers, and built up their estates' productivity to impressive levels but they had little respect for the Algerian Muslim culture. Certainly, the pressure of local European colons for more and more control over Algerian affairs negated many of the well-intentioned plans of Paris to adopt a more magnanimous attitude toward Algeria's indigenous populace. Dispossessed of their lands, the Algerian Muslims became foreigners in their own country. Their traditional economic, social, and political system was shattered as the Europeans took over the best lands.

* Government General of Algeria, *Bulletin Officiel des Actes du Gouvernement* (Paris: Imprimerie Royal, 1834-1854), Vol. I, 9; translated from the French in John Ruedy, *Land Policy in Colonial Algeria* (Berkeley and Los Angeles: University of California Press, 1967), 39-40.

(Algiers)   (September 8, 1830)

Art. 1.   All houses, stores, shops, gardens, lands, places, and establishments whatsoever formerly occupied by the Dey, the bays, or Turks who have left the territory of the Regency of Algiers, or which are managed for their accounts, as well as those belonging in any way whatsoever to Mecca or Medina, revert to the public domain and shall be managed for its profit.

Art. 2.   Persons of any nation who are holders or tenants of the said properties are obliged within three days to file declarations indicating the nature, location, and consistency of the domains of which they enjoy the use of management, together with the amount of the income or rent and the time of the last payment.

Art. 3.   This declaration shall be transcribed onto registers opened for this purpose by the municipality.

Art. 4.   Any person subject to this declaration who fails to file it within the time prescribed shall be condemned to a fine that shall not be less than one year's revenue or rent of the undeclared property, and he shall be constrained to the payment of this fine by the severest penalties.

Art. 5.   Any individual who reveals to the French government the existence of an undeclared domain property shall be entitled to half of the fine incurred by the delinquent party.

(Clauzel, General in Chief, French Army in Algeria)

26

The Creation of Protectorates, Franco-Tunisian Treaty of Qasr al-Sa'id (Bardo), 12 May 1881 *

Protectorates took many forms. Normally, a treaty which established a protectorate included provisions whereby the local ruler surrendered the conduct of foreign and military affairs to the protecting power. In more elaborate treaties stipulations regarding the regulation of financial and other internal affairs often are present. Many important functions carried out by the protecting power were not explicitly defined but left to implication. Thus, the unofficial usages and the precedents built up over time usually constituted at least

* Translation from the French by A. M. Broadley, *The Last Punic War, Tunis, Past and Present* (London: William Blackwood and Sons, 1882), Vol. I, 313-315.

as important a part of a protectorate regime as its formally defined functions. Also, the general imperial philosophy of a protecting power was reflected more in its actual administration than in the treaty creating a protectorate. Consequently, indirect rule was more a feature of British than French protectorates. The French protectorate in Tunisia rose out of border complications, financial and commercial involvement, and European diplomatic maneuvers whereby the Germans encouraged France to become more involved in colonial affairs. The treaty was signed after a combined sea-land invasion forced Muhammed al-Sadiq Bey to capitulate to a French ultimatum. It was followed in June 1883 by the Marsa Convention which clarified the nature of French control over Tunisia's internal affairs. Under the protectorate the bey was reduced to figurehead status and the Tunisian administration was placed under the direction of a French resident general. As in Algeria, much of the best rural land passed into European hands but the status of Tunisia as a legal entity was recognized and served as a focus for the growth of a Tunisian subvariety of Arab nationalism which appeared before World War I.

*   *   *

The Government of the French Republic and that of His Highness the Bey of Tunis, wishing to prevent for ever the renewal of the disturbances which have recently occurred on the frontiers of the two states *and on the coast* of the Regency (Tunisia), and being desirous of drawing closer their ancient relations of friendship and good neighbourhood, have determined to conclude a Convention to this effect, in the interest of the two High Contracting Parties.

In consequence the President of the French Republic has named as his Plenipotentiary M. le General Bréart, who has agreed with His Highness the Bey upon the following stipulations:—

ARTICLE I.

The Treaties of peace, friendship, and commerce, and all other conventions actually existing between the French Republic and His Highness the Bey of Tunis, are expressly confirmed and renewed.

ARTICLE II.

With a view of facilitating the accomplishment by the French Republic of the measures which it will have to take in order to attain the end proposed by the High Contracting Parties, His Highness the Bey of Tunis consents that the French military authorities should occupy the points which they may deem necessary to ensure the re-establishment of order and the security of the frontiers and of the coast.

This occupation shall cease when the French and Tunisian military authorities shall have recognised by common consent that the local administration is capable of guaranteeing the maintenance of order.

ARTICLE III.

The Government of the French Republic undertakes to give constant support to His Highness the Bey of Tunis against any danger which may menace the person or dynasty of His Highness, or which may compromise the tranquillity of his states.

ARTICLE IV.

The Government of the French Republic guarantees the execution of the Treaties at present existing between the Government of the Regency and the different European Powers.

ARTICLE V.

The Government of the French Republic shall be represented near His Highness the Bey of Tunis by a Minister Resident, who will watch over the execution of the present instrument, and who will be the medium of communication between the French Government and the Tunisian authorities for all affairs common to the two countries.

ARTICLE VI.

The diplomatic and consular agents of France in foreign countries will be charged with the protection of Tunisian interests and of the nationals of the Regency. In return, His Highness the Bey undertakes to conclude no act having an international character without having communicated it to the Government of the French Republic, and without having previously come to an understanding with them.

ARTICLE VII.

The Government of the French Republic and the Government of His Highness the Bey of Tunis reserve to themselves the right to fix, by a common agreement, the bases of a financial organisation of the Regency, which shall be of a nature to assure the service of the public debt and to guarantee the rights of the creditors of Tunis.

ARTICLE VIII.

A war contribution will be imposed on the unsubdued tribes on the frontier and on the coast. A further convention will settle the amount of it and the method of collecting it, for which the Government of His Highness the Bey hold themselves responsible.

ARTICLE IX.

In order to protect the Algerian possessions of the French Republic against the smuggling of arms and munitions of war, the Government of His Highness the Bey of Tunis undertakes to prohibit any introduction of arms or of munitions of war by the Island of Djerba, the Port of Gabes, or the other ports to the south of Tunis.

ARTICLE X.

The present treaty will be submitted for the ratification of the Government of the French Republic, and the instrument of ratification will be returned to His Highness the Bey with as little delay as possible.

27

The Confrontation of Imperialism with Nationalism, Lord Cromer's Critique of Egyptian Nationalism, 1906 *

This report submitted by Lord Cromer (1841-1917) near the close of his career as Britain's pro-consul in Egypt summarizes much of Cromer's, as well as official Britain's, attitude toward nationalism and self-government in Egypt and the Middle East. It was a paternalistic attitude which feared allowing too fast a pace of reform lest it disrupt the balance and cohesiveness of Egypt. Change should come only in stages lest internal stability be upset and the well-being of the mass of the people compromised. Certain modern economic and administrative prerequisites had to be created before such western notions as self-government could be profitably realized. To Cromer, therefore, the rise of Egyptian nationalism seemed premature. The movement was painted as offering an impractical program concocted by an insignificant band of semi-Westernized intellectuals, 'a few noisy individuals' who did not represent genuine Egyptian aspirations and who wished to achieve power only for their own selfish profit.

* "Reports of His Majesty's Agent and Consul General on the Finances, Administration, and Condition of Egypt and the Soudan in 1906," C. 3394, Egypt No. 1 (1907), *Sessional Papers, House of Commons, 1907,* Vol. C, 3-8.

Thus, little effort was made to associate anyone connected with the nationalist movement with the occupation and protectorate government. It would be small exaggeration to say that most varieties of Middle Eastern nationalism were similarly analyzed and treated by Western politicians during the imperial epoch. Even those imperial administrators who wished to encourage local self-government held up European standards as the ideal to be imitated. A lack of appreciation on the part of European and American leaders for the goals, content, and strength of the various Middle Eastern nationalisms continued to embitter Western-Middle Eastern relations for much of the twentieth century.

EGYPTIAN NATIONALISM

It is difficult even for those who have an extensive knowledge of Egyptian affairs to differentiate the various currents of thought which, in one form or another, are moving in the direction of creating a local public opinion favourable to the entirely novel idea of Egyptian Nationalism. I say that the idea is entirely novel, for it has to be remembered that for centuries past the Egyptians have been a subject race. Persians, Greeks, Romans, Arabs from Arabia and Bagdad, Circassians, and, finally, Ottoman Turks have successively ruled over Egypt; but we have to go back to the doubtful and obscure precedent of Pharaonic times to find an epoch when, possibly, Egypt was ruled by Egyptians. Even now Egyptian Nationalism is a plant of exotic rather than of indigenous growth. The idea, in any form which can at all be regarded as serious, is the outcome of that contact with Europe to which Nubar Pasha alluded, through the mouth of the reigning Khedive, when he said that Egypt no longer formed part of Africa. It has been evoked by the benefits which, with a rapidity probably unparalleled in history, have been conferred on the country by the introduction of Western civilization at the hands of an alien race; and it is surely the irony of political destiny that that race, or the instruments through whom it has principally acted, should be represented as the principal obstacles to the realization of schemes the conception of which is mainly due to their own action.

I have spoken of the extreme difficulty of differentiating the various opinions current in Egyptian society. In connection with this subject, I venture to utter a note of warning against rapid and sweeping generalizations in dealing with Egyptian affairs. It is too often forgotten that Egyptian society is split up into quite as numerous sections, representing different and often divergent interests and opinions, as the society of any European country. The difficulty of arriving at any sound conclusions as regards local feelings and aspirations is not, indeed, so formidable as in India, where the caste system interposes a great, if not insuperable, bar to social intercourse between Europeans and the greater part of the population. At the same time, differences of race, religion, language, and manners and customs count for much. I know of many cases of Europeans who have resided for long in Egypt, and who appear to be under the impression that they know something of Egyptian opinion, whereas, generally, all they know is the opinion of some one or more sections of Egyptian society—usually those resident in the principal towns—with whom they happen to have been thrown in contact. I hasten to add that I do not pretend to any very superior degree of knowledge. I have lived too long in the East to dogmatize about the views of the inconsistent Eastern, for whose inconsistency, moreover, I entertain much sympathy, by reason of the fact that the circumstances in which he is placed render consistency very difficult of attainment. All I ask is that the extreme difficulty of the subject should be recognized, and that, when it is recognized, some caution should be exercised lest hasty conclusions should be drawn from incomplete and often incorrect data. I know nothing more true than the following words of Professor Sayce, who is probably as qualified as any European can be to speak on the subject:—

"Those who have been in the East and have tried to mingle with the native population know well how utterly impossible it is for the European to look at the world with the same eyes as the Oriental. For a while, indeed, the European may fancy that he and the Oriental understand one another; but sooner or later a time comes when he is suddenly awakened from his dream and finds himself in the presence of a mind which is as strange to him as would be the mind of an inhabitant of Saturn."

The difficulty of dealing with this subject is, moreover, enormously enhanced by the fact that but few Egyptians have, in political or administrative affairs, a very clear idea of what they themselves want, whilst the practice of advocating two separate programmes, which are mutually destructive of each other, is the rule rather than the exception. The maxim *qui veut la fin, veut les moyens* is generally scouted. I have frequently had expressed to me by Egyptians—amongst whom I am glad to be able to count many personal friends who speak to me very frankly—a paradoxical desire to secure all the advantages of the British occupation, which they fully recognize, without the occupation itself. I have had a leading Egyptian urge me to employ fewer Europeans in the Government service, and, in the same breath, ask me to arrange that a lawsuit in which he was interested should be tried by a British Judge. I have known a warm advocate of Egyptian rights plead earnestly for the appointment of a British rather than an Egyptian engineer to superintend the distribution of water in his own province. Over and over again have I had it pointed out to me that the authority of the Egyptian Moudirs is weakened by the presence in their respective provinces of British Inspectors, whilst at the same time the withdrawal of the Inspectors would lead to disastrous consequences—conclusions in both of which I entirely agree. As to corruption, I need only say that I have known scores of cases in which individuals—often in a very high position—have inveighed bitterly against the blackmail which they have to pay to the subordinates of the Public Works and other Departments, and at the same time have refused to make any formal complaints or to mention names, thus depriving the superior authorities of the only effective arm which might enable such practices to be checked. I could multiply instances of this sort but I have said enough for my present purpose.

With these preliminary remarks, I propose to describe, to the best of my ability, the present phase of the Egyptian National movement, and to set forth my personal opinion as to the treatment which it should receive.

Whilst it would be altogether incorrect to say that the Egyptian National movement is wholly Pan-Islamic, it is certain that it is deeply tinged with Pan-Islamism. This is a fact of which I have for long been aware, and to which, if I may judge from the utterances of the local press, many Europeans in Egypt have, albeit somewhat tardily, now become alive. It would be easy, were it necessary or desirable to do so, to adduce abundant evidence in support of this statement. Here I will only say that the events of last summer merely disclosed one new feature in the Egyptian situation. Admitting, what is unquestionably the case, that religion is the main motive power in the East, and that the theocratic form of government possesses peculiar attraction for Easterns, it might still have been anticipated that the recollections of the past, and the present highly prosperous condition of Egypt as compared to the neighbouring provinces of Turkey, might have acted as a more effectual barrier to the growth of Pan-Islamism than apparently was the case. I use the word "apparently" with intention, for, in spite of all outward appearances, I am by no means convinced that Pan-Islamic sympathies extended very deep down in Egyptian society; and I am quite confident that, had there been any real prospect of effect being given to Pan-Islamic theories, a very strong and rapid revulsion of public opinion would have taken place. However this may be, it is clear that Pan-Islamism is a factor in the Egyptian situation of which account has, to a certain extent, to be taken. It is, therefore, necessary to understand what the term implies.

Pan-Islamism is generally held to mean a combination of all the Moslems throughout the world to defy and to resist the Christian Powers.

Viewed in this aspect, the movement certainly requires to be carefully watched by all European nations who have political interests in the East. It may possibly lead to sporadic outbursts of fanaticism in different parts of the world.

We were within a very measurable distance of such an outburst in Egypt last spring. I see it constantly stated that the "unrest" to which allusion was made in the House of Commons last summer was imaginary. I am wholly unable to concur in this view. The temperament of the lower classes of the Egyptian population, and notably of the urban population, is eminently mercurial. They were suddenly lashed into a fury by the inflammatory and mendacious writings in the Pan-Islamic press, and they subsided into comparative tranquillity with almost equal suddenness when the British garrison was increased, and when the writers in the vernacular press, under pressure exerted on them by the more intelligent of their own countrymen, moderated their tone. But that for some little while a situation of real danger existed I have not the smallest doubt. Very numerous reports reached me of threats uttered against Christians and Europeans. The vague rumours which, in the East, are the usual precursors of disturbance, had been current to a remarkable degree. The European inhabitants were alarmed, and began to flock into the towns. Neither was their alarm at all unreasonable. In my Report for 1905 (pp. 8-10) I described in detail the events which occurred in Alexandria towards the close of 1905. A chance quarrel between two Greeks led to a somewhat serious riot, which at once assumed an anti-Christian form. I have no hesitation in saying that if, as was by no means improbable, some adventitious incident of this sort had occurred during the height of the excitement caused by the Turko-Egyptian frontier incident, the consequences might, and probably would, have been serious. I wish to add that the idea, which I occasionally see advanced, that this "unrest" was in any degree due to the policy pursued by the British and Egyptian Governments in connection with the internal affairs of Egypt is devoid of the smallest real foundation. It was not partly, but wholly, due to the fact that, under Pan-Islamic influence, a large portion of the population had been led to believe that a wanton attack was being made on the head of the Moslem religion.

To return from this digression, if I am sceptical of Pan-Islamism producing any more serious results than sporadic outbursts of fanaticism, it is, in the first place, because I greatly doubt the possibility of Moslem co-operation and cohesion when once it becomes a question of passing from words to deeds; and, in the second place, because I am quite confident of the power of Europe, should the necessity arise, to deal effectively with the material, though not with the spiritual, aspects of the movement.

Pan-Islamism is, moreover, a convenient phrase for conveying a number of other ideas, more or less connected with its primary signification. For the purpose of my present argument, these are of greater practical importance than the wider definition to which I have alluded above.

In the first place, it means, in Egypt, more or less complete subserviency to the Sultan. A somewhat novel element is thus introduced into Egyptian political life. Until recently, the Egyptian national movement has been on distinctly anti-Turkish lines. The Arabic revolt was, in its essence, directed against Turkey and the Turks. I understand, however, that the leaders of the national movement now declare that they have no wish to draw closer the bonds between Turkey and Egypt, and that their only desire is to maintain the suzerainty of the Sultan. This language contrasts so remarkably with utterances of a very recent date that it is impossible not to entertain some suspicion that it is an afterthought due to a correct appreciation of the fact that a more extended pro-Turkish programme is calculated to alienate sympathies, which it is desirable to maintain and to foster. It would, however, be unfair to pin down the Nationalist party, as a body, to the chance utterances of a few irresponsible individuals. Accepting, therefore, this later version of the programme as correct, I have to observe that the suzerainty of the Sultan over Egypt has never, so far as I am aware, been impugned, neither does it appear probable that it will be endangered so long as all parties to the Firman—which, it has to be borne in mind, is a bilateral arrangement—take no action outside the limits of their respective rights. The Sinai Peninsula incident derived its main importance from the fact that there appeared at one time to be some risk that the Firman, and the documents which form part of it, would be violated to the detriment of Egypt.

In the second place, Pan-Islamism almost necessarily connotes a recrudescence of racial and religious animosity. Many of its adherents are, I do not doubt, inspired by genuine religious fervour. Others, again, whether from indifference verging on agnosticism, or from political and opportunist motives, or—as I trust may sometimes be the case—from having really assimilated modern ideas on the subject of religious toleration, would be willing, were such a course possible, to separate the political from the religious, and even possibly from the racial, issues. If such are their wishes and intentions, I entertain very little doubt that they will find them impossible of execution. Unless they can convince the Moslem masses of their militant Islamism, they will fail to arrest their attention or to attract their sympathy. Appeals, either overt or covert, to racial and religious passions are thus a necessity of their existence in order to insure the furtherance of their political programme.

In the third place, Pan-Islamism almost necessarily connotes an attempt to regenerate Islam on Islamic lines—in other words, to revivify and stereotype in the twentieth century the principles laid down, more than a thousand years ago, for the guidance of a primitive society. Those principles involve a recognition of slavery, laws regulating the relations of the sexes which clash with modern ideas, and, which is perhaps more important than all, that crystallization of the civil, criminal, and canonical law into one immutable whole, which has so largely contributed to arrest the progress of those countries whose populations have embraced the Moslem faith.

It is for these reasons, independent of any political considerations, that all who are interested in the work of Egyptian reform are constrained to condemn Pan-Islamism. More than this, the utmost care has to be exercised lest any natural and very legitimate sympathy for genuine nationalism may not be unconsciously attracted towards a movement which is, in reality, highly retrograde and deserving of but scant sympathy. It is at times not easy to recognize the Pan-Islamic figure under the Nationalist cloak.

I am, however, fully aware that side by side with the Pan-Islamic movement there exists another which may possibly be entitled to the designation of national. The two movements are, in fact, merged into each other, neither is it easy to state with any degree of precision where the one begins and the other ends. My conviction is that, in reality, Pan-Islamism is the predominant partner. However this may be, I proceed to discuss the position of the National movement independently of any real or imaginary connection it may have with Pan-Islamism.

It is extremely natural that the idea of creating an Egyptian Nationalism should have germinated and brought forth some fruit. The extent to which the so-called National party represents the real wishes and aspirations of the mass of the people is, indeed, more than doubtful. Over and over again have representative Egyptians protested to me strongly against the claim of the leaders of this party to the title which they have arrogated to themselves. Over and over again has it been urged on me that the party consists merely of a few noisy individuals, whose action is often due to no very reputable motives, and who in no way represent the real wishes and aspirations of their countrymen. I believe this view of the situation to be substantially correct. In any case, it may be confidently stated that the consequences which would inevitably ensue were the programme of the National party capable of rapid realization are very imperfectly understood. There can be no doubt that the recollection of past abuses is rapidly fading away. Education, moreover, as was to be anticipated, has awakened ambitions which were formerly dormant. The most humble fellah now knows that, in the eye of the law, he is the equal of the Pasha. A spirit of independence, which was formerly conspicuous by its absence, has been created. Under such circumstances, it can be no matter for surprise that the educated youth should begin to clamour for a greater share than heretofore in the government and administration of their country. Nothing could be more ungenerous than to withhold a certain amount of sympathy from these very legitimate aspirations. Nothing, on the other hand, could be more unwise than to abstain, at this early period of the National movement, from pointing out to all who are willing to listen to reason the limits which, for the time being, must be assigned to those aspirations. I am too true a friend to the Egyptian people to endeavour either to flatter or to deceive them.

I ask myself, therefore, what is it that the young Egyptians, in so far as their views are represented by the National party, wish to accomplish?

In the first place, they wish to rise to such of the higher administrative posts in the Government service as are now occupied by Europeans. I have not a word to say against this aspiration. I propose, in another portion of this Report, to deal fully with this branch of the question. Here I will only speak of the wider and more strictly political portion of the National programme. I understand that what is demanded is a wide and immediate extension of Parliamentary institutions. A good deal of misapprehension appears to exist, especially in England, as to the extent to which Parliamentary institutions already exist in Egypt. I deal with this question in another portion of my Report. For the moment I propose to confine myself to inquiring how far it would be possible or desirable to extend the powers of the Legislative Council and Assembly.

I am not aware that the Egyptian National party has ever formulated its programme in any very precise terms, but, so far as I am able to judge, they advocate the creation in Egypt of an institution similar to the British House of Commons. I have not noticed whether it is proposed to vest all power in a single Chamber, or whether it is suggested that a second Chamber, which would take the place of the French Senate or the British House of Lords, is contemplated. Neither am I quite clear as to whether it is proposed that the Egyptian Parliament should legislate, without distinction, for all the inhabitants of Egypt or only for local subjects. The former of these two methods would require the consent of all the Powers, which would certainly not be obtained. Leaving aside these doubtful but very important points, I conceive I shall be right in holding that what is proposed is, first, the creation of a Ministry responsible to the Chamber, and dependent for its existence on the maintenance of a majority; and, secondly, complete control over the finances of the country, such as that exercised by the elected Chambers in the United Kingdom and in other European countries.

The adoption of the first of these proposals would, unless I am much mistaken, produce a state of things which may without exaggeration be termed chaotic. Intrigue of all sorts would be rife. The system of bribery and corruption which was at one time so prevalent in the country, and which is even now only dying a lingering death, would receive a fresh impulse. It is more than probable that, under the specious title of free institutions, the worst evils of personal government would reappear.

The adoption of the second proposal—that of handing over complete financial control to the Chamber—would almost inevitably lead to national bankruptcy.

It requires, indeed, some mental effort to discuss these proposals seriously. Can any sane man believe that a country which has for centuries past been exposed to the worst forms of misgovernment at the hands of its rulers, from Pharaohs to Pashas, and in which, but ten years ago, only 9.5 per cent of the men and .3 per cent of the women could read and write, is capable of suddenly springing into a position which will enable it to exercise full rights of autonomy with advantage to itself and to others interested in its welfare? The idea is absurd. The programme of the National party is quite incapable of realization at present, and it may well be doubted whether, in the form in which it is now conceived, it can ever be realized. In any case, I must wholly decline to take any part in furthering proposals the adoption of which would, in my opinion, constitute a flagrant injustice, not only to the very large foreign interests involved, but also to those ten or twelve millions of Egyptians to the advancement of whose moral and material welfare I have devoted the best years of my life.

Is there, then, no hope for Egyptian Nationalism? In the form in which that idea is conceived by the Egyptian National party there is, I am convinced, little or none. But it is well for a nation, and even for practical politicians, to entertain an ideal, even although its realization may be distant and beset with many difficulties. I venture, therefore, as a counter-programme to that of the Egyptian National party, to put forward an ideal which I have for long entertained. It is, that the only possible Egyptian nationality which can ever be created must consist of all the dwellers in Egypt, irrespective of race, religion, or extraction. So long as the country was well-nigh throttled by impending bankruptcy, so long as the fate of the Soudan was uncertain, and so long as Anglo-French rivalry was in a more or less acute stage, discussions or reflections on this subject could be nothing more than academical. These obstacles have now been removed. Another, however, remains. So long as the régime of the Capitulations, in its present form, exists, not only must the Egyptians and the foreigners resident in Egypt always be divided into two separate camps, but also no thorough solidarity of interest can be established between the various communities of Europeans *inter se*. There can be no real cohesion and no concentrated action. That cohesion can only be secured by the creation of a local International Legislative Council. I dealt with this subject in my last Annual Report, and I revert to it in another portion of this Report. Apart from other grounds on which it may be defended as a reform beneficial alike to Europeans and Egyptians, I maintain that this measure will tend more than any other to create a community of interest amongst the heterogeneous population which inhabits the valley of the Nile, and that it will be a first step towards the formation of an Egyptian national spirit in the only sense in which that spirit can be evoked without detriment to the true interests of the country. I am very fully aware of the difficulties which have to be encountered before effect can be given to this proposal. Possibly some long while may yet elapse before the first European Legislative Council meets in Egypt. But I have no fear for the ultimate result. The success of the cause which I advocate does not wholly depend on the opinions of a few individuals, whatever may be their position or influence. Neither does it wholly depend on the local opinion, whether European or Egyptian, of the day. The bestowal of legislative autonomy on the Europeans resident in Egypt, to take the place of the present cumbersome and unworkable system of legislation by diplomacy, is a measure naturally indicated by the ordinary canons which apply to political evolution. The cause will certainly triumph, although the triumph may be delayed.

Before leaving the question of the Egyptian National movement, I have yet one further remark to make. Besides those who have assumed the title of Nationalist, there exists a small but increasing number of Egyptians of whom comparatively little is heard, but who deserve that title quite as much as their competitors of a different school of thought and action. I allude to the party which, for the sake of brevity, I may call the followers of the late Mufti, Sheikh Mohamed Abdou. I have in previous Reports frequently alluded to the opinions held by this section of Egyptian society—opinions which are very analogous to those advocated by the late Seyyid Ahmed, who founded the Aligarh College in India. Their fundamental idea is to reform various Moslem institutions without shaking the main pillars on which the faith of Islam rests. They are truly Nationalist in the sense of wishing to advance the interests of their countrymen and coreligionists, but they are not tainted with Pan-Islamism. Their programme, if I understand it rightly, involves not opposition to, but co-operation with, Europeans in the introduction of Western civilization into the country. The main hope of Egyptian Nationalism, in the only true and practicable sense of the word, lies, in my opinion, with those who belong to this party. In the past they have not, for reasons on which I need not dwell, but for which the British advisers of the Egyptian Government are in no way responsible, received all the encouragement they deserve. Recently, however, one of their most distinguished members (Saad Zagloul Pasha) was appointed Minister of Education. The main reason for his appointment was not, as was sometimes supposed, any dissatisfaction with the manner in which the work of the Department of Public Instruction had been conducted; still less did it indicate an intention of making any radical changes in the educational policy heretofore pursued. It was mainly due to a desire to associate an able man and enlightened Egyptian of this particular section of society with the work of Egyptian reform. The experiment, for such it is, will be watched with interest. Should it succeed, as I hope and believe will be the case, some encouragement will be afforded to move further in the same direction. Should it fail, the necessary consequence will be to throw the continuance of the work of reform to a greater extent than formerly into European, and notably into British hands. In any case there can be no retrogression. The work of introducing Western civilization into Egypt is proceeding in every Department of the State on lines which have been carefully considered, and which admit of development but not of reversal or of radical change.

28

Financial Imperialism and Its Relationship to Development, the Ottoman Public Debt Administration, 1881-1925 *

The inability of Middle Eastern governments to pay off loans utilized to finance large-scale modernization schemes prompted the establishment in the late 19th century of various types of international debt administrations in many countries including Tunisia, Egypt, Iran, and the Ottoman Empire. The Ottoman Public Debt Administration founded in 1881 was one of the most influential of those. The Ottoman government turned over the collection of certain taxes, and monopoly revenues to the Public Debt Administration to service the defaulted loans. The work of the Administration had a permanent influence upon the modernization of the Ottoman Empire and its successor, the Republic of Turkey. Financial collection and disbursement is at the heart of many governmental operations; thus a foreign-dominated body was given a large voice in determining Ottoman political as well as economic policies. The Administration's bureaucracy employed thousands of locals, trained them in modern financial and tax procedures, and thus bequeathed a well-trained core of financial officials to Turkey and other Ottoman successor states when it ceased its operations in 1925. Much of the modern sector of the Ottoman economy in 1914 was the creation of the Administration since European financiers were willing to invest in railroads, public utility companies, and even banks knowing their loans were guaranteed. The Ottoman government itself voluntarily turned over several sources of revenue for Administration collection so impressed were they with its money-amassing efficiency.

---

* a. Excerpts from, Ottoman Decree of 28 Muharram 1299 (December 20, 1881) translated in "Imperial Ottoman Debt," Turkey No. 1 (1911), *Sessional Papers House of Commons, 1911,* Vol. CIII, 20, 23-26, 28-31.

   b. Excerpts from Adam Block, *Special Report on the Public Debt followed by the Translation of the Annual Report of the Council of Administration for the Twenty Fourth Financial Period* (Istanbul: Ottoman Public Debt Administration, 1906), 9-11, 21-25, 27, 34-35, 89, 90, 100.

A. DECREE OF 28 MUHARREM, 1299
(8 [20] DECEMBER 1881)

The Imperial Ottoman Government, in pursuance of the declarations made by their representative at the Congress of Berlin at the session of the 11th July, 1878, and in accordance with the engagement which they entered into by their note of the 3rd October, 1880, have, in a subsequent note of the 23rd October of the same year, invited the holders of bonds of the Ottoman Public Debt to choose a certain number of delegates to proceed as soon as possible to Constantinople for the purpose of coming to a direct agreement with the Imperial Government as to an equitable and practical settlement of the Ottoman Public Debt as well as to the means of resuming the service of the interest and sinking fund on that debt. . . .

ARTICLE 8.

For the service of the Debt determined by article 3, the Government cede by these presents, absolutely and irrevocably, from the 1st (13th) January, 1882, and until the complete extinction of the said debt:—

1. The revenues of the monopolies and indirect taxes which form the subject of the convention of the 10th (22nd) November, 1879, which is abrogated from the 1st (13th) January, 1882, in virtue of the convention annexed to the present decree, viz.:

(*a*.) Of the monopolies of tobacco and salt produced or consumed in the vilayets of the empire enumerated in the list annexed to the convention of the 10th (22nd) November, 1879, and appended to this decree, annex 2, not including cigars, snuffs, chewing tobacco, and imported tombéki, and with the exception of the tithe and the customs duties on tobacco.

(*b*.) Of the stamp duty (varakaï-sahiha);

Of the mirié and rouhsatié duties on spirits in the vilayets of the empire enumerated in the said list, except the customs duties levied on spirits;

Of the duty on fish in Constantinople and its suburbs, according to the detail which figure in the list relating thereto; and

Of the silk tithe of the suburbs of Constantinople, as also of Adrianople, Brusa, and Samsun, according to the detail stated in the list relating thereto.

2. The silk tithes:

Of Tokat, a dependency of the Samsun administration.

Of Kavala, Yenidjeh, Eskidje, Dede Agatch, dependencies of the Adrianople administration.

Of Sarouhan, a dependency of the Sarouhan administration.

Of Yenikeui of Chile, a dependency of the Constantinople administration.

Of Kartal, Guebzé, and Daridja, dependencies of the Ismidt administration.

As also the duty on fish:

Of Banados, a dependency of the Rodosto administration.
Of Gallipoli, dependency of the Gallipoli administration.
Of Yalova, a dependency of the Kara Mussal administration.
Of Seyki, Mudania, Guemlek, Kurchunlu, Armudlu, Kapu Dagh, Marmora, Pasha-Liman, Erdek, Panderma, and Lake of Manias, dependencies of the Brusa administration.

3. The surplus of the customs receipts resulting from a modification in the tariffs in the event of a revision of the commercial treaties.

4. The surplus of revenue which will result from the general application of the tax on professions as compared with the actual receipts from the temettu tax.

The means by which the revenues mentioned in paragraphs 3 and 4 will be secured to the holders of the debt shall form the subject of special provisions.

5. The tribute of the principality of Bulgaria.

So long as this tribute shall not have been fixed by the representatives of the signatory Powers of the Treaty of Berlin, the Government shall replace it from the 1st (13th) January, 1882, by an annual sum of £T100,000 to be levied on the tobacco tithe.

Once the said tribute is fixed, should the Sublime Porte think fit to assign it in whole or in part to some other purpose, the amount thus disposed of shall be replaced by an equivalent sum to be levied on the tobacco tithe, and, in case this should not be sufficient, on some other revenue equally secure.

6. The surplus revenues of the island of Cyprus.

Should the surplus revenue of the island of Cyprus not be at the disposal of the Imperial Government it will be replaced from the 1st (13th) January, 1882, by an annual sum of £T130,000.

The Council of Administration (article 15) shall have the right to apply the surplus of the tobacco tithe, after deduction of the £T100,000 which are to replace the tribute of the principality of Bulgaria, to the payment of the aforesaid £T130,000 which are to replace the surplus revenues of the island of Cyprus; for the amount remaining uncovered on this sum, the Ministry of Finance shall furnish to the council half-yearly drafts on the General Customs Administration.

7. The revenue from Eastern Rumelia, now fixed at £T240,000, plus the arrears from the 1st (13th) March, 1880, subsequent increases of which this revenue is susceptible by the terms of article 5 of the organic statute, and the sum of £T5,000, representing the net annual proceeds of the customs of the said province. The Council of Administration (article 15) shall receive the aforesaid sums through the medium of the Imperial Ottoman Bank, in the safes of which they shall be deposited.

In the event of delay in the payments at the due dates, the Imperial Government shall use all diligence to see that the said province resumes the fulfilment of its engagements.

8. The proceeds from the duty on the tombéki up to a sum of £T50,000.

In order to ensure the receipt of this sum by the Council of Administration, the Ministry of Finance shall issue to the council half-yearly drafts on the General Customs Administration.

9. All the sums accruing to the Imperial Government as the contributive portions of Servia, Montenegro, Bulgaria, and Greece to the debt mentioned in article 3 according to the provisions of the Treaty of Berlin and article 10 of the Convention of Constantinople of the 24th May, 1881.

ARTICLE 9.

The revenues specified in paragraphs 1, 2, and 8, as also the tobacco tithe mentioned in paragraphs 5 and 6 of the preceding article, shall be administered in accordance with existing laws and regulations and the revenues mentioned in paragraphs 3 and 4 (surplus of customs and tax on professions) in accordance with the provisions to be enacted for that purpose.

Notwithstanding, the Council of Administration shall have the right to decide upon all modifications and improvements which may be introduced in the existing system of monopolies or contributions mentioned in Nos. 1 and 2 or the tobacco tithe mentioned in Nos. 5 and 6 of the preceding article, in case the said tithe should be applied to the service of the debt in pursuance of the provisions of the same article relating thereto, without going beyond the limits of the existing laws and regulations and without imposing fresh charges on Ottoman subjects. . . .

ARTICLE 10.

The net proceeds of the revenues indicated in article 8 shall be devoted wholly, on the 1st (13th) September and the 1st (13th) March of each year, from the 1st (13th) January, 1882, to the payment of interest and sinking fund of the Debt. . . .

ARTICLE 11.

There shall be assigned every year to the service of the interest four-fifths of the net proceeds of the revenues ceded to the bondholders, not including the contributive portions of Servia, Montenegro, Bulgaria, and Greece, and after deduction of the sums representing interest on the redeemed bonds. . . .

ARTICLE 12.

There shall be assigned every year for the sinking fund one-fifth of the net proceeds of the revenues ceded to the bondholders, not including the contributive portions of Servia, Montenegro, Bulgaria, and Greece, but increased by the amount representing interest upon the redeemed bonds, as stated in the preceding article....

ARTICLE 15.

A Council of Administration is established to represent the bondholders, and to act in their interests.

This council has its head office at Constantinople.

The said council shall be composed as hereinafter stated:—

One member representing the English bondholders, who also represents the Dutch bondholders, and who is to be appointed by the Council of Foreign Bondholders of London, or in default of it by the Governor of the Bank of England, or in default of him by a resolution adopted at a public meeting of English and Dutch bondholders in London;

One member representing the French bondholders;

One member representing the German bondholders;

One member representing the Austro-Hungarian bondholders;

who are to be appointed by the syndicates of the financial houses of Paris, Berlin, and Vienna, which have adhered to the communication of the Imperial Ottoman Government of the 23rd October, 1880, and, if necessary, their choice shall be approved by a general meeting of the French, German, and Austro-Hungarian bondholders in each of the three capitals designated above.

On member representing the Italian bondholders, who is to be appointed by the Roman Chamber of Commerce, constituted in the syndicate of the chambers of commerce of the kingdom, and, if necessary, its choice shall be approved by a general meeting of the Italian bondholders in Rome.

One member representing the Ottoman bondholders, who is to be appointed by a general meeting of the latter, assembled at Constantinople at the invitation of the prefect of the city.

One member representing the holders of the bonds provided for by the annexed convention, who will be appointed by the Imperial Ottoman Bank, or in default of it by a resolution adopted at a public meeting of the said bondholders in Constantinople....

Every employé in the service of the Imperial Ottoman Government, whether a foreigner or an Ottoman subject, who shall be appointed a member of the council shall be bound to resign his public functions for the whole duration of his office....

The members of the council shall be appointed for five years, and they shall sit until the installation of the new council.

They may be re-elected on the expiration of their mandate....

The members of the council shall each have a vote. Resolutions shall be taken by a majority of votes. In case of a tie, the president shall have a casting vote....

ARTICLE 16.

The Council of Administration shall have the direct administration, collection, and encashment on behalf of the bondholders and by means of agents holding its authority of the revenues and other resources enumerated in article 8, sections 1, 2, 5, 6, 7, and 9, including the tobacco tithe in the cases provided for by sections 5 and 6 of the said article, excepting, however, as regards the said tithe the obligation of rendering an account thereof to the Government, and paying annually to the Exchequer the surplus over and above the £T100,000 which shall take the place of the Bulgarian tribute, and eventually of the £T130,000 which shall take the place of the surplus revenue of the island of Cyprus.

It shall likewise have the encashment of the £T50,000 ceded on the proceeds of the tombéki duties (paragraph 8 of article 8) and of the revenues mentioned in paragraphs 3 and 4 of the said article.

The amount of the six Indirect Contributions shall be collected in cash in conformity with the regulation in force as regards the fiscal agencies of the State ("Meskukiat Nizam-namessi") promulgated on the 1st March, 1296.

It shall realise the value of the ceded revenues and other resources, and shall apply the whole amount thereof, after deduction of the costs of administration and collection, to the service of the interest and sinking fund of the bonds provided for by the annexed convention and of the debt fixed by article 3 in conformity with the distribution adopted.

The council shall have the right to farm or lease to third parties any of the ceded revenues; but in this case it shall remain directly responsible to the Imperial Government.

The council shall appoint a director-general of the administration who shall have, under the authority of the council, the management of affairs. He shall represent the council as regards third parties for the execution of any decisions, and in legal proceedings if required, subject to obtaining the necessary authorisation for appearing before the courts or other jurisdictions either as plaintiff or defendant in the name of the administration of the ceded revenues.

The council shall likewise appoint and dismiss the other employés of the administration of the ceded revenues.

The said employés shall be considered as State officials in the exercise of their duties. The Government shall take into favourable consideration every recommendation of the council as regards their rank, advancement, and promotion in the Ottoman hierarchy.

As regards duties, contributions, and taxes, the administration of the ceded revenues and its employés shall be treated on the same footing as the administrations of the State and its employés.

As regards employés of the State who shall enter the service of the Council of Administration, their position shall be fixed by a special regulation. The provisions of this regulation shall apply equally to the employés of the State who are already in the service of the administration of the six Indirect Contributions. It is understood that this regulation shall not prejudice the right of the council to appoint and dismiss any official of this administration—a right which is already exercised, in fact, by the present administration.

As regards the indemnities and other extraordinary disbursements provided for in article 13 of the convention of the 22nd November, liability shall rest with the council.

The Government shall afford the council in the exercise of its administration all general assistance compatible with the existing public institutions, and, with a view to a repression of contraband trade, they undertake to apply against it the penalties enacted by law.

In case of delay in the payments of the revenue from Eastern Roumelia, the council shall have the right to apply to the Sublime Porte and to demand the necessary measures for recovery of the arrears.

The Government shall afford to the Administration of the Council the military protection indispensable for the security of its head office and its local branches.

The Government shall continue to the council the gratuitous use of the premises which they have already placed at the disposal of the actual administration of the six Indirect Contributions.

The removable stamps and stamped papers necessary for the council's transactions shall be supplied by the Government under the supervision and at the expense of the latter.

Independently of the State employés entrusted with the policing and supervision of the service to be undertaken by the State, the council may appoint auxiliary employés responsible to none but itself, as well as secret inspectors whose duty shall be to prevent frauds punishable in conformity with the laws.

The secret inspectors of the administration shall receive, like those of the Government, the usual portion of the fines and double duties to be paid by delinquents.

The council shall make regulations concerning the resolution and dispatch of business.

It shall sign the bonds to be issued in conformity with the annexed convention to discharge the debts of the signatories of the said convention indicated in article 10.

ARTICLE 17.

The Council of Administration shall be bound to draw up and present to the Ministry of Finance two months before the commencement of each budgetary year a budget indicating the estimates of the council as to receipts and expenditure, especially as to the sums which shall be applied during the course of the said year to the service of the bonds provided for in the annexed convention and for the service of the Debt established by article 3.

This budget must conform to the existing regulations, and shall be approved by the Imperial Government within two months.

It shall be inserted in the general budget of the Empire....

B. ANNUAL REPORT, OTTOMAN PUBLIC DEBT ADMINISTRATION 1905–1906, EXCERPTS

...In the London market there is no clear perception of the position and attributions of the Ottoman Public Debt Administration, and it does not seem to be understood that the Public Debt Administraion is an independent Administration directed by a European Board...

...[a]s regards Turkish Fours [bonds] in particular, it should always be borne in mind that since the promulgation of the Decree of Mouharrem in 1881 [creating the Ottoman Public Debt Administration], both H.I.M. the Sultan and his successive Ministers have loyally observed the stipulation of the Act.

We have every reason to be grateful for the cordial support accorded to our Board by those in authority. We possess their entire confidence, and with a continuation of the loyal cooperation which we have enjoyed hitherto, there is every reason to hope that the interests entrusted to our charge will not suffer in the future. The interests of the Debt Administration and those of the Turkish Government are now identical. Since the Decree of 1903 the Treasury has a direct interest in our surplus, and will the more readily, I am convinced, give us, as in the past, all the support and assistance which is so necessary to the proper administration of the various important Revenues pledged to its creditors.

I maintain that these Revenues are still elastic. Time will show if my estimate is correct.

In the meantime the Council [of the Debt Administration] will neglect no opportunity of developing them, bearing in mind the interests of the Government and the people the same time as the interests of those who have chosen us as their representatives.

Lord Fitzmaurice has been good enough to state in a recent debate that "the Ottoman Debt Commission had been a singularly honest and successful service. ...That Commission was not a body which took a certain amount of money and handed it over to certain Bondholders. No doubt that was its first origin and what called it into existence but gradually, owing to the great skill of the financiers who had control of its operations, it had been entrusted with the collection as well as the administration of various other Revenues, and the taxes which it collected with the consent of the Ottoman Government had gradually gone on increasing." ...

I am in a position to affirm that the view is shared by many of the highest officials in this country. The financial credit of Turkey depends on our existence, . . .

The receipts from the Revenues ceded to the Bondholders by the Decree of Mouharrem now exceeds £T3,000,000, but this sum does not by any means represent the total of the sum which we collect on behalf of the Government in every part of the Empire for the service of the loans created since 1881, or for the payment of railway guarantees, etc.

. . . the fact that we are charged with these new services is worthy of notice, even to those who have no direct interest in the matter, inasmuch as it is a striking proof that the Government has complete confidence in the Administration, and that financial establishments and railway company promoters look to us alone for an effective guarantee of their undertakings in Turkey. . . .

In all, therefore, we collect a sum of £T5,516,187. Considering that the Budget of the Empire is estimated at about £T23,000,000—this is a high estimate—the Debt Administration collects roughly 24% thereof. . . . Every year fresh Revenues are ceded to us. . . .

It must not be supposed that the increase in the Revenue is due only to fresh taxation. New taxes have been imposed, it is true, some sound and some, I regret to state, hardly in accordance with the ordinary rules of political economy. But the increase is due chiefly to improved methods of collection, and secondly, in certain districts, to the economic progress taking place in the country. . . .

When Europe calls upon Turkey to reform, I am afraid it is sometimes forgotten that with restricted financial resources it is not always so easy to reorganize the administration on modern Western lines. A very distinguished diplomatist has expressed to me his astonishment that the Government manages to get along at all with the small means it possesses. At the same time, I am the first to admit that the financial measures adopted by the Government are not always profitable to the Fisc in the long run. The burden of the taxpayer is not so excessive as is generally supposed, but there are vexations and burdensome taxes which might with advantage be withdrawn; they produce little revenue, and could the Government find means to forgo them, I believe an immediate increase of the productive and purchasing power of the people would result, and the State Revenues would in the end suffer no diminution.

Th Council of Administration of the Debt has never adopted the *role* of mere bailiffs of the Bondholders clamouring for their pound of flesh. Over and over again we have come to the assistance of the Government, and time out of number we have given an impetus to industries in the country. We have never hesitated to make suggestions for the adoption of sounder methods of financial administration in general calculated to develop the resources and wealth of the country, but, I regret to state, not always with success.

I have said that the economic conditions of the country are improving. The chief factor in the improvement is the construction of railways. When I first came to this country, thirty years ago next year, there were only 1,230 kilometers of railways in existence.

Today there are 5,744 kilometers constructed and in the course of construction (I omit the Eregli-Bagdad Persian Gulf line, 1,800 kilometers, and the Hedjaz railway to Medina, 1,800 kilometers, and the prolongation of the Smyrna-Aidin railway to Egirdir, 60 kilometers, in all 3,660 kilometers). . . .

As usual where railways have been built they have brought with them increased civilization, tranquility, better administration, followed at once by increased production and prosperity. . . .

Another proof of the growing prosperity of the country is that during the last few years many public works of permanent utility have been undertaken by foreign companies (chiefly port facilities, water works, electric light, and street railway facilities). . . .

Were further proof of increasing wealth required, it would be found in the establishment of new banking establishments in the capital and in the Provinces. . . .

The total staff of the Administration in 1905-1906 was as follows:

Constantinople 1,831

Provinces 3,802

The cost in 1904-1905 (including employees engaged temporarily) was £T264,-749, as against £T259,064 in 1905-1906:—

The majority of our agents are Moslems, and there is no better employee to be found, provided the pay is good and the control severe.

We have in our employ   4,992 Moslems

509 Christians

132 Europeans

TOTAL   5,633

In the year 1905-1906 I took measures to increase the pay of our small officials, and the Council took what I considered to be a wise measure in deciding that no Provincial Agent should receive less than 400 piastres a month.

It is astonishing how with such insignificant salaries men can be found to serve us in responsible positions with absolute integrity, provided always that any irregularity is visited with immediate severity, and that there is a certainty of regular pay and employment with a pension to look forward to. It speaks well for the character of the people. . . .

Since October, 1889, the Administration of the Debt has on various occasions advanced money to the Government for urgent current needs to the amount of £T1,191,933. All these advances have been duly reimbursed.

29

Development Concessions, The D'Arcy Concession for Iranian Oil, 29 May 1901 *

Between the 1850's and World War I the grant of concessions was a device often used by Middle Eastern governments who could command only limited financial and technical resources but who were anxious to encourage large-scale development projects in their country. In return for small initial payments and possibly a modest annual rent or share of anticipated profits, European business combines undertook to construct and operate development projects for the Middle Eastern rulers. Originally, these projects concentrated on transportation and communications schemes such as the Suez Canal (opened 1869) or the Indo-European telegraph (completed 1865) but later included public utilities such as streetcar, gas, and electricity companies, land development corporations, and ultimately mineral extraction combines. The D'Arcy concession is the prototype of the Middle Eastern oil exploitation agreements and by 1932 virtually the entire Iran-Iraq-Persian Gulf region was reserved for exploitation by Western oil combines. After World War II North Africa's petroleum reserves, too, were regulated by concession agreements. As the following selection illustrates, the compensation originally received by the locals was small (although the business risks were considerable too). In the 1920's the Iranians began to agitate for an increase in their share in oil profits, the first in a series of such renegotiations that has marked the subsequent history of the Middle Eastern oil business. Destined to become the largest modern economic enterprise in the Middle East, the political as well as the economic consequences of the growth of the oil industry since the discovery of oil in commercial quantities in Iran in 1908 have been closely identified with the course of the region's modernization.

*   *   *

Between the Government of His Imperial Majesty the Shah of Persia, of the one part, and William Knox d'Arcy, of independent means, residing in London at No. 42, Grosvenor Square (hereinafter called "the Concessionnaire"), of the other part;

* "William Knox D'Arcy Oil Concession in Persia, 29 May 1901," J. C. Hurewitz, *Diplomacy in the Near and Middle East, A Documentary Record: 1535-1914* (Princeton: D. Van Nostrand, 1956), Vol. I, 249-251.

The following has by these presents been agreed on and arranged—viz.:

ART. 1. The Government of His Imperial Majesty the Shah grants to the concessionnaire by these presents a special and exclusive privilege to search for, obtain, exploit, develop, render suitable for trade, carry away and sell natural gas, petroleum, asphalt and ozokerite throughout the whole extent of the Persian Empire for a term of sixty years as from the date of these presents.

ART. 2. This privilege shall comprise the exclusive right of laying the pipe-lines necessary from the deposits where there may be found one or several of the said products up to the Persian Gulf, as also the necessary distributing branches. It shall also comprise the right of constructing and maintaining all and any wells, reservoirs, stations and pump services, accumulation services and distribution services, factories and other works and arrangements that may be deemed necessary.

ART. 3. The Imperial Persian Government grants gratuitously to the concessionnaire all uncultivated lands belonging to the State which the concessionnaire's engineers may deem necessary for the construction of the whole or any part of the above-mentioned works. As for cultivated lands belonging to the State, the concessionnaire must purchase them at the fair and current price of the province.

The Government also grants to the concessionnaire the right of acquiring all and any other lands or buildings necessary for the said purpose, with the consent of the proprietors, on such conditions as may be arranged between him and then without their being allowed to make demands of a nature to surcharge the prices ordinarily current for lands situate in their respective localities.

Holy places with all their dependencies within a radius of 200 Persian archines are formally excluded.

ART. 4. As three petroleum mines situated at Schouster, Kassre-Chirine, in the Province of Kermanschahan, and Daleki, near Bouchir, are at present let to private persons and produce an annual revenue of two thousand tomans for the benefit of the Government, it has been agreed that the three aforesaid mines shall be comprised in the Deed of Concession in conformity with Article 1, on condition that, over and above the 16 per cent mentioned in Article 10, the concessionnaire shall pay every year the fixed sum of 2,000 (two thousand) tomans to the Imperial Government.

ART. 5. The course of the pipe-lines shall be fixed by the concessionnaire and his engineers.

ART. 6. Notwithstanding what is above set forth, the privilege granted by these presents shall not extend to the provinces of Azerbadjan, Ghilan, Mazendaran, Asdrabad and Khorassan, but on the express condition that the Persian Imperial Government shall not grant to any other person the right of constructing a pipe-line to the southern rivers or to the South Coast of Persia.

ART. 7. All lands granted by these presents to the concessionnaire or that may be acquired by him in the manner provided for in Articles 3 and 4 of these presents, as also all products exported, shall be free of all imposts and taxes during the term of the present concession. All material and apparatuses necessary for the exploration, working and development of the deposits, and for the construction and development of the pipe-lines, shall enter Persia free of all taxes and Custom-House duties.

ART. 8. The concessionnaire shall immediately send out to Persia and at his own cost one or several experts with a view to their exploring the region in which there exist, as he believes, the said products, and, in the event of the report of the expert being in the opinion of the concessionnaire of a satisfactory nature, the latter shall immediately send to Persia and at his own cost all the technical staff necessary, with the working plant and machinery required for boring and sinking wells and ascertaining the value of the property.

ART. 9. The Imperial Persian Government authorises the concessionnaire to found one or several companies for the working of the concession.

The names' "statutes" and capital of the said companies shall be fixed by the concessionnaire, and the directors shall be chosen by him on the express condition that, on the formation of each company, the concessionnaire shall give official notice of such formation to the Imperial Government, through the medium of the Imperial Commissioner, and shall forward the "statutes," with information as to the places at which such company is to operate. Such company or companies shall enjoy all the rights and privileges granted to the concessionnaire, but they must assume all his engagements and responsibilities.

ART. 10. It shall be stipulated in the contract between the concessionnaire, of the one part, and the company, of the other part, that the latter is, within the term of one month as from the date of the formation of the first exploitation company, to pay the Imperial Persian Government the sum of £20,000 sterling in cash, and an additional sum of £20,000 sterling in paid-up shares of the first company founded by virtue of the foregoing article. It shall also pay the said Government annually a sum equal to 16 per cent of the annual net profits of any company or companies that may be formed in accordance with the said article.

ART. 11. The said Government shall be free to appoint an Imperial Commissioner, who shall be consulted by the concessionnaire and the directors of the companies to be formed. He shall supply all and any useful information at his disposal, and he shall inform them of the best course to be adopted in the interest of the undertaking. He shall establish, by agreement with the concessionnaire, such supervision as he may deem expedient to safeguard the interests of the Imperial Government.

The aforesaid powers of the Imperial Commissioner shall be set forth in the "statutes" of the companies to be created.

The concessionnaire shall pay the Commissioner thus appointed an annual sum of £1,000 sterling for his services as from the date of the formation of the first company.

ART. 12. The workmen employed in the service of the company shall be subject to His Imperial Majesty the Shah, except the technical staff, such as the managers, engineers, borers and foremen.

ART. 13. At any place in which it may be proved that the inhabitants of the country now obtain petroleum for their own use, the company must supply them gratuitously with the quantity of petroleum that they themselves got previously. Such quantity shall be fixed according to their own declarations, subject to the supervision of the local authority.

ART. 14. The Imperial Government binds itself to take all and any necessary measures to secure the safety and the carrying out of the object of this concession of the plant and of the apparatuses, of which mention is made, for the purposes of the undertaking of the company, and to protect the representatives, agents and servants of the company. The Imperial Government having thus fulfilled its engagements, the concessionnaire and the companies created by him shall not have power, under any pretext whatever, to claim damages from the Persian Government.

ART. 15. On the expiration of the term of the present concession, all materials, buildings and apparatuses then used by the company for the exploitation of its industry shall become the property of the said Government, and the company shall have no right to any indemnity in this connection.

ART. 16. If within the term of two years as from the present date the concessionnaire shall not have established the first of the said companies authorised by Article 9 of the present agreement, the present concession shall become null and void.

ART. 17. In the event of there arising between the parties to the present concession any dispute or difference in respect of its interpretation or the rights or responsibilities of one or the other of the parties therefrom resulting, such dispute or difference shall be submitted to two arbitrators at Teheran, one of whom shall be named by each of the parties, and to an umpire who shall be appointed by the arbitrators before they proceed to arbitrate. The decision of the arbitrators or, in the event of the latter disagreeing, that of the umpire shall be final.

ART. 18. This Act of Concession, made in duplicate, is written in the French language and translated into Persian with the same meaning.

But, in the event of there being any dispute in relation to such meaning, the French text shall alone prevail.

30

Western Missionary Activity and Educational Modernization; Excerpts from a Fund-Raising Brochure of Robert College, Istanbul, 1900 *

Probably the two areas where the activities of Western missionaries in the Middle East produced the most apparent effects was in the modernization of medical and educational practices. Missionary founded and administered educational institutions in particular introduced many future Middle Eastern leaders to modern civilization and its values. American Protestant missionaries were in the vanguard of this movement, and in addition to founding secondary schools in Ottoman, Arab, and Iranian cities, they founded collegiate institutions. Two of the most important of these were Robert College, established by Cyrus Hamlin in Istanbul in 1863, and the Syrian Protestant College, now the American University of Beirut, founded by Daniel Bliss in 1866. The colleges, like many nineteenth-century American institutions of higher learning, were more secondary schools than universities in their early days. By 1900, however, faculties of medicine, engineering, and professional education had been added to the original liberal arts courses. Although a disproportionately large percentage of the early students came from minority groups, more Muslim students began attending the missionary colleges as their reputations spread. The following section, taken from an early fund-raising brochure issued by Robert College, describes the reasons for the founding of the College and some of the practical results which attended its growth.

*   *   *

. . . In theory the College was founded in 1860, but difficulties arose, both here and in America, which postponed the actual opening until September, 1863. It was the first of many similar institutions which have been established by Americans in different parts of the world, and has served as a model for all of them. In 1869 an Iradé for its legal establishment was granted by His Imperial Majesty, the Sultan, to the Legation of the United States at Constantinople, securing to the College all the advantages bestowed by the Imperial Government upon Educational Institutions of the State.

* *Robert College, Constantinople, Turkey, 1900* (New York: the Trustees of Robert College of Constantinople, 1900), 1-9.

Origin and History of the College

Robert College was an outgrowth of American Missions in Turkey. It supplied a want which they could not meet. . . .

It was the object of the Founders to establish at Constantinople something as nearly as possible like a first-class New England college, thoroughly Christian but unsectarian and open to young men of all the nationalities and religions of the East, with the English language as the common ground upon which all could meet. It seemed a quixotic scheme to most people who knew the East. There was not a college in the Turkish Empire and very few schools of any kind, and the idea of bringing the fiercely hostile races and religions of Turkey to live together in peace in a Christian college seemed absurd. It was a bold experiment, but Mr. Robert and Dr. Hamlin were men of faith and prayer, and they "builded better than they knew." The founding of Robert College was the beginning of a new era in Turkey. . . .

Since the granting of an Imperial Charter, the Turkish Government has always respected the rights of the College and granted all additional favors that have been asked.

The College opened in 1863, in an old building in Bebec, belonging to the American Board, where there had long been a Mission School under Dr. Hamlin's direction. There were four students, all English or Americans. It was transferred in 1871 to the new building and commenced the year with 170 students of 15 nationalities. . . .

. . . The College has gone steadily forward without any interruption. It has done what it could to alleviate suffering, to protect the oppressed, to defend the right, to promote peace and good will, and especially to fit young men of these various nationalities, by a Christian education, to serve God and their country. It has won the sympathy, the confidence, and the gratitude of the people, and the very troubles which, had they been foreseen, might have discouraged its founders, have been the means of extending its influence and giving it a world-wide reputation. More than 2,000 students have spent an average of three years in the College, 345 of whom have graduated after five or six years' study.

The Graduates of the College

In the early history of the College very few of the students remained to complete their course and graduate. Their parents could not understand the necessity of so long a course of study. We have no records to show the history or the professions of the non-graduates, but we know that many of them have greatly distinguished themselves, and are now leading men in their respective communities. The graduates have played a very important part in the history of the East, especially in Bulgaria, where they have filled the highest offices of State, and exerted a vast influence in the moral, intellectual and political developments of the people.

The following table will show approximately the professions chosen by the graduates:

Preachers	12	Lawyers	36
Teachers	88	Physicians	37
Government Officials	50	Army Officers	20
Judges	14	Civil Engineers	10
Editors	12	Business Men	110

The four principal races represented in the College are the Armenian, Bulgarian, Greek, and Turkish, but we always have students of from twelve to fifteen different nationalities. . . .

PART TWO:

Seeking a Reorganized Society

5

World War I and Political Reorientation

The First World War is a watershed in the history of the modern Middle East. While it marked the end of one era and destroyed much of what remained of the traditional political order also, it created situations which have continued to influence the course of events in the region to our own day.

The Middle East became involved in the war not only because of its strategic importance but also because of the ambitions of Enver Pasha (1881-1922), Ottoman Minister of War and one of the ruling Young Turk triumvirate. Enver wished to share, at Russia's expense, the territorial spoils of what he was sure would be an eventual victory for the Central Powers. War finally came in the autumn of 1914 when Enver conspired with Admiral Souchon, the commander of the German cruisers *Goeben* and *Breslau* which had fled to Istanbul to escape the British navy, to raise the Ottoman flag on the warships and attack the Russians at Odessa. Despite misgivings and resignations the Ottoman cabinet accepted Enver's *fait accompli* and the allies declared war.

The fighting in the Middle East was important although the decisive battles of World War I took place elsewhere. In these hostilities millions of Middle Easterners were directly involved as soldiers or laborers in the contending armies; millions more of the civilian population were seriously affected by the war's desolation and dislocations. Fighting took place on a number of fronts. Some of the bloodiest confrontations resulted from an Ottoman offensive, commanded by Enver Pasha personally, against the Russians in the Caucasus. This attack, launched in the dead of winter in 1915, was an organizational fiasco. Troops sent into battle in summer uniforms froze or starved to death and after some early success the offensive simply collapsed as a Russian counterattack wiped out all its gains. More important was the fact that many thousands of Ottoman troops along with their equipment were lost; these were the best troops in the army and the Ottoman war effort never really recovered from the disaster. Another tragic aspect of the fighting in the Caucasus and eastern Anatolia was the near obliteration of the Armenians as a nation. In 1916 and 1917 hundreds of thousands of Armenians, because of their supposed allied sympathies and nationalist aims, were uprooted and forced into detention camps. Hundreds of thousands died in the operation.

The Ottoman army gave a better account of itself in other theaters. On the Sinai-Palestine front the Ottoman Fourth Army, assisted by a large number of German and Austrian advisors, early in 1915 carried the attack against the British by striking at the Suez Canal. As the British began to build up their forces in Egypt, however, the initiative passed into their hands. Nevertheless, it was not until after a second Ottoman thrust against the canal was blunted that the British began clearing the Turks out of Sinai. Finally the well-supplied but overly deliberate British army invaded Palestine only to be thrown back in April 1917 before the Ottoman entrenchments at Gaza. Only later in 1917 after Allenby took command did the British begin to clear Palestine. By that time the Ottoman army was half its former size, supplies were running low and the Arabs had begun their revolt under Sherif Husayn along the desert fringes of the Ottoman Arab provinces. The story in Iraq was similar. There, the Anglo-Indian army quickly took Basra in the autumn of 1914 but then bogged down to the point where one of their armies was captured by the Ottomans. It was 1917 before Baghdad fell before relentless British pressure. Certainly, the most glorious Ottoman victory occurred when they repulsed an allied amphibious attack at Gallipoli designed to open up the Turkish straits. This victory did much to enhance the reputation of Mustafa Kemal, the Ottoman general, who as Mustafa Kemal Atatürk was to organize the creation of a new Republic of Turkey after the war was over. Other actions of more limited import were fought at Salonika in Greece and in Iran, which although it was a neutral, had to stand by while Ottoman, Russian, and British troops fought over its territory. Still, by the time of the Mudros Armistice in 1918 the power of any Middle Eastern state to wage serious war appeared to have evaporated. "Defensive modernization" apparently had failed utterly.

Economically and socially the presence of huge European and local armies created an environment conducive to rapid change. A large-scale invasion and imposition of European technology and procedures followed after the new workshops, roads, railroads, ports, motor cars, and even airplanes introduced by the armies. Although serious economic dislocations grew almost commonplace, the war also provided the occasion for an immense demonstration of many facets of Western civilization. Unfortunately, since the demonstrators primarily were soldiers intent upon destroying an enemy, modern civilization and its representatives presented a rather grim and ruthless picture to Middle Easterners—an impression of the West still current in the area today. Consequently, the appeal of Turkish, Iranian, and the various Arab nationalisms was broadened since the fighting and the physical presence of so many Europeans dramatized the conflict between foreign and local values. As early as 1914 the Ottoman Empire's abrogation of foreign extraterritorial privileges testified to the waxing of nationalism's strength. Also, such declarations as President Wilson's Fourteen Points contributed to the nationalistic development as well as to the rise of an American popularity throughout the region that was destined to be dissipated considerably in later decades.

A most important aspect of the war was the diplomatic maneuverings which were part of it and which followed the end of hostilities. There were actually three phases in this diplomacy. Between 1914 and 1917 the Entente and Central Powers jockeyed for diplomatic advantage and traded promises for future territorial concessions. The period opened with the negotiation of the Ottoman German Alliance in 1914, an accomplishment that was countered by the anti-Ottoman, pan-Arab inspired Arab Revolt of 1916-1918 which was the immediate product of the dealings between Sherif Husayn of Mecca and Sir Henry MacMahon, the British High Commissioner in Egypt. Ultimately, of course, the revolt was an expression of Arab revulsion against the Turkish supremacy policies of the Young Turks. The period ended with the fall of the Tsarist government and Russia's consequent retreat from participation in Middle Eastern affairs, but with a compensating entry of the United States as a participant in the international politics of the region. Secondly, from 1917 to 1920 the victorious allies proceeded to carve up the Middle East. This stage opened with the Balfour Declaration of 1917 by which the London authorities promised to support the concept of a "Jewish national home" in Palestine, territory already claimed by Sherif Husayn. It closed with the signing in August of 1920 of the Treaty of Sèvres by representatives of the defeated Ottoman government. This treaty, the harshest of any of those inflicted on a member of the Central Powers, would have dismembered what was left of the Ottoman Empire and left large parts of it in the hands of allied occupation forces. But the Arabs, too, were dismayed by the peace settlements. The San Remo Conference of 1920, rather than ratifying the understandings reached in the Husayn-MacMahon correspondence which envisioned the creation of a large Arab state uniting the Arabian peninsula with the Fertile Crescent, instead established the "mandates"—in essence a variety of protectorate—over the Fertile Crescent provinces. Formally, the mandates were designed to establish eventual self-government and were creatures of the League of Nations, actually they were devices which assured British control of Palestine and Iraq and French control of Syria and Lebanon. For its part, Iran's government in 1919 signed a treaty with Great Britain, now dominant in the country since the Russian withdrawal, which would have turned that state into a virtual British protectorate. Nevertheless, the final 1920-1923 phase of World War I diplomacy in the Middle East testified to the success of nationalist inspired anti-imperialist reactions in Turkey and Iran which prevented the actual application of the partition schemes of the Allies in those countries. One can point to the signing of the Treaty of Lausanne of 1923 which recognized a free, nationalist Turkish Republic as the actual end of World War I in the Middle East.

Certainly, the most dramatic happening of the war period was the final shattering of the multinational Ottoman Empire which, despite its attempts to come to grips with the modern world, right to its end, embodied so much of the heritage of traditional Middle Eastern culture. But the disaster which overtook the house of Osman also freed Turks and Arabs to embark upon a more thoroughgoing reconstruction of their societies. For if the Ottoman ideal was dead, the new ideals of Turkish and Arab nationalism were very much alive and they, along with Iranian nationalism, became the focus of local aspirations. This is not to say that nationalism was a creed that held the loyalty of most Middle Easterners in 1918. It was not. The mass of the population was stunned by the war, its demonstration of local impotence in the face of the power of the modern world, and most seemed to be passively awaiting their fate. But those within the local populace who still had the desire to assert their independence seized upon nationalism—if they had not done so previously—as their last, best hope to avert a final cultural obliteration. Nationalists may have been a numerical minority, but they were an activist, elitist minority who soon captured the apparatus of the state in Turkey and Iran and used this machinery to create nations; nationalism was used to provide an ideological statement of the goals of the activists while the state was the means used to realize these goals. Even in the Arab world where imperial regimes held sway from the Atlantic to the Persian Gulf after World War I, various nationalisms were virtually the unchallenged creed of the educated classes including those realists who were willing to cooperate with the imperial powers in an effort to make gradual progress toward the goal of independence.

31

Assertions of Independence, Ottoman Circular Abolishing Foreign Capitulatory Rights, 9 September 1914*

Since the 1860's the Ottomans had sought to gain acquies-
cence from the powers to end the several capitulatory treaties and the various
extraterritorial privileges enjoyed by foreigners within the empire in exchange
for the establishment of a reformed legal system. The powers, however, refused
to consider this and legal reform in the Ottoman Empire was neglected under
Abdülhamid II. Under the Young Turk regime agitation for abolition of the
capitulations revived and was crowned by the circular reproduced below. This
was issued in the early days of World War I when the Ottomans hoped to
capitalize on their initial neutrality. Actually, all the powers protested the Ottoman announcement although Austria and Germany ceased to voice their objections after the Ottomans joined the Central Powers. During the war only the
American consular courts remained operating until these too closed when the
United States and the Ottomans severed diplomatic relations in April 1917 after
America joined the allies. However, with the allied victory the capitulations were
restored, a situation ratified by the Treaty of Sèvres of 1920. Nevertheless, the rise
of the Kemalist regime in Ankara and their successful struggle to expel the foreigners from Turkish soil reached ultimate fruition in the Treaty of Lausanne of
1923 which finally abolished foreign capitulatory rights. The drive to end the
capitulations, if originally an assertion of Ottoman defensiveness, by 1914 was a
symptom of the rise of Turkish nationalism.

*   *   *

The Imperial Ottoman Government, in its sentiments of hospitality and sympathy towards the subjects of the friendly Powers, had in former times determined
in a special manner the rules to which foreigners coming to the Orient to trade
there should be subject, and had communicated those rules to the Powers. Subsequently those rules, which the Sublime Porte had decreed entirely of its own accord, were interpreted as privileges, corroborated and extended by certain practices,

* *Papers Relating to the Foreign Relations of the United States, 1914* (Washington: Govt.
Printing Office, 1922), 1092-1093.

and were maintained down to our days under the name of ancient treaties (or Capitulations). Meanwhile these privileges, which on the one hand were found to be in complete opposition to the juridical rules of the century and to the principle of national sovereignty, constituted on the other hand an impediment to the progress and the development of the Ottoman Empire, just as they gave birth to certain misunderstandings in its relations with the foreign Powers; and thus they form an obstacle to the attainment of the desired degree of cordiality and sincerity in those relations.

The Ottoman Empire, surmounting all resistance, continues to march in the path of renaissance and reform which it entered upon in 1255 [A.D. 1839] by the Hatti-Humayoun of Gul-Hané, and, in order to assure for itself the place which was due it in the family of the civilized peoples of Europe, it accepted the most modern juridical principles and did not deviate from the program of supporting the edifice of the State on these foundations. The establishment of the constitutional régime demonstrates with what happy success the efforts of the Ottoman Government in the way of progress were crowned.

However, as consequences deduced from the Capitulations, the intervention of foreigners in the exercise of judiciary power, which constitutes the most important basis of the sovereignty of the State; the limitation of the legislative power, by the claim put forth that many laws could not be applied to foreigners; the fact that a criminal who has committed an offense against public security is screened from the application of the laws on the sole ground of his being of foreign nationality; or again the fact that public action is compromised by the necessity of respecting in regard to the foreign delinquent all sorts of restrictions and conditions; the fact finally that, according to the nationality of the contracting parties, a difference arising from a single contract admits of a different forum and mode of procedure—all these facts and other similar restrictive privileges constitute an insurmountable barrier to all organization of tribunals begun with a view to assuring in the country the perfect working of justice.

Likewise, that consequence of the Capitulations which renders foreigners exempt and free from taxes in the Ottoman Empire renders the Sublime Porte powerless not only to procure the necessary means for providing for the carrying out of reforms but even for satisfying current administrative needs, without having recourse to a loan. In the same order of ideas, the obstacles raised to the increase of indirect taxes result in raising the quota of direct taxes and in overburdening the Ottoman taxpayers. The fact that foreigners trading in the Ottoman Empire and enjoying there all sorts of immunities and privileges are less heavily taxed than Ottomans constitutes at the same time a manifest injustice and an infringement of the independence and dignity of the State. The Imperial Government, in spite of all these obstacles, was zealously pursuing its efforts at reform when the unforeseen outbreak of the general war brought the financial difficulties in the country to the last degree of acuteness, endangering the accomplishment of all the work which had been begun or the undertaking of which had been decided upon. Now the Sublime Porte is convinced that the only means of salvation for Turkey is to bring into being this work of reform and of development as soon as possible, and it is likewise convinced that all the steps that it takes in this direction will meet with the encouragement of all the friendly Powers.

It is on the basis of this conviction that the decision has been taken to abrogate, reckoning from October 1, 1914, the Capitulations, which up to the present have constituted a hindrance to all progress in the Empire, as well as all privileges and toleration accessory to these Capitulations or resulting from them, and to adopt as the basis of relations with all States the general principles of international law.

While having the honor of communicating the present decision, which as it is to open an era of happiness for the Ottoman Empire will for this reason, I have no doubt, be received with satisfaction by the American Government, I consider it my duty to add that the Sublime Porte, inspired exclusively in its decision by the higher interests of the Ottoman land, does not nourish, in abrogating the Capitulations, any unfriendly thought in regard to any Power and that it is quite disposed to enter upon negotiations with a view to concluding with the American Government treaties of commerce on the basis of the general principles of public international law.

32

The Ottoman Home Front, a German Correspondent's Remarks, 1917*

Dr. Stuermer, a correspondent for the *Kölnische Zeitung* stationed in Istanbul during 1915-1916, left an interesting account of the internal situation within the Ottoman Empire during the First World War. Wartime attempts to curb inflation and to reform the Ottoman monetary system were symptomatic of the severe financial strains which the war brought. Also the war stimulated the growth of Turkish nationalism to the point where even the German allies of the Ottoman Empire were subjected to the inconveniences rising from a wholesale Turkification campaign. By 1917, the empire was in a very

* Harry Stuermer, *Two War Years in Constantinople,* tr. from German by E. Allen (New York: George H. Doran Co., 1917), 121-124, 154-157.

weak state; lack of food and medicines was as rampant among the civilian population as among the troops.

*   *   *

On the financial side, apart from Turkey's enormous debt to Germany, the wonderful attempt at a reform and standardisation of the coinage in the middle of May 1916 is worthy of mention. The reform, which was a simplification of huge economic value of the tremendously complicated money system and introduced a theoretical gold unit, must be regarded chiefly as a war measure to prevent the rapid deterioration of Turkish paper money.

This last attempt, as was obvious after a few months' trial, was entirely unsuccessful, and even hastened the fall of paper money, for the population soon discovered at the back of these drastic measures the thinly veiled anxiety of the Government lest there should be a further deterioration. Dire punishments, such as the closing down of money-changers' businesses and arraignment before a military court for the slightest offence, were meted out to anyone found guilty of changing gold or even silver for paper.

In November 1916, however, it was an open secret that, in spite of all these prohibitions, there was no difficulty in the inland provinces and in Syria and Palestine in changing a gold pound for two or more paper pounds. In still more unfrequented spots no paper money would be accepted, so that the whole trade of the country simply came to a standstill. Even in Constantinople at the beginning of December 1916, paper stood to gold as 100 to 175.

The Anatolian population still went gaily on, burying all the available silver *medjidiehs* and even nickel piastres in their clay pots in the ground, ... The people, too, could not but remember what had happened with the "Kaime" [a paper money issue, ed.] after the Turko-Russian war, when thousands who had believed in the assurances of the Government suddenly found themselves penniless. In Constantinople it was a favorite joke to take one of the new pound, half-pound, or quarter-pound notes issued under German paper, not gold, guarantee and printed only on one side and say, "This (pointing to the right side) is the present value, and that (blank side) will be the value on the conclusion of peace."

Even those who were better informed, however, and sat at the receipt of custom, did exactly the same ... ; no idea of patriotism prevented them from collecting everything metal they could lay their hands on, and, in spite of all threats of punishment—which could never overtake them!—, paying the highest price in paper money for every gold piece they could get. Their argument was: "One must of course have something to live on in the time directly following the conclusion of peace." In ordinary trade and commerce, filthy, torn paper notes, down to a paper piastre, came more and more to be practically the only exchange....

As early as the summer 1915 there were clear outward indications in the streets of Constantinople of a smouldering nationalism ready to break out at any moment. Turkey, under the leadership of Talaat Bey, pursued her course along the well trodden paths, and the first sphere in which there was evidence of an attempt at forcible Turkification was the language. Somewhere toward the end of 1915 Talaat suddenly ordered the removal of all French and English inscriptions, shop signs, etc., even in the middle of European Pera. In tram cars and at stopping-places the French text was blocked out; boards with public police warnings in French were either removed altogether or replaced by unreadable Turkish scrawls; the street indications were simply abolished. The authorities apparently thought it preferable that the Levantine public should get into the wrong tramcar, should break their legs getting out, pick flowers in the park and wander round helplessly in a maze of unnamed streets rather than that the spirit of forcible Turkification should make even the least sacrifice to comfort.

Of the thousand inhabitants of Pera, not ten can read Turkish; but under the pressure of the official order and for fear of brutal assault or some kind of under-hand treatment in case of non-compliance, the inhabitants really surpassed themselves, and before one could turn, all the names over the shops had been painted over and replaced by wonderful Turkish characters that looked like decorative shields or something of the kind painted in the red and white of the national colors. If one had not noted the entrance to the shop and the look of the window very carefully, one might wander helplessly up and down the Grand Rue de Pera if one wanted to buy something in a particular shop.

But the German . . . was highly delighted in spite of the extraordinary difficulty of communal life. "Away with French and English," he would shout. "God punish England; hurrah, our Turkish brothers are helping us and favoring the extension of our German language!"

The answer to these pan-German expansion politicians and language fanatics, whose spiritual home was round the beertables of the "Teutonia," was provided by a second decree of Talaat's some weeks later when all German notices had to disappear. A few, who would not believe the order, held out obstinately, and the signs remained in German till they were either supplemented in 1916, on a very clear hint from Stamboul, by the obligatory Turkish language or later quite supplanted. . . .

Then came the famous language regulations, which even went so far—with a year of grace granted owing to the extraordinary difficulties of the Turkish script —as to decree that in the offices of all trade undertakings of any public interest whatsoever, such as banks, newspapers, transport agencies, etc., the Turkish language should be used exclusively for bookkeeping and any written communication with customers. . . . Old and trusty employees suddenly found themselves faced with the choice of learning the difficult Turkish script or being turned out in a year's time. The possibility—indeed, the necessity—of employing Turkish hands in European businesses suddenly came within the range of practical politics—and that was exactly what the Turkish Government wanted. . . .

33

The Arab Revolt and Its Aims, Selections from the Husayn-MacMahon Correspondence, July 1915 to March 1916 *

The Sherif of Mecca, Husayn, had toyed with the idea of revolting against the Ottomans even before the outbreak of World War I, given the increasing control the Young Turks were asserting over his autonomous regime. Once hostilities began, negotiations between Husayn and the British High Commissioner in Egypt, Sir Henry MacMahon, were carried on by correspondence. Ten letters, the famous Husayn-MacMahon Correspondence, were exchanged between July 1915 and March 1916. The British quickly agreed to supply arms, money, and military advice to Husayn in return for his aid against the Ottomans. An ambiguous political settlement which meant one thing to the British and another to the Arabs was also reached. Generally, the British agreed to support the creation of a large Arab state but reserved Palestine, Syria, and Iraq for special status. Beginning his revolt in June 1916, Husayn counted upon the Arabs of Syria and Palestine, who were indignant over Jemal Pasha's harsh rule and Turkification efforts there to aid his cause. Aided by his sons, Faysal 'Abdallah and 'Ali, as well as by Col. T. E. Lawrence, a British military advisor, Husayn's forces proceeded to cut the Hijaz Railway, provide valuable aid to Allenby's offensive into Palestine and Syria, and to occupy Damascus. The fact that the expectations of the Arabs raised by the Husayn-MacMahon correspondence and Arab success in battle were dashed after the war did much to stimulate the growth of Arab nationalism and their disillusionment with Western liberalism and treaty-making.

*   *   *

NO. 1.

Translation of a letter from the Sherif of Mecca to Sir Henry MacMahon, His Majesty's High Commissioner at Cairo.

To his Honour: *July* 14, 1915.

WHEREAS the whole of the Arab nation without any exception have decided in these last years to live, and to accomplish their freedom, and grasp the reins of

* "Correspondence between Sir Henry MacMahon . . . , His Majesty's High Commissioner at Cairo, and the Sherif Hussein of Mecca," Miscellaneous No. 3 (1939) (Cmd. 5957), *Sessional Papers, House of Commons, 1938-39*, Vol. XIV, Letter 1, 3-4, Letter 9, 15-17.

their administration both in theory and practice; and whereas they have found and felt that it is to the interest of the Government of Great Britain to support them and aid them to the attainment of their firm and lawful intentions (which are based upon the maintenance of the honour and dignity of their life) without any ulterior motives whatsoever unconnected with this object;

And whereas it is to their (the Arabs') interest also to prefer the assistance of the Government of Great Britain in consideration of their geographical position and economic interests, and also of the attitude of the above-mentioned Government, which is known to both nations and therefore need not be emphasised;

For these reasons the Arab nation see fit to limit themselves, as time is short, to asking the Government of Great Britain, if it should think fit, for the approval, through her deputy or representative, of the following fundamental propositions, leaving out all things considered secondary in comparison with these, so that it may prepare all means necessary for attaining this noble purpose, until such time as it finds occasion for making the actual negotiations:—

Firstly.—England to acknowledge the independence of the Arab countries, bounded on the north by Mersina and Adana up to the 37° of latitude, on which degree fall Birijik, Urfa, Mardin, Midiat. Jezirat (Ibn 'Umar), Amadia, up to the border of Persia; on the east by the borders of Persia up to the Gulf of Basra; on the south by the Indian Ocean, with the exception of the position of Aden to remain as it is; on the west by the Red Sea, the Mediterranean Sea up to Mersina. England to approve of the proclamation of an Arab Khalifate of Islam.

Secondly.—The Arab Government of the Sherif to acknowledge that England shall have the preference in all economic enterprises in the Arab countries whenever conditions of enterprises are otherwise equal.

Thirdly.—For the security of this Arab independence and the certainty of such preference of economic enterprises, both high contracting parties to offer mutual assistance, to the best ability of their military and naval forces, to face any foreign Power which may attack either party. Peace not to be decided without agreement of both parties.

Fourthly.—If one of the parties enters upon an aggressive conflict, the other party to assume a neutral attitude, and in case of such party wishing the other to join forces, both to meet and discuss the conditions.

Fifthly.—England to acknowledge the abolition of foreign privileges in the Arab countries, and to assist the Government of the Sherif in an International Convention for confirming such abolition.

Sixthly.—Articles 3 and 4 of this treaty to remain in vigour for fifteen years, and, if either wishes it to be renewed, one year's notice before lapse of treaty to be given.

Consequently, and as the whole of the Arab nation have (praise be to God) agreed and united for the attainment, at all costs and finally, of this noble object, they beg the Government of Great Britain to answer them positively or negatively in a period of thirty days after receiving this intimation; and if this period should lapse before they receive an answer, they reserve to themselves complete freedom of action. Moreover, we (the Sherif's family) will consider ourselves free in word and deed from the bonds of our previous declaration which we made through Ali Effendi.

NO. 9.

Translation of a letter from the Sherif of Mecca to Sir H. MacMahon, His Majesty's High Commissioner at Cairo.

February 18, 1916.

(In the name of the Merciful, the Compassionate!)
To the most noble His Excellency the High Commissioner. May God protect him.
(After compliments and respects.)

WE received your Excellency's letter dated 25th Rabi El Awal, and its contents filled us with the utmost pleasure and satisfaction at the attainment of the required understanding and the intimacy desired. I ask God to make easy our purposes and prosper our endeavours. Your Excellency will understand the work that is being done, and the reasons for it from the following:—

Firstly.—We had informed your Excellency that we had sent one of our sons to Syria to command the operations deemed necessary there. We have received a detailed report from him stating that the tyrannies of the Government there have not left of the persons upon whom they could depend, whether of the different ranks of soldiers or of others, save only a few, and those of secondary importance; and that he is awaiting the arrival of the forces announced from different places, especially from the people of the country and the surrounding Arab regions as Aleppo and the south of Mosul, whose total is calculated at not less than 100,000, by their estimate; and he intends, if the majority of the forces mentioned are Arab, to begin the movement by them; and, if otherwise, that is, of the Turks or others, he will observe their advance to the Canal, and when they begin to fight, his movements upon them will be different to what they expect.

Secondly.—We purposed sending our eldest son to Medina with sufficient forces to strengthen his brother (who is) in Syria, and with every possibility of occupying the railway line, or carrying out such operations as circumstances may admit. This is the beginning of the principal movement, and we are satisfied in its beginning with what we had levied as guards to keep the interior of the country quiet; they are of the people of Hejaz only, for many reasons, which it would take too long to set forth; chiefly the difficulties in the way of providing their necessities with secrecy and speed (although this precaution was not necessary) and to make it easy to bring reinforcements when needed; this is the summary of what you wished to understand. In my opinion it is sufficient, and it is to be taken as a foundation and a standard as to our actions in the face of all changes and unforeseen events which the sequence of events may show. It remains for us to state what we need at present:—

Firstly.—The amount of £50,000 in gold for the monthly pay of the troops levied, and other things the necessity of which needs no explanation. We beg you to send it with all possible haste.

Secondly.—20,000 sacks of rice, 15,000 sacks of flour, 3,000 sacks of barley, 150 sacks of coffee, 150 sacks of sugar, 5,000 rifles of the modern pattern and the necessary ammunition, and 100 boxes of the two sample cartridges (enclosed) and of Martini-Henry cartridges and "Aza," that is those of the rifles of the factory of St. Etienne in France, for the use of those two kinds of rifles of our tribes; it would not be amiss to send 500 boxes of both kinds.

Thirdly.—We think it better that the place of deposit of all these things should be Port Sudan.

Fourthly.—As the above provisions and munitions are not needed until the beginning of the movement (of which we will inform you officially), they should remain at the above place, and when we need them we will inform the Governor there of the place to which they may be conveyed, and of the intermediaries who will carry orders for receiving them.

Fifthly.—The money required should be sent at once to the Governor of Port Sudan, and a confidential agent will be sent by us to receive it, either all at once, or in two instalments, according as he is able, and this ($\substack{V \\ Q}$) is the (secret) sign to be recognised for accepting the man.

Sixthly.—Our envoy who will receive the money will be sent to Port Sudan in three weeks' time, that is to say, he will be there on the 5th Jamad Awal (9th March) with a letter from us addressed to Al Khawaga Elias Effendi, saying that he (Elias) will pay him, in accordance with the letter, the rent of our properties, and the signature will be clear in our name, but we will instruct him to ask for the Governor of the place, whom you will apprise of this person's arrival. After perusal of the letter, the money should be given to him on condition that no discussion whatever is to be made with him of any question concerning us. We beg you most emphatically not to tell him anything, keeping this affair secret, and he should be treated apparently as if he were nothing out of the way.

Let it not be thought that our appointment of another man results from lack of confidence in the bearer; it is only to avoid waste of time, for we are appointing him to a task elsewhere. At the same time we beg you not to embark or send him in a steamer, or officially, the means already arranged being sufficient.

Seventhly.—Our representative, bearer of the present letter, has been definitely instructed to ensure the arrival of this, and I think that his mission this time is finished since the condition of things is known both in general and in detail, and there is no need for sending anyone else. In case of need for sending information, it will come from us; yet as our next representative will reach you after three weeks, you may prepare instructions for him to take back. Yet let him be treated simply in appearance.

Eighthly.—Let the British Government consider this military expenditure in accordance with the books which will be furnished it, explaining how the money has been spent.

To conclude, my best and numberless salutations beyond all increase.
14 *Rabi al Akhar*, 1334.

34

The Evolution of Zionism, from the Basle Program to the Balfour Declaration, 1897-1917*

Modern Zionism was born among the Jewish communities of central and eastern Europe. It united an urge to revive the ancient Hebrew culture with a political reaction against the rise of various exclusive European nationalisms. The movement, initially diverse in its aims and organization, was welded into a coherent force by Theodor Herzl (1860-1904), a Viennese literary figure. The essential content of the Zionist program was summarized at the First International Zionist Congress organized by Herzl at Basle in 1897. Its heart was a call for the creation of a Jewish homeland in Palestine sustained by emigration and the support of a world-wide organization. By World War I migration to Palestine had resulted in the settling of some 80,000 European Jews there. During the war both the Central Powers and the Allies actively courted Jewish support. In 1917 the Zionists gained important French advocacy for the idea of a Jewish national home. Next, Chaim Weizmann (1874-1952), a Russian-born Manchester chemistry professor who had solved a difficult munitions problem for the British government, coordinated a drive to gain British support for Zionist aims. Ultimately, the appeal succeeded and the Balfour declaration, actually a semi-public letter to Baron Rothschild, promised British governmental backing for a Jewish national home in Palestine. Thus, another nationalism was injected into the Middle East.

* a. "The Basle Program of the First International Zionist Congress," *Protokoll des I. Zionistenkongresses in Basel vom 29 bis 31 August 1897* (Prague: World Zionist Congress, 1911), 131;

b. "Letter of Foreign Minister Balfour to Lord Rothschild, 2 November 1917," *The Times* (London: 9 November 1917).

A. THE ZIONIST BASLE PROGRAM, 31 AUGUST 1897

The goal of Zionism is the establishment for the Jewish people of a home in Palestine guaranteed by public law. The Congress anticipates the following means to reach that goal:

1. The promotion, in suitable ways, of the colonization of Palestine by Jewish agricultural and industrial workers.

2. The organizing and uniting of all Jews by means of suitable institutions, local and international, in compliance with the laws of all countries.

3. The strengthening and encouraging of Jewish national sentiment and awareness.

4. Introductory moves towards receiving governmental approval where necessary, for the realization of Zionism's goal.

B. THE BALFOUR DECLARATION, 2 NOVEMBER 1917

Foreign Office
November 2nd, 1917

Dear Lord Rothschild,

I have much pleasure in conveying to you, on behalf of His Majesty's Government, the following declaration of sympathy with Jewish Zionist aspirations which has been submitted to, and approved by, the Cabinet:

"His Majesty's Government view with favour the establishment in Palestine of a national home for the Jewish people, and will use their best endeavours to facilitate the achievement of this object, it being clearly understood that nothing shall be done which may prejudice the civil and religious rights of existing non-Jewish communities in Palestine, or the rights and political status enjoyed by Jews in any other country."

I shall be grateful if you would bring this declaration to the knowledge of the Zionist Federation.

Yours Sincerely,

ARTHUR JAMES BALFOUR

35

The Establishment of the British Occupation Administration in Iraq[*]

The British occupied Basra and the districts of the Ottoman province of Iraq bordering the Persian Gulf early in the war. With occupation came the necessity of establishing a political administration to govern the local Arab population. Relying heavily upon administrative procedures and personnel taken from the Anglo-Indian government, the British scrapped much although not all of the established Ottoman system. In the important area of land tenure and ownership the British preserved Ottoman practices. Because practically all of the Ottoman officials fled as the British advanced the new regime depended heavily upon military decrees, hasty improvisation, and a few educated Arabs who were recruited to form the basis of a new local civil service. By 1917 just as the administration of Basra and vicinity was beginning to work fairly smoothly the British took Baghdad and had to install a new government there. The main problem facing the occupation authorities was lack of trained officials. Consequently, damaging mistakes were made and uprisings were common especially in rural areas as the local population chaffed under direct rule by European military administrators. Nevertheless, when the mandate Kingdom of Iraq was founded in 1921 much of its political apparatus was inherited from the occupation regime and precedents established by it were incorporated into the Arab administration.

*   *   *

The initial difficulties in setting up civil administration in the occupied territories were greatly enhanced by the fact that, except for a few Arab subordinates, all the former Turkish officials had fled, taking with them the most recent documents and registers. Nevertheless, immediately after our arrival in Basrah a beginning was made in establishing a system of government which should be consonant with the spirit of our proclamations. The British military authorities had at first no leisure to make any arrangements with regard to fiscal and revenue matters except in respect of customs, but towards the middle of January a Revenue Commissioner, Mr. Henry Dobbs, I.C.S., arrived in Basrah from India, and such records as had been left by the Turks were overhauled. They were mostly out

---

[*] Iraq Civil Commissioner, *Review of the Civil Administration of Mesopotamia*, Cmd. 1061 (London: H.M.S.O., 1920), 5-8, 14-15, 18-20.

of date and were lying mixed with masses of lumber on the floors of the Turkish offices, the only papers in any kind of order being the registers of title-deeds to land and registered documents. Their escape was fortunate, as their loss would have been a severe blow to landowners and traders of the province. The administration was confronted with the task of setting the whole of a strange and complicated system on its legs as quickly as possible without the aid of the most recent records or of the most experienced officials, while the remaining records took many weeks to reduce to order. At the same time the nearness of the enemy's forces caused a feeling of insecurity among the people, and made many of them hesitate to compromise themselves by helping the authorities and reluctant to pay their taxes. Moreover, the exactions of the Turks before leaving, the confusion into which the administration had for some months been thrown, and the dislocation of trade by the stoppage of commerce with Baghdad on the one side and with India and Europe on the other, coupled with an unusually bad date season, had temporarily deprived the population of cash and credit. The administration of civil justice was in abeyance, so that the recovery of debts and rents, except by consent, was impossible. It was necessary to set up temporarily some sort of revenue and fiscal administration. To this end it was decided to keep intact the Turkish system, to which the people were accustomed, but to free it from corruption and abuses and increase its efficiency. The number of alien officials introduced was deliberately kept low. All other appointments were filled by the more honest of the ex-official people of the country, the large majority being Mussalmans. This would have been in any case inevitable, as the records of the departments were all in Turkish; the language of vernacular records and receipts, together with all other official business, was, however, changed to Arabic, a measure which satisfied local sentiment. One of the curses of the Turkish régime was the number of its officials; checks, counter-checks and delays being multiplied in order to provide occupation for fresh appointments. In consequence, no one did even half an honest day's work, and idleness pervaded every office. Under the British organisation only the minimum number of officials were re-employed.

On the whole the people adapted themselves with surprising alacrity to the new order. During the four months which elapsed between the capture of Qurnah and the crucial battle of Shu'aibah, in spite of the fact that a large Turkish force lay almost at the gates of Basrah, the life of the town went on undisturbed, the bazaars were busy and the streets safe. It was the best answer which could be given to Turkish propaganda and reflected no little credit on the native population. . . .

The victory at Shu'aibah removed the pressure of immediate danger, and within three months the advance up the two rivers had more than tripled the area under our control. Military Governors under the senior local military officer were appointed to 'Amarah and Nasiriyah, and Assistant Political Officers were placed in charge of the political and revenue administration of the districts. The Assistant Political Officers were responsible to the Chief Political Officer for purposes of civil administration, and worked directly under the local military authorities for the purchase of supplies and in measures connected with the safe preservation of the line of communications.

The confusion which reigned in the Ottoman administration was due as much to a radically bad system as to the inefficiency of the Turkish staff. Financially, the budget of the two provinces of Basrah and Baghdad had, until two or three years before the British occupation, presented a deficit which had been converted into a small surplus, probably as the result not of improvement in method, but of financial readjustments and increased taxation. How complicated were the existing financial arrangements may be judged by the fact that no less than five departments of government, apart from the general revenue, were independently collecting monies and remitting them to Constantinople. These departments were, firstly, the Régie, a foreign concession; secondly, the Auqaf, the department of Pious Bequests; thirdly, the Sanniyah or Crown lands, which since the constitution of 1908 had been administered as State lands; fourthly, the Ottoman Debt, to the service of which 12 petty taxes were allocated besides 3 per cent on customs; and, fifthly, the International Board of Health, which collected so-called quarantine fees impartially from the dead and from the living. The net result of these five excrescences was that the normal life of the people was interfered with at almost every step and that no unification of system or taxation was possible. References to Constantinople on petty details of administration were incessant, and the hope of local autonomy which had come to birth in the Arab provinces of the Turkish Empire after the revolution of 1908 could not, even if it had received official approval, have taken practical shape.

There was a complete cleavage between the executive and revenue sides of the administration. The executive officers provided force for the collection of taxes, but they had no other concern with the revenue system. Taxes were collected usually by farming or by subordinate officials appointed annually to collect a specific tax. With few exceptions all demands were fluctuating. They were fixed each year by assessments or by counts of the objects subject to taxation, such as sheep, buffaloes and camels, or date and fruit trees, or, in the case of crops, by estimation of the yield. The greater part of this work was done by a temporary official, who had no interest in his particular employment beyond making the most of its short duration. There was no one permanently responsible for the probity of the collector in any area, and the system invited peculation and corruption. The invitation was seldom refused.

The Turkish administrative system was thus one of watertight compartments, each in separate correspondence with a head departmental office at Constantinople; war conditions and the breaking off of relations with the Turkish capital made it easy to put at end to a scheme which was manifestly incompatible with efficiency. The Sanniyah or Crown lands were merged in the Revenue Department. The Régie, a hostile trading concern, ceased to exist, and the regulation of the tobacco trade, of which there was little till the occupation of Baghdad brought us into contact with tobacco-growing areas, fell under the direction of the same department, together with other miscellaneous revenues. Many of these miscellaneous revenues had been allocated to the public debt and collected by its officers; the administration of the debt was therefore allotted to the Revenue Department, until in 1917 the separate organisation of the debt was terminated. Quarantine, which may have had its uses in Turkish times in connection with the annual influx of pilgrims, chiefly from Persia, was no longer needed, since pilgrimage had been intermitted by the war and the port authorities dealt with arrivals by sea. In addition, Auqaf and Education were included, like Customs, in the Revenue Department. Such amalgamation was inevitable at first owing to the lack of British officers and of qualified Arab assistants, but it was not intended to be otherwise than a temporary expedient; and with the increase of staff and the development of administration, Customs, Auqaf and Education became separate units. The Revenue Department at Administrative Headquarters worked locally through the Political Officers of the district, which put an end to the former division between the executive and revenue branches of the administration. As for the methods of collecting taxation, the gradual extinction of the tax-farmer was the desired goal, together with the substitution of a fixed for a fluctuating demand, but neither aim could be achieved at once....

On the occupation of Basrah the collection and assessment of Customs duty was undertaken by Messrs. Gray, Mackenzie & Co., but after the fall of 'Amarah imports greatly increased and the firm asked to be relieved of the work. An officer of the Indian Imperial Customs Service, Mr. Watkins, was deputed to Basrah as Collector of Customs, a post which he continued to hold until he became Chief Collector of Customs to the Force and subsequently also Secretary for Commerce. He undertook the organisation of the Department with much zeal and efficiency. Customs were left under the supervision of the Revenue Commissioner and passed under that of the Revenue Board, which replaced the Revenue Commissioner in February 1917....

The re-establishment of judicial administration was subject to the same difficulty which hampered the civil authorities in other departments, namely, that practically all Turkish judicial officers had left their posts before the occupation of Basrah. Those who remained were not willing to continue their functions and no other staff which had experience of Turkish law was available. As the Capitulations had been abolished by the Turks at the outbreak of war no claim that they should be revived in the occupied territories, at all events during the war, was to be admitted. Alien enemy firms established in Basrah, exclusive of the indigenous population, which was regarded as friendly, ceased to do business on the occupation of the town, and their affairs were taken over by the Department of Hostile Trading Concerns, which was responsible to the Chief Political Officer.

In August 1915, for the purpose of providing for the administration of civil and criminal justice for the civil population, the Army Commander promulgated a code, known as the 'Iraq Occupied Territories Code, which was based on the Indian Civil and Criminal Codes. Powers were taken therein to enforce any Indian law, as well as to introduce such amendments as might be necessitated by local conditions, and courts were started in Basrah.

The course pursued was open to objections, but it had the great advantage of providing without delay machinery which would not otherwise have been forthcoming, and without such immediate provision the activities of the community would in many directions have been brought to a standstill. The practice of the new courts was so far superior to that of the courts they superseded, and the Indian codes so much better and simpler than the Turkish that no objection was raised to the substitution of the Indian for the Turkish judicial system. The people, accustomed to the dilatory processes of the Turks, were amazed and delighted with the expedition shown in the execution of justice.

The bulk of the criminal work did not come into the courts. Serious cases were tried by Military Commissions, but there was a consensus of opinion that serious crime was remarkably rare, that which existed being mainly theft or robbery under arms. The Deputy Military Governors of Basrah and 'Ashar disposed of most of the criminal suits. Until after the occupation of Baghdad, no courts existed in the Basrah Wilayat outside Basrah town. In 'Amarah and Nasiriyah disputes of all kinds were decided by Military Governors, while in the rural districts the same powers were exercised by Political Officers. In all these cases limitations were set to the sentences which could be imposed.

Outside the towns the tribal population had not been wont to resort to the Ottoman courts, in spite of all attempts on the Ottoman Government to induce or force them to do so. In point of fact, over the greater part of Mesopotamia it was not the Turkish judicial authorities who had regulated the relations between man and man or assigned the penalties for breaches in their observance. Behind all legal paraphernalia lay the old sanctions, understood and respected because they were the natural outcome of social needs. The shaikh in his tent heard the plaint of petitioners seated round his coffee hearth and gave his verdict with what acumen he might possess, guided by a due regard for tribal custom; the local saiyid, strong in his reputation for a greater familiarity than that of other men with the revealed ordinances of the Almighty, and yet stronger in the wisdom brought by long experience in arbitration, delivered his awards on disputes grave or trivial, and the decisions thus reached were generally consonant with natural justice and always conformable with the habits of thought of the contending parties.

This system of local justice was recognised by us to be a strong weapon on the side of order and good conduct. Just as it was the habit of the British Military Governors when hearing cases to call in the mukhtars, the headmen of the town quarters, and ask them to take part in the proceedings, so the Political Officers

turned to the shaikhs of tribe and village and obtained their opinion. This practice was extended by an enactment called the Tribal Disputes Regulation, issued
with the approval of the Army Commander in February 1916. It was laid down
herein that when a dispute occurred in which either of the parties was a tribes-
man, the Political Officer might refer it to a majlis, or tribal court, consisting of
shaikhs or arbiters selected according to tribal usage. Unless the findings of this
body were manifestly unjust or at variance with the facts of the case, the Political
Officer would pass judgment in general accordance with it. . . .

It may fairly be said that the extension of the administration usually succeeded
in fulfilling a double function. Not only was efficiency increased, but close personal
contact was established between the governors and the governed, and confidence
grew correspondingly. A good example of the results which followed on more
intimate relations between British officers and the people of the country, and did
their share in turn in strengthening these relations, was the Shabanah. These
tribal guards were enrolled and paid by the local Political Officer to help in the
preservation of order and the protection of the lines of communication. They also
carried messages, went on errands and served as a kind of bodyguard. They were
enlisted through their shaikhs and organised under two grades of native non-
commissioned officers, but the organisation of the force varied according to the
requirements of the district. On the Tigris below 'Amarah, where the estates held
by individual shaikhs are large and the principle of local authority well understood, each shaikh provided the men for his section of the river. As the force
thus composed consisted of separate tribal elements, no single non-commissioned
officer was put at its head. On the other hand, in the Hammar Lake, between
Qurnah and Nasiriyah, where the tribal units were small and conspicuous for a
prevailing anarchy, it was thought inadvisable to post Shabanah in their own districts as they were liable to be preoccupied by private feuds rather than to devote
themselves to their official duties. Nor were the Shabanah organised on a tribal
basis in the Suq district, where the main part of the force was kept at headquarters, but three small units were placed under friendly shaikhs near the town.
Both Suq and Nasiriyah were provided with a body of tribal horse—originally
enrolled at Nasiriyah under the military authorities. . . .

Medical facilities, integrity in the administration of justice, the gradual abolition
of the tax-farmer, the stabilising of taxation on a fair basis, the repairing of
mosque and village, together with a sympathetic handling of the tribes, these
were the most effective means of meeting Turkish and German propaganda, but
steps were taken to provide the reading public, a very small portion of the community, with news from sources less tainted than those of the enemy. A Government press was instituted at Basrah, and when the great initial difficulties in pro-
curing material had been surmounted, a vernacular paper, both in Arabic and
Persian, was published daily. The news conveyed was mainly derived from
Reuters, but local well-wishers were encouraged to contribute; for example, valu-

able articles on the treatment by the Turks of the Shi'ah holy towns were received from a respected saiyid. If the circulation was not very large the paper reached a wider public than the numbers bought would seem to indicate, for in a population almost wholly illiterate it is the habit for one who has an acquaintance with letters to read the news aloud to the company gathered round him in the coffee shop, and one copy will therefore serve to instruct a group of listeners. As the press became better equipped, vernacular pamphlets and broad sheets, reproductions of important native documents, such as a petition against the Turks sent by the Shi'ahs of Najaf and Karbala to Persia, were issued from it. Besides the vernacular and English daily papers the press gradually accomplished more and more current official work, both civil and military, to the alleviation of offices where typists were permanently too few and stenographers almost unknown.

Arrangements were made for the circulation of reputable Egyptian vernacular papers, which were imported and distributed, for the most part, free of charge. They were appreciated by the very small public who read anything beyond the daily telegrams. . . .

Whatever care might be taken to keep the pressure of war conditions from the inhabitants of the occupied territories, so long as they observed neutrality, it was impossible to avoid the infliction of some inconveniences. Of these, perhaps the most pressing was the blockade, essential to prevent goods reaching enemy hands from the markets of Basrah, 'Amarah and Nasiriyah, which were now well stocked. It extended to Kuwait and Najd and into Persia, and thus, besides being a severe restriction on the population of the 'Iraq, threatened on several occasions to embroil us with trusted friends whose subjects could not forgo the tempting profits of illicit trade. A minor but galling grievance was the requisitioning of houses for military and civil use; more serious, but equally unavoidable, was the demand for native labour. Dykes, railways, roads, the work of the port, growing daily more considerable, the laying out of camps and other military necessities, obliged us to draw the agricultural population away from the palm gardens and arable lands, where the surplus available was smaller than the supply called for. Not many of these works were of public benefit, and some were even directly contrary to local interests, though the exigencies of the campaign demanded them. All was done that could be done to lighten the burden by providing that the labourers should return periodically to their home after short terms of work, and by making arrangements for their being lodged in well-arranged camps, and adequately paid and fed. Arab labour when properly handled was found to compare favourably with that of the Indian labour corps employed in the country. Arab, Persian and Kurdish labour corps were formed under the control of British officers, who quickly learnt how to make themselves popular with the men under their command, and thereby to get the best work out of them. The organisation of labour, begun under civil auspices, was converted in 1916 into a military department, since most of the work required was for military purposes; but the task of providing labour through the shaikhs by persuasion or demand remained with the local Political Officer, who, while he recognised the inevitable requirement, sometimes groaned under it.

36

The Post-War Settlement, The League of Nations Mandate for Syria and Lebanon, 24 July 1922 *

The political reorganization of the Middle East that followed World War I produced a myriad of treaties and other documents. "Definitive treaties" were drawn, then ignored, and ultimately replaced by other definitive treaties. Among the hardier settlements were the various mandate agreements of which there were three: a French mandate for Syria and Lebanon and British mandates for Iraq and for Palestine (from which Transjordan was separated in 1922). The mandates were designed to provide for the administration of former Central Power territory under the general supervision of the League of Nations. The various mandate agreements were similar in their provisions regarding military and foreign affairs, internal administration, and the responsibilities of the League of Nations Council. The actual administration of the Middle Eastern mandates was vested in either Britain or France. These states, despite their charge to prepare the mandates for eventual independence, actually treated them as protectorates, components of their imperial systems. Iraq achieved *dejure* independence in 1932 but a treaty of alliance still bound her closely to Britain. The Palestine mandate was vexed from the start by the Arab-Zionist contest for supremacy there. In Syria and Lebanon, France's repressive administration was punctuated by numerous uprisings which were severely dealt with by the military as sundry officials and precedents borrowed from North Africa were imposed upon the two countries. The French relied upon divide-and-rule tactics and split the area into six units, an action which served to accentuate existing divisions in Syrian society. Nationalist spokesmen often were harassed and parliamentary life in Syria-Lebanon was marked by rancour and numerous suspensions of legislatures by the French High Commissioner. Independence finally came to the two states during World War II.

* *Mandate for Syria and Lebanon* (Geneva: League of Nations, 1922); text also available in Helen Davis, *Constitutions, Electoral Laws, Treaties of States in the Near and Middle East* (Durham: Duke University Press, 1953), 283-290.

The Council of the League of Nations:

Whereas the Principal Allied Powers have agreed that the territory of Syria and the Lebanon, which formerly belonged to the Turkish Empire, shall, within such boundaries as may be fixed by the said Powers, be entrusted to a Mandatory charged with the duty of rendering administrative advice and assistance to the population, in accordance with the provisions of Article 22 (paragraph 4) of the Covenant of the League of Nations; and

Whereas the Principal Allied Powers have decided that the mandate for the territory referred to above should be conferred on the Government of the French Republic, which has accepted it; and

Whereas the terms of this mandate, which are defined in the articles below, have also been accepted by the Government of the French Republic and submitted to the Council of the League for approval; and

Whereas the Government of the French Republic has undertaken to exercise this mandate on behalf of the League of Nations, in conformity with the following provisions; and

Whereas by the afore-mentioned Article 22 (paragraph 8), it is provided that the degree of authority, control or administration to be exercised by the Mandatory, not having been previously agreed upon by the Members of the League, shall be explicitly defined by the Council of the League of Nations;

Confirming the said mandate, defines its terms as follows:

Art. 1. The Mandatory shall frame, within a period of three years from the coming into force of this mandate, an organic law for Syria and the Lebanon.

This organic law shall be framed in agreement with the native authorities and shall take into account the rights, interests, and wishes of all the population inhabiting the said territory. The Mandatory shall further enact measures to facilitate the progressive development of Syria and the Lebanon as independent States. Pending the coming into effect of the organic law, the Government of Syria and the Lebanon shall be conducted in accordance with the spirit of this mandate.

The Mandatory shall, as far as circumstances permit, encourage local autonomy.

Art. 2. The Mandatory may maintain its troops in the said territory for its defence. It shall further be empowered, until the entry into force of the organic law and the re-establishment of public security, to organise such local militia as may be necessary for the defence of the territory, and to employ this militia for defence and also for the maintenance of order. These local forces may only be recruited from the inhabitants of the said territory.

The said militia shall thereafter be under the local authorities, subject to the authority and the control which the Mandatory shall retain over these forces. It shall not be used for purposes other than those above specified save with the consent of the Mandatory.

Nothing shall preclude Syria and the Lebanon from contributing to the cost of the maintenance of the forces of the Mandatory stationed in the territory.

The Mandatory shall at all times possess the right to make use of the ports, railways and means of communication of Syria and the Lebanon for the passage of its troops and of all materials, supplies and fuel.

Art. 3. The Mandatory shall be entrusted with the exclusive control of the foreign relations of Syria and the Lebanon and with the right to issue exequaturs to the consuls appointed by foreign Powers. Nationals of Syria and the Lebanon living outside the limits of the territory shall be under the diplomatic and consular protection of the Mandatory.

Art. 4. The Mandatory shall be responsible for seeing that no part of the territory of Syria and the Lebanon is ceded or leased or in any way placed under the control of a foreign Power.

Art. 5. The privileges and immunities of foreigners, including the benefits of consular jurisdiction and protection as formerly enjoyed by Capitulation or usage in the Ottoman Empire, shall not be applicable in Syria and the Lebanon. Foreign consular tribunals shall, however, continue to perform their duties until the coming into force of the new legal organisation provided for in Article 6.

Unless the Powers whose nationals enjoyed the afore-mentioned privileges and immunities on August 1st, 1914, shall have previously renounced the right to their re-establishment, or shall have agreed to their non-application during a specified period, these privileges and immunities shall at the expiration of the mandate be immediately re-established in their entirety or with such modifications as may have been agreed upon between the Powers concerned.

Art. 6. The Mandatory shall establish in Syria and the Lebanon a judicial system which shall assure to natives as well as to foreigners a complete guarantee of their rights.

Respect for the personal status of the various peoples and for their religious interests shall be fully guaranteed. In particular, the control and administration of Wakfs shall be exercised in complete accordance with religious law and the dispositions of the founders.

Art. 7. Pending the conclusion of special extradition agreements, the extradition treaties at present in force between foreign Powers and the Mandatory shall apply within the territory of Syria and the Lebanon.

Art. 8. The Mandatory shall ensure to all complete freedom of conscience and the free exercise of all forms of worship which are consonant with public order and morality. No discrimination of any kind shall be made between the inhabitants of Syria and the Lebanon on the ground of differences in race, religion, or language.

The Mandatory shall encourage public instruction, which shall be given through the medium of the native languages in use in the territory of Syria and the Lebanon.

The right of each community to maintain its own schools for the instruction and education of its own members in its own language, while conforming to such educational requirements of a general nature as the administration may impose, shall not be denied or impaired.

Art. 9. The Mandatory shall refrain from all interference in the administration of the Councils of management (*Conseils de fabrique*) or in the management of religious communities and sacred shrines belonging to the various religions, the immunity of which has been expressly guaranteed.

Art. 10. The supervision exercised by the Mandatory over the religious missions in Syria and the Lebanon shall be limited to the maintenance of public order and good government; the activities of these religious missions shall in no way be restricted, nor shall their members be subjected to any restrictive measures on the ground of nationality, provided that their activities are confined to the domain of religion.

The religious missions may also concern themselves with education and relief, subject to the general right of regulation and control by the Mandatory or of the local government, in regard to education, public instruction and charitable relief.

Art. 11. The Mandatory shall see that there is no discrimination in Syria or the Lebanon against the nationals, including societies and associations, of any State Member of the League of Nations as compared with its own nationals, including societies and associations, or with the nationals of any other foreign State in matters concerning taxation or commerce, the exercise of professions or industries, or navigation, or in the treatment of ships or aircraft. Similarly, there shall be no discrimination in Syria or the Lebanon against goods originating in or destined for any of the said States; there shall be freedom of transit, under equitable conditions, across the said territory.

Subject to the above, the Mandatory may impose or cause to be imposed by the local governments such taxes and Customs duties as it may consider necessary. The Mandatory, or the local governments acting under its advice, may also conclude on grounds of contiguity any special Customs arrangements with an adjoining country.

The Mandatory may take or cause to be taken, subject to the provisions of paragraph I of this article, such steps as it may think best to ensure the development of the natural resources of the said territory and to safeguard the interests of the local population.

Concessions for the development of these natural resources shall be granted without distinction of nationality between the nationals of all States Members of the League of Nations, but on condition that they do not infringe upon the authority of the local government. Concessions in the nature of a general monopoly shall not be granted. This clause shall in no way limit the right of the Mandatory to create monopolies of a purely fiscal character in the interest of the territory of Syria and the Lebanon, and with a view to assuring to the territory the fiscal resources which would appear best adapted to the local needs, or, in certain cases, with a view to developing the natural resources either directly by the State or through an organisation under its control, provided that this does not involve either directly or indirectly the creation of a monopoly of the natural resources in favour of the Mandatory or its nationals, nor involve any preferential treatment which would be incompatible with the economic, commercial and industrial equality guaranteed above.

Art. 12. The Mandatory shall adhere, on behalf of Syria and the Lebanon, to any general international agreement already existing, or which may be concluded hereafter with the approval of the League of Nations, in respect of the following: the slave trade, the traffic in drugs, the traffic in arms and ammunition, commercial equality, freedom of transit and navigation, aerial navigation, postal, telegraphic or wireless communications, and measures for the protection of literature, art or industries.

Art. 13. The Mandatory shall secure the adhesion of Syria and the Lebanon, so far as social, religious and other conditions permit, to such measures of common utility as may be adopted by the League of Nations for preventing and combating disease, including diseases of animals and plants.

Art. 14. The Mandatory shall draw up and put into force within twelve months from this date a law of antiquities in conformity with the following provisions. This law shall ensure equality of treatment in the matter of excavations and archaeological research to the nationals of all States Members of the League Nations.

(1) «Antiquity» means any construction or any product of human activity earlier than the year 1700 A.D.

(2) The law for the protection of antiquities shall proceed by encouragement rather than by threat.

Any person who, having discovered an antiquity without being furnished with the authorisation referred to in paragraph 5, reports the same to an official of the competent Department, shall be rewarded according to the value of the discovery.

(3) No antiquity may be disposed of except to the competent Department, unless this Department renounces the acquisition of any such antiquity.

No antiquity may leave the country without an export license from the said Department.

(4) Any person who maliciously or negligently destroys or damages an antiquity shall be liable to a penalty to be fixed.

(5) No clearing of ground or digging with the object of finding antiquities shall be permitted, under penalty of fine, except to persons authorised by the competent Department.

(6) Equitable terms shall be fixed for expropriation, temporary or permanent, of lands which might be of historical or archaeological interest.

(7) Authorisation to excavate shall only be granted to persons who show suffi-

cient guarantees of archaeological experience. The Mandatory shall not, in granting these authorisations, act in such a way as to exclude scholars of any nation without good grounds.

(8) The proceeds of excavations may be divided between the excavator and the competent Department in a proportion fixed by that Department. If division seems impossible for scientific reasons, the excavator shall receive a fair indemnity in lieu of a part of the find.

Art. 15. Upon the coming into force of the organic law referred to in Article 1, an arrangement shall be made between the Mandatory and the local governments for reimbursement by the latter of all expenses incurred by the Mandatory in organising the administration, developing local resources, and carrying out permanent public works, of which the country retains the benefit. Such arrangement shall be communicated to the Council of the League of Nations.

Art. 16. French and Arabic shall be the official languages of Syria and the Lebanon.

Art. 17. The Mandatory shall make to the Council of the League of Nations an annual report to the satisfaction of the Council as to the measures taken during the year to carry out the provisions of this mandate. Copies of all laws and regulations promulgated during the year shall be attached to the said report.

Art. 18. The consent of the Council of the League of Nations is required for any modification of the terms of this mandate.

Art. 19. On the termination of the mandate, the Council of the League of Nations shall use its influence to safeguard for the future the fulfilment by the Government of Syria and the Lebanon of the financial obligations, including pensions and allowances, regularly assumed by the administration of Syria or of the Lebanon during the period of the mandate.

Art. 20. The Mandatory agrees that if any dispute whatever should arise between the Mandatory and another Member of the League of Nations relating to the interpretation or the application of the provisions of the mandate, such dispute, if it cannot be settled by negotiation, shall be submitted to the Permanent Court of International Justice provided for by Article 14 of the Covenant of the League of Nations.

The present instrument shall be deposited in original in the archives of the League of Nations and certified copies shall be forwarded by the Secretary-General of the League of Nations to all Members of the League.

Done at London on the twenty-fourth of July, 1922.

6

Assertions of National Identity

Although the Mudros armistice of 30 October 1918, stilled the fighting of World War I in the Middle East, peace initially was a time of chaos in the region. Everywhere the Allies were in the ascendancy with their troops occupying extensive territories from Morocco to Afghanistan. North Africa seemed more under the domination of France, Italy, and Spain than ever while, with the exception of Syria which was a French sphere, pro-British administrations were either already in control or in the process of being installed in the eastern Arab states, Turkey and Iran. Even Afghanistan and Central Asia were threatened with a British take-over. It seemed as if the defeated and demoralized bastions of Islam in the Middle East were about to accept the proposition that European civilization had won the final battle in their long history of armed confrontation.

But in May 1919, two events occurred four days apart that were destined to mark not only the revival of resistance in the Middle East to Western hegemony over the region but also the intention of the various peoples of the region to assert their separate national identities. On May 15, 1919—with unofficial Allied blessings—a Greek army landed at Izmir on Turkey's Aegean coast, occupied the city, and began to drive inland. The Greek aim was to annex a large part of the eastern Aegean littoral, Thrace, and, hopefully, even Istanbul itself. This was the so-called "great idea" which, if realized, would have recreated the medieval Greek Byzantine empire. The Turkish people reacted immediately and almost instinctively to the invasion for the Greeks were a former non-Muslim subject nationality and hence looked down upon by most Turks. Demonstrations rocked Turkish cities and guerrillas threw themselves against the advancing Greeks. But the sultan's government in Allied-occupied Istanbul failed to offer either the example of defiance or the practical leadership which the country was calling for to oppose the Greek challenge and this failure sealed the eventual doom of the Ottoman dynasty.

Yet, at that grave time a leader did emerge. On 19 May 1919, the greatest of the Ottoman military heroes of World War I, Mustafa Kemal Pasha, landed at the Black Sea port of Samsun. Ignoring orders to facilitate the demobilization of what was left of Ottoman military power in north-central Anatolia, Mustafa Kemal instead began organizing a political and military resistance to the Allied design to reduce the Ottoman Empire—Turkey—to the status of an impotent, truncated mummy kingdom. By January 1920 numbers of Ottoman military officers and civil servants had joined Kemal, in the Anatolian city of Ankara, the nucleus of a nationalist government and a national army had been formed, and a program emphasizing the need to safeguard Turkey's basic territorial integrity and political independence had been widely publicized. Indeed, for a time, the Kemalists even gained the temporary adherence of the sultan's government to the nationalist program as attested by the Ottoman Parliament's assent in January 1920, to the Turkish National Pact, a manifesto of nationalist aims. At this point the Allied occupation authorities grew alarmed, suppressed the Ottoman Parliament, and arrested all accessible nationalists. In the summer of 1920 this was followed by the imposition of the draconian Treaty of Sèvres on the moribund Ottoman government, which also was induced to denounce the Kemalist regime and sentence its leaders to death *in absentia*.

By summer 1920, the Kemalists were fighting for their lives against the Greeks, the French, the sultan's forces, and the Armenians. Nevertheless, during the winter of 1920-1921 the tide began to turn as most Turks, chagrined by the Treaty of Sèvres, accepted the Kemalists as their last hope to avoid eclipse as a people. Moreover, Kemal profited from a diplomatic falling-out among the Allies who finally realized that Anatolia was not going to fall into their hands like a ripe plum. The war-weary Italians and French evacuated Turkish territory leaving behind large quantities of arms and supplies. Simultaneously, eastern Anatolia was secured as the Kemalist armies crushed the Armenian separatists' forces while the Kemalists and the Soviets arranged a mutually advantageous rapprochement. Still, the formidable, British-backed Greek army remained poised to snuff out Kemalist dreams and in the summer of 1921 it mounted its final grand offensive to eliminate the nationalist army. The decisive battles were fought close to the nationalist capital at Ankara along the Sakarya River where Mustafa Kemal won a great victory.

The final phase of the Turkish War of Independence in the summer and fall of

1922 saw the Greek army, hamstrung by political dissension at home, collapse utterly. In September, the Greeks evacuated Izmir and left the Turks triumphant in western Anatolia. After this, an armistice was arranged with the British who still held the straits area. Complete and final recognition of a Turkish state embodying nationalist, modernizing goals under the leadership of Mustafa Kemal came with the signing of the Lausanne Treaty in July 1923. Already, the previous November, the last Ottoman sultan, Mehmed VI, had fled aboard a British warship and in October the sultanate was abolished.

In Iran, too, a nationalist revival and dynastic overturn occurred between 1919 and 1925. Iran emerged from World War I with vast stretches of the country in the hands of local war lords and British troops. The central Qajar administration was corrupt and so weak that its writ meant little outside Teheran itself. Indeed, the government, in return for a large subsidy, agreed in August 1919 to turn Iran virtually into a British protectorate. Moreover, in the Caspian provinces and in Azerbaijan several communist-aided regimes threatened to detach themselves from allegiance to Teheran or even to march on the capital and turn Iran itself into a Soviet republic. Reaction to this prevailing chaos centered among the reformist intellectuals and in the so-called Persian Cossack Division, a Tsarist creation which by 1920 had expelled its Russian officers, and was under the command of a shrewd Persian soldier imbued with strong patriotism, Reza Khan (1878-1944). By the end of 1920, the Cossack Division had blunted the local communist threat. For their part, the British, because they believed themselves over-committed in the Middle East, decided to concentrate their imperial interests in Iran at the Khuzistan oil fields and the Persian Gulf littoral. It was at that stage that Reza Khan and certain nationalist reformist elements led by Sayyid Zia al-Din Tabataba'i combined their strength and took advantage of the political vacuum in Teheran to engineer a successful coup d'etat on 21 February 1921. The manifestos that accompanied the coup emphasized a preoccupation with achieving national integrity, unity, and a reformed administration. The coup initiated a new activist era in Iran's history—a definite thrust toward reorganizing Iran on a modern, nationalist basis. Reza Khan, as war minister, emerged as the real power in the new regime and Tabataba'i was ousted from the prime ministership within three months of the coup. Between 1921 and 1925, Reza Khan created the modern Iranian army, and used it as a unifying force which ultimately gave Iran its first genuinely centralized government; even the British surrendered political control of the south rather than risk war with Reza Khan's nationalists. So, in one sense, modern Iran, like Prussia, was the creation of its army. Finally, in December 1925, after deposing the last Qajar monarch, Reza Khan took Iran's throne for himself and became Reza Shah, founder of the Pahlavi dynasty.

In both Turkey and Iran, strong nationalist resistance after World War I convinced the imperial powers, especially the British, that the potential rewards for enforcing their will in those countries were not worth the risks of war. In the

Arab world, however, such was not to be the case. Certainly, there were Arab nationalist agitations for full independence after the war. Sundry delegations from Egypt and the Fertile Crescent presented their demands to the Paris Peace Conference in 1919. But these appeals were not coordinated and Arab nationalism was revealed as not one but several separate movements. The frustration of Arab hopes at the peace conference combined with postwar economic and political dislocations provoked serious uprisings in several Arab states between 1919 and 1921, notably in Iraq, Syria, Palestine, and Egypt. In North Africa full-scale rebellions broke out in Libya and in the Rif mountains of Morocco which were repressed only with much bloodshed. Still, if the French and Italians met unrest with severe repression, the British tried to accommodate some of the Arab demands. Thus, in 1922, Britain abdicated supervision of Egypt's internal administration (although retaining the means to assure her strategic interests) by unilaterally declaring Egypt an independent kingdom. Also, she gave a large measure of self-govern- to her Iraq and Transjordan mandates.

In the mid-1920's, the period of nationalist resistance to the World War I peace settlement gave way to a time of groping for the proper formulas upon which a reconstructed political, economic, and social order could be erected in the Middle East. This time of searching was dominated by political concerns such as the strengthening of modernizing leadership and the state apparatus, and extended into the early 1950's. While matters of economic development received some attention, the upper-class elitist leadership that directed the several indigenous political structures of the Middle East during those years paid little practical regard to the question of ensuring social justice for the mass of the population. It was more a time for clarifying goals than achieving them.

The fact that there were several striking similarities in the situations of Turkey and Iran during the 1925-1950 period should not obscure significant differences between the recent history of the two countries. Both Mustafa Kemal (who took the surname, Atatürk, "Father of the Turks," in 1934) and Reza Shah emerged from military backgrounds, forging nationalist and modernizing authoritarian and centralist regimes to ensure that foreign control of their countries, once cast off, could not reassert itself. But Atatürk inherited a country that was far better prepared to accept a modernization program than did Reza Shah. Many of Atatürk's changes were based on plans that had been discussed or even partially effected in some cases before 1914, while Reza Shah's projects were new to Iran. Most important, Atatürk inherited a functioning state apparatus, staffed with educated, dedicated soldiers and civil servants while Reza Shah had to create both a modern army as well as a civil service. Even on the ideological level Turkish nationalism was the active creed of a significant minority of Turks after World War I, while Reza Shah preached the cult of Iranian nationalism from a more limited base. Thus, Reza Shah used the ancient Iranian institution of monarchy—one might say he depended upon history—to support nationalism and to make his innovations more palatable to Iran's people.

In 1923, when Mustafa Kemal was free to turn his attention toward Turkey's internal problems he faced the immediate tasks of reconstructing the country's political apparatus and consolidating the ideal of Turkish nationalism by asserting the modernizing ideology of his revolution. These complex tasks occupied most of Atatürk's time until 1935. His regime was quasi-democratic in that it recognized the principle of popular sovereignty as expressed through a Grand National Assembly selected by a restricted electorate which in turn chose the President of the Republic. In actuality, however, Atatürk was an authoritarian figure whose rule was buttressed by the loyalty of the army, the patriotic devotion of the civil bureaucracy to their national duty, and a political alliance with the non-traditionalist urban and rural elite who monopolized the positions of administrative, economic, and intellectual power in Turkey. Atatürk was convinced that the main obstacle to his goals was the influence wielded by Turkey's elaborately organized Islamic religious establishment which was effective right down to the neighborhood level. Atatürk believed, in common with much upper-class opinion, that the role played by religion in Turkey's modern history had been harmful in that it hindered the country's modernization. Consequently, despite the unifying function that Islamic loyalties had provided during the War for Independence, as soon as the war ended Atatürk moved against religion. First, in 1924, he abolished the office of caliph which, although the sultanate had been abrogated in 1923, was still in the hands of an Ottoman prince, Abdülmejid. This act was followed by the suppression of Islamic religious seminaries and the removal of many of the outward expressions of Muslim piety from at least the urban scene. In the 1930's, economic development and the achieving of the chimerical goal of economic self-sufficiency became a major concern, but World War II intervened before the state injected itself decisively into economic life. Atatürk's death in 1938 signaled the impending loosening of authoritarian controls although during the emergency of World War II Ismet Inönü, Atatürk's successor as president, was able to retain most of his predecessor's powers if not his influence. Between 1945 and 1950, however, a multiparty system emerged within the context of acceptance of the ideal of a modernizing nation state. This process culminated in 1950 when the Democratic Party, in a free election, united commercial and landed elite leadership with lower-class urban and peasant votes to oust the Republicans, Atatürk's party, from office.

Reza Shah, while he retained a rubber stamp Majlis (parliament), ruled with even more of an iron hand than did Atatürk and based his administration on the army given the absence of a well-developed civil service. To build a civil bureaucracy numbers of young Iranians were sent abroad for training but after these intellectuals returned many became bitter against the shah's stern authoritarianism.

Still, the shah's problem was indeed largely a military one, the need to subdue the semi-independent tribes and rural areas so that a real national entity could emerge from Iran's diverse elements. Economic development was encouraged by the shah who invested state funds in projects that included small processing plants but emphasized communications. A national airline, roads, and the Trans-Iranian railway, a spectacular engineering feat that included over 4000 bridges and 200 tunnels, were built to encourage national unification. Reza Shah always had to contend with a strong foreign presence in Iran in the guise of the Anglo-Iranian Oil Company. Finally, his regime apparently failed to achieve its paramount objective given Iran's occupation and his deposition in 1941 by Britain and Russia during World War II. But his essential success was demonstrated during the Azerbaijan crisis of 1946 when Iranian nationalism would not tolerate partition when the Soviets tried to set up a puppet state in the north. Reza Shah's removal from power allowed the Iranians to revive experiments with parliamentary government during the 1940's; moreover, private entrepreneurs enjoyed far more liberty to nurture their economic and political power than previously. Meanwhile, the new ruler, Muhammad Reza Shah tried to assume the role of compromiser among the various factions unleashed by his father's fall. This experiment faltered between 1951 and 1953 when anti-foreign nationalist passions whipped up by Muhammad Mussaddiq (1879-1967) over the issue of control of Iran's oil wealth almost dethroned the shah. Nevertheless, in the decisive moment Iran's army—the creation of the Pahlavi dynasty—stood by their monarch and in so doing inaugurated a new period of royal supremacy and sponsorship of modernization.

Generally, the history of the Arab states from the mid-1920's to the early 1950's was marked by a growing pessimism and a disillusioned retreat from faith in the appropriateness of Western liberal institutions. From Morocco to the Persian Gulf the Arab world was fragmented into more than twenty separate governments, all dominated by European pro-consuls with the exception of independent Saudi Arabia and Yemen, which ironically were among the least modern of the Arab states. In the French and Italian colonies in North Africa the culture of the mother country was propagandized at the expense of local mores. Political assimilation, too, was in vogue as the theory that Algeria was as much a part of France as Provence was popularized. In Egypt and the Fertile Crescent, however, governments under Arab leaders, albeit under various forms of European tutelage, did exist. These governments and the other facets of Arab society, however, were the province of an upper-class political elite. In Syria and Iraq ex-Ottoman Arab civil and military officials were much in evidence while in Egypt members of the landowning and court-connected professional upper class monopolized public and private positions of influence. Nevertheless, in the final analysis, many of these men were sincere nationalists who did press successfully for a gradual relaxation of imperialist restraints. Yet, they adhered to a peculiar upper-class parochially oriented nationalism calculated to preserve the internal political status-quo and virtually ignored the social discontents of the Arab masses. The many local versions of Arab nationalism were reinforced during the 1920-1950 years by the operating of separate political, educational, and military establishments in the various Arab states. Thus, the identity of states such as Syria or Jordan was exaggerated and a vested interest in their continued existence arose among the numerous bureaucrats and others whose livelihoods and prestige depended upon serving the administrative needs of the many Arab sovereignties.

The confrontation between parochial and pan-Arab nationalisms was punctuated by protracted arguments among intellectuals. Thus, in Egypt, Taha Husayn (b. 1889) and others, asserted the existence of a separate Egyptian identity that could be traced to pharaonic times and had more in common with the Mediterranean than the Arab world. An interesting and persistent variation on this theme was encountered in Lebanon, where Phoenician origins were claimed although Lebanon's role as a bridge between the Mediterranean and Arab worlds also was stressed. A leading theoretician of pan-Arab nationalism was Sati' al-Husri (b. 1879), an Arab intellectual who spent many years in Ottoman service and whose theories of Arab nationalism borrowed much from Young Turk ideas. Al-Husri and those of similar bent articulated much of the basic content of today's Arab nationalism in the 1920-30's. They preached that the Arabs constituted one nation united by a common language and culture that stretched from Morocco's Atlantic shores to Oman's coast on the Indian Ocean. They embellished and glorified Arab history and held that Islam was particularly identified with the Arabs. However, other philosophies, too, owed a debt to Islam. This was particularly true of the Muslim Brotherhood, founded in 1929, which mixed anti-foreignism, ultra-Islamic legalism, and sympathy for the plight of the masses with an efficient political organization which pioneered as the first mass doctrinal party in the Arab world. In the 1930's a number of extremist parties appeared, including those inspired by communist and quasi-fascist as well as Arab nationalists' ideals and stimulated by the rise of totalitarianism in Europe. These groups in general were energized in their activities by prevailing opposition to British-French supremacy and to the increasing strength of Zionism in Palestine.

Another major cause for the rise of extremist groups was the continual erosion of confidence in liberal, parliamentary democracy in most of the Arab world. In Egypt, for example, parliament was restored in 1923 together with a legally independent constitutional monarchy. But in practice, parliamentary democracy seemed a farce as upper class politicians used the chamber as a debating society. King Fu'ad (1917-1936) was a royal dictator who skillfully manipulated his government. His corrupt, playboy son, King Faruq (1936-1952) came to symbolize the faults of the monarchy and the constitution to many ashamed Egyptians. Similar so-called parliamentary regimes existed in other Arab countries. By World War II confidence in liberal democracy was failing rapidly because of the inefficiency, corruption, lack of social consciousness and seeming cooperation with imperialism that marked these regimes. Moreover, many pan-Arabists were displeased with the Arab League's establishment in 1945 as a loose confederation of cooperating but fully independent states.

Nevertheless, World War II's end and the consequent weakening of the European imperial powers initiated a process which brought the gradual collapse of the apparatus of Western imperialism in the Middle East. In the eastern Arab world the mandate system was abandoned in the 1940's while the preferential treaties which still bound states such as Iraq and Egypt to Britain were casualties of the 1950's. In the western Arab world the rise of nationalism in Tunisia, Morocco, and Algeria reached its culmination in the early 1950's with the outbreak of armed insurrection against continued French supremacy. The growth of nationalism in North Africa was the result of an amalgamation of Islamic-inspired groups reacting against French down-grading of Muslim culture with young intellectuals, largely French educated, who were infected by the virus of nationalism during their student days. Tunisia, since the mid-19th century a center of reformist thought, was the first of the Maghrib states to express a nationalist consciousness just prior to World War I. The moderate nationalist Dustur (Constitution) Party was formed after World War I and served as the organizational springboard for Habib Bourguiba's (b. 1903) Neo-Dustur movement which appeared in 1934. By 1946 Tunisian nationalists amalgamated into a coalition under Bourguiba's leadership which, after encountering French intransigence, finally succeeded in securing Tunisia's full freedom in 1955. In Morocco, nationalism became an organized movement in the 1920's, amalgamated into a "national front" in 1937, and a decade later received the full backing of the ruler, Muhammad V (1927-1961), who subsequently assumed leadership of the nationalist movement and, after a period of exile, presided over its triumph in 1955. Algerian nationalism had to contend with the counter-nationalism of the French settlers, a confrontation which instigated the costly, bloody Algerian War of 1954-1962 but, again, ended with a victory for local nationalism.

Arab nationalism was not successful in its contest with another European-born nationalism, however, as Zionism consolidated its claim to Palestine and forged the independent state of Israel in 1948. During the 1930's Zionism's impetus (as well as Arab antipathy against it) was intensified when its leaders as well as many Zionist sympathizers in Europe and America reacted to the horrors of Nazi persecutions of the European Jewish communities by intensifying their efforts to facilitate Jewish settlement in Palestine. The British holders of the Palestine mandate tried to moderate the growing bitterness that characterized Jewish-Arab relations in Palestine by stabilizing the country's population at a ratio that would have left the Arabs in the majority. However, Arab opinion was not happy with the mechanics of the British scheme while Zionists rejected it altogether with a call for unrestricted Jewish emigration. After World War II, open fighting broke out between Palestine's Arab and Jewish communities with the exhausted British being unable to either halt or mediate the civil war. After a United Nations mediation attempt calling for partition failed, the British announced they were surrendering the mandate and evacuating Palestine on 15 May 1948. On that date the Zionist leadership declared the State of Israel and massive fighting involving the armies of the surrounding Arab states broke out. The 1948 Arab-Israeli War resulted in a hard-fought Israeli victory but continued border trouble, punctuated by two more outbreaks of open war in 1956 and 1967, has since marked Arab-Israeli relations. Besides its security problems, internal Israeli politics have concentrated upon questions of economic development and integration of Israel's disparate population into a homogeneous nationality. For the Arabs, too, the presence of an Israeli nation in their midst stimulated nationalism by engendering much soul-searching and encouraging efforts to revolutionize and thereby modernize and strengthen Arab society.

37

The Assertion of Turkish Independence and National Integrity, from the Organization of a Nationalist Regime to the Turkish National Pact, 1 June 1919– 28 January 1920 *

No sooner had Mustafa Kemal landed in Samsun on 19 May 1919, to become Inspector General of the Ottoman Third Army in Anatolia than he moved to rally Turkish nationalist sentiment into a force capable of resisting Allied and Greek imperial ambitions. Quickly he amalgamated the scattered "Societies for the Defense of Rights," Turkish nationalist resistance groups, into a nationalist political apparatus, and began to reorganize demoralized Otto-

---

* a. "Circular telegram of Mustafa Kemal Pasha, 21 June 1919," Kemal Atatürk, *Nutuk* (Ankara: Ministry of Education, 1950), Vol. I, 30-31; translated into English as *A Speech Delivered by Ghazi Mustapha Kemal, President of the Turkish Republic,* October 1927 (Leipzig: K. F. Koehler, 1929), 31.

b. "The Turkish National Pact," translated in Arnold J. Toynbee, *The Western Question in Greece and Turkey* (London: Constable, 1922), 209-210; also found in J. C. Hurewitz *Diplomacy in the Near and Middle East* (Princeton: D. Van Nostrand, 1956), Vol. II, 74-75.

man military units into a nationalist army. Not the least of his accomplishments was his articulation of Turkish fears and goals into an easily understood, practical program of action which he circulated widely in coded telegraph messages. Late in June 1919, only a month after his Samsun landing, he summoned a congress which met late in July and converted itself into a proto-nationalist government. The Kemalists convened first at Erzerum in July and August, Sivas in September, and finally settled in Ankara, the seat of an arsenal and the head of a rail-link to Istanbul, late in 1919. All these inland cities were relatively secure from direct foreign intimidation. Meanwhile, a gauge of the strength of nationalist sentiment was provided by the nationwide Ottoman parliamentary elections held in December 1919, which returned a majority of Kemalist supporters. After assembling, Parliament approved a summary of nationalist aims, the so-called Turkish National Pact of January 1920, which signaled to the world the nature and strength of Turkey's renewed resolve.

A. MUSTAFA KEMAL'S CIRCULAR TELEGRAM CALLING FOR THE CREATION OF A TURKISH NATIONALIST GOVERNMENT, 21 JUNE 1919

1. The integrity of the country; the independence of the nation being in imminent jeopardy.
2. The Central Ottoman Government is unequal to the task for which it has assumed responsibility; the consequence being that our nation is not considered at all.
3. The energy and the will of the nation alone can save its independence.
4. It is absolutely necessary that a National Assembly shall be formed to protect the country from foreign influence and be independent of all control, so that it will be free to examine the position of the nation and assert its rights before the whole world.
5. It has been decided to convene a national congress forthwith at Sivas, which from every point of view is the safest place in Anatolia for that purpose.
6. Every district in all the vilayets provinces must, therefore, immediately send those delegates each who possess the confidence of the nation, and they must start without delay, so that they may arrive as soon as possible.
7. To avoid any danger, this must be kept a national secret and the delegates must travel incognito through all the districts, if it should be considered necessary to do so.
8. On the 10th July a congress of the Eastern Provinces will meet at Erzerum. If the delegates from the other provinces can reach Sivas in time, the members of the congress at Erzerum will also start for Sivas in order that they may be present at the general meeting.

B. THE TURKISH NATIONAL PACT, 28 JANUARY 1920

The Members of the Ottoman Chamber of Deputies recognise and affirm that the independence of the State and the future of the Nation can be assured by complete respect for the following principles, which represent the maximum of sacrifice which can be undertaken in order to achieve a just and lasting peace, and that the continued existence of a stable Ottoman Sultanate and society is impossible outside of the said principles:

ART. 1. Inasmuch as it is necessary that the destinies of the portions of the Turkish Empire which are populated exclusively by an Arab majority, and which on the conclusion of the armistice of the 30th October 1918 were in the occupation of enemy forces, should be determined in accordance with the votes which shall be freely given by the inhabitants, the whole of those parts whether within or outside the said armistice line which are inhabited by an Ottoman Moslem majority, united in religion, in race and in aim, imbued with sentiments of mutual respect for each other and of sacrifice, and wholly respectful of each other's racial and social rights and surrounding conditions, form a whole which does not admit of division for any reason in truth or in ordinance.

ART. 2. We accept that, in the case of the three [Kurdish] Sandjaks which united themselves by a general vote to the mother country when they first were free, recourse should again be had, if necssary, to a free popular vote.

ART. 3. The determination of the juridical status of Western Thrace also, which has been made dependent on the Turkish peace, must be effected in accordance with the votes which shall be given by the inhabitants in complete freedom.

ART. 4. The security of the city of Constantinople, which is the seat of the Caliphate of Islam, the capital of the Sultanate, and the headquarters of the Ottoman Government, and of the Sea of Marmora must be protected from every danger. Provided this principle is maintained, whatever decision may be arrived at jointly by us and all other Governments concerned, regarding the opening of the Bosphorus to the commerce and traffic of the world, is valid.

ART. 5. The rights of minorities as defined in the treaties concluded between the Entente Powers and their enemies and certain of their associates shall be confirmed and assured by us—in reliance on the belief that the Moslem minorities in neighbouring countries also will have the benefit of the same rights.

ART. 6. It is a fundamental condition of our life and continued existence that we, like every country, should enjoy complete independence and liberty in the matter of assuring the means of our development, in order that our national and economic development should be rendered possible and that it should be possible to conduct affairs in the form of a more up-to-date regular administration.

For this reason we are opposed to restrictions inimical to our development in political, judicial, financial, and other matters.

The conditions of settlement of our proved debts shall likewise not be contrary to these principles.

38

The Assertion of Iranian Independence and National Integrity, Reza Khan's Proclamation Announcing the Coup d'Etat, 21 February 1921 *

The coup d'etat of February 1921, was the culmination of efforts to prevent the main implication of the Anglo-Iranian treaty of 1919—British supremacy in Iran—from being realized. Also it was a milestone in the rise of Reza Khan (later Reza Shah) to supreme power in Iran. The proclamation, which was issued after the coup's success was assured, is very interesting in that it summarized the dual preoccupations with ensuring national unity and with creating a reformed political order that have characterized Iranian nationalism. Also, it illustrates the disgust expressed in Iranian learned circles at the corruption and inefficiency of the Qajar administration. Too, the proclamation indicates Reza Khan's reliance upon the military, a hallmark of his twenty-year period of supremacy in Iran. Although the liberal reformist hopes expressed in the document undoubtedly reflected the influence of Zia al-Din Tabataba'i, Reza Khan's chief collaborator in the coup and the nationalist regime's first prime minister, the fact that the puscht was backed by the Persian Cossack Division—which under Reza Khan's aegis was to become the nucleus of a new national Iranian army—must have provided much of the manifesto's real impact. The nationalists' first act upon achieving power was to denounce the Anglo-Persian treaty of 1919, which had never been ratified, and to conclude a treaty of friendship with the Soviets, who, in order to strike a blow against the British by encouraging a nationalist Iranian government, agreed to cease supporting the various communist-inspired regimes operating in the northern provinces and to cancel all Tsarist concessions and debt obligations binding upon Iran.

*   *   *

'Compatriots, the sacred duties of sacrifice for our King and Country in the bloody, death-laden fields made by a larger and better equipped enemy force to

* Translated in Peter Avery, *Modern Iran* (New York: Frederick A. Praeger, 1965), 229-231.

invade Iran and threaten its capital—these sacred duties were heartily and coura-geously accepted by the brave men of the Cossack Force. For this was the only force properly organised in Iran to be capable of undertaking the defense of the country and it was the men of this force who, lacking clothes, lacking boots, lacking food, lacking adequate arms, made their chests and faces shields against the shot-scattering canon, and stood testimony to the glory and honour of Iran, driving the invader from the gates of Qazvin to the shores of the sea.

'Had the sacrifices and service, rendered without regard to life, of the Cossack Army not attained the desired result and had we been unable to save the sacred soil of our land and the violated dignity of Gilani brothers from the hand of the foe, it would have been through no fault of ours. No, had our efforts been barren it would have been due to the treachery of the officers and of those people who entrusted the direction of our business to them. Yet we may boast with pride that the effusion of Cossack blood was able to save our country's capital from enemy capture. Had the foreign traitors been able to nullify the sacrifices of Iran's sons it would have been due to this, that our own traitors among us had become playthings in their hands and panderers to their, and others', whims. At the time of our retreat from the Gilan marshes under fire from the enemy's guns, we felt that the source and origin of all Iran's misfortunes was the vileness of that army of our own traitors. At the time when we were shedding our blood before the invading host, by the honour of that same pure and holy blood did we swear that on the first available opportunity we would shed our blood to uproot these selfish, pampered traitors and release the people of Iran from the coils of the magic spell cast over them by a handful of thieves.

'God's will and the royal desire found that this opportunity was ready for us and so it is that we are here in Tehran. We have not seized Tehran, for it would be impossible for us to raise our arms in the place honoured by the presence of our blessed Prince and Sovereign. We have only come to Tehran, and we have done this to cleanse and purify our capital to be fit to become the seat of a true guardianship of the realm and the centre of government; government that shall devote itself only to Iran; government that shall be not simply the spectator of the nation's misfortunes and humiliation; government that shall consider among the first blessings of the country the glorification and expansion of the army; that shall know the army's strength and well-being to be the country's sole means of salvation. Government that shall not make the treasury of Muslims the means of satisfying the lusts of idle, pampered parasites without honour. Government that shall not make the splendid abode of Muslim people the centre of infamy and the base for tyranny and tight-fisted extortion. Government under whose jurisdiction thousands of the country's children shall not die of hunger and misery. Government that will permit no difference to appear between the protection of the honour and chastity of a Gilani, Tabrizi, or Kirmani and the protection of its own sisters and mothers. Government that will not add to the nation's wretchedness for the sake of embellishing and glorifying a limited few. Government that shall never be the tool of foreign politicians.

'We are soldiers and ready to make the supreme sacrifice. We are prepared to shed our blood to realise these aspirations. Our only desire is the strength and glory of the Army for the safe-keeping of our sacred King and Country. The moment such a government has been formed and the means of ensuring the nation's honour, freedom, repose, and progress have become manifest and the nation is no longer treated as a flock of muted sheep, that is the moment when we shall be able to look to the future with confidence. As we have shown, we shall fulfil the duty of defending the country—with all our military brethren in the Gendarmerie and Police Battalions who have also with sad hearts shared in the sacrifices of the Cossack Division and possess the utmost sincerity of purpose—and we shall not permit those hostile to the army's happy development to sow division among us. We are all loyal to the Shah, ready to lay down our lives: all sons of Iran, servants of the realm. Long live the Shah of Iran. Long may the Iranian Nation endure. Long may the Army and the Brave Cossacks of Iran be strong and glorious. Head of the Imperial Royal Cossack Division and Commander-in-Chief, Reza.'

39

The Assertion of Egyptian Independence, the Program of the Egyptian Wafd, 1919 *

The Egyptian Wafd (delegation) began as a coalition of nationalist leaders, men who were committed to a parochial-Egyptian rather than a pan-Arab concept of nationalism. The delegation was formed in order to press the Egyptian nationalist case at the Paris Peace Conference and to negotiate with Britain about the issue of Egyptian independence after World War I. Originally, the British were cool to the Wafd and actively hindered its operation but the outbreak of serious riots in Egypt in 1919 changed their mind. The riots were caused by a mixture of social and economic discontents stimulated by wartime dislocation of Egyptian life as well as by nationalist agitation for an end to the British protectorate. Actually, the Wafd split soon after its formation. A conservative group entered into serious talks with the British which eventually led in 1922 to Britain's renunciation of their protectorate and the declaration of an 'in-

* Translated in Muhammad Khalil, *The Arab States and the Arab League* (Beirut: Khayats, 1962), Vol. I, 659-661.

dependent' kingdom of Egypt. The more radical group under Sa'd Zaghlul (1860-1927) formed a broad-based nationalist party which retained the same 'Wafd' and was destined to remain far and away the most powerful political party in Egypt (at least in the numerical sense) until the 1952 revolution. When the constitution of the kingdom of Egypt was promulgated by King Fu'ad in 1923, the Wafd formed the majority in parliament and Zaghlul became prime minister. He was forced out of office, however, by the combined maneuverings of the British, who were unwilling to tolerate Zaghlul's ultra-nationalist stance on issues such as the Sudan or the stationing of British troops in Egypt, and the king, who jealously guarded his royal prerogatives and did not want to contribute to the rise of a potential rival focus of political power.

*   *   *

(1) A delegation by the name of "The Egyptian Wafd"...has been formed (and composed) of Messrs. Sa'd Zaghlul Pasha, 'Ali Sha'rawy Pasha, 'Abd al-'Aziz Fahmi Bey, Muhammad 'Ali Bey, 'Abd al-Latif al-Mikbaty Bey, Muhammad Mahmud Pasha, Ahmad Lutfi as-Sayyid Bey, Isma'il Sidqy Pasha, Sinwat Hanna Bey, Hamad Pasha al-Basil, George Khayyat Bey, Mahmud Abu an-Nasr Bey, Mustafa an-Nahhas Bey, and Dr. Hafiz 'Afify Bey.

(2) The task of this delegation: to seek, by legitimate, peaceful means, wherever (the delegation) may find it possible to seek—the complete independence of Egypt.

(3) The Egyptian Wafd derives its strength from the wishes of the inhabitants of Egypt, expressed by them directly or through their delegates at the parliamentary bodies.

(4) This Wafd shall last so long as the work for which it has been commissioned shall last, and it shall end whenever (that work) shall end.

(5) The Wafd may not act improperly in respect of the task for which it has been commissioned. For neither the Wafd nor any one of its members may, in their demands, go beyond the limits of the mandate from which they derive their strength; this is: the complete independence of Egypt, together with (all) the concomitant details.

(6) Each member of the Wafd shall swear that he will carry out his task for the purpose for which he has been commissioned, that he will collaborate in the work, and that he will not divulge the secrets of the Wafd.

(7) Should anything happen which may make the withdrawal of one of the members necessary, this (withdrawal) shall be (effected) by a decision of at least three-quarters of the (members of the) Wafd. A member may resign at any time he wants, without having the right to claim back the sums he had already paid.

(8) The Wafd may co-opt other members, provided that, in selecting them, it pays due regard to the advantage which may result from their participation with it in the work.

(9) The Wafd may travel to any destination if it considers that travelling to that (destination) is of benefit to the Egyptian cause. It may delegate some of its members to travel to any destination whenever it finds that this is useful.

(10) Decisions shall be issued by a majority of votes. In case of the equality of (these votes) the opinion of the party having the president on its side shall prevail.

(11) The Wafd shall designate a president, a secretary and a treasurer. Each of these may have an assistant from among the members.

(12) The Wafd may appoint, from among its members, anyone it may consider (fit) to carry out certain functions. It may (also) appoint committees and fix the number of their members and their competences.

(13) The President shall represent the Wafd and shall preside over its meetings, as well as maintain its order and supervise the activities of the committees, over those (of) members holding posts (in the Wafd), and over the work of the Secretariat and the Treasurer.

(14) The Secretary shall assume the clerical work of the Wafd, and shall be entrusted with the archives, minutes, books and other papers of the Wafd, other than those relating to accounts papers.

(15) The Treasurer shall keep the funds collected in the name of the general expenses of the Wafd, either with him or at the bank to be designated by the Wafd. It shall (also) supervise the accounting work, and shall be responsible for all dealings with the funds of the Wafd.

(16) The Wafd shall be considered to be in a state of continuous session. Its regular meetings shall be held upon the invitation of the president. When necessary, it may adopt any urgent decisions which it may consider (fit); in this case it shall submit these to the first regular session in order to have them included in the minutes.

(17) The minutes of meetings shall include, in addition to the summary, all deliberations and decisions. Notes shall also be made of every important discussion related to the task of the Wafd.

(18) The minutes shall be approved at the next meeting, and shall be signed after their approval by the president and the secretary.

(19) The Secretary shall adopt, in addition to the minutes, a register in which he shall daily note down (all) important events, journeys and activities. This register shall be approved daily by the president.

(20) No member of the Wafd may hold discussions with any public persons in the name of the Wafd except when he has (beforehand) submitted to the president the question over which the discussion will take place. Following the end of the discussion he shall put down the discussion in writing and (then) submit it to the president. Should the member not be able to acquaint the president with the discussion before it (takes place), he should explain to the person with whom he is having such discussion that he is not speaking for the Wafd in his discussion.

(21) Every member shall meet his own expenses for travel or accommodation. He may not ask save for the expenses he may have incurred in connection with matters related to the task of the Wafd.

(22) No (amount) may be expended out of the funds of the Wafd save by a decision of the Wafd. Expenditure vouchers shall be signed by the President and the Treasurer. The Wafd shall allocate a sum in the nature of a permanent loan to be spent on urgent matters, provided that the Wafd should approve all expenditure following the exhaustion of the amount of the loan and (also) ask for the allocation of another (amount).

(23) The Wafd may be accompanied by paid employees in order to help in administrative or clerical matters; these (employees) shall, by the nature of their work, be under the supervision of the Secretary or Treasurer, all being under the management of the President. The employees shall swear that they will not divulge (any) secret coming to their knowledge by virtue of their offices.

(24) The funds of the Wafd shall consist of the proceeds of donations paid by its members or by others who want to help in the work of the Wafd.

(25) The remainder of the funds of the Wafd following the completion of its task shall be spent on one of the public Egyptian affairs in accordance with the decision of the Wafd at the time.

(26) The Wafd shall appoint a committee to be called the Central Committee of the Egyptian Wafd. Its members shall be chosen from among the prominent and patriotic personages; its task shall be the collection of contributions in the name of the Wafd, as well as the sending of these (contributions) to it and the conduct of correspondence with the Wafd concerning matters relating to its task.

40

Assertions of Arab Nationalism, Resolutions of the General Syrian Congress, 2 July 1919*

At the end of World War I the Arab nationalists who had participated in the Arab Revolt under the titular leadership of Amir Faysal occupied most of present day Jordan and inland Syria including Damascus. The nationalists proceeded to organize a government and eventually declared Faysal 'King of Syria.' Nevertheless, as early as the spring of 1919 the Syrians learned of

* Translation in, Nuri as-Sa'id, *Arab Independence and Unity* (Baghdad: Government Press, 1943), 73-74.

the project to place Syria under a French mandate and raised vehement objections to the prospect. These received an articulated form in the resolutions of a General Syrian Congress which included representatives from Palestine, Lebanon, and Syria. The resolutions, which were passed on to the American King-Crane Commission which was investigating the situation in Syria at the time, called for the creation of a greater Syrian state and were willing to allow some sort of loose American mandate that would be restricted to channeling technical assistance into the country. The French claims were categorically rejected as were Zionist claims to a separate Jewish commonwealth in Palestine. Nevertheless, the French mandate was imposed and in 1920 the French military expelled Faysal's government from Syria by force, the beginning of a two-decade-long period of troubled French ascendancy in the Levant.

*   *   *

(Damascus, *July* 2, 1919)

We, the undersigned, members of the General Syrian Congress assembled in Damascus on the 2nd of July, 1919, and composed of delegations from the three zones, namely the southern, eastern and western, and furnished with credentials duly authorising us to represent the Moslem, Christian and Jewish inhabitants of our respective districts, have resolved to submit the following as defining the aspirations of the people who have chosen us to place them before the American Section of the Inter-Allied Commission. With the exception of the fifth clause, which was passed by a large majority, the Resolutions which follow were all adopted unanimously:—

(1) We desire full and absolute political independence for Syria within the following boundaries: on the north, the Taurus Range; on the south, a line running from Rafah to al-Jauf and following the Syria-Hejaz border below 'Aqaba; on the east, the boundary formed by the Euphrates and Khabur rivers and a line stretching from some distance cast of Abu-Kamal to some distance east of al-Jauf; on the west, the Mediterranean Sea.

(2) We desire the Government of Syria to be a constitutional monarchy based on principles of democratic and broadly decentralised rule which shall safeguard the rights of minorities, and we wish that the Amir Faisal who has striven so nobly for our liberation and enjoyed our full confidence and trust be our King.

(3) In view of the fact that the Arab inhabitants of Syria are not less fitted or gifted than were certain other nations (such as the Bulgarians, Serbs, Greeks and Rumanians) when granted independence, we protest against Article XXII of the Covenant of the League of Nations which relegates us to the standing of insufficiently developed races requiring the tutelage of a mandatory power.

(4) If, for whatever reason that might remain undisclosed to us, the Peace Conference were to ignore this legitimate protest, we shall regard the mandate mentioned in the Covenant of the League of Nations as implying to [no] more than

the rendering of assistance in the technical and economic fields without impairment of our absolute independence. We rely on President Wilson's declarations that his object in entering the War was to put an end to acquisitive designs for imperialistic purposes. In our desire that our country should not be made a field for colonisation, and in the belief that the American nation is devoid of colonial ambitions and has no political designs on our country, we resolve to seek assistance in the technical and economic fields from the United States of America on the understanding that the duration of such assistance shall not exceed twenty years.

(5) In the event of the United States finding herself unable to accede to our request for assistance, we would seek it from Great Britain, provided always that it will not be allowed to impair the unity and absolute independence of our country and that its duration should not exceed the period mentioned in the preceding clause.

(6) We do not recognise to the French Government any right to any part of Syria, and we reject all proposals that France should give us assistance or exercise authority in any portion of the country.

(7) We reject the claims of the Zionists for the establishment of a Jewish commonwealth in that part of southern Syria which is known as Palestine, and we are opposed to Jewish immigration into any part of the country. We do not acknowledge that they have a title, and we regard their claims as a grave menace to our national, political and economic life. Our Jewish fellow-citizens shall continue to enjoy the rights and to bear the responsibilities which are ours in common.

(8) We desire that there should be no dismemberment of Syria and no separation of Palestine or the coastal region in the west or the Lebanon from the mother country; and we ask that the unity of the country be maintained under any circumstances.

(9) We desire that Iraq should enjoy complete independence, and that no economic barriers be placed between the two countries.

(10) The basic principles proclaimed by President Wilson in condemnation of secret treaties cause us to enter an emphatic protest against any agreement providing for the dismemberment of Syria and against any undertaking envisaging the recognition of Zionism in southern Syria; and we ask for the explicit annulment of all such agreements and undertakings.

The lofty principles proclaimed by President Wilson encourage us to believe that the determining consideration in the settlement of our own future will be the real desires of our people; and that we may look to President Wilson and the liberal American nation, who are known for their sincere and generous sympathy with the aspirations of weak nations, for help in the fulfilment of our hopes.

We also fully believe that the Peace Conference will recognise that we would not have risen against Turkish rule under which we enjoyed civic and political privileges, as well as rights of representation, had it not been that the Turks denied us our right to a national existence. We believe that the Peace Conference will meet our desires in full, if only to ensure that our political privileges may not be less, after the sacrifices of life which we have made in the cause of our freedom, than they were before the War.

We desire to be allowed to send a delegation to represent us at the Peace Conference, advocate our claims and secure the fulfilment of our aspirations.

41

Organizing the Turkish National State, the Abolition of the Ottoman Caliphate, 3 March 1924 *

In October 1923, Mustafa Kemal gained the final reluctant assent of the Grand National Assembly to the abolition of the office of sultan and their subsequent approval of the proclamation of a republic with himself as president. Moreover, the capital was shifted from Istanbul, filled as it was with shades and physical reminders of an imperial, Islamic heritage, to Ankara deep in the Turkish heartland, a symbol of the new Turkey that was to be built. Nevertheless, although the office of sultan was dead, the office of caliph, supposedly a religious but not a political dignity, had been retained, occupied by the scholarly Ottoman prince, Abdülmejid (Abdülmecid, 1923-1924). Increasingly, Mustafa Kemal viewed the caliphate as a focus around which traditionalists and others opposed to his goals were rallying. Indeed, many Turks did view Abdülmejid rather than Kemal as the legitimate head of state as well as the head of Islam. Finally, in March 1924, the Kemalists acted and received the Assembly's assent to the suppression of the caliphate and the banishment of the Ottoman royal house. Abdülmejid was then placed aboard the Orient Express for the ride westward. The abolition of the caliphate had repercussions throughout the Islamic world and served to emphasize that the old age was indeed gone and irrecoverable; it strengthened the thrust of those who were building modern nation states throughout the Middle East.

* Kemal Atatürk, *Nutuk* (Ankara: Ministry of Education, 1950), Vol. II, 846-851; translated into English as, *A Speech Delivered by Ghazi Mustapha Kemal, President of the Turkish Republic, October 1927* (Leipzig: K. F. Koehler, 1929), 681-686.

During my stay [in Izmir] I believed that the moment for the abolition of the Caliphate had arrived. I will try to follow the course of this affair as it actually happened.

On the 22ⁿᵈ January, 1924, I received from Ismet Pasha, President of the Council of Ministers, a telegram in cipher which I will read to you in full:

Telegram in cipher.
To His Excellency the President of the Turkish Republic.

The First Secretary of the Caliph sends me the following: For some time there have been articles in the newspapers concerning the situation of the Caliphate and the person of the Caliph, which give rise to misunderstandings. The Caliph is very much afflicted about the articles which seem to lower his authority without reason, and particularly the fact that the leaders of the Government coming from time to time to Stanbul, as well as the official corporations, avoid him. The Caliph had thought of making his feelings and wishes on this question known either by sending a Chamberlain to Angora or by requesting that a trustworthy person should be sent to him, but he declares that he has abandoned this idea, because he was afraid that this step might be misinterpreted.

The General Secretary writes at length about the question of allocations, and asks that the question should be examined and the necessary steps taken in this matter according to the communications of the Government of the 15ᵗʰ April, 1923, which stated that the Ministry of Finance would help if the expenses were beyond the means of the Treasury of the Caliphate or outside the obligations of the Caliphate. The question will be discussed in the Council of Ministers. I shall have the honour of informing Your Excellency of the result of the discussion.

(Signed) Ismet.

In reply to this telegram, being myself by the side of the instrument, I sent the following reply to Ismet Pasha:

At the instrument. Smyrna.
To His Excellency Ismet Pasha, President of the Council of Ministers, Angora.
Reply to the telegram in cipher of 22ⁿᵈ January, 1924.

It is to the attitude and manner of acting of the Caliph himself that the origin of the misunderstandings and the unfavourable interpretations regarding the Caliphate and the person of the Caliph must be attributed. In his private life and especially in his public appearances the Caliph seems to follow the system of the Sultans, his ancestors. As a proof: the Friday ceremonies, the relations of the Caliph to foreign representatives to whom he sends officials; his drivings out in great pomp; his private life in the Palace where he goes even so far as to receive dismissed officers to whose complaints he is listening, mixing his own tears with theirs. When the Caliph considers his situation, placing himself face to face with the Turkish Republic and the Turkish people, he must adopt as a measure of comparison the situation of the Caliphate and the Caliph towards the British Kingdom and the Mohamedan population of India, of the Government of Afghanistan and the people of Afghanistan. The Caliph himself and the whole world must know in a categoric manner that the Caliph and the office of the Caliph as they are now maintained and exist, have in reality neither a material nor a political meaning or any right of existence. The Turkish Republic cannot allow itself to be influenced by fallacies and cannot expose its independence and existence to danger.

To complete the analysis, the dignity of the Caliphate can have no other importance for us than that of an historical memory. The demand of the Caliph that the dignitaries of the Turkish Republic and the official corporations should enter into connection with him constitutes a flagrant violation of the independence of the Republic. The fact that he wants to send his First Chamberlain to Angora or his demand to inform the Government of his feelings and his wishes through a trustworthy person sent to him, shows likewise that he is taking up a position antagonistic to the Government of the Republic. He has no competency for doing this. It is also suggested that he should commission his First Secretary to act as mediator in the correspondence between him and the Government of the Republic. The First Secretary must be told that he must abstain from such impudence. Allocations inferior to those of the President of the Turkish Republic must suffice to secure the means of subsistence of the Caliph. Luxury and pomp are out of place. The question is only to secure a decent living for the Caliph. I do not understand what is meant by the "treasure of the Caliphate." The Caliphate has no treasure, and ought not to have any. If this should be an inheritance of his ancestors, I request you to make inquiries and to give me official and clear information about this question. What are the obligations which the Caliph cannot fulfil with the allocations he receives, and what promises and declarations have been made to him through the communication of the Government dated the 15th April? I ask you to inform me of this. A duty which the Government ought to have fulfilled hitherto is to specify and fix the place of residence of the Caliph. There are a great number of palaces in Constantinople which have been built with the money raised from the bread of the people, and the furniture and valuable objects they contain; in short, all is given over to destruction, because the Government has not exactly defined the situation. Rumours are spread to the effect that persons who are attached to the Caliph are selling here and there at Pera the most precious objects of the palaces. The Government must take the treasures which still remain under its guard. If there is a reason for selling anything it is for the Government to do so. It is necessary to submit the administrative functions of the Caliphate to a serious examination and reorganisation, for the fact that there are "First Chamberlains" and "First Secretaries" always sustains the dream of power in the mind of the Caliph.

If the French to-day, a hundred years after the Revolution, are still of the opinion that it would be dangerous for their independence and sovereignty to allow members of the royal family and their confidants to come to France, we, on our part, in the attitude which we have to adopt in view of a dynasty and its confidants who are eager to see on the horizon the sun of absolute power rise again, cannot sacrifice the Republic for considerations of courtesy and sophism. The Caliph must be told exactly who he is and what his office represents and must content himself with this situation. I ask you to proceed in such a manner that the Government takes fundamental and serious steps and to inform me of this.

(Signed) Ghazi Mustapha Kemal,
President of the Turkish Republic.

After this exchange of correspondence Ismet Pasha and Kiasim Pasha, Minister of War, arrived at Smyrna for the "Kriegspiel." Fewsi Pasha, Chief of the General Staff, was already there. We agreed about the necessity of suppressing the Caliphate. We had decided at the same time to suppress also the Ministry for Religious Affairs and the "Evkaf" * and to unify public instruction.

On the 1st March, 1924, I had to open the Assembly.

We had returned to Angora on the 23rd February. I informed the competent authorities of my resolutions.

The discussion about the Budget began in the Assembly. This afforded us an opportunity of occupying ourselves for a short time with the question of the allocations to the members of the dynasty and the Budget of the Ministry for Religious Affairs and the Evkaf. My comrades began to make remarks and criticisms aiming at attaining the proposed aid. The debate was intentionally prolonged. In the speech which I delivered on the 1st March, the fifth anniversary of the opening of the Assembly, I especially emphasised the three following points:

1. The nation demands that now, in the future, for ever and unconditionally the Republic shall be protected from every attack. The wish of the nation can be expressed through the fact that the Republic will be founded a moment earlier and completely on the whole of the positive principles which have been put to the test.

2. We declare that it is necessary without loss of time to apply the principle of unity of instruction and education which has been decided by the vote of the nation.

3. We also recognise that it is indispensable in order to secure the revival of the Islamic Faith, to disengage it from the condition of being a political instrument, which it has been for centuries through habit.

The group of the Party was invited to a sitting on the 2nd March. The three

---

* Religious institutions which represented a considerable value.

points I have just mentioned were brought forward and discussed. We were united in principle. Amongst other matters received, the following motions were read on the 3rd March during the first sitting of the Assembly:

1. Draft of the law of Sheikh Safvet Effendi and fifty of his colleagues concerning the abolition of the Caliphate and the expulsion of the Ottoman dynasty from Turkish territory.

2. Draft of the law of Halil Hulki Effendi, deputy for Seerd, and fifty of his colleagues concerning the suppression of the Ministry for Religious Affairs, of the Evkaf and the Ministry of the General Staff.

3. Motion of Vassif Bey, deputy for Saruchan, and fifty of his colleagues concerning the unification of instruction.

Fethi Bey, who presided, announced: "Gentlemen, there are proposals with numerous signatures, demanding immediate discussion of these questions of law. I put this demand to the vote."

Without referring it to commissions Fethi Bey immediately put the motions to the vote, and they were accepted.

The first objection was raised by Halid Bey, deputy for Kastamuni. One or two joined him in the course of the discussion. Numerous important speakers ascended the platform and gave long explanations in favour of the propositions. Besides the signatories of the motions the late Sejid Bey and Ismet Pasha made convincing speeches which were of a highly scientific nature and which will always be worthy of being studied and borne in mind. The discussion lasted for nearly five hours. When the discussion closed at 6.45 p.m. the Grand National Assembly had promulgated the Laws No. 429, 430 and 431.

In virtue of these laws the "Grand National Assembly of Turkey and the Government formed by it is authorised to give legal form to the stipulations which are in force in the Turkish Republic with reference to public affairs and to carry through their application. The Ministry for Religious Affairs and the Evkaf have been suppressed."

All scientific and educational institutions in Turkish territory ..., all ecclesiastical schools, are transferred to the Ministry of Public Instruction.

The Caliph is declared deposed and the dignity abolished. All members of the deposed Ottoman dynasty are for ever forbidden to reside within the frontiers of the territory of the Turkish Republic.

Certain persons who wrongly believed that it was necessary, for religious and political reasons to maintain the Caliphate, proposed at the last moment when the decisions were to be taken, that I should assume the office of the Caliphate.

I immediately gave a negative reply to these men.

Let me emphasise another point which arose: When the Grand National Assembly had abolished the Caliphate, Rassih Effendi, an ecclesiastic and deputy for Adalia, was president of the deputation of the Red Half-Moon, which was in India. He came back to Angora viâ Egypt. After soliciting an interview with me, he made statements to the effect that "the Mohamedans in the countries through which he had been travelling demanded that I should become Caliph, and that the competent Mohamedan bodies had commissioned him to inform me of this desire."

In the reply which I gave to Rassih Effendi, I expressed my thanks for the benevolence and affection which the Mohamedans had shown me and said: "You are a Doctor of Religious Right. You know that Caliph signifies Chief of the State. How can I accept the proposals and desires of people who are governed by kings and emperors? If I should declare myself ready to accept this office, would the sovereigns of those people consent to it? The orders of the Caliph must be obeyed and his interdictions submitted to. Are those who want to make me Caliph in a position to execute my orders? Consequently, would it not be ridiculous to rig me up with an illusionary rôle which has neither sense nor right of existence?"

Gentlemen, I must frankly and categorically declare that those who continue to occupy themselves with the chimera of the Caliphate and thereby mislead the Mohamedan world, are nothing but enemies of the Mohamedan world, and especially of Turkey. They are only ignorant or blind men who could attach hopes to such jugglery.

Is it from love of our faith that such people as Rauf Bey, Tsherkess Edhem and Reshid, all the "Hundred and Fifty," all members of the deposed dynasty of the Sultanate and the Caliphate with their adherents, all enemies of Turkey, are working with so much bitterness? Is the aim of those who are working so energetically against us, sheltering themselves under the words "holy revolution," but who use means such as murderous attempts, and gangs of brigands, and who maintain organisation centres at our frontiers, who have always made the destruction of Turkey their aim—is this aim actually a holy one? Indeed, to believe this would mean that we were possessed of unmitigated ignorance and boundless blindness.

From now onwards it will not be so easy to suppose that the Mohamedan peoples and the Turkish nation would have fallen to such a low level as to continue in the abuse of the purity of the conscience and the tenderness of the sentiments of the Mohamedan world to criminal aims. Impudence has its limits.

42

The Kemalist Ideology, Program of the People's Republican Party of Turkey, May 1935 *

By 1935, the political and ideological framework of the Turkish Republic was essentially completed. At that point Turks were turning toward reconstructing their economic and social environment. Turkey's basically capitalistic economic structure had been a cause of concern ever since 1930 when the effects of the Great Depression began to upset her trade. *Ad hoc* measures taken to protect the economy resulted in much of the economy coming under some degree of government supervision. Then, in the early 1930's various opinions on how best to stimulate economic self-sufficiency began to coalesce. The result was the emergence of "etatism" which simply implied that the government would oversee the economy in general and supply capital for needed projects which could not attract private investment. The tale of Turkish state enterprise in the 1930's is not happy. Agriculture, the real basis of the Turkish economy, was ignored in favor of wasteful often inefficient industrial development projects. Nevertheless, the best summary of Turkey's enlarged perspective is the 1935 Republican Party "platform." Also, this is an early example of the program manifestos issued by mass doctrinal parties that have become a characteristic of Middle Eastern political propaganda. Since Turkey under Atatürk was a one-party state, the platform is a statement of the Kemalist elite's goals at their maturity. Many of the intentions of the program remained unrealized because the deterioration of the world's international climate in the late 1930's diverted the Turkish leadership once more to questions involving national security.

ADOPTED BY THE FOURTH GRAND CONGRESS OF THE PARTY, MAY 1935

Introduction

The fundamental ideas that constitute the basis of the Program of the Republican Party of the People are evident in the acts and realizations which have taken place from the beginning of our Revolution until today.

* *C.H.P. Programi* (Ankara: Cumhuriyet Halk Partisi, 1935); translated into English as *Program of the People's Party of the Republic* (Ankara: People's Republican Party, 1935), adopted by fourth party congress.

On the other hand, the main ideas have been formulated in the general principles of the Statutes of the Party, adopted also by the Grand Congress of the Party in 1927, as well as in the Declaration published on the occasion of the elections to the Grand National Assembly in 1931.

The main lines of our intentions, not only for a few years, but for the future as well, are here put together in a compact form. All of these principles which are the fundamentals of the Party constitute Kamâlism.

Part I

Principles

1—The Fatherland
2—The Nation
3—The Constitution of the State
4—The Public Rights

1—The Fatherland. The Fatherland is the sacred country within our present political boundaries, where the Turkish Nation lives with its ancient and illustrious history, and with its past glories still living in the depths of its soil.

The Fatherland is a Unity which does not accept separation under any circumstance.

2—The Nation. The Nation is the political Unit composed of citizens bound together with the bonds of language, culture and ideal.

3—Constitutional Organization of the State. Turkey is a nationalist, populist, *étatist,* secular [*laïque*], and revolutionary Republic.

The form of administration of the Turkish nation is based on the principle of the unity of power. There is only one Sovereignty, and it belongs to the nation without restriction or condition.

The Grand National Assembly exercises the right of sovereignty in the name of the nation. The legislative authority and the executive power are embodied in the Grand National Assembly. The Assembly exercises its legislative power itself. It leaves its executive authority to the President of the Republic, elected from among its members, and to the Council of Ministers appointed by him. The courts in Turkey are independent.

The Party is convinced that this is the most suitable of all State organizations.

4—Public Rights.

(a) It is one of the important principles of our Party to safeguard the individual and social rights of liberty, of equality, of inviolabilty, and of property. These rights are within the bounds of the State's authority. The activity of the individuals and of legal persons shall not be in contradiction with the interests of the public. Laws are made in accordance with this principle.

(b) The Party does not make any distinction between men and women in giving rights and duties to citizens.

(c) The Law on the election of deputies shall be renewed. We find it more suitable to the real requirements of democracy to leave the citizen free to elect electors whom he knows well and trusts, in accordance with the general conditions of our country. The election of the deputies shall take place in this manner.

PART II

THE ESSENTIAL CHARACTERISTICS OF THE
REPUBLICAN PARTY OF THE PEOPLE

5—The Republican Party of the People is: (a) Republican (b) Nationalist (c) Populist (d) *Étatist* (e) Secular (f) Revolutionary.

(a) The Party is convinced that the Republic is the form of government which represents and realizes most safely the ideal of national sovereignty. With this unshakable conviction, the Party defends, with all its means, the Republic against all danger.

(b) The Party considers it essential to preserve the special character and the entirely independent identity of the Turkish social community in the sense explained in Art. 2. The Party follows, in the meantime, a way parallel to and in harmony with all the modern nations in the way of progress and development, and in international contacts and relations.

(c) The source of Will and Sovereignty is the Nation. The Party considers it an important principle that this Will and Sovereignty be used to regulate the proper fulfillment of the mutual duties of the citizen to the State and of the State to the citizen.

We consider the individuals who accept an absolute equality before the Law, and who recognize no privileges for any individual, family, class, or community, to be of the people and for the people (populist).

It is one of our main principles to consider the people of the Turkish Republic, not as composed of different classes, but as a community divided into various professions according to the requirements of the division of labor for the individual and social life of the Turkish people.

The farmers, handicraftsmen, laborers and workmen, people exercising free professions, industrialists, merchants, and public servants are the main groups of work constituting the Turkish community. The functioning of each of these groups is essential to the life and happiness of the others and of the community.

The aims of our Party, with this principle, are to secure social order and solidarity instead of class conflict, and to establish harmony of interests. The benefits are to be proportionate to the aptitude to the amount of work.

(d) Although considering private work and activity a basic idea, it is one of our main principles to interest the State acitvely in matters where the general and vital interests of the nation are in question, especially in the economic field, in order to lead the nation and the country to prosperity in as short a time as possible.

The interest of the State in economic matters is to be an actual builder, as well as to encourage private enterprises, and also to regulate and control the work that is being done.

The determination of the economic matters to be undertaken by the State depends upon the requirements of the greatest public interest of the nation. If the enterprise, which the State itself decides to undertake actively as a result of this necessity, is in the hands of private entrepreneurs, its appropriation shall, each time, depend upon the enactment of a law, which will indicate the way in which the State shall indemnify the loss sustained by the private enterprise as a result of this appropriation. In the estimation of the loss the possibility of future earnings shall not be taken into consideration.

(e) The Party considers it a principle to have the laws, regulations, and methods in the administration of the State prepared and applied in conformity with the needs of the world and on the basis of the fundamentals and methods provided for modern civilization by Science and Technique.

As the conception of religion is a matter of conscience, the Party considers it to be one of the chief factors of the success of our nation in contemporary progress, to separate ideas of religion from politics, and from the affairs of the world and of the State.

(f) The Party does not consider itself bound by progressive and evolutionary principles in finding measures in the State administration. The Party holds it essential to remain faithful to the principles born of revolutions which our nation has made with great sacrifices, and to defend these principles which have since been elaborated.

Part III

Economy

Agriculture, Industry, Mines, Forests, Commerce and Public Works

6—Liquid capital is important in Economy. The only source of normal capital is national work and saving. Therefore, the essential principle of our Party is to increase work, and to instill the idea of saving in the individual, the family, and in general, in State, local and national administrations.

7—The problems of credit shall be looked after with the importance proportionate to the needs. The cheapness and ease of interest and discount in credit transactions is our main desire.

(a) The Party attaches great importance to the security of credit in the country. We are convinced that this can only be achieved by giving preference to real and strong guaranties. We are also convinced that this is the only means of limiting the desire to use credit in business to real business men.

(b) It is right to provide for the seasonal credit needs of small farmers by means of agricultural credit coöperatives, and the yearly credit needs of farm owners by means of mortgage credit.

(c) The methods of granting credit against crops, live stock, agricultural implements, and machinery shall be systematized.

(d) It shall be provided that the day of payment of farm credits be postponed until after such time when the crop can be sold to the best advantage, without pressure on the part of the buyers.

(e) The credit needs of miners, industrialists, handicraftsmen, small traders, fishers, and sponge fishers shall be provided for.

(f) The methods of providing credit for industrialists, and against machinery and implements for sea products shall be systematized.

(g) Our Party considers it an important principle to enable citizens to become home owners. It attaches great importance to widening the basis of real estate credit, which at present is narrow, and favors devoting for the moment that part of the resources of the Real Estate Bank reserved for new constructions to the building of dwellings. The Real Estate Bank cannot grant credit for new buildings to be constructed for the purpose of acquiring revenue. Credit can be granted against existing buildings on condition that the proceeds are not devoted to the construction of buildings for rent. In this way the use of the existing capital, for the purpose in question is generalized. On the other hand, we consider necessary the establishment and existence of a Real Estate Credit Organization on the model of Crédit Foncier as soon as possible.

8—It is one of the principles of our Party to fight Usury.

9—The problems of insurance shall receive our attention proportionate to their importance.

10—Our Party considers the encouragement of coöperative undertakings as one of its main principles. We think it important to establish and increase the number of credit and sales coöperatives which will benefit the agricultural producers with the real value of their products. The Agricultural Bank of Turkey is the Mother Bank of agricultural coöperatives.

11—It is our aim to render the Agricultural Bank more useful especially to the economy of the peasant and farmer, and to see that it is owned in such a way as to secure its control on a legal basis.

12—It is our obligation to regulate our balance of payments, and to keep our foreign trade in balance.

Our principle in foreign trade and commercial agreements is to buy the products of those who buy our products.

13—The small and the large industries shall enjoy protection in harmony with the interests of the producers of raw materials.

14—Every economic enterprise shall harmonize with united national work as well as with the general interest. This harmony is also the principle in the union of work between the employer and worker.

With the Labor Law the mutual relations of workers and employers shall be regulated. Labor conflicts shall be dealt with by means of conciliation, and where this is impossible, through the arbitration of Reconciliation Agencies to be set up by the State. Strikes and lockouts shall be prohibited.

We are interested in the life and rights of the nationalist Turkish workers within the framework of these principles. The Labor Laws to be promulgated shall conform to these principles.

15—The industries which the State or individuals shall establish for the industrialization of the country shall conform to a general program. The items of the State program shall follow one another in such a way as to render the country an industrial unit.

The industrial undertakings shall not be concentrated in certain parts of the country, but shall, instead, be spread all over the country, taking into consideration the economic factors.

In order to prevent conflict of interest between producers and consumers of industrial products, the State shall organize price control. Apart from this, financial and technical control shall be established for the State factories.

The financial control of establishments, the majority or totality of whose capital belongs to the State, shall be organized in such a way as to conform to their commercial character. We shall emphasize the rationalization of work.

Trusts or Cartels which establish unity of price against the consumers shall not be allowed. Those undertaken for the purpose of rationalization are excepted.

16—All kinds of commercial activity are useful in the development of the Country. The owners of capital who work normally and on a technical basis shall be encouraged and protected.

17—We consider exportation one of the important national activities and the regulation of foreign trade one of our main economic duties. We shall render fruitful the activities of those engaged in commerce. We shall be closely interested in facilitating the sale of our national products and manufactured articles, in safeguarding their reputation, in insuring their export, and in measures to be taken for their standardization. We desire to let our foreign trade function in accordance with an exportation policy which conforms to the necessities and requirements of different markets. We also want to strengthen our foreign trade with State aid. We shall have organizations which will furnish those engaged in the export trade with information they need to succeed in their work.

18—We consider it a good policy to create, when necessary, free zones which will benefit the State in foreign trade transits.

19—We shall always consider carefully the port, dock, quay, and loading and unloading tariffs which shall be made to conform to the requirements of national economy.

20—We shall attach importance to fishing and sponge fishing. The development of the fishing industry, as well as the improvement of the present system of dealing in fish, which is against the benefit of both producers and consumers, is necessary.

21—We shall encourage the canning industry.

22—We consider the tourist trade (*tourisme*) a means of making Turkey known and liked abroad, and a means of benefiting Turkish economy.

23—In our economic considerations we shall consider a general principle the rule of absolute usefulness and profitability from the economic point of view in all affairs of State relating to any ministry or authority. We consider it important to improve, in time, old laws and methods on this point.

Our Party, besides attaching this importance to economic matters, considers Economics one of the important branches of State affairs, each of which has a special importance for us.

24—We shall endeavor to develop and regulate transportation by land, sea, and air. We consider it one of the economic needs of the country to bring about a harmony in the exploitation and tariffs of these three kinds of transportation so that they may benefit the country to their full extent.

We shall further the State Navigation Administration according to an extensive program. In this connection, we attach importance to freight shipping.

25—Extensive water schemes which will serve our economic purpose are our ideal. To complete our small water schemes is one of our first aims.

26—Our public works shall follow a practical and productive program in all its branches. Among these, we shall continue the railway construction work, which is a means of bringing prosperity and strength to the country.

We shall consider the necessity of beginning the construction of ports at convenient times.

Work shall continue on Vilâyet roads and on a practical program to provide the country with bridges and a net of roads built with modern technique, and connecting the different parts of the country.

In building roads, economic considerations shall be given importance, and they shall be constructed perpendicular to the railway lines in order to feed them with traffic. Considerations of national defense and security shall also be taken into account in their construction.

27—We shall organize matters relating to the post, telegraph, telephone, and wireless in such a way as to render them technically perfect, and corresponding to the needs of the country. We shall constantly increase the telephone connections between the cities.

28—The following matters shall be considered:

Not to let the price of wheat, which is first in quantity and value among our agricultural products, fall below its worth.

To widen and strengthen the measures to counteract the changes that may take place to the disadvantage of producers and consumers.

To this end, we shall continue the work of constructing grain elevators and warehouses, already begun. It is a duty to keep sufficient grain stocks to suffice in case of national defense or unexpected drought.

29—We attach great importance to reducing our agricultural products and our fruits to types suitable for exportation, and to producing the quantity of raw materials needed for our home industry. To this end, we shall work intensively on the improvement of seeds, tree nurseries, and tree grafting.

30—The advancement of the agricultural industry is one of our main tasks.

31—In order to protect the work of producers we shall fight the diseases and enemies of plants and animals.

32—To exploit and to render valuable our underground wealth, our water power, and our forests shall be a special part of our work. We consider the electrification of the whole country one of the main items in the progress of the Turkish Fatherland. We shall continue our researches in order to determine the real value and extent of our wealth in this category. It is our aim to found a financial establishment to take care of these enterprises. These undertakings are the main fields of application of the *étatist* qualification of our Party.

33—We shall endeavor to encourage, ameliorate, and increase the breeding and rearing of livestock, and to advance the livestock industry.

34—It is one of the principal aims of our Party to render each Turkish farmer owner of sufficient land. It is necessary to enact special laws of appropriation in order to distribute land to farmers owning no land.

35—The geographic situation of our country and the standard of civilization and the duty of our nation require that our citizens consider sea mindedness important from the points of view of sport, health, defense and general economy. The Party believes in the necessity of considering this in all national and governmental affairs.

PART IV

FINANCE

36—The principal idea of finance in our Party is a budget based on continued and real balance. We consider regular payments important for the Treasury, and a principle in the tax payments of the citizens.

37—It is our aim to place the imposition of taxes on an indirect and net revenue basis. Our efforts shall continue, in the meantime, to better our fiscal laws with the view of rendering them practical and applicable without disregarding the capacity of the nation for payment.

38—It is one of the matters which we consider important, to try and to put our customs tariffs and formalities on a basis more in harmony with the economic interests of the nation.

39—We consider suppression of smuggling a means of protecting the rights and authority of the Turkish Treasury.

40—The State Monopolies constitute a source of revenue to the State Treasury, and serve the national economy by protecting the value of the products which enter their field of activity.

PART V

NATIONAL EDUCATION AND INSTRUCTION

41—Our main principles for national education and instruction are as follows:

(a) The cornerstone of our cultural policy is the suppression of ignorance. In the field of public instruction a policy of teaching and training more children and citizens every day shall be followed.

(b) The training of strongly republican, nationalist, populist, *étatist,* and secular citizens must be fostered in every stage of education.

To respect, and make others respect the Turkish nation, the Grand National Assembly of Turkey, and the Turkish State must be taught as a duty to which very one must be very sensitive.

(c) It is our great desire to attach importance to intellectual as well as physical development, and especially to elevate the character to the high level inspired by our great national history.

(d) The method followed in education and instruction is to render Learning an instrument in the hands of citizens for guaranteeing success in material life.

(e) Education must be high, national, patriotic, and far from all sorts of superstition and foreign ideas.

(f) We are convinced that it is important to treat the students in all institutions of education and instruction tactfully, in order not to hinder their capacity for enterprise. On the other hand, it is important to accustom them to serious discipline and order, and to a sincere conception of morals, in order to prevent their being faulty in life.

(g) Our Party lays an extraordinary importance upon the citizens' knowing our great history. This learning is the sacred essence that nourishes the indestructible resistance of the Turk against all currents that may prejudice the national existence, his capacity and power, and his sentiments of self-confidence.

(h) We shall continue our serious work in rendering the Turkish language a perfect and ordered national language.

42—Our main ideas about the schools are the following:

(a) The normal primary education consists of five years. The number of primary schools in cities, villages, or groups of villages shall be increased according to a regular program of application, and according to the needs. In the village schools ideas on hygiene, better living, agriculture and industry that have a bearing upon the region in question shall be taught.

(b) Village schools of three or four terms shall be opened to give the village children, in a short time, the essential learning required in practical life. A plan shall be made to establish such schools and to increase their number.

These schools shall be of a separate type from those which propose to prepare the children for higher education. It is necessary to begin the education in these village schools at a maturer age, to continue it without interruption, and to have it controlled by the State in the same manner as the military service duty.

(c) The professional and trade schools, as well as the night trade schools, shall be increased to cope with the needs of the country, and necessary new courses shall be instituted.

(d) We are convinced of the necessity of having secondary schools in capitals of Vilâyets and in the regions of *kazas* wherever it is necessary, following the principle of spreading secondary education through the country. We shall endeavor to create organizations to provide boarding facilities which shall enable the children of the country to benefit from these schools in peace and security.

(e) We shall strengthen and complete our Lycées in every way, so that they may prepare students fully qualified for higher education.

(f) The University and our schools for higher education shall be brought to a state of perfection where they can give the results expected of them. We are thinking of increasing the number of Universities.

43—Boarding facilities of a practical nature for the ordinary primary schools for the children of several thinly populated villages, as well as for the special type village schools, shall be established and protected.

44—The fine arts, and especially music, shall be given an importance in accordance with the high expression of our Revolution.

45—Importance shall be attached to collecting historical objects in order to enrich our Museums. For this purpose, we shall undertake excavations, classify the works of antiquity, and preserve them where they stand, if necessary.

46—Matters in connection with books, publications and libraries are important for the Party. We want to establish and increase the number of libraries in cities and villages.

47—Our Public Instruction policy shall be organized after a plan taking into consideration the present and future requirements of education. After this plan, all the degrees of education, shall be informed according to the needs of professions and trades.

48—We consider it important to give the masses a continuous adult education, outside the classical school education, in harmony with the advancement of new Turkey. The State shall protect with all possible means the People's Houses which are working to this end.

49—The Party shall found a Museum of the Revolution. We consider this an effective means of instilling the revolutionary culture in the people.

50—The Turkish youth shall be organized in a national organization so as to bring them together in clean ethics and a high love of Fatherland and Revolution. They shall be given a physical education that will foster their joy, health, and their belief in themselves and in the nation. The youth shall be brought up with the conviction of considering the defense of the Revolution and of the Fatherland with all its requisites of independence, the highest duty of youth. They shall be taught to be ready to sacrifice everything in order to fulfill this duty.

In order that this fundamental education shall attain its full results, high qualities requisite for success, such as thinking, making decisions and taking the initiative shall be developed in the Turkish youth. In the meantime, they shall be required to work under strict discipline, which is the sole means of accomplishing every difficult task.

The sports organizations in Turkey shall be established and furthered in accordance with these principles. The connection and coöperation of the ideals of the new youth organization with the University, the Schools and Institutes, People's Houses, the factories and establishments, employing a number of workers together, shall be organized.

Uniformity in physical and revolutionary education, as well as in matters relating to sports in the country, shall be considered.

It shall be made obligatory for everybody in schools, government institutions, in private establishments, and factories to take part in physical education according to their age. The sport fields and organizations necessary for physical education shall be established. In securing the sport fields, the municipalities and local administrations shall be led to take a special interest.

51—The Party considers the radio to be one of the most valuable instruments for the political and cultural education of the nation. We shall erect powerful broadcasting stations, and shall provide for the easy purchase of cheap receiving sets. We shall consider it our task to render the moving pictures in the country useful to the nation.

52—The national opera and the national theater are among our important tasks.

Part VI

Social Life and Public Health

53—The conservation of the institution of family is essential in Turkish social life.

54—The increase of our population and the bringing up of a strong and healthy future generation are among tasks which we must always take into important consideration.

55—We shall work under a definite program, and with scientific methods, to improve the hygienic conditions and drinking water supplies of our cities, towns, and villages; to improve the housing conditions in our villages, and to increase the hygienic knowledge of our villagers.

56—The Party is deeply interested in the life of children and in the health of their mothers. To this end, we shall continue to work according to the following main lines:

(a) To increase the number of maternity homes, to open maternity wards in State hospitals, to provide gratuitous maternity help, and to use every means of persuasion, imparting advice in child care, as well as to increase the number of scientifically trained midwives and visiting nurses.

(b) To increase the number of baby homes, examination and consultation centers for babies, day nurseries and homes for orphans in cities and towns.

(c) To protect the working mothers and their children in the workmen's districts.

57—The orphans, needy old people, and invalids are under the protection and tutelage of the nation.

58—We shall endeavor to provide the social and hygienic needs of workers and their families. We shall especially continue to open day nurseries in workmen's districts for women who have to earn their living.

59—Matters relating to public hygiene have a special importance for our Party. Work in this connection shall be widened continuously and in proportion to general needs.

60—We shall continue the fight against contagious diseases such as Malaria, Syphilis, and Trachoma.

Part VII

Interior, Judicial, and Foreign Policy, Public Servants, People Engaged in Free Professions

61—The basis of our work is to establish and provide for the functioning of a governmental authority. This authority must be unshakable before any event or influence, and shall protect all the results of the Revolution, the full security of the citizens, and national order and discipline, by means of its internal and judicial organization and its laws.

62—Among the tasks of applying our principle to increase our population, we shall provide all help and facility to Turks who may come from outside the country.

63—We shall elaborate and complete the law on the organization of the courts of justice, in a manner most suitable to the needs of the public and to the interests of the country.

We shall widen the scope of the simple, rapid and practical judicial procedure which offers security.

We shall take measures to guarantee rapidly and easily the desired results in matters relating to judicial execution and notification.

We shall endeavor to separate the prisoners from the people under arrest, and to turn the prisons into reformatories.

64—Peace in the country and peace in the world is one of our main principles.

65—The public servants who devote their life to their duty with all their attention and care, always considering the high interests of the nation, are worthy of all peace and prosperity.

66—No association shall be founded in Turkey with the purpose of propagating ideas of class distinction, or of class conflict. Those who receive salary or pay for their services from the State, local administrations, municipalities, or establishments attached to the State, cannot use the identity of their position in order to found associations, in the quality and identity of the office they hold.

67—Organizations carrying the name of Students' Associations can, in no way, engage in politics, nor can they, in any way, engage in activity against the administration of the School, Faculty or Institute to which they belong.

68—We shall make a point of organizing the Turkish workers and members of different trades within the main existence of the nation, and in such a way as to render them useful and invigorating to it, in accordance with the attitude outlined in the Party Program.

69—Associations with internationalist intentions shall not be founded, and it shall be forbidden to found associations with their center outside the country. The decision of the Council of Ministers is necessary to found associations to create unity among nations that shall be deemed by the State to be of use, or to open branches of such associations already in existence.

70—The services of people exercising free professions useful and necessary for the national Turkish existence are appreciated by the Party. It is our duty to keep their field of activity open and secure, in order that they may reap the benefits of their capacity and effort.

71—We consider the village important from every point of view in the life of new Turkey. The health and happiness of the peasants, their understanding of the revolution and of culture, and their force in the economic field, are to be considered important from the point of view of our available working forces.

Part VIII

Defense of the Fatherland

72—The defense of the Fatherland is the most sacred of national duties. All the living and inanimate resources of the country shall be used to this end in case of necessity. The Party has accepted the principle of applying obligatory military service equally to all citizens. The Turkish army is above all political considerations and influences. We consider it important that the army possess the power to fulfill successfully, at every moment, the high duty confided in it, and that it be equipped with means in conformity with modern advancement.

73—We especially take care that the army of the Republic, which is the unshakable foundation of the high State organization, and which protects and guards the national ideal, the national existence, and the Revolution, as well as its valuable members, be always honored and respected.

43

The Multi-Party Experiment in Turkey, Excerpts from a Democratic Party Election Manifesto, 1950 *

The liberalization of the Turkish political atmosphere that followed the end of World War II permitted the rise of political parties and their competition with the government backed People's Republican Party of President Ismet Inönü (b. 1884). The most important of the more than twenty new groupings was the People's Democratic Party, led by Celal Bayar, a former economic advisor and prime minister under Atatürk. The Democrats attracted the support of many of those elements in Turkish society which had amassed grievances against the ruling bureaucracy and its political arm, the People's Republican Party, during their years of dominance under Atatürk and Inönü. Most of these discontents seemed to revolve around resentment against bureaucratic meddling, statist restraints on economic life, and the uncompromising anticlericalism of the government. The discontented united into a broad coalition of commercial and agricultural entrepreneurs, urban workers, peasants, and nonestablishment intellectuals. It succeeded in electing a large Democratic majority in the elections of 1950. President Inönü did not try to overturn the vote and allowed himself to be turned out of office. Thus, the election of 1950 was the beginning of a new era in Turkey's history and it demonstrated how far the political modernization of the country had progressed since the establishment of the republic.

*   *   *

It is important for Turkey's security, and even for world peace, that friend and foe alike understand that a change in government will cause not the slightest

* "The Democratic Party Election Manifesto, excerpts," *Middle Eastern Affairs* (New York: Council for Middle Eastern Affairs, 1950), Vol. I, No. 5, May 1950, 149-150.

change in our foreign policy, which expresses the views of the whole Turkish nation. We are convinced that Turkish foreign policy, based on a traditional alliance with Great Britain and France and on the closest possible friendship and cooperation with the United States, is an important factor for world peace and democracy. It is our most sincere desire continually to make stronger the political and economic relations which bind Turkey to her allies and to her great friend of the United States in an atmosphere of complete understanding.

In this connection it is necessary to mention also the subject of our national defense, a major mainstay of our foreign policy. In the present critical world situation, where peace and security have still to be established five years after the end of the war, and where we are faced with the somber designs against our country entertained by one of our close neighbors, it is a sacred national duty to keep a very watchful eye on our requirements for national defense, the very basis of our existence.

To accelerate the development of private enterprise and the increase of national wealth, it is necessary to put a definite stop to a policy whereby national resources are either frozen, or wasted by the state in non-productive fields of activity.

We are in urgent need of the initiative, capital, and technical know-how that can be provided from abroad, but it is a mistake to believe that foreign capital will be invested in a country where there are but limited scope for development and inadequate guarantees for private enterprise. We have a tremendous amount of work to do, and cannot afford to waste the long years that a stubborn reliance exclusively on our own resources would require; it is well to remember that progress today is forging ahead incomparably faster than in any other era in history.

One of the major reasons for our present economic difficulties is the failure to inspire confidence in the minds of investors. This failure can be traced to arbitrary forms of taxation such as the Capital Levy, and to the obstacles to foreign investment in Turkey.

There is no doubt that our proposed economic and financial policy will serve to raise the general standard of living by reorganizing the economic machinery so as to increase production and hence national income. We see no other way to improve the lot of the peasants, the working classes, and the great majority of individuals with a small or fixed income, all of whom suffer from the present high cost of living.

The Democratic Party will naturally consider it as its primary duty to safeguard the reforms and democratic developments which are now such a permanent feature of our national life. To this end we are resolved to make certain changes in the Constitution which will render it impossible for single-party rule ever to return.

The Democratic Party's record during the past five years is sufficient guarantee that a change in the government can be effected without the slightest moral or material disturbance within the country. No single citizen, no particular class or category will be adversely affected in any way by a change in government; but everyone will be better off because of the numerous benefits which will result from the application of progressive policies based on the will of the peeople themselves.

44

Organizing the Iranian National State, a Poem Praising Reza Shah's Monarchy, 1926 *

Historically, a key to Iranian realities has been Persian poetry. Many poems have dealt with current political problems and they are probably more influential in molding mass sentiment than more prosaic pronouncements and explanations. In the following selection the well-known poet Pur-i-Da'ud, welcomed the rise of Reza Shah and the Pahlavi House and the fall of the Qajar 'dynasty. The poet dwells on the Turkish, non-Iranian descent of the old ruling family and contrasts this with the pure Iranian origins of Reza Shah, "this son of the land." But the propagandization of Iranian nationalism is mixed with many traditional references. This mixture of old with new was characteristic of Reza Shah's use of the monarchy, an institution which was popularized as the national Iranian form of government and as the summary of the essence of the Iranian nation. He emphasized the pre-Islamic heritage of Iran, and identified the monarchy with this heritage as well as with the idea that Iran was great only when ruled by a great native-born king. Reza Shah's monarchy was a traditionalist veil behind which the work of building up a modern centralized political apparatus was conducted. History, as well as the copying of ancient Iranian motifs in public art and architecture was all used to support a modern nationalist cult.

HARK! A messenger has brought the good news that Ahmad
  Shāh of Īrān has been deposed
And the royal throne cleared of this occupant, the devil of an
  offender, a brigand and a Turkomān of the Qāchār tribe.

* Pūr-i-Dā'ūd, "Poem," translated by Hadi Hasan, *A Golden Treasury of Persian Poetry* (Delhi: Publications Division, Ministry of Information and Broadcasting, Government of India, 1966), 222-223.

With this happy tidings render thy thanks to God, for we have
freed ourselves once more from the ignominy of alien rule.

Because of this tribe and its seven kings of Turkish descent,
old Īran had become a heap of ruins—

An abode of owls. And from that debris was going up to
heaven the wail of a people, senseless, homeless, lifeless,

Sad, emaciated, dejected, distracted—the gift of the rule of the
Qāchārs.

Save a (crushing) tax naught else from an alien ruler can come;
save a (venomous) sting naught else from a snake and a
scorpion can come;

Save harm and loss what else from a brigand or a thief can
come? The strength and skill of a lion from a jackal
cannot come;

The justice and splendour of Parwīz from the Qāchār cannot
come: from the rose-bush the rose you'll get and thorn
from the thorn.

This dynasty was threatening our national existence: with its
heavy load, the beams of our house were sagging.

Universal became fooling, idling, drinking, begging, joking,
sinning, bluffing;

Sufīism, materialism, egoism: and the urge to steal, lie, cheat,
hate and slay.

Name a single king from this House who was just: name one
who was capable, wise and illustrious.

Can a ravished land boast of gold and silver? Or guns,
troops, mail, hood and shield?

In a parched and arid land where is verdure and fruit?
Where field, where harvest, where wheat, where granary?

Sardār Sipah cleared the house of its alien occupant. This son
of the land soothed the bereaved motherland.

He struggled like a man and charged from all sides till he had
unseated the Qāchār from the Peacock Throne.

He gave a new Constitution and a new social order: may the
Hurmuz in heaven be his protector on earth.

45

Iran and the National Front, a Speech by Prime Minister Muhammad Musaddiq, 27 September 1951 *

Muhammad Musaddiq rode to power in Iran atop a wave of anti-foreignism and nationalism. His rise to the prime ministership was accomplished in the fluid political environment of post World War II Iran when Musaddiq gained the reputation of being an honest, uncompromising champion of Iranian nationalism. He supported the efforts to expel the Russians from Azerbaijan in 1946 and he became prime minister on the strength of his equally vehement opposition to Britain's preponderance, as represented by the Anglo-Iranian Oil Company, in southern Iran. In 1951, the issue of the oil company's control of Iran's richest natural resource came to a head as the Iranian government decided to safeguard the nation's interests and increase national income by nationalizing the oil fields. The British, supported by other oil-consuming nations, resisted this unilateral action by refusing to buy Iranian oil, an action which threatened Iran with bankruptcy and the curtailment of her development plans. Musaddiq, who first recommended nationalization to the Majlis, became prime minister in 1951 in the midst of the dispute, supported by an outpouring of nationalist fervor from all classes. A master of crowd appeal, he was hailed as the man who "kicked out" the British. But the rise of Musaddiq also represented an attempt to limit the prerogatives of the monarchy. Musaddiq himself had family ties to the deposed Qajars and had been an opponent of Reza Shah. Thus, the activities of Mussaddiq's National Front were animated by a curious blend of anti-foreign, constitutional, and personal motivations. Musaddiq's luster began to dim as his increasingly authoritarian stance coupled with spreading economic chaos drained away support. Finally, in 1953, his attempt to wrest control of the army from the shah brought the confrontation that led to his fall.

*   *   *

"... In my opinion wherever a crowd is gathered of men of good will and patriotic feelings a true Majless is to be found there; and where a group of people,

* *Speech of Prime Minister Muhammad Mossadegh on Baharestan Square, 27 September 1951* (Teheran: Foreign Ministry of Iran, 1951), 1-6.

opposed to the interests of the country are assembled that place is not considered as a Majless.

"My dear countrymen," the Prime Minister continued, "you are well aware that we did our utmost for a peaceful settlement of the oil dispute through negotiations (cheers of the crowd). Dear countrymen, I openly declare that the Iranian people will not give up their rights through the exercise of force (enthusiastic cheers of the crowd). The Iranian people have realised very well how they have been oppressed for half a century and now will not give up their lawful rights (cheers of the crowd and shouts of "long live Dr. Mossadegh"). A limited number of Majless deputies," the Prime Minister went on, "have imagined that through yielding to the desires of foreigners our people would give up their legitimate rights through pressure brought upon them. The Iranian people have come to know that by forming a ruling class separated from them they will not give up their rights (enthusiastic cheers)." Then the Prime Minister paused and produced a list and showing it to the people said, "My dear countrymen, according to official figures the former usurping company has only paid us 110 million pounds during the 40 years of its operations, i.e., since 1912 when the company has started its exploitation activities it has only paid us £110,943,798 in the way of royalties, taxes and dividends due to the Iranian Government for its 20% shares in the company. Countrymen," the Prime Minister continued, "we were prepared to keep the British technical experts in the South so as not to disturb the international peace; we were prepared to compensate the former Company for all losses arising out of the nationalisation of its installations, and settle the whole issue on a sound basis, i.e., either to pay for the shares of the company according to their quoted value at the international markets, or alternatively to follow the practice of those countries who have nationalised their mineral resources, leaving the choice to the company to choose either one of the two ways which guarantees its interests best. We were prepared to put an end to all the claims of the company and the counter-claims of the Iranian Government, in a manner mutually satisfactory to both parties. We also declared our readiness to supply Great Britain yearly its oil requirements on the basis of the average of the oil received by it during the last three years, and for a period of time which would be mutually agreed upon; furthermore we agreed to earmark 50% of the value of the oil given to them for the amortization of the claims of the former company as judged by one of the two above-mentioned standards. We also gave the British another advantage to transfer to them the quantities of oil bought by our other customers, provided they produced duly signed orders from them. We showed our readiness to establish anew sincere relations between the two Governments; our main intention was simply to recover our legal rights, i.e., the profits of our oil resources from a cruel usurper, and to use the same for the amelioration of the lot of fifteen million poor people, to give them what is due to them in the way of health and education." (At this moment loud applause and shouts were uttered by the audience accompanied by clappings which lasted for several minutes). The Prime Minister went on and said, "The British Government did not show any willingness to accept our just and equitable proposals." (The crowds shouted, "Death upon the British, death upon the British.") Then the Prime Minister, moved by feelings of the audience, said to them, "I don't want to hear you utter any words like this 'Death upon the British'; but I admonish you to pray to God Almighty to lead the British to the path of justice to recognise our lawful rights; and that God may open their eyes to see our miseries. (At this juncture the great multitude who were gathered in the Parliament Square started to weep.)

"My dear countrymen, there was a time when the British Government was following a laudable policy in Iran; and that was at the beginning of our constitutional movement. When the British Government realised that certain mean and treacherous elements in our population had become the tools of the despotic Government of the Tzars of Russia, it immediately decided to back up the liberal movement in Iran, and consequently through great sacrifices of our liberty-loving people who gave their lives for this purpose a constitutional regime was established in our country. This was a very wise rôle which was played by the British Government; but unfortunately as time went on, this laudable attitude was changed, and the British Government entered into partition agreements with the Government of the Tzars based on zones of influence. Then the First World War began and subsequently a communistic régime appeared in Russia. The British Government instead of backing the patriotic and liberal elements of this country (i.e., that portion of the population who had the preservation of our country's independence at heart), paved the way for the establishment of a dictatorial Government which deprived all the people of their human rights of freedom; not being content with this, the British Government before making the Coup d'Etat intended to impose upon the Iranian people a protectorate, while taking advantage of the confused state of affairs in Soviet Russia who was at the time absorbed in its internal difficulties. This agreement did not materialise through your patriotic sentiments, my dear brothers. Furthermore the appearance of the U. S. S. R. as a new factor in world politics and also the declaration of the Government of the United States of America for the formation of a League of Nationals through which the rights of the small nations were to be defended all combined to neutralise the proposed agreement. Dear countrymen, I have fought this imperialism during the life of the 14th Majless (Approval of the crowd). I have opposed the credentials of Sayed Ziadin Tabatabai, the employment of Dr. Millspaugh and the Sadre Government, and also the tri-party commission; in short I have been a vigilant fighter against everything which endangered the freedom of our country and our people.

"In the 14th Majless my countrymen were not so enlightened regarding these vital questions as they are now to come and help me in the passage of the new

Electoral Bill submitted by me to the Parliament, and to show their persistence in achieving this goal. My only aim has been to prevent the recurrence of a situation in which we would have no Majless; but on the other hand I have always desired to see in continued existence a centre in which opinions could be expressed freely. Countrymen, political parties, patriots, I must declare that you were negligent in this affair; because during the last days of the life of that Majless some people decided to close this place, which was the refuge of the people, against the will of the Majority of the nation. Consequently the Majless was dissolved and a period of uncertainty followed. What should not have been done was done by those who brought about this situation; to mention one case, the budget deficit of 3,000 million rials is the outcome of the unlawful activities of the Government during the period at which the Parliament was closed.

"When the new Elections for the 15th Majless started in Tehran my political friends and myself took refuge in the Imperial Court to secure the non-interference of the Government in the National elections, but we were met with a negative reply. A few days after we left the Imperial Court somebody came and told me, 'Do you know that the British Embassy was back of this movement of your taking refuge in the Imperial Court.' My reply was of course a resolute 'no'; but I added if the British Embassy had written to me to go and take refuge in the Imperial Court for securing the freedom of the National Elections I, for one, would not have refused. Suppose the British Embassy had told me to observe my religious fasting; do you think I should have refused to do so because the utterance was made by the British Embassy. On the contrary I should have observed my religious injunctions irrespective of the source which reminded me to do so. Then I enquired the person what made you think that the British Embassy was back of our movement of taking refuge in the Imperial Court? In reply he said 'because they had told the Soviet Russians that in case the Tehran Elections were free from interference the returns might not be helpful to the passage of the proposed mixed Irano-Russian Oil Company agreement.'

"Therefore the elections should be under the control of the Government; so that neither the Tudeh Party could send any members nor those who intended to oppose the above-mentioned agreement.

"When the Elections for the 16th Majless started I was totally disappointed because all our efforts during the 14th and 15th Majless elections were futile; but when the time came for the Tehran elections I said to myself let us do our best, may be the desired goal will be achieved. Hence I requested many of you, dear countrymen, to assemble before the Imperial Court to obtain our rights of free franchise. You responded to my call and showed your national maturity in a very admirable manner." (At this moment the Premier was overcome by his feeling and the drops of tears appeared on his cheeks, which made everybody cry.) The Prime Minister then continued and said, "My dear countrymen, your opponents who were awaiting for any disturbance were dismayed, because they had in mind to put under arrest anybody who broke the peace of the audience as a rioter and inflict upon him all sorts of punishment.

"But fortunately nothing of the sort happened and peace was preserved. A few of us only went to the Court with a plea to have the Minister of Interior, Dr. Eghbal, removed from his office; as our request was not complied with we left the Court. Instead of that we entered into a fearful campaign to succeed in the elections. As a result of this campaign myself and a few members of the National front (whom you all know well) were elected; and because of the continuation of our campaign in Majless, while being in minority *we took the reins of the Government.* Who has ever heard of an opposition to have taken the Government in its hands!" (To this remark one of the people retorted with a shout: "You were the Majority and not the opposition.")

"The coming into power of the opposition," stated the Prime Minister, "was only due to the backing of you, my dear countrymen, who are the well wishers of our fatherland. For our part I must say that we accepted the responsibilities of the Government for the sole purpose of recovering the lost rights of the Iranian people, we accepted the heavy duties of the Government in order to put an end to the exploitation of our people by others. It is quite surprising that a handful of persons try in vain to show that your sentiments are aroused through the intrigues of the Government. Do tell me frankly has any member of the Government ever given you any instruction or even has spoken to anyone of you?" The reply was "Never, never." "The fact that the opposition has come into power is a good proof that your sentiments are genuine. It came to my knowledge that the British Ambassador had called on His Excellency Taghi-zadeh, the President of the Senate, three day ago; and had expressed his surprise at the fact that an Opposition had come into existence in Majless, while such an opposition did not exist in the senate. He had furthermore explicitly stated that as long as Dr. Mossadegh is in power the British Government is not ready to enter into negotiations with the Iranian Government." At this juncture the multitude showed their sentiments towards the Prime Minister by saying, "Long live Dr. Mossadegh, and long live his Government."

A bouquet was presented to him by one of the audience; the Premier put the flowers on his head and then returned them to the person who had made the offer. The Premier then went on and said, "His Excellency Mr. Taghi-zadeh gave the appropriate reply to the said Honourable Ambassador stressing the fact that no foreign intervention is permissible in the internal affairs of Iran.

"Now I want to tell you, my dear countrymen, that it is impossible for the present Government to take any steps contrary to your welfare; and as long as a vote of non-confidence is not given by both houses this Government shall continue its fight with all severity and persistence to recover your rights." (While great roars of applause were rending the air in the Baharestan Square, the Premier went back to the Majless building and thence returned to his residence.)

46

The Decay of Liberal Ideals in the Arab World, the Decree of King Fu'ad I Suspending the Egyptian Constitution of 1923, 22 October 1930 *

Although a liberal constitution was issued by King Fu'ad in 1923, the monarch's reign (1917-1922 as sultan, 1922-1936 as king) was not characterized by the maturing of liberal parliamentary practices or democracy in Egypt. In fact, King Fu'ad was an authoritarian figure who ruled through minor parties and relied upon the extensive use of decree. He feared particularly the popular nationalist Wafd party and constantly sought to undercut the influence of its leaders, Sa'd Zaghlul and Mustafa al-Nahhas. Especially, after the spread of the Great Depression in the 1930's Fu'ad acted as a royal dictator rather than a constitutional monarch. An excellent example of this tendency is provided by 'Royal Order No. 70' which decreed the replacement of the 1923 constitution with a new, more restrictive document. While the king eventually restored the 1923 constitution in 1935, by that time his dominance of governmental machinery was assured. The king may have been an energetic patron of art, learning and even educational modernization, but his interest in economic development was restricted largely to building up the royal fortune. Social affairs interested him hardly at all. King Fu'ad can serve as a symbol of the attitudes and methods employed by many Arab leaders in the 1920-1950 period. Though he tried to diminish British political influence in Egypt he sought also to enhance his own powers. The government he headed and bequeathed to his son, King Faruq (1936-1952) was a bizarre representative of liberal, democratic values.

*   *   *

We Fu'ad the First, King of Egypt,

Having considered our Order No. 42, of 1923,

And since our most cherished desire and the greatest aim of our determination is to ensure the welfare of our people, in an orderly and peaceable manner,

* "Royal Order No. 70 Establishing a Constitutional Regime for Egypt," translated by Muhammad Khalil, *The Arab States and the Arab League* (Beirut: Khayats, 1962), Vol. I, 475-476.

And taking due note of the experience of the past seven years, and acting in accordance with the necessity of reconciling the basic theories and the conditions and needs of the country,

And having considered the letter and statement submitted to us by the Cabinet on October 21, 1930,

Order as follows:

Article 1. The present Constitution shall cease to be operative, and shall be replaced by the Constitution annexed to this Order.

The two Houses existing at present shall be dissolved.

Article 2. Subject to the application of Articles 48 and 60, as provided for in the next Article, the new Constitution shall become effective as from the day Parliament assembles.

Article 3. From the date of the publication of the Constitution and until Parliament assembles, legislative power, together with the other powers assigned to Parliament by virtue of the Constitution, shall be vested in us and exercised by us, in accordance with Articles 48 and 60 of the Constitution, by means of decrees (issued) by us, provided, however, that the provisions embodied in these (decrees) shall not contravene the basic principles established by the Constitution.

Article 4. During the period referred to in the preceding Article, it shall be permissible, for the sake of maintaining public order, religion or morals, to suppress or abolish any newspaper or periodical, by a decision (qarar) of the Minister of Interior, following two warnings, or by a decision of the Council of Ministers without a warning.

Article 5. Laws promulgated between June 21, 1930, and the meeting of Parliament, shall be submitted to the two Houses during the first session of Parliament; if they are not so submitted they shall cease to have effect in future.

The laws (so) submitted may not be repealed or amended except by a law.

Article 6. All (legal) principles established by laws, decrees, orders, regulations and decisions, ... and, similarly, all (legislation) passed and acts and measures taken, in conformity with the rules and procedures in force until the publication of our Order No. 42, of 1923, as well as all (legal) principles established by those decrees considered valid by Law No. 2, of 1926, shall continue to be effective, provided, however, that their operation shall be consistent with the principles of freedom and equality guaranteed by the Constitution. All this (shall take place) without prejudice to the right of the legislative power to repeal and modify (the above), within the limits of its competence, provided, however, that such (right) does not prejudice the principle established by Article 27 of the Constitution, concerning the non-retroactivity of laws.

All (legal) principles, as well as all (legislation) passed and acts and measures taken, in conformity with the rules and procedures established by our Order No. 46, of 1928, shall also continue to be effective, provided, however, that this does not prejudice the right of the legislative power mentioned in the preceding paragraph. (All these) shall continue to have retroactive legal effect.

The same shall apply to the (legal) principles and to all (legislation) passed and acts and measures taken since June 21, 1930, and until the publication of the (present) Constitution.

Article 7. Our Ministers shall carry out this our Order and the Constitution annexed thereto, each in so far as he is concerned.

Issued at the Muntazah Palace, on Jumada al-'Ula 30, 1349 A.H. (October 22, 1930), in two copies, one of which shall be kept at our Court, and the other, at the office of the Prime Minister; (and has been given the number of 70, 1930).

(Counter-signed): ISMA'IL SIDQI, Prime Minister   *(Signed) FU'AD*

47

The Rise of Mass Doctrinal Parties, the Program of Hassan al-Banna and the Muslim Brotherhood, 1936 *

This pamphlet, addressed to King Faruq, Prime Minister Nahhas, and the other notables of the Arab world, summarizes the aims of Shaykh Hassan al-Banna (1906-1940), Supreme Guide of the Muslim Brotherhood. The Muslim Brotherhood was and is a many-faceted organization. In some respects it is a modernized Sufi (Muslim fraternity) organization that offers a blueprint for social and economic reorganization according to commonly understood Muslim principles and a vehicle for resistance to foreign control. Much of its early success can be attributed to the imaginative leadership and attractive personality of Shaykh al-Banna, who combined a sound grounding in fundamentalist Islamic teachings with credentials as an activist in the Egyptian struggle against imperialism. By the time of al-Banna's assassination in 1949, the Brotherhood counted some two million members, many of them from the lower middle class, in Egypt, Sudan, Syria, and most other Arab countries. When it rose in the 1930's it offered an attractive alternative to the vaguely liberal parliamentary regimes then governing much of the Arab East. The Brotherhood was instrumental in pioneering the ideology and technique of mass political organization

* Translated from *Naḥw al-Nūr* (Towards the Light) (Cairo: Jam'īyat al-'Ikhwān al-Muslimīn, 1936), 38-48.

used by the revolutionary regimes which rose in the Arab world in the 1950's. It is significant that members of 'Abd al-Nasir's Free Officers movement were at one time or another closely connected with the Brotherhood and that the Free Officers borrowed heavily from its secret, cellular structure before the 1952 revolution and from its techniques for appealing to the masses after the uprising. Indeed, 'Abd al-Nasir and other similar leaders stole the Brotherhood's thunder not only organizationally but also in their concern for pan-Arab unity and social justice for the masses. The Brotherhood's underground still operates and, although it has declined in popularity, it remains a factor in Arab politics.

TOWARD AN EFFECTIVE REFORM

After having studied the ideals which ought to inspire a renascent nation on the spiritual level, we wish to offer, in conclusion, some practical suggestions. We will list here only the chapter headings because we know very well that each suggestion will require profound study as well as the special attention of experts; we know also that the needs of the nation are enormous; we do not believe that the fulfilling of the needs and the aspirations of the country will be an easy thing; what is more, we do not think that these goals can be reached in one journey or two. We realize the obstacles which these problems must overcome. The task will require a great deal of patience, a great deal of ability, and a willing tenacity.

But one thing is certain: resolve will lead to success. A dedicated nation, working to accomplish the right, will certainly reach, with God's help, the goals toward which it strives.

The following are the chapter headings for a reform based upon the true spirit of Islam:

I. In the political, judicial, and administrative fields:

    1st. To prohibit political parties and to direct the forces of the nation toward the formation of a united front;

    2nd. To reform the law in such a way that it will be entirely in accordance with Islamic legal practice;

    3rd. To build up the army, to increase the number of youth groups; to instill in youth the spirit of holy struggle, faith, and self-sacrifice;

    4th. To strengthen the ties among Islamic countries and more particularly among Arab countries which is a necessary step toward serious examination of the question of the defunct "Caliphate";

    5th. To propagate an Islamic spirit within the civil administration so that all officials will understand the need for applying the teachings of Islam;

    6th. To supervise the personal conduct of officials because the private life and the administrative life of these officials forms an indivisible whole;

7th. To advance the hours of work in summer and in winter so that the accomplishment of religious obligations will be eased and to prevent all useless staying up late at night;

8th. To condemn corruption and influence peddling; to reward only competence and merit;

9th. Government will act in conformity to the law and to Islamic principles; the carrying out of ceremonies, receptions, and official meetings, as well as the administration of prisons and hospitals should not be contrary to Islamic teachings. The scheduling of government services ought to take account of the hours set aside for prayer.

10th. To train and to use the "Azharis," that is to say, the graduates of Al-Azhar University [a Cairo institution specializing in Islamic learning, ed.], for military and civil roles;

II. In the fields of social and everyday practical life:

1st. The people should respect public mores: this ought to be the object of special attention—to strongly condemn attacks upon public mores and morality;

2nd. To find a solution for the problems of women, a solution that will allow her to progress and which will protect her while conforming to Islamic principles. This very important social question should not be ignored because it has become the subject of polemics and of more or less unsupported and exaggerated opinion;

3rd. To root out clandestine or public prostitution and to consider fornication as a reprehensible crime the authors of which should be punished;

4th. To prohibit all games of chance (gaming, lotteries, races, golf);

5th. To stop the use of alcohol and intoxicants—these obliterate the painful consequences of people's evil deeds;

6th. To stop attacks on modesty, to educate women, to provide quality education for female teachers, school pupils, students, and doctors;

7th. To prepare instructional programs for girls; to develop an educational program for girls different than the one for boys;

8th. Male students should not be mixed with female students—any relationship between unmarried men and women is considered to be wrong until it is approved;

9th. To encourage marriage and procreation—to develop legislation to safeguard the family and to solve marriage problems;

10th. To close dance halls; to forbid dancing;

11th. To censor theatre productions and films; to be severe in approving films;

12th. To supervise and to approve music;

13th. To approve programs, songs, and subjects before they are released, to use radio to encourage national education;

14th. To confiscate malicious articles and books as well as magazines displaying a grotesque character or spreading frivolity;

15th. To carefully organize vacation centers;

16th. To change the hours when public cafes are opened or closed, to watch the activities of those who habituate them—to direct these people towards wholesome pursuits, to prevent people from spending too much time in these cafes;

17th. To use the cafes as centers to teach reading and writing to illiterates, to seek help in this task from primary school teachers and students;

18th. To combat the bad practices which are prejudicial to the economy and to the morale of the nation, to direct the people toward good customs and praiseworthy projects such as marriage, orphanages, births, and festivals; the government should provide the example for this;

19th. To bring to trial those who break the laws of Islam, who do not fast, who do not pray, and who insult religion;

20th. To transfer village primary schools to the mosque and to carry on all beneficial activities there (selecting officers, matters of health, interested support for young children learning their religious duties, introducing the old to science);

21st. Religious teaching should constitute the essential subject matter to be taught in all educational establishments and faculties;

22nd. To memorize the Koran in state schools—this condition will be essential in order to obtain diplomas with a religious or philosophical specialty—in every school students should learn part of the Koran;

23rd. To develop a policy designed to raise the level of teaching, to unify the different teaching specialties, to bring together the different branches of culture—emphasis should be put upon teaching morality and physics;

24th. Interested support for teaching the Arabic language in all grades—absolute priority to be given to Arabic over foreign languages (primary teaching);

25th. To study the history of Islam, the nation, and Muslim civilization;

26th. To study the best way to allow people to dress progressively and in an identical manner;

27th. To combat foreign customs (in the realm of vocabulary, customs, dress, nursing) and to Egyptianize all of these (one finds these customs among the well-to-do members of society);

28th. To orient journalism toward wholesome things, to encourage writers and authors who should study specifically Muslim and Oriental subjects;

29th. To safeguard public health through every kind of publicity—increasing the number of hospitals, doctors, and out-patient clinics;

30th. To call particular attention to the problems of village life (administration, hygiene, water supply, education, recreation, morality).

III. The economic field:

1st. Organization of the "zakat tax" according to Islamic precepts, using zakat proceeds for welfare projects such as aiding the indigent, the poor, orphans; the zakat should also be used to strengthen the army;

2nd. To prevent the practice of usury, to direct banks to implement this policy; the government should provide an example by giving up the "interest" fixed by banks for servicing a personal loan or an industrial loan, etc.;

3rd. To facilitate and to increase the number of economic enterprises and to employ the jobless there, to employ for the nation's benefit the skills possessed by the foreigners in these enterprises;

4th. To protect workers against monopoly companies, to require these companies to obey the law, the public should share in all profits;

5th. Aid for low-ranking employees and enlargement of their pay, lowering the income of high-ranking employees;

6th. Reducing the number of posts for employees, to be satisfied with a job necessary for the country, payment of employees should be apportioned on a fair basis;

7th. To encourage agricultural and industrial works, to improve the situation of the peasants and industrial workers;

8th. To give special attention to the technical and social needs of the workers, to raise their level of life and aid their class;

9th. Exploitation of certain natural resources (unworked land, neglected mines; etc.);

10th. To give priority to projects whose accomplishment is vital to the country. . . .

48

The Progress of Pan-Arab Nationalism Between the Wars, a View by Sati' al-Husri*

Among the most important apostles of pan-Arab nationalism is Sati' al-Husri (b. 1879) a man whose lifetime has spanned virtually the entire period of the creed's development. Al-Husri, born into an Aleppo family, was educated and worked in Ottoman Istanbul where his understanding of nationalist theory was influenced by the ideas of Ziya Gökalp and other pioneers of Turkish nationalism. From 1918 until 1941, he was associated with the Hashimite governments in Syria and Iraq and he served as a high official in the Iraqi Ministry of Education. In the 1930's, he engaged in intellectual jousts with champions of various parochial versions of Arab nationalism. The most important of these encounters were his arguments popularizing the pan-Arab view of nationalism against Egyptian particularists, including the formidable Taha Husayn. Al-Husri's views won wide acceptance among the younger generation of Arab nationalists who, when they achieved power in the 1950's, tried to accomplish a pan-Arab program. Thus, al-Husri was instrumental in enlarging the basic theoretical context within which Arab national development would occur after World War II. Moreover, as early as the 1930's, his theories provided a practical framework for opposing British and French political supremacy and Zionist activities in Palestine. The combination of theoretical ideals with concrete proposals to cope with existing problems is a characteristic of al-Husri's writings.

*   *   *

The Arab Revolt [of 1916-1918] ... was designed to guarantee the independence of all the Arab provinces in the hope of creating an independent state uniting all of these provinces under one flag.

But the peace treaties and the establishment of the mandates shattered this dream and partitioned those Arab provinces which were detached from the Ottoman sultanate into seven political units: one was placed entirely under foreign domination, two others became completely independent; the other four ultimately were each endowed with an autonomous administration under mandatory control.

* Sati' al-Ḥusri, *Muḥāḍarat fī Nushū' al-Fikrah al-Qawmīyah* (Lectures Upon the Origins of the Idea of Nationalism) (Cairo: Maṭba'at al-Risālah, 1951), 225-238.

The establishment of Arab states in this way encouraged those "regional tendencies" inherent in each of them. These tendencies have countered Arab nationalist
thinking, have impeded its development, and even at certain times and in certain situations, threatened its ruin.

Some succeeding events strengthened particular regional tendencies, others
aided general nationalist thinking. The conflict which rages between the two
opposing and contradictory movements still exists today.

But to understand the movement of events we have to look at each of the
two movements separately since the end of the First World War.

First, we should say that regionalism has profited from the status quo while
nationalism has sought the realization of a dream. Regionalism supported the
frontiers which were drawn and worked to preserve and strengthen them by any
means while nationalism considered them to be temporary and supported those
movements which ignored or reduced them. Each of these two tendencies derived
its strength from certain happenings and other events.

Regionalism is particularly influential among the common people and suits the
interest of those seeking self-gain the best. Each state has obvious and real characteristics as well as a concrete power: it has an individual flag which all the
world can see, police and an army, individual identity cards and passports, a
political administration with money and with special assemblies. But nationalist
thought, within the context of great numbers of states, is private in its orientation
for it exists inside these states as a spiritual concept present inside the soul and
preoccupying it.

Finally, the state also passes laws, organizes the economy, and directs culture.
Thus, the existence of a number of different states naturally results in a more or
less wide separation of peoples despite the indivisibility of the nation to which
they belong.

All of this actually happened in the Arab countries after their division into
several states. Each of them was founded within a different environment than
that which prevailed during the establishment of the others. Some countries were
placed under the mandate of one state while other brother countries were
mandated to another state and ruled in a totally different type of situation. That is
why the people of these states began to grow apart and move away from each
other given so many regimes with their several administrative, judicial, economic,
and cultural organizations.

In each state a group of leaders, managers, and politicians formed with the
help of existing conditions. This group preached in favor of the status quo and
impeded any change in the situation.

To these internal factors must be added the external factors. The occupying
mandatory powers generally were opposed to a reunification of the Arab peoples.
It was in their interest that the people were isolated from each other and that
differences among them were augmented and strengthened. Consequently, they

expended all their efforts to restrain the rise of Arab nationalist thought. This was a particular preoccupation of France. She struggled against Arab nationalist sentiment with all the propaganda tools at her disposal. "Syrians are not Arabs although they speak Arabic. The Lebanese have nothing in common with the Arabs or the Syrians: they are Phoenicians. In particular, the Christians among them are the most distant from the Arabs and from Arabism because they are the descendants of the Crusaders who came to Syria and Lebanon from several European countries, especially from France." Such were the ideas which during their mandate the French enforced and inculcated in the press, and the schools, and also in religious sermons. They succeeded in influencing some people who were the agents of regionalist propaganda and the enemies of Arab nationalism.

Nevertheless, the factors explained above did not prevail entirely because there were others beside which encouraged completely opposite actions. Many of those turned aside hindrances, stimulated improved general understanding and unity, and struggled against the causes of division.

The development of communications was the most important of these factors. The opening of an automobile route across the Syrian desert played a role in this. This route reduced distances considerably, for to go from Damascus to Baghdad once took about three weeks. After the opening of this route the time was reduced to two days, then to one, and ultimately to eight hours. Finally, after air connections were inaugurated it was reduced even more to about two hours.

It is not necessary to point out that one such development of transport considerably reinforces nationalist thought and weakens divisive regionalist tendencies while enlarging the limits of cultural relations.

Moreover, it is undeniable that the tourist traffic to Lebanon also has played a considerable part in this development. It has been one of "the factors opposing separatism," for it encourages a better understanding among the several Arab countries and facilitates their rapprochement. We must say that Lebanon's geographic situation and climate have made the country a natural summering place for the Arabs especially since the development of communications and transport. Every year many Iraqis, Syrians, Palestinians, and Egyptians, accompanied by their families, travel to Lebanon to spend the summer or to vacation there. Naturally, they come to know Lebanon and the Lebanese. Also, they mingle with each other there despite the different passports which they carry and the countries from which they originate. The meetings that occur in this way set up new mutual bonds and stimulate a result contrary to those causes of divisiveness which have been mentioned already.

I should add to these two "semi-materialistic" factors, the cultural influences such as the press, radio, poetry, literature, and the theatre which are not blocked by political frontiers but which surmount them and bloom naturally in all the different countries where Arabic is spoken.

It is understandable, for all these reasons, that a common feeling formed almost spontaneously in the different Arab countries.

Moreover, to these "passive" influences we have to add active influences. Some nationalists began to write poems, compose hymns, make speeches and lectures, and to publish books and articles in order to spread nationalist ideas, to strengthen nationalist sentiment, and to struggle against regional tendencies. In addition, they occupied themselves in establishing associations, and founding clubs in order to extend the range of their activities and to enhance their influence among the population.

Finally, some governments themselves assumed the role of diffusing the idea of Arab nationalism. They introduced into the programs of some schools, studies which clearly encouraged this goal.

These works and these attempts were undertaken first inside each separate state, then later, by men from different countries working in permanent organizations or participating in periodic congresses. Ultimately, the Arab states themselves also took an active part in these works and efforts.

This was the way in which Egypt began to play a very important role....

Egypt began to interest itself in Arab problems during the second quarter of the century, especially after the second half of the third decade. Its participation in the Arab nationalist movement opened in "the history of the birth of nationalist thought among the Arabs," a new chapter marking a new phase of development.

In this next phase, nationalist thinking was no longer associated only with certain clubs and groups operating within each separate Arab state but also was the subject of discussion within associations and groups made up of citizens from all the Arab countries and it was their main interest.

The Arab Medical Congress which has met for nearly a week each year since 1937, the creation of the General Federation of Arab Medical Associations, in 1941, the Congress of Arab Lawyers convened in 1944, also the Congress of Arab Engineers which met for the first time in 1945, formed major parts of the new movement.

These general Arab congresses contented themselves at first only with scientific and cultural problems but they enlarged their scope until political affairs were included in their discussions. Such was the case with the General Palestinian Arab Congress which was held at Bludan in 1937 and which assembled delegates and representatives from all Arab countries to discuss what actions should be taken to combat Zionism.

Following these popular congresses, governments also began to feel the necessity of collaborating and cooperating to safeguard common Arab interests. The holding of the Round Table Conference at London in 1939 to examine Palestinian problems was the first expression of this sentiment as official representatives of all the Arab states took part.

It is not necessary to explain that all these associations and popular and governmental organizations prepared the way for the formation of a permanant organ concerned with matters of interest to the Arab states.

The questions which concerned Palestine, for one thing, and the violent crises which upset the Arab world during the Second World War, for another, led the Arab governments to feel strongly the necessity for increasing cooperation among them.

Naturally, it was that powerful feeling which led to the establishment of the League of Arab States. As is known, the League was founded officially in 1945, after talks and exchanges of notes which took place during the year 1944 ...

49

Inter-Arab Cooperation, the Alexandria Protocol and the Arab League, 7 October 1944 *

The impulse toward the creation of a regional organization of Arab states was a result of British attempts to gain Arab war-time cooperation in exchange for support of the goal of Arab unity combined with Arab desires to facilitate some degree of collaboration or even unification among the several Arab states. In 1943, the Iraqi prime minister, Nuri al-Sa'id (1888-1958), presented a plan for amalgamation of Syria, Lebanon, Palestine, and Transjordan into a single Greater Syria, the latter's close federation with Iraq, and the creation of a League of Arab States. With British encouragement, diplomats representing several Arab states held conversations which led to the summoning of a 'General Arab Conference' at Alexandria in the autumn of 1944. The 'Protocol' issued by the conference called for the creation of an Arab League that would be a cooperative association of independent Arab states rather than a vehicle for unification or federation of the several Arab countries. While the 'Protocol' expressed a hope that the League could "consolidate" in the future its endorsement of the facts of Arab political division disappointed many idealistic pan-Arabists. Nevertheless, given continued Arab political disunity, the Arab League since its formal foundation in 1945, has been the chief vehicle for promoting inter-Arab state coop-

* "The Alexandria Protocol," *The Arab World* (New York: Arab Information Center, April 1959), 15-16.

eration. Moreover, it has provided increasingly valuable support for intellectual, social, and economic modernization projects in the Arab world.

The chiefs and members of the Syrian, Trans-Jordanian, Iraqi, Lebanese and Egyptian delegations at the Preliminary Committee of the General Arab Conference,

Anxious to strengthen and consolidate the ties which bind all Arab countries and to direct them toward the welfare of the Arab world, to improve its conditions, insure its future, and realize its hopes and aspirations,

And in response to Arab public opinion in all Arab countries,

Have met at Alexandria from Shawwal 8, 1363 (September 25, 1944), in the form of a Preliminary Committee of the General Arab Conference, and have agreed as follows:

1. League of Arab States

A League will be formed of the independent Arab States which consent to join the League. It will have a council which will be known as the "Council of the League of Arab States," in which all participating states will be represented on an equal footing.

The object of the League will be to control the execution of the agreements which the above states will conclude; to hold periodic meetings which will strengthen the relations between those states; to coordinate their political plans so as to insure their cooperation, and protect their independence and sovereignty against every aggression by suitable means; and to supervise in a general way the affairs and interests of the Arab countries.

The decisions of the Council will be binding on those who have accepted them except in cases where a disagreement arises between two member states of the League in which the two parties shall refer their dispute to the Council for solution. In this case the decision of the Council of the League will be binding.

In no case will resort to force to settle a dispute between any two member states of the League be allowed. But every state shall be free to conclude with any other member state of the League, or other powers, special agreements which do not contradict the text or spirit of the present dispositions.

In no case will the adoption of a foreign policy which may be prejudicial to the policy of the League or an individual member state be allowed.

The Council will intervene in every dispute which may lead to war between a member state of the League and any other member state or power, so as to reconcile them.

A subcommittee will be formed of the members of the Preliminary Committee to prepare a draft of the statutes of the Council of the League and to examine the political questions which may be the object of agreement among Arab States.

2. COOPERATION IN ECONOMIC, CULTURAL, SOCIAL AND OTHER MATTERS

A. The Arab States represented on the Preliminary Committee shall closely cooperate in the following matters:

(1) Economic and financial matters, i.e., commercial exchange, customs, currency, agriculture, and industry.

(2) Communications, i.e., railways, roads, aviation, navigation, posts and telegraphs.

(3) Cultural matters.

(4) Questions of nationality, passports, visas, execution of judgments, extradition of criminals, etc.

(5) Social questions.

(6) Questions of public health.

B. A subcommittee of experts for each of the above subjects will be formed in which the states which have participated in the Preliminary Committee will be represented. This subcommittee will prepare draft regulations for cooperation in the above matters, describing the extent and means of that collaboration.

C. A committee for coordination and editing will be formed whose object will be to control the work of the other subcommittees, to coordinate that part of the work which is accomplished, and to prepare drafts of agreements which will be submitted to the various governments.

D. When all the subcommittees have acommplished their work the Preliminary Committee will meet to examine the work of the subcommittee as a preliminary step toward the holding of a General Arab Conference.

3. CONSOLIDATION OF THESE TIES IN THE FUTURE

While expressing its satisfaction at such a happy step, the Committee hopes that Arab States will be able in the future to consolidate that step by other steps, especially if postwar events should result in institutions which bind various Powers more closely together.

4. A SPECIAL RESOLUTION CONCERNING LEBANON

The Arab States represented on the Preliminary Committee emphasize their respect of the independence and sovereignty of Lebanon in its present frontiers, which the governments of the above States have already recognized in consequence of Lebanon's adoption of an independent policy, which the Government of that country announced in its program of October 7, 1943, unanimously approved by the Lebanese Chamber of Deputies.

5. A Special Resolution Concerning Palestine

A. The Committee is of the opinion that Palestine constitutes an important part of the Arab World and that the rights of the Arabs in Palestine cannot be touched without prejudice to peace and stability in the Arab World.

The Committee also is of the opinion that the pledges binding the British Government and providing for the cessation of Jewish immigration, the preservation of Arab lands, and the achievement of independence for Palestine are permanent Arab rights whose prompt implementation would constitute a step toward the desired goal and toward the stabilization of peace and security.

The Committee declares its support of the cause of the Arabs of Palestine and its willingness to work for the achievement of their legitimate aim and the safeguarding of their just rights.

The Committee also declares that it is second to none in regretting the woes which have been inflicted upon the Jews of Europe by European dictatorial states. But the question of these Jews should not be confused with Zionism, for there can be no greater injustice and aggression than solving the problem of the Jews of Europe by another injustice, i.e., by inflicting injustice on the Arabs of Palestine of various religions and denominations.

B. The special proposal concerning the participation of the Arab Governments and peoples in the "Arab National Fund" to safeguard the lands of the Arabs of Palestine shall be referred to the committee of financial and economic affairs to examine it from all its angles and to submit the results of that examination to the Preliminary Committee in its next meeting.

In faith of which this protocol has been signed at Faruq I University at Alexandria on Saturday, Shawwal 20, 1363 (October 7, 1944).

50

The Maturing of Nationalism in Morocco from the Founding of the Moroccan National Party to King Muhammad V's Assumption of Nationalist Leadership, 1937-1947 *

Nationalism in Morocco emerged from an amalgamation of the Salafiyah movement, which was inspired by ideals of Islamic fundamentalism and Arab unity as propagated in the Qarawiyin University in Fez, with the efforts of young Moroccan intellectuals educated in France and Cairo. It received its first concrete expression in the reaction to the 'Berber Edict,' issued by the French protectorate authorities in May 1930, which encouraged Berber separatism and contained anti-Arab and anti-Islamic implications. The *Kutlat al-Amal al-Watani* (National Action Bloc) formed by a coalition of Muslim divines and educated Arab townsmen channeled the response against French divide-and-rule tactics designed to attract rural Berber elements to French policy and culture. Although the Kutlah was repressed by the French resident general in March of 1937, it reemerged in a new guise, the *Hizb al-Watani* (National Party), a few months later. The National Party's 'Covenant', issued in October 1937, which looked toward the gradual accomplishment of independence did much to popularize nationalist sentiment. However, a new repression and the outbreak of World War II postponed the further organization of Moroccan nationalism until the end of hostilities. At that point, Sultan (later King) Muhammad V (1927-1961) assumed the leadership of the nationalist cause. This was made most apparent in a royal visit to Tangier, a city then under international administration but officially part of the monarch's realm, in April 1947. During his tour the sultan made a series of speeches, many of which were phrased as religious sermons since the ruler was both the official spiritual and political head of Morocco. These

---

* a. "Moroccan National Covenant of the National Party, 7 Sha'ban 1356/13 October 1937," in 'Alāl al-Fāsi, *Al-Harakāt al-Istiqlālīyah-fi al-Maghrib al-'Arabi* (Cairo: Maṭba'at al-Risālah, 1948), 253-255; English translation by Hazem Zaki Nuseibeh, *The Independence Movements in Arab North Africa* (Washington: American Council of Learned Societies, 1954; New York: Farrar, Straus and Giroux), 188-190.

   b. "Statement of 12 April 1947 of Muhammad V to Foreign Journalists at Tangier," al-Fāsi, *Al-Harakāt . . .*, 360; English translation in, *Independence Movements . . .*, 275-276.

directly challenged the French and Spanish protectorates by pointing to the basically Arab character of Morocco and its cultural ties to other Arab states, the need to reunify the country, and the need to organize a free, democratic government. Muhammad V's efforts earned him exile in 1953, but in 1955, a hero's return to his country as king of an independent Morocco.

A. MOROCCAN NATIONAL COVENANT OF THE NATIONAL PARTY, 7 SHA'BAN 1356 (13 OCTOBER 1937)

The conferees, assembled in the house of the brother Ahmad al-Sharqāwi, the evening on Wednesday the seventh of Sha'ban 1356 A.H. (October 13, 1937), representing the branches of the party in the regions of Oujda, Taza, Burkan, Fez, Mekens, Wazān, Sidi Qāsim, Sidi Yehya, Qunaytera, Cela, Rabat, Casablanca, Jadīdah, Āsifi, Suwayrah, Settat, and Marrakech—

In view of the material and the moral crises through which our Moroccan land is passing at the present time and which have resulted from the policy of discrimination and oppression pursued by the Residency-General;

Whereas the protectorate had failed to live up to its promises, made on many occasions, concerning the implementation of Morocco's urgent demands, in spite of the country's dire need for action in the fields of relief, social welfare, and justice;

In view of the painful events in Meknes, is the course of which the blood of freedom-loving martyrs was spilled, fire was opened on the unarmed crowds, and many an innocent person was arrested for trial before military tribunals, their only guilt being their solidarity with the prisoners who had resisted the spoliation of their water rights;

In view of the persecutions, resorted to by the authorities, in the Bawādi [tribal areas] of Morocco against any one who joins or contacts our movement, and where hundreds have been imprisoned, tortured, and bound in iron chains, where livestock was let loose and house holdings were destroyed; and whereas the administration had let loose a regular cavalry force upon the abode of Matarnāgha of Bani Yāzagha where they committed the most heinous crimes including the destruction of tents, the plundering of properties and livestock, the raping of women, and the torturing of the innocent.

Whereas the authorities had given a free hand to Bayyāz, Glaoui, and their associates, to oppress Moroccans by means of imprisonment, exile, torture, flogging, iron chains, and rape; whereas their attacks extended to the 'Ulemas of the Sharī'ah law and other religious dignitaries, the closing down of Koranic schools, the banishment of their teachers, the desecration of their books, the confiscation of the national press, and the imposition of punishment and fines upon those who read them;

Whereas the responsible authorities had permitted a missionary pilgrimage to the church of St. Theresa, as patroness of the missionaries at al-Khumīsāt, and had forbidden students of Āyat Urbīl of the Zamūr tribe to hold their annual Koranic celebration, except on condition that they refrained from reciting the Koran and from including in their prayers solicitations for His Majesty the Sultan; whereas previous to that they had banned celebrations in Marrakech, on the anniversary of the Prophet's birthday, which proves that the spirit of the Berber policy still dominates the administration of the protectorate;

Whereas the Moroccan press has been choked by censorship, suspension, and confiscation;

Whereas the government has turned down all applications for the establishment of various societies and associations;

Whereas the hired pro-colonial press has been levelling accusations and depicting our movement in a manner contrary to facts;—and having listened to the statements of the National Party pertaining to the aforementioned, and having studied the situation in all its ramifications, the conferees have resolved:

1. To condemn in the name of the Moroccan people all the dastardly persecutions committed in Meknes, Marrakech, Bani Yazāgha, and the Moroccan Bawādi; to protest against these barbarous acts, which represent the spirit of the Dark Ages, and to demand the release of all internees and the expeditious payment of compensation to all the victims and their families for the losses inflicted upon them.

2. To protest in the strongest terms against the persecution of the Moroccan press and resolve to combat all measures and attempts designed to suspend, confiscate, or censor the press; to demand for the Moroccan press the same rights that are accorded to the foreign press in Morocco.

3. To condemn the persistent refusal of the Residency to concede to Moroccans the right to form associations whatever be their aims.

4. To place responsibility for this policy upon the reactionary spirit which permeates the protectorate circles and which had in the past stirred the indignation of Morocco and the Muslim world.

5. To pledge themselves to resist these iniquitous policies by all effective and legitimate means, and leave decisions as to methods and timing to the responsible leaders of the party.

6. To condemn all the false accusations and the tendentious fabrications attributed to our movement by reactionary circles and the colonial press; and to declare that the movement has no connection with any foreign element and should not be regarded as responsible except for what emanates from those responsible in the National Party.

7. To resolve that no understanding with the government is possible so long as liberties are suppressed and persecutions persists and so long as the urgent demands of Morocco have not been met; to consider His Majesty the King's patron-

age of his people and the sympathetic attitude of the libertarians in the French democratic camp as facilitating the attainment of these objectives.

8. To pledge God to carry out the contents of this Covenant and declare their readiness to offer the necessary sacrifices with a view to this end.

B. STATEMENT OF KING MUHAMMAD V IN TANGIER, 12 APRIL 1947

Before we leave Tangier, the diplomatic capital of Morocco, it gives us pleasure to address our thanks to all the inhabitants for their expressions of fidelity and loyalty; in the reception accorded to us, Tangier has fulfilled our confidence in her as a Moroccan city staunchly attached to the throne of her king. She has thus proved that Morocco is a unity whose symbol is the crown; may this journey expedite a solution of the question of Tangier.

Morocco is anxious to maintain good relations in the future with all the states that have struggled for freedom and still continue to support it; she is most anxious to attain her full rights.

Needless to say, Morocco is an Arab country closely attached to the Arab East; it is natural, therefore, that these ties grow closer and stronger, particularly so since the Arab League has become an organization playing an important role in world politics.

We are convinced that the role of culture is important in the achievement of closer ties; therefore, we are endeavoring to promote the enlightenment of the Moroccan people, principally through the establishment of educational institutions having identical curricula with those of the educational colleges of Egypt, Syria, Lebanon, and Iraq; we have also endeavored since our accession to the throne to accord our subjects [the] democratic rights, and we are confident of achieving all our aspirations.

51

The Erosion of Imperialism, Manifesto of the National Tunisian Conference, 23 August 1946 *

Tunisia was the first North African country to nurture a nationalist movement. However, after its beginnings, prior to World War I, the nationalists were fragmented into several competing, relatively ineffective bodies. During World War II, Tunisia's nominal ruler, Munsif Bey (1942-1943) began to organize nationalist sentiment, but was deposed by the French. Nevertheless, Habib Bourguiba, leader of the Neo-Dustur party, after returning from exile in 1943, started another drive to amalgamate nationalist strength. His efforts were rewarded in 1946, when a conference was held including delegates from the Neo-Dustur and old Dustur parties, the Tunisian Trade Union Federation, and the faculty of Zaytunah University. Although the French authorities scattered the meeeting it was able to issue a manifesto which called for complete unconditional independence, a point which had split Tunisian nationalists previously. Moreover, Bourguiba became the chairman of the nationalist coalition. The coalition's efforts eventually included direction of armed resistance to continued French protection and were crowned with success in 1955, when Tunisia gained internal autonomy to be followed by full independence a year later.

*   *   *

Whereas Tunisia had been, prior to 1881, an independent state linked to the Islamic Caliphate primarily by spiritual rather than by political bonds;

Whereas Tunisian sovereignty had been internationally recognized as evidenced by the treaties into which it had entered with the various powers;

Whereas France, after defending the independence of Tunisian from the Ottoman state, had forced the acceptance of her occupation by a treaty imposed by brazen force upon King Muhammad al-Sādiq, in which treaty the people of Tunisia had never acquiesced;

Whereas the Treaty of Bardo did not exclude the Tunisian state from the international community and did not divest it of its internal or external authority;

* "Manifesto of the National Tunisian Conference, 23 August 1946," in 'Alāl al-Fāsi, Al-Harakāt al-Istiqlālīyah-fi al-Maghrib al-'Arabi (Cairo: Maṭba'at al-Risālah, 1948), 89-92; English translation by Hazem Zaki Nuseibeh, The Independence Movements in Arab North Africa (Washington: American Council of Learned Societies, 1954; New York: Farrar, Straus and Giroux), 75-77.

Whereas the occupation—after sixty-five years—had turned into a system of colonial exploitation, in which Tunisia has been divested of her sovereignty and her wealth systematically plundered, while both the spirit and the letter of the Treaties of Bardo and of Marsa did not contemplate more than a temporary trusteeship;

Whereas the protecting authority had not confined itself to the duties of supervision but had replaced the protected state in the direct management of government and public affairs;

Whereas the French authority had seized legislative functions belonging to His Majesty the Bey with the result that the latter had become a mere honorary official whose private liberty is curtailed, while Tunisian ministers of state had been reduced to mere dignitaries for ceremonial purposes; whereas governors had been reduced to mere tools for implementing the orders of French civil controllers, while all jurisdiction had been transferred from Tunisian to French officials whose experience or integrity have not in most cases been free of aspersions;

Whereas France, which had been officially obligated to protect the person and the family of the Bey, had violated her pledge once more by forcibly ejecting the legitimate sovereign of the land. His Majesty the Bey al-Munsif, thereby committing a breach of one of the basic tenets of the Islamic religion;

Whereas these aggressions had given rise to an unstable administrative system which is neither fully taken over nor autonomous, and in which location of authority and responsibility is non-existent;

Whereas France since the imposition of the occupation had pursued a policy of impoverishing the people and plundering their best lands and of allocating more than two-thirds of the budget for the administrative apparatus (almost wholly French), a budget over which the people have no control and which is based on per capita levies rather than on wealth; whereas Tunisia has been subjected to currency, customs, and commercial policies that are detrimental to her economic well-being and place the country in an unfavorable position in its dealing with foreign countries;

Whereas the policy of impoverishment is the consequence of the colonization of the country by colonists and officials, of enticing the people to assimilation, of granting naturalization to Maltese, English, White Russians, Spanish Republicans, and even in the latter phase to Italians, with a view to increasing the number of French citizens in proportion to the indigenous population and of destroying the Tunisian character of the country.

Whereas the financial extravagance indulged in in pursuance of this policy has led to the failure of the protecting power to meet its social obligations towards the Arab population—such as adequate nutrition, housing, medical care, and education.

Whereas the protecting authority had neglected its humanitarian obligations for the benefit of the capitalist exploiters who dominate the country and had failed in its alleged civilizing mission by virtue of which it sought to justify the imposition of its protectorate;

Whereas the representation of the French Tunisian community in the French Parliament constitutes a further aggression against Tunisian sovereignty and a serious breach of the international obligations underlying the occupation;

Whereas the people of Tunisia have been denied in their own country the most fundamental freedoms, that is, the freedom of thought, speech, publication, association, and movement, and have lived for twenty years under military law.

Whereas the protecting state had failed in its obligation to safeguard the security of the country and had delivered it over to the Axis Powers, while the Tunisians had expended their blood on every occasion in defense of France and her allies.

Whereas the Treaty of Bardo had specifically stipulated that the protectorate was essentially an ad hoc arrangement and that French interests arising therefrom could not under any circumstances assume the character of permanence;

Whereas on the other hand, the interests of a protecting power should not stand in the way of the people's inalienable rights to determine freely their own fate;

Whereas colonialism is rightly regarded as a cause of international animosities and conflicts, and considering that the United Nations had explicitly and unequivocally condemned it, and had announced as one of its war-aims the right of all peoples to choose the form of government acceptable to them together with the restoration of independence and sovereignty to the peoples from whom they had been forcibly alienated;

Whereas this new principle has been reiterated and recognized at the various world conferences, and France had been one of the colonial powers which had assented to the principle that no nation has the right to rule over peoples under its authority indefinitely;

For all these reasons, the Tunisian National Conference declares that the protectorate regime is a political and economic system totally incompatible with the sovereignty of the Tunisian nation and its vital interests, and that this colonial regime has shown its bankruptcy before the world after an experiment lasting sixty-five years. The conference also declares the unflinching determination of the people to restore their complete independence and to join as a sovereign state the League of Arab States and the United Nations, and to demand participation in the peace conference.

52

The Clash of Zionism and Arab Nationalism, Nuri al-Sa'id's Description of Arab Frustrations, 13 February 1939 *

During the 1930's, conditions in Palestine progressively deteriorated as pressure built up to provide there a haven for European Jewish victims of Nazi persecution. These desires collided with those of the local Arab population who feared that they were becoming a minority and second-class citizens in their own country. Virtual civil war broke out in 1936, during which Arab organizational weaknesses became apparent. For their part, the disorders prompted the determined Zionists to begin organizing an underground army and political administration. With war looming in Europe, Britain tried to quiet Palestine by limiting Jewish immigration, but Arab objections to other aspects of the proposed British solution meant that nobody was satisfied with the situation. More than in most modern international disputes, the struggle for Palestine and its successor Arab-Israeli dispute has been marked by bitter passion, inflexibility of policy, adherence to unsupported suppositions, and fears that compromise can only bring imminent betrayal. The following excerpt displays some of the specific Arab fears as seen in the 1930's. These are expressed not by a radical anti-imperialist, but by an old-line ally of the British. Still, the mixture of betrayed outrage and despair that generally charged Arab views on Palestine is apparent in the speech.

*   *   *

But I cannot help feeling that it is most unfortunate that this Conference has to be held at a time when the Jews of Europe are suffering such unparalleled misfortune. When England, Holland, France and America are endeavouring to find places of refuge for the unfortunate Jews who are being expelled from European countries it is particularly unfortunate that the Arabs should have to resist their further entry into Palestine. Ever since the Arabs became an Empire and a ruling race the Jews have been guaranteed protection within their dominions. When Christendom rejected the Jews Islam sheltered them. It is exceedingly un-

* Excerpts from, "Speech by General Nuri al-Sa'id at the Palestine Conference, London, 13 February 1939," in Nuri as-Sa'id, *Arab Independence and Unity* (Baghdad: Government Press, 1943), 50-51, 55-58.

fortunate that at this miserable period in Jewish history the Arabs, of all people, should appear to be intolerant.

As a representative of a State in which Jews are equal citizens with Arabs I do not want the present unfortunate state of the Jews in Europe to be used as a reason for denying justice to the Arabs, who have never in all their history been intolerant towards the Jews.

The interest which the Government of Iraq takes in the settlement of the present dispute in Palestine is very real and lively. Not only is she a close neighbour of Palestine but until the post-war policy was initiated in that country the composition of her population was not dissimilar. Both countries are predominantly Arab in character and both contain large Jewish communities. Both formed part of the pre-war Ottoman Empire and were governed by the same laws. Their culture, customs and local institutions are almost identical. So I must preface my remarks with some observations on the position of the Jews in the pre-war Ottoman Empire and in Iraq up to the present day. Throughout the Ottoman Empire were scattered numerous Jewish communities whose numbers were estimated at 800,000 in 1912. They were mostly centred in the towns but a few agricultural communities did exist. Many of the communities were large ones, that in Iraq amounting to 70,000. These Jews were organised as a community (millet), and were race-conscious, maintaining their religion, their language and their racial purity. Though the Zionist movement existed before the war in Europe, we in the Ottoman Empire, though aware of its existence, regarded it as a spiritual symbolic movement quite unassociated with politics. There was certainly no movement of Jews from within the Ottoman Empire to Palestin. The Jews were very contented, prosperous subjects of the Ottoman Empire, and happy to remain in the various provinces which had sheltered them for centuries. Ottoman Jews had no sympathy with Zionism and such migration as did take place was to such centres as Bombay, Calcutta, Shanghai and London, in all of which places Jews from Baghdad and other parts of the Ottoman Empire established large and prosperous business houses. No Jews from Iraq or other parts of the Ottoman Empire ever went to Palestine to settle. Palestine was not regarded by the Jews in other parts of the Ottoman Empire as a particularly desirable place in which to settle or a land to which they must return.

The Jews, moreover, identified themselves very much with the life of the district in which they lived. For example, those in Iraq would consider themselves Iraqi Jews and as much concerned with the life of the Arabs who surrounded them, and with whom they had daily contacts, as with Jewry in other parts of the Ottoman Empire....

In 1916 Arab officers and men who had served in the Turkish Army volunteered for service in the forces of King Hussein, relying on the promises made by Great Britain in the McMahon correspondence to create an Arab State which would include Palestine. The regular contingents of trained troops were almost entirely composed of Palestinians, Syrians and Iraqis, they bore the brunt of the fighting.

When we in this Army heard of the Balfour Declaration at the end of 1917 we were near Aqaba and the news caused consternation throughout the whole of the Arab force. We took counsel together and declared that we must abandon the fight for Arab independence in co-operation with the forces of Great Britain until we received assurances that the McMahon pledges would be carried out. King Hussein had already protested against the Balfour Declaration, and in January 1918 received from Commander Hogarth of the Arab Bureau, who had been sent by His Majesty's Government to Jedda, specific assurances that the Balfour Declaration would not conflict with the political and economic freedom promised to the Arabs in the MacMahon correspondence. He was further assured by His Majesty's Government through Commander Hogarth that the Balfour Declaration envisaged no more than a restricted settlement of Jews in Palestine for spiritual and cultural reasons, and that no Jewish State was contemplated. King Hussein communicated these assurances to the Arab forces who in consequence continued to fight side by side with the British.

A similar Declaration was made to Arab leaders in Cairo in June 1918 in an official statement issued on the authority of the Foreign Office and known as "the Declaration to the Seven." In this statement His Majesty's Government promised that the future government of Palestine would be based upon the principle "of the consent of the governed."

In view of these explanations the Arabs for the remainder of the war prosecuted their campaign against the Turks, confident that at the conclusion of hostilities Palestine would be a part of the Arab State. Haji Amin al Husseini, the present Grand Mufti, actively recruited volunteers in Palestine from among the Arabs to join the forces of King Feisal. He openly promised them that Palestine would be part of the Arab State, and these promises were known to the British Officers, who actively assisted him in his efforts to recruit Palestinian Arabs. All the British officers with whom the Arabs fighting in the Hejaz, Palestine and Syria came in contact shared their views, and though Zionist propaganda in Europe and America was, as we now know, giving a totally different interpretation of the Balfour Declaration, the Arabs were encouraged by Great Britain to believe that Palestine would in future enjoy self-government as part of the Arab State. The Anglo-French Declaration of November 1918 did nothing to disabuse them of this belief. After the Armistice, when Zionist aspirations became known, Arab alarm was revived. The Arab leaders themselves were fully employed consolidating the positions captured in Syria against any possible recurrence of the war and in creating an Arab State in Syria. They were content to leave the administration of Palestine temporarily in the hands of their Allies, the British, whom they still trusted to carry out their promises in respect to Palestine when peace should be finally declared.

At the Peace conference, however, they discovered for the first time that the British Government was prepared to give the Jews a far different "National Home" in Palestine than the British Government had explained to the Arabs. This led to the conversations between the late King Feisal and Lord Curzon in 1919 to which I have already referred. That this Arab view of the meaning attached to the Balfour Declaration at the time it was made in 1917 is correct is confirmed by the "Statement of Policy in Palestine" isued by the Colonial Office in 1922 which defines "The Jewish National Home" as "a centre in which the Jewish people as a whole may take, on grounds of religion and race, an interest and a pride." The Jews were to be allowed to establish in Palestine a religious and cultural centre and not a political state embracing all Palestine and to be populated by mass immigration of Jews to the eventual exclusion of all Arabs.

But though the Colonial Office, in 1922, gave this definition of the National Home, the British Government had in that year accepted from the League of Nations the Palestinian Mandate, a document which the British and Zionists had jointly drafted and which contemplated the establishment in Palestine of a Jewish National Home of a totally different kind. From 1919 the Arab leaders and the people of Palestine had viewed with alarm the growing Zionist pretensions. They had protested repeatedly against them but were always told to wait until the League of Nations decided what the future of Palestine was to be. When the Mandate was proclaimed and their worst fears justified they refused all co-operation with Great Britain, feeling that they had been betrayed. They could not possibly accept any offer by Great Britain of palliatives such as mock legislative councils until their basic claims under the McMahon promises were admitted and accepted by Great Britain without qualification.

In consequence the Arabs have consistently refused to recognise the Mandate for Palestine. For several years, however, opposition in Palestine, though active, was not violent, and Great Britain had a chance to set up self-governing institutions had she so desired. But the administration of Palestine by Great Britain was not even in accordance with the Mandate. Article 2 of the Mandate, which is the most important article, imposes two equal duties upon the Mandatory: first, the establishment of the Jewish National Home, and secondly, the development of self-governing institutions. Other articles impose other duties, but they are only designed to further these two objects. One of these secondary duties is that of facilitating Jewish immigration under suitable conditions and without prejudice to the rights and position of other sections of the population.

During the past eighteen years the Mandatory Power has encouraged Jewish immigration to the maximum degree possible and in every manner, natural and artificial. Moreover, the Jewish Agency, the official body set up to co-operate with the Government on this and other matters, has admitted conniving at the entry into Palestine of even those Jews whose entry into Palestine was considered undesirable and whom the regulations of the Government did not allow to enter.

In addition to encouraging Jewish immigration, the Government of Palestine has faithfully carried out the obligations to secure the establishment of the Jewish Nation Home. Hebrew has become an official language and large numbers of foreign Jews with no Palestinian status have been employed in the Government services. Zionist bodies have been allowed to acquire large tracts of land and to control the sources of minerals and of electric power, no option being allowed either to Arabs or the Palestine administration to share in the resources of their country.

As a result, during the past eighteen years over 300,000 Jews have migrated to Palestine—that small country. We want to know when, if ever, this immigration will cease. Do the British promises to the Jews entail a continuous, never-ending stream of Jewish immigrants into Palestine? At what date will the promises made to the Jews in the Balfour Declaration come to an end? Jewish immigration, according to the Mandate, should be conditioned by the rights and position of other sections of the population of Palestine. According to the reports of the Shaw Commission, and the Hope-Simpson Inquiry, the economic capacity of Palestine to absorb further immigrants came to an end in 1930.

But nothing has been done to further the second objective laid down in Article 2 of the Mandate—the development of self-governing institutions. The Palestinian Arabs have not been given any share in the government of their own country. No institutions have been set up to prepare them for self-government. They are farther from the ideal of self-government now than they were in 1920. For eighteen years they have been ruled by a peculiar combination of Crown Colony Government and Zionism co-operating very closely, to the total exclusion of Arabs. All this has gone on notwithstanding the fact that in the Passfield White Paper it was declared: "It is the considered opinion of His Majesty's Government that the time has now come when the important question of the establishment of a measure of self-government in Palestine must, in the interest of the community as a whole, be taken in hand without further delay." The Passfield White Paper sets forth the advantages to be gained by the development of self-governing institutions, but the Zionists were hostile to any effort on the part of the Mandatory Power to carry out this duty of promoting self-governing institutions in spite of the fact that this duty of promoting self-governing institutions was laid down in Article 2 of the Mandate and was of equal importance with that of creating a Jewish National Home. Zionist policy was naturally animated by a desire to delay the promotion of self-governing institutions in Palestine until the day when, by intensive mass immigration of Jews, they had established in Palestine sufficient Jews to outnumber the Arabs.

In 1930, following the reports of the Shaw Commission and the Hope-Simpson Inquiry, Lord Passfield, then Colonial Secretary, issued a White Paper in which he accepted many of the Arab claims and proposed what amounted to a new policy in Palestine. Though it did not meet all the Arab demands it roused their hopes that a new era would open in Palestine. Unfortunately, Zionist agitation and political pressure in England compelled the Prime Minister to give public assurances to the Zionist leader, Dr. Weiszmann, that British policy in Palestine would not be radically changed. This letter to Dr. Weiszmann of February 1931, though laid before the House of Commons, has not the status of a Command Paper, and the late Mr. Ramsay MacDonald was particularly anxious that the letter should not have the same status as the dominating document—the Passfield White Paper. But in the result British policy in Palestine continued unchanged, and in consequence the Arabs have been compelled to regard this letter as the ruling declaration of British policy.

Since that date the Arabs of Palestine have been in despair. Convinced that no report of any Commission that was favourable to the Arab claims would be acted upon by Great Britain, the Arabs of Palestine felt that it was impossible any longer to work with the Mandatory Power.

This failure of the Mandatory Power to fulfil the specific duty imposed by the Mandate to promote self-governing institutions has, in the opinion of all Arabs, led to the present breakdown in the administration of the country. In the White Paper Lord Passfield asserted that it is a primary duty of the Administration to ensure peace, order and good government in Palestine. This elementary duty the Mandatory Power has failed to do. Her policy has alienated the goodwill of the Arab majority and open rebellion has resulted. The civil authorities have had to call in the aid of the military and air forces to hold down the country and the ordinary liberties of the subjects have been suspended.

53

The Clash of Zionism and Arab Nationalism, the Biltmore Zionist Program, 11 May 1942*

In May of 1942, a conference that included Weizmann, Ben Gurion, and major British and American Zionist leaders was held in New York's Hotel Biltmore. Convinced of Arab intransigence, British duplicity, and meeting at a time when Hitler had converted his persecution into wholesale genocide of Europe's Jews, the conference concluded that the concept of a Jewish National Home did not hold enough guarantees for the survival of the Jews as a people. Hence the conference altered Zionists' goals to embrace full independence—that

* *Book of Documents Submitted to the General Assembly of the United Nations* (Jewish Agency for Palestine, 1947), 226-227; see also J. C. Hurewitz, *Diplomacy in the Near and Middle East* (Princeton: D. Van Nostrand, 1956), 234-235.

"Palestine be established as a Jewish Commonwealth." It also called for removal of all restrictions on Jewish immigration and land purchases as well as the creation of a Jewish military force flying its own flag to fight the Axis. The confrontation of Zionist and Arab nationalisms over control of Palestine became a total deadlock by the end of World War II, as both sides began girding themselves for the armed struggle they felt certain would come. The British, meanwhile, found themselves trying to reconcile two ambitions that were irreconcilable.

*   *   *

1. American Zionists assembled in this Extraordinary Conference reaffirm their unequivocal devotion to the cause of democratic freedom and international justice to which the people of the United States, allied with the other United Nations, have dedicated themselves, and give expression to their faith in the ultimate victory of humanity and justice over lawlessless and brute force.

2. This Conference offers a message of hope and encouragement to their fellow Jews in the Ghettos and concentration camps of Hitler-dominated Europe and prays that their hour of liberation may not be far distant.

3. The Conference sends its warmest greetings to the Jewish Agency Executive in Jerusalem, to the Va'ad Leumi, and to the whole Yishuv in Palestine, and expresses its profound admiration for their steadfastness and achievements in the face of peril and great difficulties. The Jewish men and women in field and factory, and the thousands of Jewish soldiers of Palestine in the Near East who have acquitted themselves with honor and distinction in Greece, Ethiopia, Syria, Libya and on other battlefields, have shown themselves worthy of their people and ready to assume the rights and responsibilities of nationhood.

4. In our generation, and in particular in the course of the past twenty years, the Jewish people have awakened and transformed their ancient homeland; from 50,000 at the end of the last war their numbers have increased to more than 500,000. They have made the waste places to bear fruit and the desert to blossom. Their pioneering achievements in agriculture and in industry, embodying new patterns of cooperative endeavor, have written a notable page in the history of colonization.

5. In the new values thus created, their Arab neighbors in Palestine have shared. The Jewish people in its own work of national redemption welcomes the economic, agricultural and national development of the Arab peoples and states. The Conference reaffirms the stand previously adopted at Congresses of the World Zionist Organization, expressing the readiness and the desire of the Jewish people for full cooperation with their Arab neighbors.

6. The Conference calls for the fulfilment of the original purpose of the Balfour Declaration and the Mandate which *"recognizing the historical connection of the Jewish people with Palestine"* was to afford them the opportunity, as stated by President Wilson, to found there a Jewish Commonwealth.

The Conference affirms its unalterable rejection of the White Paper of May 1939 and denies its moral or legal validity. The White Paper seeks to limit, and in fact to nullify, Jewish rights to immigration and settlement in Palestine, and, as stated by Mr. Winston Churchill in the House of Commons in May 1939, constitutes "a breach and repudiation of the Balfour Declaration." The policy of the White Paper is cruel and indefensible in its denial of sanctuary to Jews fleeing from Nazi persecution; and at a time when Palestine has become a focal point in the war front of the United Nations, and Palestine Jewry must provide all available manpower for farm and factory and camp, it is in direct conflict with the interests of the allied war effort.

7. In the struggle against the forces of aggression and tyranny, of which Jews were the earliest victims, and which now menace the Jewish National Home, recognition must be given to the right of the Jews of Palestine to play their full part in the war effort and in the defense of their country, through a Jewish military force fighting under its own flag and under the high command of the United Nations.

8. The Conference declares that the new world order that will follow victory cannot be established on foundations of peace, justice and equality, unless the problem of Jewish homelessness is finally solved.

The Conference urges that the gates of Palestine be opened; that the Jewish Agency be vested with control of immigration into Palestine and with the necessary authority for upbuilding the country, including the development of its unoccupied and uncultivated lands; and that Palestine be established as a Jewish Commonwealth integrated in the structure of the new democratic world.

Then and only then will the age-old wrong to the Jewish people be righted.

54

The Realization of Zionism, Proclamation of Independence of the State of Israel, 14 May 1948 *

The independence of Israel was declared on the evening before the British gave up the Palestine mandate and evacuated their last troops. The proclamation summarizes the essential content of Zionism and its claim to Palestine. The ceremony was an emotion-filled experience held in a small hall

* "Proclamation of the State of Israel, 14 May 1948," *Israel Government Yearbook* 5711 (Tel Aviv: State of Israel, Office of Information, 1950), 43-45.

in Tel Aviv's Museum; it took seventeen minutes for Israel's first prime minister, David Ben Gurion (b. 1886) to read the declaration. Civil strife, including pitched battles, had shattered Palestine's peace for months but the departure of the British brought the immediate entry into the country of military formations detached from the newly organized national armies of the adjacent Arab states. So began the 1948 Arab-Israeli War, the first of three major encounters fought between Arab and Israeli troops in 1948, 1956, and 1967, all of which ended with Israeli military victories. With the proclamation of an independent Israel, the various Zionist political organizations existing in Palestine were invested as Israel's government.

*   *   *

THE LAND OF ISRAEL was the birthplace of the Jewish people. Here their spiritual, religious and national identity was formed. Here they achieved independence and created a culture of national and universal significance. Here they wrote and gave the Bible to the world.

Exiled from the Land of Israel the Jewish people remained faithful to it in all the countries of their dispersion, never ceasing to pray and hope for their return and the restoration of their national freedom. Impelled by this historic association, Jews strove throughout the centuries to go back to the land of their fathers and regain their statehood. In recent decades they returned in their masses. They reclaimed the wilderness, revived their language, built cities and villages, and established a vigorous and ever-growing community, with its own economic and cultural life. They sought peace yet were prepared to defend themselves. They brought the blessings of progress to all inhabitants of the country and looked forward to sovereign independence.

In the year 1897 the First Zionist Congress, inspired by Theodor Herzl's vision of the Jewish State, proclaimed the right of the Jewish people to national revival in their own country.

This right was acknowledged by the Balfour Declaration of November 2, 1917, and reaffirmed by the Mandate of the League of Nations, which gave explicit international recognition to the historic connection of the Jewish people with Palestine and their right to reconstitute their National Home.

The recent holocaust, which engulfed millions of Jews in Europe, proved anew the need to solve the problem of the homelessness and lack of independence of the Jewish people by means of the reestablishment of the Jewish State, which would open the gates to all Jews and endow the Jewish people with equality of status among the family of nations.

The survivors of the disastrous slaughter in Europe, and also Jews from other lands, have not desisted from their efforts to reach Eretz-Yisrael, in face of difficulties, obstacles and perils; and have not ceased to urge their right to a life of dignity, freedom and honest toil in their ancestral land.

In the Second World War the Jewish people in Palestine made their full contribution to the struggle of the freedom-loving nations against the Nazi evil. The sacrifices of their soldiers and their war effort gained them the right to rank with the nations which founded the United Nations.

On November 29, 1947, the General Assembly of the United Nations adopted a Resolution requiring the establishment of a Jewish State in Palestine. The General Assembly called upon the inhabitants of the country to take all the necessary steps on their part to put the plan into effect. This recognition by the United Nations of the right of the Jewish people to establish their independent State is unassailable.

It is the natural right of the Jewish people to lead, as do all other nations, an independent existence in its sovereign State.

ACCORDINGLY WE, the members of the National Council, representing the Jewish people in Palestine and the World Zionist Movement, are met together in solemn assembly today, the day of termination of the British Mandate for Palestine; and by virtue of the natural and historic right of the Jewish people and of the Resolution of the General Assembly of the United Nations.

WE HEREBY PROCLAIM the establishment of the Jewish State in Palestine, to be called Medinath Yisrael (The State of Israel).

WE HEREBY DECLARE that, as from the termination of the Mandate at midnight, the 14th—15th May, 1948, and pending the setting up of the duly elected bodies of the State in accordance with a Constitution, to be drawn up by the Constituent Assembly not later than the 1st October, 1948, the National Council shall act as the Provisional Government of the Jewish State, which shall be known as Israel.

THE STATE OF ISRAEL will be open to the immigration of Jews from all countries of their dispersion; will promote the development of the country for the benefit of all its inhabitants; will be based on the principles of liberty, justice and peace as conceived by the Prophets of Israel; will uphold the full social and political equality of all its citizens, without distinction of religion, race or sex; will guarantee freedom of religion, conscience, education and culture; will safeguard the Holy Places of all religions; and will loyally uphold the principles of the United Nations Charter.

THE STATE OF ISRAEL will be ready to cooperate with the organs and representatives of the United Nations in the implementation of the Resolution of the Assembly of November 29, 1947, and will take steps to bring about the Economic Union over the whole of Palestine.

We appeal to the United Nations to assist the Jewish people in the building of its State and to admit Israel into the family of nations. In the midst of wanton aggression, we yet call upon the Arab inhabitants of the State of Israel to preserve the ways of peace and play their part in the development of the State, on the basis of full and equal citizenship and due representation in all its bodies and institutions—provisional and permanent.

We extend our hand in peace and neighbourliness to all the neighbouring states and their peoples, and invite them to cooperate with the independent Jewish nation for the common good of all. The State of Israel is prepared to make its contribution to the progress of the Middle East as a whole.

Our call goes out to the Jewish people all over the world to rally to our side in the task of immigration and development and to stand by us in the great struggle for the fulfillment of the dream of generations for the redemption of Israel.

With trust in Almighty God, we set our hand to this Declaration, at this Session of the Provisional State Council, on the soil of the Homeland, in the city of Tel Aviv, on this Sabbath eve, the fifth of Iyar, 5708, the fourteenth day of May, 1948.

Signed:

D. Ben Gurion, Daniel Auster, Mordechai Ben Tov, Itzhak Ben Zvi, Eliahu Berlin, P. Bernstein, Rabbi Zeev Gold, Meir Grabosvky, Y. Greenbaum, Abraham Granovsky, Eliahu Dobkin, Meir Vilner, Zorah Warhaftig, Herzl Vardi, Rachel Cohen, Kalman Kahana, S. Kovashi, Itzhak Meir Levin, M. D. Levinstein, Zvi Luria, Golda Myerson, Nahum Nir-Raffalkes, Zvi Segal, Yehuda Leib Hacohen Fishman, David Zvi Pinhas, Aharon Zisling, Moshe Kolodni, E. Kaplan, A. Katzenelson, Felix Rosenblut, D. Remez, B. Repetur, Mordecai Shattner, Ben Zion Sternberg, Bechor Shitreet, Moshe Shapira, Moshe Shertok.

55

The Arab Reaction to Israel's Creation, Constantine Zurayq's Call for a New Order, 1948 *

Arab reactions to the success of Zionism in Palestine have varied. Understandably, the bitterest thoughts were harbored among younger Palestinians. Feelings ranged from anger to shame, from despair to resolve to undo the defeat, and usually were an amalgam of such emotions. While many writers

* Qunsṭanṭīn (Constantine) Zurayq, *Ma'na al-Naḳba* (Bayrut: Dar al 'Ulm al-Malāyin, 1948), 42-43, 50-55; English translation by R. Bayly Winder, *The Meaning of the Disaster* (Beirut: Khayats College Book Cooperative, 1956), 34-35, 41-45.

searched for scapegoats and pointed an accusing finger at the West, particularly Britain and the United States, or at their own leaders, others singled out the shortcomings of Arab society, still half traditional in attitude, operation, and structure. Constantine Zurayq's analysis is of the latter school and it was very instrumental in preparing the psychology of young, educated Arab nationalists for a revolution in their political system and their social and economic order. He lays stress on the role that would have to be played by the modernly oriented elite if regeneration was to succeed. The book was prophetic in many ways and the ideas it helped to propagate have determined much of the course of Arab history since the early 1950's.

*   *   *

The explanation of the victory which the Zionists have achieved—and only a person who deceives and blinds himself can deny the victory—lies not in the superiority of one people over another, but rather in the superiority of one system over another. The reason for this victory is that the roots of Zionism are grounded in modern Western life while we for the most part are still distant from this life and hostile to it. They live in the present and for the future while we continue to dream the dreams of the past and to stupefy ourselves with its fading glory.

Only a united, progressive, Arab national being will avert the Zionist danger, or for that matter any other danger which has aggressive designs on us. The first principle, then, in the long range Arab struggle is the establishment of this being, which, as I have said above, will not be achieved unless there is a fundamental transformation in Arab life. It follows that the external struggle to repel the dangers of aggression is linked with the internal struggle to establish a sound Arab being. In fact the latter is the pivot of the former and is essential to its success....

There remains one more question: where is the road to this all-inclusive revolution which, on the broadcast scale and to the greatest extent, will assure national progress?

There are some obvious roads which will lead to this revolution and which will aid it. They include: the encouragement of local initiative in the exploitation of the area's resources, the propagation of knowledge and culture by all [available] means, broadening the extent of political, social, and intellectual liberties, and the reform of administrative procedures, as well as other courses of action leading toward development and progress.

However, these courses of action, despite their far-reaching influence on the revolution to which we look forward, are limited from two points of view. The first is that they are slow to take effect and need extended effort over a long period of time in order to bring about the fundamental change which is desired in our present situation. But we are in a situation where we cannot allow time and effort the liberty to do their work slowly and calmly. The external and internal dangers which threaten our existence do not permit us to wait for gradual evolution; instead, they impose on us, if we want to be secure and to survive, a plunge forward —a [real] revolution. Secondly, the aforementioned courses of action need people who will discover, strengthen, and universalize them; they need sincere, able workers and creative leaders. These courses of action will for their part help to bring forth such leaders. They in turn, when found, will control and direct these policies with a view to multiplying their results and strengthening their effect in bringing about the fundamental change which is sought.

The factors making for progress, like all the forces of life, are interrelated and interdependent. A cause produces a result, and this result in its turn may become a cause and thus strengthen and support the first cause. It is not reasonable to want to eliminate those evolutionary factors which we have mentioned, such as propagating knowledge and so forth, but there is no doubt that the point of departure for that change and revolution at which we must today aim is no other than those who lead and shape, the creative elite which can grasp these means and push them hard along that single road which we seek.

This elite, on whose shoulders this most serious task will be laid, or which rather will seize it by force, must have already realized within itself the progress and the revolution which it seeks within society. For he who is motivated by impulse rather than by faith cannot inculcate faith in the nation no matter how loud his voice or how flowery his speech. He who has not liberated himself but remains a slave to impulses and ambitions cannot liberate any one else no matter how exalted his position or how great his authority. He whose mind is obscured and in the corner of whose brain the spider of fanaticism and reaction nests will never bring light to his nation nor will he propagate tolerance, co-operation, and unity in his society no matter what the color of the garment he wears.

Therefore, the initial condition for the success of revolutionary and progressive action is that its leaders and masters be progressive in their souls and revolutionary down to the marrow of their bones. Each of those who apply themselves to this most serious task must measure himself by this scale and evaluate himself on this basis. The people in general—and the cultured and liberated in particular—must test their leaders by this touchstone. Those whose metal is pure will be worthy of leadership, whereas those whose metal shows debasement will be condemned and rejected.

This elite must, as a prerequisite of its existence, organize and unify itself into well-knit parties and organizations. These must stand on a unified and pure doctrine and must be bound by a strong, sound loyalty to which the elite will subjugate all its divergent tendencies and in which it will willingly and freely believe. One view of the history of the various awakenings in the world demonstrates most clearly that a bringing together of the forces of these struggling elites within party organizations and the like is the greatest factor in creating the awakening and transforming the situation.

As another prerequisite of its own existence this elite must create true leadership and produce those individuals who build states, create nations, and make history. These are the ones who sow their seeds deep in the very life of the people and whose sights are at the same time set on what ought to be. They continue to work, with the support of those who believe as they do and who associate themselves with them, until they or their successors complete the fashioning of a new life and the rebuilding of a shattered being. These are those who live every minute of their lives under pressure from their consciences and in fear of the judgment of history. These are the sufis—Sufis not because they are ascetic and abstinent, but because they step forward and accept [the challenge]—who are not striving for personal satisfaction and happiness, but who will receive both through the immersion of the self in the larger entity of the fatherland. In a word these, and other reformers like them, are they without whom a nation does not exist, a civilization does not flourish, and human life has no flavor or meaning.

An Arab national life, united and progressive, which as we have said contains within itself the fundamental solution of the Palestine problem and in fact of the Arab problem in its entirety, will remain a dream and a potentiality if it is not first realized in the souls of the nation's struggling elite—led by true leaders drawn from it—and in the system which this elite sets up, and in the parties and institutions which it establishes.

As one looks around himself, he finds that this point of departure is still slight and that the struggling elite which we seek is still small and scattered. It has not become strong as a result of enlightened vision and fire-tested struggle. The hostile forces of imperialism, and the ruling classes and their temptations have collaborated to weaken and scatter it. Some individuals within it have left an impression, but as an organized group it has had no clear or palpable effect.

The young men of this nation look around in all directions, but on the one hand they do not find their ideal within the present leadership, nor on the other hand do the struggles of the disjointed nationalist cliques satisfy their eager ambition; thus despair overcomes them, and perplexity overflows in their souls. They end either by doubting their own nation and despairing of the potentialities of their people, in which case they follow a path leading toward satisfaction of desire and yielding to temptation, or else they fall prey to some destructive movement and find their consolation in uproar and disturbance for its own sake, regardless of result. No one can escape these dangers and preserve his faith and belief except the few who have strong spirits and sound sinews. But even these are in danger of dispersal and disintegration after the tragedy of Palestine!

However, whatever the case may be and no matter how weak and disunited our struggling elites may be at this time, there is absolutely no doubt that they *are* the point of departure, the beginning of the road, and the source of hope.

7

Creating a New Economic and Social Order

By the early 1950's, a new style of leadership was either clearly dominant or struggling to gain control in most Middle Eastern countries. Also, a subtle but profoundly important shift took place in the late 1950's and 1960's, away from preoccupation with achieving immediate political goals such as building modern administrative apparatus or struggling against the vestiges of imperalism, toward concentration on economic and social development. Of course, this trend manifested itself over an extended period and took more or less time in various parts of the Middle East; indeed, in some areas—many of the Persian Gulf principalities, for instance—it hardly had begun even in the late 1960's. Nevertheless, in monarchies such as Kuwayt, Saudi Arabia, and Libya, more real social and economic modernization often may have been accomplished behind the traditionalist facade of a patriarchial monarchy than in avowedly revolutionary states such as Syria. Oil-rich Kuwayt has one of the most advanced social welfare systems in the world, while Syria's exists largely on paper.

In the Arab world the shift began with the successful anti-monarchial Egyptian revolution of 1952 which was an outgrowth of the old regime's failure in the 1948 Arab-Israel war. It was led by Gamal 'Abd al-Nasir (b. 1918) and other military officers and set off a succession of rebellions and coups in several other Arab countries aimed at seizing the existing state apparatus and using it to cure social and economic ills. Initially, most of the coups were directed against the old upper-class leadership encrusted with Western associations and manners. The new leadership was usually made up of young army officers and spiced with a sprinkling of technocrats representing the educated sector of the lower middle class. As a group, they were far more concerned with gaining international respect for the Arabs, and achieving social justice and large-scale economic development (which usually implied reorganization of the agricultural system and industrialization) than they were with preserving what to them were discredited parliamentary regimes, responsive only to upper-class factions and the civil liberties that the parliamentary regimes applauded but did not often apply. Moreover, the new leaders, coming from a lower strata of society than their predecessors, usually displayed a folksy Islamic pietism that helped them to communicate with the masses and win a much larger measure of popular support than previous Arab governments had enjoyed. However, many Arab countries—Iraq is a good example—have been visited by a second wave of coups which reflect tactical disagreements and a consequent jockeying for supremacy among competing factions within the new leadership itself. Invariably, the new leadership has declared its support for the concept of pan-Arab unity, although the difficulties of achieving this goal, given the geographic immensity and the differing regional attitudes encountered in the Arab world, have become apparent to all. The Arab world can best be compared to a 4000 mile long archipelago composed of separate islands of cultivation and settlement separated from one another by vast distances of desert; just the technological difficulty of connecting the various islands or regions into which the Arab world is divided challenges even the most modern communication capabilities.

'Abd al-Nasir became the symbol of the Arab desire for unity. Between 1954 and 1956, he negotiated Britain's final withdrawal from Egypt and followed this with the diplomatic triumphs of the nationalization of the Suez Canal and the frustration of the combined Anglo-French-Israeli attack on Egypt. Arab pride in 'Abd al-Nasir's image as a "new Saladin" was concretely expressed in the experiment that joined Egypt and Syria between 1958 and 1961 in the United Arab Republic. But the break-up of this union in 1961 indicates that although the many Arab states now enjoy full political sovereignty, neither 'Abd al-Nasir nor any other Arab leader has found the formula to achieve the other main goals of Arab nationalism: unity, an acceptable solution of the Palestine dilemma, and a viable new political order that will press social and economic development.

The Arabs are far from achieving a consensus on what kind of political system should be created to guide the new order. Consequently, the Arab world is still divided politically and philosophically by the disputes of a myriad of competing ideologies, some of which have captured control of one or another of the Arab state administrations. These ideologies—actually formulas to guide future change —range over radical revolutionary statements such as those distributed by Algeria's regime or the Syrian Ba'th (Resurrection) Party; the authoritarian, statist philosophy of 'Abd al-Nasir's Egypt; the pragmatic, moderate statism of Bourguiba's

Tunisia; the liberal, parliamentary beliefs still dominant in Lebanon; or the conservative gradualism espoused by monarchial regimes in the Arabian peninsula. Many of these ideologies rather loosely use the term "socialist" to describe their basic goals. Moreover, the prevailing climate of ideological ferment has been charged also by the ramifications of political disputes among the several local polities by the Arab-Israeli imbroglio, as well as by continued great power ambitions and rivalry in the Middle East. If the dominant Arab response to these international pressures has been to stress independence and neutrality or to accept Soviet aid designed to counter the lingering influence of the West, then on the other hand Turkey and Iran, in order to preserve their independence were willing to accept American aid to counter Soviet influence.

Turkey, Iran, and Israel too, have been affected by the same basic concern expressed in the Arab states during the 1950's and 1960's to encourage social and economic modernization. Moreover, in those nations, various formulas for change have competed with one another. During the period, Afghanistan, also, after an abortive attempt under King Amanullah (1919-1929) to initiate modernization before the country had achieved meaningful political unity, made significant strides after 1950 toward forging a genuine Afghan nationalism, building a modern communications network, and stimulating agricultural development.

In Turkey, the Democratic party began its ten years of supremacy amidst optimistic hopes that a liberalization of political, economic, and religious life would be achieved. However, the freedom offered to private commercial and agricultural entrepreneurs to participate in Turkey's economic development by the mid-1950's had evolved into a near monopoly of power by a wealthy oligarchy. For a few years, all classes benefited from economic boom but unbalanced expansion, inflation, and finally, long, sharp looks by American aid officials at questionable projects began to take the gloss off the economic picture. In the late 1950's, Turkish intellectuals began to dispute the entrepreneurial oligarchy's aims, especially its lack of concern about the growing social disequilibrium in Turkey. In the late 1950's even the old elite, the military and civil servants who had dominated Turkey under Atatürk, espoused the cause of social justice being preached by the intellectuals. The ruling Democratic oligarchy answered these protests with political and intellectual repression. Finally, the coalition of the discontented gained the support of the military and unseated the Democratic Party regime in the coup d'etat of 27 May 1960, an event which ushered in the Second Turkish Republic. After some hesitation, the army restored civilian rule and a new constitution was adopted in 1961. Under the new dispensation, the diversity of modern Turkish thought—its flowering in many branches—has been most apparent and constitutes a measure of how profound the country's modernization has been. While the old style nationalism and even Islamic piety remain strong among the masses, the more sophisticated elements of the population are grappling with complex blueprints for economic and social developments, which emphasize various statist, socialist, or private initiative based solutions to Turkey's problems. Also, after the close cooperation with the Western bloc that characterized the 1945-1960 years, there has been a resurgence of isolationism and even a restrained anti-Westernism stimulated in large part by popular discontent with the way Turkey's NATO allies reacted to the Cyprus dispute of 1963-1967.

Mild anti-Westernism also is a factor among some Iranians who blame American support for the fact that the shah, in his zeal to modernize Iran, has commanded the financial resources to initiate many of his programs without first gaining full parliamentary backing for his plans. After the fall of the Mussadiq government in 1953, Muhammad Reza Shah assumed a far more active role in governing his realm than he had during the first decade of his reign. While the middle 1950's were spent increasing the efficiency of Iran's army and security establishment—in part a reward for their crucial support in the crisis of 1953— in the late 1950's the shah turned his efforts toward facilitating economic and social modernization. Since then the touchstone of the Iranian political problem has revolved around the fact that while most shades of opinion agree on the desirability of converting the regime into a true constitutional monarchy, there is also general concurrence that the country must undergo rapid, comprehensive development of its economic capabilities and social structure. However, in the late 1950's and early 1960's the shah's land reform program was subjected to determined attack in the majlis, which reflected the fact that the landowning classes held the majority there. The impasse was broken in 1961 when the shah decreed a reform program without submitting the project to parliamentary deliberation. Moreover, the shah sought to legitimize his "white-revolution" by adopting the device of referring his programs to direct plebiscite votes, again bypassing parliament. So far, the traditional loyalty of the rural masses to the concept of monarchy combined with the strong support of the Iranian army, always a main prop of the Pahlavi dynasty, has enabled the shah to move ahead in his own fashion and to disregard widespread grumbling among the wealthy and intellectual classes.

Despite the concern evidenced in Middle Eastern countries for stimulating modernization, genuinely modern attitudes are characteristic of only a small (although a growing) percentage of the population. Conversely, traditionalism guides but a limited (and a decreasing) part of the populace. Actually it seems that most people and institutions are animated by cultural amalgams that are mixtures of old and new. Moreover, change is occurring at different rates of speed according to the place and the institution in question. Consequently, the environmental and value factors that guide Middle Eastern life are presently in acute disequilibrium. The fact that improved health standards have stimulated rapid population growth has compounded the prevailing imbalance. One aspect of this is seen in the relationship between the area's cities which have been more influenced by modernization than the tradition-bound countryside. In common with the situation in most modernizing societies, the Middle East's cities are attracting many rural emigrants and the municipalities have been hard put to provide the services needed to integrate the new arrivals. Governments in the Middle East have encouraged much of this urbanization and social mobility by concentrating many of their modernization projects in the urban areas where a skilled work force can be more easily recruited. Modern educational facilities, for instance, are far more plentiful in the cities than in isolated villages. In Turkey, relatively more modern than most Middle Eastern countries, serious efforts to extend the state educational network into the countryside did not begin until the late 1940's and early 1950's. Probably the most spectacular efforts to alter rural, social, and economic patterns were the land reform schemes that were introduced in many Middle Eastern countries during the 1950's. These projects have achieved only limited practical success, but they are good indicators of the thrust of change during recent years.

Generally, Middle Eastern countries, most of which are not well endowed with resources, have come to rely upon statist economic policies in order to make the most of scarce savings. The underdeveloped agricultural economies of the area traditionally have not produced much excess income that can be saved for reinvestment. Large-scale development projects have been financed chiefly by one of two methods. Projects such as the Trans-Iranian railway were paid for by enforced savings that were extracted from the population, especially the peasantry, through increasing taxes. Foreign aid in the form of long-term credits from Western governments and the Soviets or investment concessions to private concerns has been another leading source of money. The Soviets financed the Aswan High Dam project in Egypt while private American investors supplied the risk capital to develop the oil fields of Saudi Arabia and other Middle Eastern states. Indeed, oil royalties now are another large source of development capital. Decisions concerning how savings will be invested also have been heavily influenced by statist politics. In some countries, such as Iran and Turkey, private business, especially in services such as insurance or in consumer industry such as food processing, has been encouraged in order to diversify the economy. On the other hand, 'Abd al-Nasir's "Arab Socialism" has eliminated much of the private sector of the Egyptian economy, which until 1952 was controlled largely by foreign business interests. But everywhere in the Middle East, aspirations have far outrun the human and material resources available for social and economic development.

56

Formulas for Change, The Evolution of Nasserism, 1952-1962 *

When 'Abd al-Nasir led the Free Officers to power in Egypt in 1952, he was not clear on how to regenerate Egyptian society. Originally, friendly to the West, and desirous of freeing Egypt's political life from royalist restraints and corruption, eventually he concluded that Egypt's potential role in the world could be accomplished only if the country cut its close ties with the West and radically restructured its internal life. The searching, tentative nature of the leader's thinking during his early days in power, is well reflected in the *Philosophy of the Revolution* where he used a theatrical analogy comparing Egypt to a stage role seeking a heroic actor to realize its promise. In the years that followed, he digested the ideas of many Arab politicians and intellectuals and eventually molded them into the statement of mature Nasserism which was contained in the 'National Charter of 1962'. But certain characteristic attitudes have colored 'Abd al-Nasir's ideological approach from 1952 until today. These include a preoccupation with asserting Arab and Egyptian dignity through the promotion of pan-Arab unity and freedom from foreign control as well as a strong concern for nurturing the social and economic well-being of the Egyptian and Arab masses. At times the implications of these attitudes in terms of practical, day to day politics have collided because the strong foreign policy required to promote Arab dignity and freedom can easily monopolize the scarce energies and resources needed to accomplish domestic social and economic development. In all his programs 'Abd al-Nasir has relied heavily on statist practices (dubbed 'Arab socialism' in 1961) and the centralized bureaucracy which, although inherited from previous Egyptian regimes, he has improved.

* a. Jamāl 'Abd al-Nāṣir, *Falsafat al-Thawrah* (Cairo: 1952); English translation, Gamal Abdel Nasser, *The Philosophy of the Revolution* (Cairo: Dar al-Ma'ref, N.D. 1954?), 20-21, 54-56.

   b. Jamāl 'Abd al-Nāṣir, *Al-Mīthāq al-Watanī* (The National Charter); English translation *The Charter presented by President Gamal Abdel Nasser, May 21, 1962* (Cairo: United Arab Republic, Information Department, 1962); résumé in, Alan W. Horton, "The Charter for National Action of the U.A.R.," *American Universities Field Staff Reports North African Series* (New York: 1962), Vol. IX, No. 5.

A. EXCERPTS FROM "THE PHILOSOPHY OF THE REVOLUTION"

I confess that after July 23rd [1952, the date of the Egyptian Revolution, ed.] I suffered fits in which I accused myself, my colleagues and the rest of the army of rashness and folly we committed on July 23rd.

Prior to that date I imagined that the whole nation was on tip-toes and prepared for action, that it awaited the advance of the vanguard and the storming of the outside walls for it to pour down in a solid phalanx marching faithfully to the great goal. I thought we were only the pioneers and the commandos, that we would only be in the front for a few hours, and that we would be soon followed by the solid masses marching to the goal. My imagination often carried me away. I felt I could hear the rattle of their solid, orderly rows as they marched onwards to the main front. My faith was such as to render everything I heard a concrete fact and not a mere vision.

After July 23rd I was shocked by the reality. The vanguard performed its task; it stormed the walls of the fort of tyranny; it forced Farouk to abdicate and stood by expecting the mass formations to arrive at their ultimate object. It waited and waited. Endless crowds showed up, but how different is the reality from the vision! The multitudes that arrived were dispersed followers and contrasted remnants. The holy march towards the great goal was interrupted. A dismal picture, horrible and threatening, then presented itself. I felt my heart charged with sorrow and dripping with bitterness. The mission of the vanguard had not ended. In fact it was just beginning at that very hour. We needed discipline but found chaos behind our lines. We needed unity but found dissensions. We needed action but found nothing but surrender and idleness. It was from this source and no other that the revolution derived its motto....

I survey our conditions and find out we are in a group of circles which should be the theatre of our activity and in which we try to move as much as we can.

Fate does not play jokes. Events are not produced haphazardly. Existence cannot come out of nothing.

We cannot look stupidly at a map of the world not realising our place therein and the role determined to us by that place. Neither can we ignore that there is an Arab circle surrounding us and that this circle is as much a part of us as we are a part of it, that our history has been mixed with it and that its interests are linked with ours. These are actual facts and not mere words.

Can we ignore that there is a continent of Africa in which fate has placed us and which is destined today to witness a terrible struggle on its future? This struggle will affect us whether we want or not.

Can we ignore that there is a Moslem world with which we are tied by bonds which are not only forged by religious faith but also tightened by the facts of history? I said once that fate plays no jokes. It is not in vain that our country lies to the Southwest of Asia close to the Arab world, whose life is intermingled with ours. It is not in vain that our country lies in the North East of Africa, a position from which it gives upon the dark continent wherein rages today the most violent struggle between white colonisers and black natives for the possession of its inexhaustible resources. It is not in vain that Islamic civilization and Islamic heritage, which the Mongols ravaged in their conquest of the old Islamic Capitals, retreated and sought refuge in Egypt where they found shelter and safety as a result of the counterattack with which Egypt repelled the invasion of these Tartars at Ein Galout.

All these are fundamental facts, whose roots lie deeply in our life; whatever we do, we cannot forget them or run away from them.

I see no reason why, as I sit alone in my study with my thoughts wandering away, I should recall, at this stage of my thinking, a well-known story by the Italian poet Luigi Pirandelli which he called, "Six Personalities in Search of Actors".

The annals of history are full of heroes who carved for themselves great and heroic roles and played them on momentous occasions on the stage. History is also charged with great heroic roles which do not find actors to play them on the stage. I do not know why I always imagine that in this region in which we live there is a role wandering aimlessly about seeking an actor to play it. I do not know why this role, tired of roaming about in this vast region which extends to every place around us, should at last settle down, weary and worn out, on our frontiers beckoning us to move, to dress up for it and to perform it since there is nobody else who can do so.

Here I hasten to point out that this role is not a leading role. It is one of interplay of reactions and experiments with all these factors aiming at exploding this terrific energy latent in every sphere around us and at the creation, in this region, of a tremendous power capable of lifting this region up and making it play its positive role in the construction of the future of humanity.

There is no doubt that the Arab circle is the most important and the most closely connected with us. Its history merges with ours. We have suffered the same hardships, lived the same crises and when we fell prostrate under the spikes of the horses of conquerors they lay with us.

Religion also fused this circle with us. The centres of religious enlightenment radiated from Mecca, from Koufa and later from Cairo. . . .

B. EXCERPTS FROM "THE NATIONAL CHARTER" OF THE UNITED ARAB REPUBLIC, 1962

Chapter I—A General View

On July 23, 1952, the Egyptian people first realized their potential for revolutionary change. Prior to that date foreign invaders were in occupation, an alien royal family ruled by whim, feudalists owned the land, and capitalists exploited the country's wealth and dominated its government. Political leaders who attempted to organize the people's struggle were lured by class privileges into cooperation with the forces dominating Egypt. Similarly, the army was weakened and diverted from supporting the national struggle—and the dominating forces were even on the verge of using the army to suppress the struggle.

On July 23, 1952, the Egyptian people raised their heads with faith and pride. Their revolutionary march began with no political organization and with an incomplete blueprint for revolutionary change. They had only six principles:

1) Destruction of imperialism and its traitorous Egyptian stooges—in the face of British occupation of the Canal Zone.
2) Ending of feudalism—in the face of feudalism's domination of the land and those on the land.
3) Ending of monopoly and the domination of capital over the government—in the face of the exploitation of resources to serve the interests of capitalists.
4) Establishment of social justice—in the face of the exploitation and despotism arising from the existing situation.
5) Building of a powerful national army—in the face of conspiracies to weaken it and use it against the revolutionary front.
6) Establishment of a sound democratic system—in the face of the political forgery that tried to veil the landmarks of true nationalism....

Chapter II—On the Necessity of the Revolution

Experience has shown that revolution is the only means to a better Arab future, free of the elements of suppression and exploitation that have long dominated the Arab nation and that will never surrender their power except by nationalist force. Revolution is the only way to deal with underdevelopment—conventional methods are no longer adequate to cope with the gap between the Arab nation and the advanced countries. The nation's material and spiritual potentialities must be mobilized—including a mobilization of scientific talent.

The Arab Revolution needs to equip itself with three powers:

1) A mentality based on scientific conviction arising from enlightened thought and free discussion—unaffected by forces of fanaticism and terrorism.
2) A freedom of movement for rapid adaptation to the changing circumstances of the Arab struggle—providing such movement observes the objectives and moral ideals of the struggle.
3) A clarity of perception of revolutionary objectives—eliminating the possibility of emotional and energy-wasting diversions.

The objectives of the struggle are a true expression of the Arab national conscience: freedom, socialism, and unity. Freedom has come to mean freedom of the nation and freedom of the citizen. Socialism has become both a means and an end, namely, sufficiency and justice. Unity has come to be the popular call for the restoration of the Arab nation that has been torn apart by its enemies. . . .

Chapter V—True Democracy

True democracy can be outlined as follows:

1) Political democracy cannot be separated from social democracy. Nobody can be regarded as free to vote without three guarantees: freedom from exploitation in all its forms; equal opportunity for a fair share of the national wealth; and freedom from all anxiety concerning future security.

2) Political democracy cannot exist under the domination of any one class. Class strife always exists in some measure, but peaceful solutions are possible within the framework of national unity. Democratic interaction between the various working forces (namely, peasants, workers, soldiers, intellectuals, and national capital) is alone capable of replacing reactionary democracy by true democracy.

3) Co-operation between the representative working forces creates a national unity that makes possible the Arab Socialist Union—which will constitute the ultimate authority, the driving force, and the guardian of the Revolution. The new constitution must guarantee that popular forces find expression in the following ways:

   a) Popular and political organizations based on free and direct elections must truly represent the popular forces. Peasants and workers must fill half the seats in political and popular organizations at all levels—including the Representative Assembly.

   b) The authority of elected popular councils must always be raised above the authority of the executive machinery of the state—at all levels.

   c) A new political organization, within the framework of the Arab Socialist Union, must recruit leaders and organize their efforts, clarify the revolutionary aspirations of the masses, and endeavor to satisfy the needs of the masses.

   d) Collective leadership must guard against the possible excesses of the individual and ensure the reign of true democracy.

4) Popular organizations, especially co-operatives and trade unions, can play an effective and influential role in promoting true democracy. These organizations are now free to form a vanguard of national democratic action. And it is now time that agricultural labor unions were established.

5) Criticism and self-criticism are important guarantees of freedom. The greatest obstacle to effective criticism is the infiltration of reactionary elements

into political organizations. By eliminating reactionary influences, the people ensure not only effective political action but also a free press (which now belongs to the people).

6) Revolutionary conceptions of true democracy must contribute decisively to the formation of citizens—especially with respect to education and to administrative regulations. Educational curricula should enable the individual to reshape his life; laws should be re-drafted to fit a new situation, and justice should cease to be an expensive commodity.

Chapter VI—The Inevitability of the Socialist Solution

Socialism is the way to social freedom; social freedom means equal opportunity to every citizen to obtain a fair share of the national wealth. The national wealth must be not only redistributed but also, and equally importantly, expanded.

The socialist solution to the problems of social and economic underdevelopment is an historical inevitability. Attempts at capitalist solutions have failed to achieve progress. Because of the development of capitalist monopolies in the advanced countries, local capitalism cannot compete without customs protection paid for by the masses and without making itself an appendage to world capitalism. The widening gap between the underdeveloped and the advanced states no longer permits that progress should be left to desultory individual efforts sustained only by the profit motive. Individual efforts cannot meet the three requirements of progress:

1) Assembling of the national savings.
2) Use of all experiences of modern science for the efficient exploitation of national savings.
3) Drafting of an over-all plan for production.

Expansion and redistribution of the natural wealth cannot be left to private, voluntary efforts—hence the necessity of people's control over all the tools of production and over the disposition of surplus in accordance with scientific planning.

But control over all the tools of production does not mean the nationalization of all the means of production, the abolition of private ownership, or interference with the rights of inheritance. Control can be achieved in two ways:

1) Creation of an efficient public sector that can provide leadership for economic progress and bear the main responsibility for planned development.
2) Existence of a private sector that without unfair exploitation can contribute its share to national development within the planned framework for economic progress.

Efficient socialist planning guarantees the just and proper use of all national resources—material, natural, and human. Efficient socialist planning permits increased production, increased consumption of goods and services, and increase of savings for new investment. With reference to effective socialist control, the lessons of history indicate the following:

1) In the field of production in general—the backbone of the production effort should be within the framework of public ownership (railways, roads, ports, airports, dams, transport, and other public services).

2) In the field of industry—most heavy and medium industry, including mining, should be publicly owned. Although some private ownership can be allowed here, and more in light industry, the public sector must always be able to guide the private sector to serve the public interest.

3) In the field of trade—foreign trade must be under the control of the people. The public sector should manage three-fourths of the country's export-import trade; the private sector should be encouraged to manage the balance. In the coming eight years the public sector should take over one-fourth of internal trade—it being understood that internal trade constitutes services and distribution against reasonable, nonexploiting profit.

4) In the field of finance—banks and insurance companies should be publicly owned.

5) In the domain of land—a distinction should be made between exploiting ownership and nonexploiting ownership; the latter serves the national economy while serving the interests of the owners themselves. The present agrarian reform laws limit individual ownership to 100 feddans; the spirit of these laws implies that the limitation should apply to an entire family (father, mother, minor children) in order to avoid clusters of family ownership. Hence, the families affected should within the coming eight years sell their excess land for cash to agricultural co-operative societies or to others. With reference to ownership of buildings, present laws effectively prevent exploitation by owners. . . .

The great importance of the public sector cannot, however, eliminate the private sector. The latter must now renovate itself and make a new and creative effort based on service rather than parasitic exploitation.

Chapter VII—Concerning Production and Society

Production is the true test of dynamic Arab power. By production we can end our underdevelopment, move rapidly toward progress, face and overcome difficulties and intrigues, and finally achieve victory over all enemies.

The battle of production, the battle to double the national income every ten years, is threatened chiefly by the increase in population. Family planning on scientific lines is necessary. Also necessary is the tremendous will to work and to produce—within the framework of a new society based on new values.

In the agricultural sector, Arab socialism does not believe in the nationalization of land but in individual ownership within limits that prevent feudalism. It believes also in agricultural co-operation in terms of credit, use of modern machinery, and marketing. The production battle in the rural areas has a threefold focus:

1) The horizontal extension of agriculture—the reclamation of desert and wasteland and the use of every drop of Nile water for irrigation.
2) The vertical extension of agriculture—the increase in productivity of land already under cultivation by means of increased application of scientific methods.
3) The industrialization and mechanization of agriculture.

Simultaneously, village life and mentality must be changed in a revolutionary and decisive way.

In the industrial sector, the latest scientific achievements and the newest equipment must compensate for present underdevelopment. Our natural and mineral wealth must be further explored. Raw materials must be processed in Egypt. Consumer industries must be further developed not only to save foreign currency but also to earn foreign currency by export. For social reasons heavy industry must be kept in balance with consumer industries. The workman now has a minimum wage and a seven-hour working day; he must respond to these new rights and privileges by a corresponding increase in his duties—particularly his responsibilty to produce. Labor unions can now take on increased responsibilities as well.

The basis of the drive toward increased production in both agriculture and industry is an increase in motivation and the establishment of the fundamental structure basic to production. Revolutionary motivation supplies the spark for improvement in all spheres. Efficient communications networks can perform miracles in terms of the unity and organization of production.

One role of the private sector (i.e., of nonexploiting national capital) is to render public ownership more effective by providing an invigorating competitive element. The socialist laws of July 1961 did not seek to destroy the private sector but sought to:

1) Create greater economic equality among citizens and contribute to the dissolution of class distinctions.
2) Increase the efficiency of the public sector, consolidate its capacity to shoulder the responsibility of planning, and enable it to play its leading role in socialist industrial development.

The private sector is limited only by the socialist laws now in force (or by those deemed necessary by popular authorities elected in the future) and is free, within the socialist framework, to promote economic development and to make reasonable nonexploiting profits.

Foreign aid, regardless of source, is accepted in order of priority as follows:

(1) unconditional aid; (2) unconditional loans; and (3) foreign investment for limited periods and unavoidable circumstances requiring international experience. Foreign aid may be viewed as an optional tax on those states with a colonial past, a compensation to the peoples who were exploited for so long.

The object of production is to provide services to society. As production and national investment increase, greater equality of opportunity is offered to the citizen. The citizen's basic rights are:

1) The right to good medical care. Health insurance must be held by each citizen.
2) The right to education that suits abilities and talents.
3) The right to secure the job that suits educational background, abilities, and interests. There should be both a minimum wage and a maximum income.
4) The right to security and rest in the event of old age or sickness.

Women must be regarded as equal to men. The family unit is basic to society and must be fostered.

The freedom of religious belief must be regarded as sacred in our new national culture with its new values. The only danger arises from reactionary attemps to exploit religion, but all religions contain a message of progress and bestow on the individual unlimited capacity for serving truth, goodness, and love.

For the individual, freedom is the greatest stimulus to all good exertion and is the basis of faith—which without freedom would become fanaticism. The individual must be free to shape his destiny, determine his position in society, express his opinion, and take an active part in his society's evolution. Law must be subservient to freedom. But no individual can be free unless he is saved from exploitation—hence, social freedom is the only way to political freedom.

Freedom of speech is the foundation of democracy; the prevalence of law is its final guarantee.

The new society, which is now being built on the basis of sufficiency and justice, needs the armed forces as a shield to defend the reconstruction of Egyptian society against external dangers. A strong army is a necessity, but the needs of defense should never have precedence over the needs of development—because without economic and social development no army can withstand the strain of long campaigns. . . .

Chapter X—Foreign Policy

The foreign policy of the people of the UAR is a true reflection of national principles.

1) War on imperialism and domination—whatever the methods they may use. The determination to end the Israeli aggression on the land of Palestine is a determination to eliminate a dangerous pocket of imperialist resistance to the

Arab struggle. The stand against racial discrimination represents a stand against a method of imperialist exploitation.

2) Consolidation of peace—peace offering the best protection for national progress. Nonalignment and positive neutrality offer the greatest hope for peace.

3) International co-operation for prosperity—since the prosperity of all peoples affects the prosperity of each. Peace must ultimately be based on comparable prosperity and on the narrowing of those economic gaps that sow the seeds of hatred.

International co-operation means (1) an end to the harboring of scientific secrets; (2) the peaceful use of atomic energy; (3) the transfer of funds now used for armaments to a budget for service to humanity; and (4) a call to international economic blocs not to obstruct the attempts at economic progress of less advanced nations. It means also that the UAR adheres not only to the concept of Arab unity but also to Pan-Africanism, Afro-Asian solidarity, the spiritual bonds of the Islamic world, and the Charter of the United Nations.

57

Formulas for Change, The Program of the Ba'th (Arab Socialist Resurrection) Party, 1963 *

The Ba'th party originated in Syria in the early 1940's as a reaction against the failings and callousness of upper-class-dominated parliamentary government. Its chief theoretician has been Michel Aflaq, a French-educated Syrian Christian who abandoned an early allegiance to communism. The party's main preoccupation from the beginning has been with revolutionizing the social and economic order on the basis of nationalization of the economy, redistribution of wealth, and worker participation in management. The Ba'th achieved power in Syria in 1958 but fear of a communist take-over led them to instigate the country's ill-starred union with Egypt. By 1963, the Ba'th in close conjunction with sympathizers in the military, had regained supremacy in Syria and taken control in Iraq. Theoretically, the Ba'thist attraction has been its strong advocacy

* "Text of the Published Deliberations of the Sixth National Congress of the Ba'th," translated by the Center for Near Eastern and North African Studies, University of Michigan, Ann Arbor, Michigan; original Arabic text in, *Al-Nahār* (Beirut: 29 October 1963).

of pan-Arab nationalism, and its socialist-statist development policy which has gained the support of intellectuals if not the masses. A major point of disagreement between Nasserites and Ba'thists has been the latter's insistence on collective, regionally decentralized leadership. However, the Ba'th leadership has proven far more adept in political maneuvering and theorizing than in actual administration and they have failed so far to realize any of their main aims except to smash the power of the old middle class. Indeed, by the late 1960's Syria's once prospering economy was in precarious state and the statist-oriented military wing of the Ba'th had achieved preponderance.

PARTY MATTERS AND THE PARTY'S RELATIONSHIP WITH THE MASSES AND THE AUTHORITY OF THE STATE

PRINCIPLE OF COLLECTIVE LEADERSHIP:

1. The Congress studied the question of Party organization in general, and emphasized the importance of maintaining the principle of collective leadership in the Party, since collective leadership represents Party democracy "at the summit." The Congress agreed also that the experience of the Party has confirmed the wisdom of the principle "of democratic centralization" as applied by the Party. The Congress considers that only the establishment of a balance between centralization on the one hand and democracy on the other will permit the Party and the masses to exercise an effective responsibility; it considers also that this balance guarantees the unity of the Party and its momentum on the one hand, and the realization of its democracy and flexibility on the other.

SOCIALIST STRUCTURE OF THE PARTY

2. In making a deep study of the Party's situation in Syria and Iraq, the Party gave special attention to the circumstances of the socialist revolution put forth by the popular masses. The Congress emphasized that the Party's socialist composition will leave its imprint on the revolution itself. Therefore, the Party decided that the socialist goals of the Party must be put into operation right away, because a thorough socialist revolution must use the workers and peasants as the basis for the Revolution and the Party simultaneously.

RIGHT OF THE POPULAR MASSES TO CRITICIZE THE PARTY

3. Under the prevailing conditions, where the Party is in power in each of the Syrian and Iraqi Regions, the Congress cautioned against the infiltration of opportunist elements into the Party. It also cautioned against the possibility that some elements of the party might succumb to the temptations of power, and the danger of turning the heads of these elements, making them feel superior to the non-party masses. The Congress emphasized that membership in the Party means

no more than an awareness of the wide and great responsibility assumed by members toward the Party. The Congress reminded the Party members of their duty to give their concern to themselves solely with their responsibilities. As to the rights of Party members, they are the same rights enjoyed by any citizen, without any addition or privilege. The Congress emphasized the right of the non-party popular masses to criticize the Party and to watch over its members. The Congress considers criticism, besides being a natural right of the masses, a guarantee of the operation of the process of rectification and interaction between the masses on the one hand and the Party and the State machinery on the other. The Congress also considers this watch as a curb on the temptations of power and on the excess manifestation of authority by the party's members, and as a means to prevent the occurrence of bourgeois manifestations by them. The Congress also stressed the necessity of paying careful attention to the quality and moral character of members of the Party, and emphasized the need for strict standards in agreeing to their affiliation and the need to prolong the period of party experimentation so as to be able to ascertain during this period the moral fitness and general aptitude of the candidates.

PARTY'S RELATIONSHIP WITH THE STATE MACHINERY

With respect to the relation between the party and the state machinery, the Congress decided upon the need for making a complete distinction between the Party and the state machinery. It warned against the danger of the state machinery swallowing up the Party, and against the possibility of the Party becoming submerged in the detailed and every-day affairs of the work of the state machinery. The Congress considers the Party as the leader of the state machinery and as the director of general policy and basic administration questions. The Congress emphasized the need for the majority of the Party leaders to give their full time to party affairs. . . .

SOCIALIST TRANSFORMATION WITHIN A DEMOCRATIC CONTEXT

6. The Congress discussed the questions of socialist transformation in the Syrian and Iraqi Regions, and decided to proceed with the task of a socialist transformation of society on a democratic basis with the participation of the popular masses. After a scientific analysis of the social, political and class conditions in the Syrian and Iraqi Regions, the Congress emphasized that the Party's dedication to the cause of the masses is preparing for the establishment of a democratic, rational, and revolutionary experience, which will be reflected not only in the two Regions but in the entire Arab country. This will be because it is preparing a realistic and objective experience which will be able to interact with the other experiences in the Arab country.

Forces of the Socialist Revolution

7.   In accordance with a scientific analysis of the political and economic circumstances in the two Regions, the Congress has reached basic conclusions as to the bourgeois middle class, which has become incapable of playing a constructive role on the economic level. Its opportunism renders it qualified only to play the role of an ally of the new imperialism. The Congress considers the workers, the peasants, the revolutionary intelligentsia, and the petty bourgeoisie to be the forces whose alliance will support the socialist revolution in its first stage.

Workers' Democratic Management

8.   In an attempt to indicate the possible horizons of the socialist evolution in the two Regions, and in the light of other revolutionary socialist experiences in the world, the Congress emphasized the need to bring about a democratic system of administration of the means of production by the workers. The Congress considers that this type of administration may enable the development of socialism in the two Regions to by-pass the stage of state capitalism experienced by most socialist experiments. The Congress emphasized the need for being alert to the dangers of bureaucracy and the continual need to curb it and control it.

State Machinery and Its Relationship with the Party and the People

9.   The Congress gave special attention to the subject of developing the state machinery and the relationship between it and the Party in particular, and between it and the popular masses in general. The Congress adopted a detailed policy to promote the revolutionary and democratic evolution of this machinery, to enable it to participate effectively in the socialist transformation. The Congress emphasized that its task is to promote evolution, not amputation. Evolution is the basis and the jumping-off point. Amputation is an exceptional course. The Congress adopted this policy both from human considerations and from its belief in the conscience of the citizen on the other hand.

10.   With respect to the question of land, the Congress adopted resolutions which countered the problem of land in a revolutionary and social manner. It agreed on the necessity of regarding the problem of land from a revolutionary outlook. It considers the agricultural revolution to be an essential step towards speedy development in the industrial sector. It considers a policy of collective farms, independently run by the peasants on land covered by Agrarian Reform, to be the sound socialist course toward developing social progress in the rural areas. It considers the establishment of these farms as a revolutionary goal towards which the Party strives. It considers the participation of peasants in the execution of the agricultural revolution to be a basic condition for the success of this revolution.

Socialist Planning

11. In its resolution, the Congress emphasized the necessity for socialist planning on regional and Arab levels, because this is the only effective means to utilize all the national, natural, and human resources in a scientific and realistic manner. It emphasized the importance of industrialization and economic development in the most important sectors to guarantee the real development of the national economy and to avoid external achievements which do not contribute to the development of production.

Socialist Policy in the Field of Services

12. The Congress adopted in its resolutions a socialist policy in the field of services. It drew attention to the open contradiction between the aspects of extravagance and waste in the state machinery and the standard of living of the popular masses. It emphasized that austerity is the duty of the well-to-do classes and of the state machinery in particular. The Congress dealt with education questions, and emphasized the need to make compulsory education a real fact. It also stressed the necessity of overcoming illiteracy, and of giving education a national and scientific aspect so as to give the coming generation a deep, complete, and coordinated understanding of human knowledge. The Congress also agreed on the need to coordinate education so as to give the requirements of development and specialization a high priority. The Congress decided to expand scientific faculties in universities, and to raise the standards of teaching in the universities. The Congress decided to expand services in the rural areas and in the remote and poor provinces. The Congress also considered that providing free medical treatment to citizens is a fundamental element of socialism, and it laid down the guidelines for executing this policy, starting with the expansion of the teaching of medicine and with the expansion of medical services given by the state, in order to liquidate the private sector in the field of medicine.

The National Guard and Its Revolutionary Tasks

13. The Congress studied the experience of the National Guards, and it considers this experience, despite its drawbacks and some mistakes that accompanied it, a bulwark for the protection of the revolution, to be developed and expanded so as to be able to perform revolutionary tasks in the field of socialist construction and in awakening the Arab popular masses. The Congress emphasized the necessity of taking a firm stand towards any errors into which the National Guard members may fall.

The Congress decided that labor, student, professional, and feminine popular organizations should have full freedom within a socialist and national framework. It emphasized the need for them to be independent of the state authority, so long as that authority is marching towards the socialist transformation and so long as the current situation has not yet been transformed into a socialist reality. The Congress considers the independence of these organizations to be a necessity dictated by the interests of those groups and classes. The Congress agreed to the right of the working class to go on strike.

IDEOLOGICAL EDUCATION IN THE ARMY

14. The Congress gave special attention to the ideological and doctrinal education of the Army. It emphasized the right of the military elements to exercise their full political rights. The Congress considers that an organic merger of the military and civilian revolutionary vanguards will bring about an ideological interaction between them, permitting unity of thought, permitting a direct and realistic joint approach to the problems of creating a socialist structure, and permitting a merger of the Army and the people into a joint revolutionary venture. The Congress concluded that the introduction of doctrinal education in the Army will create a new revolutionary understanding of discipline between the superior and his subordinate. The Congress emphasized also the importance of compulsory military service in an under-developed country, so that such service may become a training-ground for the peasant enlisted men, contributing to the overcoming of illiteracy and mental under-development in the rural areas....

POSITION TOWARD 'ABD AL-NASSER's SYSTEM

20. The Congress studied 'Abd al-Nasser's system in its positive and negative aspects. It emphasized the necessity of the presence of the UAR, with its overall and specific gravity, in any unity. The Congress considers that the positive aspects in Nasser's system drive the Party to accept Nasser's system as a partner in the unity but not as its foundation. The Congress considered that only such a form would give an opportunity to the operation of rectification and interaction between the Arab experiences. The Congress emphasized that it was Nasser himself who imposed on the Party a struggle which is only justified by the nature of the dictatorial and autocratic system of government which he himself exercises. The Congress drew attention in its resolutions to the fact that the present circumstances of Arab struggle require that this struggle be stopped, and that points of meeting and understanding be created between the liberative Arab movements on the level of the entire Arab country....

58

Formulas for Change, Habib Bourguiba and Tunisia's Pragmatic Statism, 1961 *

Habib Bourguiba has led Tunisia as prime minister and as president since the nation gained its freedom in 1955. His approach to the problems of government has been unique in the Arab world and it reflects the fact that Tunisia is a country with an old, well-developed sense of self-identity and, unlike most other Middle Eastern countries, there is a high level of genuine consensus backing government policy. A comprehensive program of social and economic reforms that has borrowed much from Kemalist Turkey and European social democracy has pushed Tunisian development. A large measure of secularization including the abolition of religious tribunals also has been carried out. Tunisians even are being pressed to adopt last names as the Turks did in the 1930's. Bourguiba has made a sustained effort to explain his plans to the people. Women and rural elements as well as the educated urban elite are involved in carrying out national programs. Bourguiba, while giving perfunctory loyalty to the pan-Arab ideal has concentrated his efforts on Tunisian, and to a much lesser extent North African, affairs. His development programs are marked by pragmatic rather than strict, doctrinaire planning. He has tried to avoid rigid categories and has sought reconciliation with most individuals or groups (such as the old-line middle-class elite) who have opposed him. Also, he has accepted limited Western foreign aid. Nevertheless, Tunisia is a state which tolerates only a single ideological party with mass membership and its progress has depended upon the leadership's reliance upon a moderate statism.

Tunisia Solves Real Problems

. . . In many underdeveloped countries, as you know, the rulers camouflage interior problems. They are always in quest of outlets to canalize the peoples passions. If, at times, interior reforms such as agrarian reform is envisaged, the publicity and fuss that is made is out of proportion with the planned project. It becomes a part of the means put into action in order to excite and encourage the people's passions in order to save appearances. The myth of the stability of

---

* Habib Bourguiba, *Building a New Tunisia* (Tunis: Secretariat of State for Information, 1961), a speech delivered 21 January 1961, excerpts.

the regime is thus upheld. Those, who by exciting the masses by the radio and other means of propaganda turn them into an instrument of power, are forced to constantly denounce the enemies. The most fashionable enemy at the moment is colonialism. It is attacked all over.

The day a nation accedes to independence it rids itself of colonialism. A new and imaginary colonialism is created in order to denounce it and thus a new outlet is found....

... This "mystique" of a struggle to the end against imaginary enemies is accompanied by a similar "mystique" of endless victories. This is repeated to a point where we begin to wonder why the battle continues in spite of so many victories. Success follows success over colonialism, zionism and heaven knows what more....

When the Hour for Settling Accounts Comes

I am sure that before long, in a few months or years, the people's eyes will be opened. These familiar "victories" will no longer fool anyone. We will see that Israel has calmly pursued her task of division. That misery has increased and the situation worsened. We will find that the population has grown larger while production has remained stationary. The problems facing underdeveloped countries in the second half of the twentieth century have not changed. The dangers have inevitably increased. What will happen when the time for settling these accounts comes? The people can be abused by sterile struggles and imaginary success only for a certain time. Lies do not lead one far. These are not lasting methods.

Tunisia enjoys the respect of all because she does not use these methods. We are respected by the two blocs as well as by the neutrals. We are both enterprising and serious, the leaders of this country are revolted by untruthfulness and thus do not mislead the people, even if they tried to do so the people would not be misled. The Tunisian rulers are not in need of using such methods in order to reinforce their authority. The man who is at the head of this state is not an unknown who came to power by a military putsch or a coup d'etat. He has no need to assert his authority by artificial personal success and prestige or by conflicts with the whole world. We are not in need of feeding the people with illusions. Our prestige is due to the cohesion of the people and the efficiency of our methods....

New Thinking in Tunisia

The success of our work in the interior of the country is due to a large extent, to the new spirit, the method of conceiving, and the enthusiasm we have created in the people for the success of this task.

We have built factories and houses, we have revived fallow land and dug wells. But before doing this we addressed the people, in order to canalize their sentiments we appealed to reason and good sense. We exerted all efforts so that the people should grasp the importance of the struggle for economic prosperity.

We had previously mobilized the people against colonialism. We persuaded them to revolt against humiliations and the indignity of their conditions. Once that battle was won, the struggle against misery was yet to be fought. This was no easy matter and required a total reconversion of the minds. The leaders, those responsible, the civil servants, the people all have acquired a new awareness of the problems they are facing. The economic struggle is the most important of all. The scale of values was changed and thus the accomplished task immense.

The people have answered my appeal and prepared themselves to combat misery. The same people who shook off their resignation and apathy and followed me in the struggle for national liberation.

I know that certain elements of the population still maintain their old scale of values, they hang around the mosques, discuss, criticize and look for defects. They still give dissertations on the question of fasting months before the month of Ramadan. These discussions take place in houses of prayer. This does not matter as they count for very little.

A Respectable Country Among Advanced Countries

The young members and the leaders of the party and national organisations and the great majority of the people are convinced that the economic and social struggle comes first. They know that it is not less important than the struggle for liberty and sovereignty. They are revolted when the find that independent Tunisia suffers from economic backwardness. They know that if they remain behind they will be wiped off the map, or at the best, humiliated to the end of time.

They are persuaded that Tunisia is capable of conquering underdevelopment.

This consciousness explains that mobilization of Tunisian energies. It is not a mobilization that is directed against imaginary enemies, but rather towards constructive work, a rational organization of efforts, the application of programs of action and a full exploitation of human possibilities and technical know-how. This is the secret of Tunisia's advance and the method by which we will rapidly reach the stage all Tunisians hope for: a respectable position among the advanced countries. By this I do not mean countries who, for appearances' sake, maintain splendid embassies and build luxurious ministries in order to impress their visitors. I mean by "advanced" countries that have high standards of living.

Our conception of the economic struggle we are engaged in, our methods and points of view, reinforce our sovereignty and increase our prestige as well as safeguard us from exterior dangers. . . .

I believe we are on the right path. We are seeing to the establishment of the technical and financial means, the mobilization of men and resources. As for the financial side, I have already told you that we must not rely solely on foreign aid, whether from public or private sources. I have already given you the reasons. The greater the foreign aid, the greater is the restriction on freedom of movement and the harder it is to remain uncommitted.... Tunisia has a strong dislike to following in the wake of any power whatsoever, especially at a time when the world is torn by hatred and group antagonisms....

We Must Rely on Ourselves First of All

This is why we have chosen to rely on ourselves in the first place. We have no objection to foreign aid, provided it is reasonable. I say reasonable and not unconditional, intentionally. For aid is never accompanied by clearly stipulated conditions at the outset. To accept aid on the pretext that there are no conditions is to take people for fools. What actually happens is that the country receiving aid becomes more and more dependent, despite the fact that there are no definite conditions, until the time comes when it feels its hands are really tied and it is no longer able to appreciate matters solely from the point of view of the national interest....

This path is not likely to tempt us. However, we see no inconvenience in accepting foreign aid provided it is reasonable and of unquestioned value and provided it strengthens our bonds of friendship with other countries without hampering our freedom of judgment and choice....

Free Investment Instead of Useless Luxury

When, in a low-income nation, the state arbitrarily decides the proportion of investment to be drawn from private incomes, there will inevitably be a certain amount of compulsion, hardship, and frustration....

As the person responsible for the destinies of the Tunisian people I should like to avoid having recourse to compulsion and to authoritarian solutions in order to decide what proportion of individual incomes should be set aside for investment. This is why I believe it my duty to make suggestions and arouse a sense of responsibility. It should be clearly understood that I shall not hesitate to use a minimum of compulsion should it be seen that the sacrifices voluntarily made by individuals are not sufficient to establish a rhythm of progress in the country, which would enable it to overcome underdevelopment. In this eventuality I should ask you to accept these compulsions. You know they will be justified. You can be certain that if I have to use authoritarian means, I shall do so only where strictly necessary. I do not despise man, and I do not claim to make the people happy, regardless of the cost. I do not wish to scatter families on the pretext of putting everyone to work. Work is not an end in itself. Personally, I believe that the state should serve the individual, not the other way around....

It is therefore essential, if we are to coordinate our work properly, to determine our aims precisely, organize our resources and decide the various stages. This will be the function of the Plan. . . .

Planning thus appears as the control of action by reason. By this I mean reason based on competence and complete disinterestedness. . . .

59

Formulas for Change, Agreement to Create a Federation of Arab Principalities in the Persian Gulf, 27 February 1968 *

A conservative formula for channeling change is represented in the document reproduced below. The prime stimulus for the 'federation' of the nine signatory principalities is the fear of their rulers that as soon as Britain gives up its protectorate in the Persian Gulf in 1971, their tiny realms will be swallowed up by one of the large neighboring states or their thrones will be overturned in revolutions. These fears are intensified by the fact that most of these small states sit atop a fortune in oil deposits. Moreover, both Saudi Arabia and Iran have long-simmering claims to one or another of the signatory states; Iran for instance has insisted since the nineteenth century that Bahrayn is legally part of the Iranian empire. Although, in the circumstances it would seem that a federation might be a natural answer to the dilemma of the Gulf principalities, such may not be the case. Historically, these states—actually most are city states— have a long history of tribal animosities, meddling in each other's internal af- fairs, as well as border and maritime trade warfare. Accordingly almost as soon as the principalities agreed to federate they began to polarize into rival blocs that reflected their traditional alliance structure. Finally, the richest of all the Gulf principalities, Kuwayt, did not join the federation, nor did the large Sul- tanate of Muscat and Oman, possibly because their rulers seek a more influential role in determining the Federation's future than formal adherence to its pact would offer.

*   *   *

1.   There shall be established a Federation of the contracting Arab Emirates † of the Arabian Gulf which shall be called 'The Federation of the Arab Emirates.'

---

* "Federation of Arab Emirates Agreement of 27 February 1968," *Arab Report and Record* (London: 1968), Issue 5, 1-15 March 1968, 59.

† Bahrain, Qatar, Abu Dhabi, Dubai, Al-Shariqah, 'Ajman, Umm al-Qaywayn, Ras al-Khaymah, Al-Fujayrah.

The purpose of this Federation is to cement ties between them in all fields, to coordinate plans for their development and prosperity, to reinforce the respect of each one of them for the independence and sovereignty of the others, to unify their foreign policies and representation, and to strengthen the collective defense of their countries with a view to safeguarding their security, safety and mutual interests in such manner as to ensure the fulfillment of their aspirations and realize the hopes of the greater Arab homeland.

2. The Affairs of the Federation shall be supervised by a Council called the Supreme Council, which shall be composed of the Rulers of the Emirates. The Council shall draw up a permanent charter for the Federation, and formulate higher policy on international, political, cultural and other affairs. The Council shall be responsible for issuing the requisite federal laws and shall take its decisions by a unanimous vote.

3. The chairmanship of the Supreme Council shall rotate annually among the Rulers of the Emirates and the Chairman shall represent the Federation both internally and before foreign states.

4. The general budget of the federation shall be issued by a decision of the Supreme Council; the sources of revenue and the share to be contributed by each of the Emirates shall be fixed by law.

5. The Supreme Council shall be assisted in the exercise of its powers by a Council called the Federal Council which shall be the executive organ of the Federation. The Federal Council shall carry out its functions in conformity with the higher policy determined by the Supreme Council and with the federal laws. Decisions of the Federal Council shall not be deemed to be final unless approved by the Supreme Council.

6. The Councils and Agencies required to assist the Federal Council in the performance of its functions shall be set up and organized by federal laws.

7. The contracting Emirates shall cooperate in strengthening their military capabilities in accordance with the right of legitimate defense, both individual and collective, of their existence and their common duty to repel any armed aggression to which anyone of them may be subjected. The Emirates shall also cooperate, according to their resources and needs, in developing their individual or collective means of defense to meet this obligation.

8. The Federation shall have a supreme court called the Supreme Federal Court and its formation; organization and functions shall be defined by law.

9. The Supreme Council shall issue a decision determining the permanent headquarters of the Federation of the Arab Emirates.

10. The government of each Emirate shall take care of its own affairs which do not fall within the scope of the Federation's prerogatives.

11. This agreement may be amended by a decision of the Supreme Council of the Federation, but any decision in respect of such amendment may only be

taken at the session following the one at which the amendment in question was put forward.

12. This agreement shall come into effect as from the First Day of Muharram 1388, corresponding to 30 March 1968, according to the systems in force in each member Emirate and pending the drawing up of a charter for the Federation.

60

Formulas for Change, Reform Directives of the Turkish National Unity Committee, September 1960 *

After the Turkish revolution of 27 May 1960, a military-dominated Committee of National Unity temporarily became the chief policy-making body of the new "Second Turkish Republic." During the summer of 1960, the Committee, in consultation with Turkish political and intellectual leaders, produced a set of sixteen 'directives' to guide the reconstruction of Turkish political life. The need for increased social services and a return to economic planning are emphasized in the restored Kemalism advocated by the new regime. The document's vagueness about political forms reflected the debate then raging, concerning the degree of statism as opposed to parliamentarianism and free enterprise that should be allowed if Turkey were to achieve true social justice and sustained economic development.

When the Constitution of 1961 finally was drawn it provided for a democratic parliamentary government but in order to assure a voice for all points of view a system of proportional representation was included. The refurbishing of democracy was not accepted by all groups some of which stated that the country's continued modernization and social integration could be assured only if an Atatürk style elitist government was restored. Above all, Turkey's second republic has witnessed an outpouring of ideological commentary ranging from conservative Islamic to left-wing Socialist in orientation.

*   *   *

I. BASIC CONCEPT: The purpose of the movement of national unity is to take Turkey and the Turkish nation in hand as a whole, establish an impartial, clean

---

* "Committee of National Unity's Directives to the Government," text in *News from Turkey* (New York: Turkish Information Office, New York), Vol. 13, No. 28, 15 September 1960.

and meritorious administration based on the reforms of Atatürk, resolve the short-term problems of the day, lay down the foundation necessary for the solution of long-range problems and work towards their implementation so far as is permitted by time and available means, and, by the Fall of 1961 at the latest, to transfer these preparations and the administration of the country to the new government.

II. Fundamental Principles in the Application of the Basic Concept

A. *Structure of the State*: Laws will be drawn up and agencies established for the reorganization of the State in conformity with a democratic rule of law and the rational principles and procedures best suited to the national structure.

B. *State and Other Public Administrations and Agencies*

1. The structure and administrations of existing agencies will be reorganized within the shortest possible time to conform to the principles of justice, morality and productivity.

2. Radical measures will be adopted and effective controls instituted to ensure that these agencies shall continue to function in accordance with the basic points set forth above.

III. National Defense

A. National defense policy will be laid down and applied in such manner as will implement the strategic concept that is in keeping with national policy.

B. A quick start will be made to reorganize the Armed Forces in accordance with the requirements of modern warfare.

C. Laws and measures will be formulated and implemented within the shortest possible time to ensure that the Armed Forces shall always remain sufficiently vigorous and strong to maintain the historic traditions of the nation and fully guarantee the future security of the State.

D. Social conditions for Armed Forces personnel will be expanded, and their needs met in a satisfactory manner.

IV. Education

The aim of national education in Turkey is to meet the country's needs in line with contemporary developments, and to prepare the student for his role in life.

A. The mobilization of resources for people's and primary education will be taken in hand on a priority basis; the support and assistance of the Army, youth, and enlightened citizens will be utilized for the attainment of this objective; and provision will be made for maximum State support in this field.

B. Vocational and technical schools will be improved and expanded to meet the needs of the national movement for recovery.

C. The necesary social and economic measures will be adopted with dispatch to ensure that university and other higher education students may pursue their studies without financial distress.

D. Teachers will be given a status that befits their standing in Turkish society.

V. Agriculture

A. While protecting rights of individual ownership, measures will be adopted to provide land for landless citizens and to ensure that all land is worked in the most productive manner possible. Importance will be attached to investments in agriculture, and personal initiative will be encouraged.

B. Most radical means will be adopted and implemented with dispatch for the preservation and development of existing forests; efforts will be exerted to provide improved social conditions and better means of livelihood for citizens located in forest areas.

C. The matter will be taken up earnestly of providing trees for inhabited areas that are presently bare of foliage.

D. The raising will be encouraged of livestock useful from the viewpoint of human consumption or the export trade, measures will be adopted to reduce mortality, and the transportation of livestock on the hoof or during shipment in scientifically processed form will be reorganized on a priority basis. In this connection, it will be ensured without fail that fish and fish products shall become available at low cost and constitute also an item of profitable export trade.

VI. Resettlement and Housing

A. Appropriate studies will be carried out for the realization of a policy of resettlement conforming to the agricultural and social requirements of the country.

B. Measures will be adopted to ensure that the problem of housing, one of the country's most important needs, ceases to be a subject of economic exploitation. Priority will be given to the construction of collective but rational housing projects calculated to meet the needs of large numbers of citizens.

VII. Health and Social Problems

A. Medical care and measures for the preservation of health will be reorganized in keeping with the social and economic structures of the country in such manner as will make it possible to meet the nationwide need for preventive medicine and permit intervention where necessary from the viewpoint of social justice and equity.

B. Necessary laws and agencies and improvements will be provided to open up and maintain new fields of activity for workers, to ensure that their labor brings in a fair return compatible with social equity, and to guarantee their future.

C. Men of religion will be given the true position and esteem to which they are entitled in Turkish society; religious institutions and the religious training of citizens will be developed in the best possible manner compatible with the principle of freedom of conscience; and every possibility will be obviated of religion being exploited for political purposes.

D. Priority will be given to the problem of ensuring that civil service personnel shall be appointed in accordance with the principles applicable to the functions which they are to perform, that their social and economic needs shall be met in line with contemporary standards, that there shall be created a proper spirit of relations with the public and also an adequate comprehension of what mental attitude and volume of productivity befits a civil service employee.

VIII. Finance

A. Measures will be formulated and implemented with dispatch to put an end to waste and needless luxury in all aspects of national and social life, with the necessary example being set by all public administrations and agencies and particularly by those attached to the State.

B. There will be applied a balanced credit policy calculated to assist and support a stable currency and national recovery.

C. Taxation will be based on an equitable and adequate system aiming at the attainment of stable national recovery. The new policy for taxation will be applied at the proper time, which is to be determined with due consideration of the citizen's ability to pay.

D. National recovery will be reconciled in the best possible manner with budgetary resources: there will be no effort to force the issue.

E. All necessary measures will be adopted to ensure the utmost benefit from possibilities of foreign private investments and foreign aid.

IX. Commerce and Industry

Existing laws will be rendered adequate to ensure that all enterprises of a commercial and industrial nature shall be developed by way of a balanced mentality of etatism that embodies guidance, encouragement and assistance calculated to enhance their worth and open up new possibilities. Investments and credits for commerce and industry will be planned and implemented within the framework of this basic concept.

X. Public Works

A. Studies and planning will be carried out with dispatch for the enhancement, preservation and development of soil and water resources. These will be implemented on the basis of strict priorities based only on considerations of economic feasibility, freedom from political influences, and suitability from the viewpoint of imperative social needs. Imperative need will be the sole deciding factor for approval of any construction project.

B. All necessary technical and financial assistance and encouragement will be provided on a high priority basis to expand the volume of production, improve quality, and ensure the spoilage-free shipment of products that have a high export value. Public works activities will be extended also to areas where social and cultural conditions need to be improved.

XI. Village Uplift

A. Technical assistance will be provided for the construction of sanitary and modern housing.

B. Institutions (such as Village Uplift Centers) will be established and activated to furnish the personnel, materials and other requirements to assist villagers in the realm of hygienic, social, cultural and economic uplift.

C. Necessary principles will be formulated and implemented within a short time to provide farmland for villagers, as well as pastureland and potable water and adequate roads for the villages themselves.

D. Ways and means will be found to enhance the value of labor on the part of the villager, and to occupy his spare time to best advantage.

XII. Communications

A. The establishment, provision, organization and administration of communications systems and equipment will be ensured within the framework of a national policy to be formulated for communications.

B. Social and economic needs as well as considerations of national defense will be reconciled to best advantage in the establishment and operation of a communications network.

C. Comfortable, economical and safe transportation will be ensured and maintained by way of strict controls on every means of communications operated by the state, by private companies, or by individuals.

XIII. Domestic Policy

Laws and agencies for the implementation of domestic policies will be reformed and continued with an impartial approach that is above all party politics and calculated solely to ensure the security and tranquillity of every citizen.

XIV. Foreign Policy

Turkey's foreign policy will be based on her national interests, international peace and security, genuine faith in freedom and tranquillity, and sincere observance of existing agreements. Turkey will maintain relations of friendship and good will with her neighbors; she will support the struggles of nations for freedom.

XV. Concept of National Unity

Faithful to the concept that the national integrity of the Turkish nation stems from the factors of national independence, freedom, and faith without regard to race, religion, language or creed, a rigorous struggle will be waged against any and every activity that is of a divisive and injurious nature.

XVI. THE GOVERNMENT'S PROGRAM

The program to be prepared by the government shall conform to the essence of the directives outlined above and to the fundamental concepts of the Committee of National Unity with respect to national problems; it shall contain proposals pertaining to all necessary laws and regulations, agencies, and plans, as well as to the manner of their implementation with due regard to time, place, and prospects of realization.

61

Formulas for Change, Muhammad Reza Shah's "Six Principles of the White Revolution" January 1963 *

Muhammad Reza Shah's "White Revolution" speech was the culmination of his struggle with the Iranian land-holding class and their allies who were entrenched in control of the majlis. It was a direct appeal to the peasants and urban workers to support the land distribution and profit-sharing scheme which was opposed by the landowners. It called for a national referendum on the shah's economic and social reform proposals. The shah countered suggestions that he was bypassing parliament and illegally contravening the constitution by offering an interesting constitutional argument of his own—that since the powers in the country were derived from the people then the people should decide directly whether to approve or reject his program. The electoral reforms included in the 'Six Principles' were designed to convert the traditional loyalty of the peasantry for the shah into pro-monarchy strength in the majlis—another check on the landowners. A particularly significant aspect of the shah's desire to extend the benefits of modernization into the countryside was his literacy corps

* a. Muhammad Reza Shah Pahlavi, excerpts from "Speech to Congress of the Board of Directors of Rural Cooperatives and Agricultural Representatives, Teheran, 9 January 1963," in Ali Ashgar Shamin, *Iran in the Reign of His Majesty Mohammad Reza Shah Pahlavi* (Teheran: Central Council, Celebration of the 25th Century of the Foundation of the Iranian Empire, 1965), translated into English by Dr. Aladin Pazargadi, 178-180.

b. Muhammad Reza Shah Pahlavi, excerpts from "Message of the King to the Nation on 28th January 1963," *Ibid.*, 180-182.

which was to be staffed by drafting secondary school graduates and sending them into the rural villages as teachers.

A. MUHAMMAD REZA SHAH'S SPEECH, 9 JANUARY 1963, EXCERPTS

"...Here, by virtue of my responsibility as king, and my loyalty to the oath I have taken for the preservation of the rights and exaltation of the Iranian nation, I cannot be an indifferent observer in the campaign of divine powers against evil forces, for I am carrying the banner of this battle.

"To prevent every power from re-establishing the system of the serfdom of the peasant in this country, and letting a small group plunder the national wealth, I consider it my duty as the head of the Triple Powers, to refer directly to the people on the basis of Article 27 (1) and Article 26 of the Supplementary Law to the Constitution which declares 'the powers in the country are derived from the people,' and to ask before the election of the two Houses of the nation, which overrules the Parliament and is the source of all national power, to affirm and establish these reforms by means of a referendum before the election of the two Houses of Parliament, so that in future no private interest, no one and no group can efface the traces of these reforms which have liberated the peasant from the slavery of landlords and masters, and are the safeguards of a better, fairer and more progressive future for the working classes, for the welfare of honest civil servants, and for the prosperity of tradesmen, and the preservation of national wealth.

"I desire that these laws which have been enforced for the realization of a great historical transformation in Iran, should receive the direct approval of the nation.

"The principles which I, as king and head of the triple Powers, submit to the referendum, and ask for the positive vote of the nation in their establishment are as follows:—

1. The abolition of the system of master and serf by the ratification of the land reform based on the amended law of land reform, approved on 9th January 1962, together with its appendages.
2. The ratification of the Law of Nationalization of Forests in the whole country.
3. The ratification of the Law for the sale of governmental factory shares as a covering for the land reform.
4. The ratification of the Law making workers share in the profits of productive and industrial organizations.
5. The Amended Law of Elections.
6. The Bill for the creation of the Literacy Corps in order to facilitate the enforcement of the Law of Compulsory General Instruction."

B. MUHAMMAD REZA SHAH'S MESSAGE TO THE NATION, 28 JANUARY 1963, EXCERPTS

". . . My heart is full of joy at the positive answer which you have given to my call. I had asked you to give your explicit and decisive answer to definite questions which have a vital and direct connection with the destiny of this country; and you have shown by your vote that you have fully understood the significance of this national approval. It is your sense of discernment that makes my faith in the future of this country firmer and more unshakable.

"My dear people, to-day we have turned a new leaf of our history together. This history has already been full of brilliant and proud pages written during many centuries by the hands of the self-sacrificing, patriotic and noble men of this country. But perhaps it has never happened during these long periods that the foundations of Iranian society should be so fundamentally transformed, to assume a new form based on social justice and to follow the road to progress and honour.

"With God's will and your enterprise we will make such a country in this part of the world that it shall rival the most advanced countries in every respect. We will make a country that shall be the land of free man and women, where the genius of the Iranian can manifest itself and its eternal originality which is the secret of the survival of this country and nation, more fully than ever before, and in a rich environment free from corruption. For the chains of slavery have now been broken, and 75 percent of the population of this country who were enslaved before, are now enjoying the blessing of freedom. This group and other members of this nation will be able to vote freely for the first time in the future elections, and take part with authority in determining their own destiny. There is no doubt that in future all Iranian men and women will make use of the new social conditions and endeavour side by side to create a flourishing and prosperous Iran.

"This social and national change which has taken place in Iran to-day is indeed a great revolution which is at the same time legal and sacred. It is legal because the King who is empowered to make laws, asked for your approval, and you, the Iranian nation from whom all powers are derived according to the Constitution, approved this legal and national revolution, and put your signature to it by your decision and crushing vote. . . .

"On the other hand this revolution is a sacred one because all its principles are based on both the lofty teachings of Islam, namely justice and equity, and the most progressive principles and ideals of modern civilization. Nevertheless, I, as your king and the person responsible for the destiny of this nation, consider it necessary to point out that while we have attained the greatest individual and national glory, we should never be proud or suppose that our work is at an end. On the contrary it is more than ever necessary that we should engage in creative activities with a high morale and a firm resolution, so that every individual from whatever class may serve the future Iran in accordance with the approved laws and within the limits of his effort and capital, and reap a proportionate benefit from the blessings and potentialities offered by this country.

"The way I have shown you is the only proper, logical and honourable one before us to safeguard the progress of this ancient and proud country. I am sure ... that with the social maturity that you have shown, and with the deep and firm spirit of nationalism which is inherent in every one of you people of this country, you will give a positive answer to any call for your own welfare and that of future generations.

"March on towards the future which will lead Iran and Iranians to the height of greatness and happiness.

"May the God of Iran always support and defend you."

62

Aspects of Economic Change, an Egyptian Assessment of Their Economic Progress, 1952-1964 *

The increasing involvement of Arab governments in the complexities of economic development is exemplified by the official assessment of Egyptian economic progress that follows. Egypt has concentrated upon reorganizing its agricultural structure through land reform and the Aswan High Dam project which will give the country a million feddans of new land and produce prodigious amounts of electric power for new industry as well. Already there has been some industrial expansion particularly in textiles, metallurgy, and secondary processing. Meanwhile, in 1961 the sweeping 'Arab Socialism' program was decreed which nationalized all large industry, banks, and business concerns. Nevertheless, Egypt, in common with most Arab countries, has not achieved a rate of economic growth rapid enough to raise the living standards of its people appreciably. There remains, beyond the statistics, a traditional rural subsistence economy that still holds most Middle Easterners in its grip.

* "Social and Economic Progress in Egypt since 1952," *Research Project on Employment and Unemployment Among the Educated* (Cairo: United Arab Republic, Institute of National Planning, 1964), compilation supervised by Dr. M. Hamza, Final Report, 18-26.

Social and Economic Progress in Egypt since 1952

Compared to its prototypes in Egypt and its counterparts in many neighbouring countries, the Egyptian revolution of July 23rd 1952 is distinguished by extending its vision and activities beyond the political sphere. It has been [acutely] aware of the indisputable fact that the political system in any state is but a direct reflection of the prevailing economic state of affairs and an accurate expression of the interests controlling this economic state. In consequence, the Revolutionary Government initiated drastic social and economic changes in the country as early as 1952.

Agricultural Development

In September 1952, the Revolution decreed the Agrarian Reform Law. According to this law, the cultivated land in Egypt was redistributed so as to achieve social justice. The limit of land holding was then fixed at 200 feddans. Later in 1961, it was fixed at 100 feddans. It was provided that in each village, the land should be distributed among farmers (each of whom was entitled to have a small holding from 2 to 5 feddans). A million people profited from the law. About ¾ million acres were taken and redistributed among 120 thousand families. The Law defined the relationship between the landowner and the tenant by limiting the rent to seven times the tax; it gave the tenant the right to keep half the crop in an associated lease. Also, the Land Reform Law provided that the wages of agricultural workers in the various agricultural districts should be fixed each year by the government. The law linked the acquisition of land with the co-operative membership. Cooperatives were formed immediately after the redistribution of land. Their number amounted in 1960 to 326 and their capital to £E1,270,947.

It was deemed necessary that land reform measures should be accompanied by a number of supporting projects and services. A project was initiated for the distribution of cattle among those who were not in possession of any livestock against reasonable prices to be paid in small annual instalments, over a period of five years. To assist the peasants of the land reform area in marketing their milk, collecting centres have been established especially near big cities where dairy plants exist. A project for livestock insurance has been initiated. Centres for stud bulls and artificial insemination, together with veterinary centres to provide medical care and treatment for the livestock and poultry were established. Also, a project for the distribution of pedigree chicks was commenced in 1954, whereby a hatching centre with an incubator having a hatching capacity of 600,000 eggs was established.

Mechanization of agriculture has come to the fore among the services offered by the Land Reform Agency. In 1960, there were in use 475 tractors, 135 threshing machines, and 5,000 items of dusting and spraying equipment, in addition to a good number of irrigation and water lifting machines. Various agricultural operations are conducted at reasonable charges through the land reform cooperatives. Also of equal importance is the project initiated by the Agency for the improvement of irrigation and drainage facilities, which was necessitated to some extent by the measures undertaken for the consolidation of the holdings. A network of canals and drains has been established in an area totaling 122,555 feddans at a cost of £E572,000.

In the social field several services are being rendered to the peasants. The housing project is considered of particular significance as it represents an entirely new approach in tackling one of the main problems of the rural areas. The Land Reform Agency contracts houses for peasants who are in need of proper housing facilities. It incurs the entire cost which is to be reimbursed in long term instalments. The number of houses being built up to 1960 reached 1,469 costing a sum of £E482,846.

The Agrarian Reform Laws and the projects based on them do not tell but one part of the picture of agricultural progress in Egypt after the Revolution. Through Nile control work Egypt is asking at present its "mighty river to give more than in the past." The average annual discharge of the Nile is 83 milliard cubic meters of which only 48 milliard cubic meters are used for irrigation and the surplus goes to the sea during the flood period. Annual storage projects provided only 8 million cubic meters of water which in addition to the natural discharge of the Nile during the low period could meet the water requirements of the country. In order to offset this deficit the idea of building the High Dam as Aswan germinated.

The High Dam Project, the first stage of which has been undertaken, is the corner-stone of the new water policy as well as the agricultural expansion projects, as it will store 130 milliard cubic meters of water.

The Project will enable Egypt to do the following:
1. Expand the cultivated area by 2 million feddans and thus bring about an increase of £E50 million in the national income.
2. Ensure cultivation in the dry years and bring irrigation waters at the prescribed times for the different products.
3. Make drainage of Upper Egypt possible without the added cost of present drainage stations or the establishment of future ones.
4. Decrease the level of subterranean waters in the Delta and Lower Egypt and facilitating means of irrigation and decreasing their cost.

The stringent natural limitations on the existing available lands and water resources in Egypt have made it imperative to rationalise their use with a view to increasing productivity to the highest possible degree. A well-rounded programme has been drafted for this purpose. This programme included the carrying out of a soil and land classification survey, the establishment of a soil salinity and a plant nutrition laboratory, the judicious use of irrigation water, the improvement of drainage on agricultural land and the development of underground water resources.

Also, a short and long term programme for land reclamation has been started after the Revolution. The short term programme was started in 1953 and was scheduled to bring under cultivation an area of 300,000 feddans. The long term programme visualised the reclamation of 585,000 during the period from 1960 to 1965, in addition to the one million feddans which will depend on the waters that will be made available after the construction of the high dam. It also includes the conversion of 700,000 feddans from basin to perennial irrigation.

Furthermore, the Government established in 1957 the General Desert Development Authority as a body responsible for developing the long neglected desert land. Investigations and research on subterranean waters in the Western Desert opened the way to vital project in the sector extending parallel to the Nile from Aswan to the Qattara Depression, namely the New Valley Project. This project will cultivate 3.5 million feddans. Ten thousand acres have already been cultivated and are yielding crops. Around 30,000 feddans are almost ready for cultivation. Three main towns, 60 villages and 12 administrative centres will be constructed. A cooperative society will be established in each of the Valley's villages for the promotion of handicrafts based on available local materials.

Industrial Development

As indicated earlier the main problem confronting Egypt arises from the excessive pressure of the population on the land. This problem has two alternative solutions: either to make available more land or to provide other means in order to absorb the surplus population. Here industrialization becomes a necessity.

The Revolutionary Government come to view industrial and agricultural development as complementary to each other. In consequence, industrial projects have gone hand in hand with agricultural projects.

Although the development of industry in Egypt dates from the early thirties, yet the first attempt towards achieving a broad industrial development was taken after 1952 and particularly after 1956 when a Five-Year-Plan was drawn up at a total cost of £E330 million. This resulted in a continuous increase of industrial production that covered almost all the needs of consumption and allowed to dispense with many imports. Thus, while the value of industrial production was only £E314 million in 1956, it rose to £E656 in 1960, thereby making an increase of 290 per cent over the 1952 figures.

The increase in production, within this period 1952-1960, included all the industrial sectors: cotton spinning increased from 56,000 tons to 105,000 tons, cotton textiles increased from 40,000 tons to 75,000 tons, flax spinning and weaving increased from 800 tons to 1,100 tons, jute spinning and weaving increased from 3,300 tons to 25,000, ready-made clothes increased from 10,000 tons to 16,000 tons, sugar production increased from 189,000 tons to 337,000 tons, production of lime nitrate nitrogen fertilizer increased from 111,000 tons to 255,000 tons, super-phosphate fertilizers increased from 106,000 tons to 190,000 tons, glass increased from 3,850 tons to 11,500 tons, cement increased from 950,000 tons to 2,047,000 tons.

Moreover, a number of important new industries were established; most important of which were the iron industry which produced in 1960 approximately 160,-000 tons, the rubber industry which produced 480,000 tyres, the pharmaceuticals industry which produced 2,000 tons, the insecticides industry which produced 5,100 tons, the bicycle industry which produced 4,000 bicycles, the sewing machines industry which produced 3,300 machines, the butagaz stoves industry which produced 47,000 stoves, the butagaz bottles industry which produced 23,000 bottles, the railway cars industry which produced 500 cars, the kerosene stoves industry which produced 150,000 stoves, the radio sets industry which produced 64,000 sets, the refrigerator industry which produced 15,000 refrigerators and the nitrogen fertilizer industry which produced 75,000 tons.

In addition, a number of foodstuffs industries were established such as pasteurized milk, canned fruits and frozen shrimps. A number of important principal industrial were contracted for to consolidate some other industries such as the petrochemical industry and the motor-cars industry.

Considering it a very important goal to furnish jobs for the greatest number of citizens, about 15,600 workers and employers have already been given jobs in these various industries. They earn annual salaries amounting to three million pounds. Also, about 32,800 persons were given jobs in the projects of the first industrial programme which started production before the end of June 1960. They earn annual wages and salaries amounting to 6.4 million pounds. It is expected to increase the number of persons employed when factories achieve full acceleration in their works. However, the results of the execution of the industrial programme has begun to appear.

Along with the noticeable increase achieved in the quantity of the various industrial products and in the number of those who are employed in industry, efforts have been directed since 1952 to improve labour conditions and raise worker standards. In December 1952 a law was issued amending the individual contract of Service and the Conciliation and Arbitration Laws which raised the amount of service leave indemnities and increased annual leaves. Other privileges included the right of the dismissed worker to ask the court for suspension of the discharge decision.

Between 1955 and 1958 laws were enacted regulating the employment of the unemployed, and creating a savings and insurance fund for workers. Interest was also taken in developing insurance and compensation for labour accidents and occupational diseases.

In 1959, the various labour laws were grouped in one unified legislation which provided for more benefits to labour.

Finally, a set of socialist revolutionary laws were issued in July 1961. Some of these laws governed workers' and labour affairs. The Company law was modified to provide for the payment to company staffs and labour of a 25% share in the profits, and for the representation of such staffs and labour on boards of director. Working hours in industrial establishments were fixed at 42 a week, and the number of additional labour to be employed by every such establishment in consequence of the shorter working day measure was duly fixed. A total of 28,361 workers were actually employed in 370 firms out of the 28,440 workers scheduled to be engaged.

The Ten-Year Plan

The state adopted the policy of planning, in order that it might ensure the regularity of work and the exploitation of all capacities to the best possible ability.

Consequently, a comprehensive development plan for the United Arab Republic aiming at doubling the national income in ten years was ratified in 1960. The plan is divided into two stages each lasting for five years. The first Five-Year Plan was authorized by Republic Law No. 1327 in 1960. It was decided to carry this out in annual stages. The plan is elastic enough to permit any alterations in order to adjust the national economic development in the field of production, consumption and investment.

The increase in national income differs among the various sectors according to the change in production which will be achieved. It will decrease economic dependence upon agriculture. Thus it will change the economical foundation and support it through industrialization in order to achieve balanced growth.

The plan is to increase the national income to 40 per cent in the first stage from £E1282 million in 1959/60 up to £E1795 million in the year 1964/65; and it will be doubled by the year 1969/70.

Industry is considered the corner-stone in the growth plan. Therefore £E579 million are to be invested. In agriculture £E392 million are to be invested in the Five-Year Plan. The national income from the agriculture sector is expected to rise from £E400 million in the base year to £E512 million in the fifth year.

It is estimated that the plan will eliminate unemployment at present and in the future with the increase of the population. Thus it is expected that the number of those employed will rise from 6 million in the base year to 7 million in the year 1964/65. But the improvement of labour circumstances will be more obvious in the second stage of the plan when expansion in agriculture is assisted by the waters of the High Dam.

In order to achieve a balanced growth of the national income at the end of the Plan, it needed to gather together all the technical energies and available materials. By Law 117 all banks and insurance companies were nationalised to bring savings and financing within the Plan. Other firm whose activities were essential for the State to execute the plan, including companies trading in timber, wood, building materials, metals, electricity, transport, tourism, etc., were nationalised. By Law 118, it was decided that the government should share in 50% of the capital in some industrial and trade firms. Thus, activities can be directed for the public interest. Law 119 regulated the possession of the private sector in the shares of some companies. It forbids any person except public organisations and establishments to possess more than ten thousand pounds of shares in companies mentioned in this law. The possession of more than this amount reverts to the state.

To regulate the distribution of incomes, the Government issued on the 19th of July 1961, additional laws for social justice. Besides distributing one quarter of their net profit among employees and labourers, joint stock companies and other firms were requested to fix five thousand pounds as the maximum for annual salaries and fees. The income tax was altered so that the maximum tax on incomes which exceed ten thousand pounds per annum rose to 90%.

It is in the light of these socio-economic developments that the facts of this report, educational and otherwise, should be understood. Educational policy and planning have been made to meet the requirements of these economic reforms. Also, the situation of supply and demand in the field of labour has changed according to these changes. Education is now held responsible for bridging the gap between demand and supply in the market of labour, and is directed to discharge this responsibility with utmost possible efficiency.

63

Aspects of Economic Change, Saudi Arabian Reactions to the Presence of American Oil Operations, 1958 *

Middle Eastern countries generally display a wary suspicion of foreign business operations within their borders. Foreign oil companies in particular have attracted close watch because of the immense economic power they

* "Press Interview on Saudi Oil" (Interview of Shaykh Abdallah al-Tariki, Director General of Petroleum and Mineral Affairs, by Sulaiman al-Qadi), translated by Center for Near Eastern and North African Studies, University of Michigan, Ann Arbor, Michigan; original Arabic text in *Al-Bilad al-Saudiyyah* (Jidda: 18 December 1958), No. 2929.

control. During the early 1950's concern for finding financial resources for their economic and social development coupled with the urge to assert their national identity and freedom from foreign control led a number of countries to flirt with the idea of nationalizing large foreign economic holdings. However, the harrowing economic crisis endured by Iran after nationalization of the Anglo-Iranian Oil Company in 1951 dissuaded most would be proponents of nationalization from action. Nevertheless, all oil-producing countries have adopted one or all of the following stances: agitation for a larger share of oil profits, strict regulation of oil company operations, fragmentation of large concessions into several smaller ones, and encouragement of local 'national oil companies' to take over oil operations when they gain the necessary technical capabilities; native owned companies, for instance, have assumed a large share of local distribution and marketing functions. In countries such as Saudi Arabia the oil company has been almost an equal partner to the nation in economic development, although not without complications as the following selection illustrates.

*   *   *

Q. What are the main functions of the Directorate General of Petroleum and Mineral Affairs?

A. The main functions of the Directorate General of Petroleum and Mineral Affairs are to implement the concessions presently granted to companies to try to define the conditions under which new concessions will be granted, and to issue an oil law defining the relationship between Government and concessionaire. One of the most important functions of the Directorate is to search for minerals and try to exploit them either by the Government, nationally owned companies, or foreign capital, in order to insure sources for the Government to depend upon besides oil. This directorate considers the establishment of petrochemical industries as one of its most important duties. This is a vast new field which includes the exploitation of natural gas dissolved in liquid petroleum when it is underground where pressure and temperatures are low. We believe here that this program deserves great consideration and with it we should start the industrialization of this country. Most of this gas which is not injected is burned in the air and is lost by the country. Therefore, we feel that the Government and concessionary companies should take care of this gas and turn it to a source from which the investor and the country might both benefit.

Q. The press has been referring to the existence of differences between the Saudi Arab Government and the Arabian American Oil Company regarding the Government's share of the profits derived from the activities of the company or its owners in connection with the transport, refinery, and marketing of the oil in the world markets. We believe that our readers are entitled to know the truth about this. Will you kindly explain this subject in a way that would be understood by readers?

A. It is true that there is a difference between us and the Arabian American Oil Company in the interpretation of the concession agreement. We say that we have the right to benefit from all the revenue derived from our oil from the time it is extracted from the well to the day it is consumed as fuel in vehicles, and factories. In other words we believe that we have the right to all profits which result from such activities, and that we should take part in all expenses required for such activities so as to make direct contact with customer and consumer. In our opinion, this will be a guarantee for the future of our country as we will have direct contact with the markets which will enable us to deal with the countries concerned in the manner that will insure our interests. However, Aramco believes that this way does not—at the present time insure the interests of either the country or the company and its owners, especially since the owners undertake the marketing of the oil and most of its transport, and risk the profit or loss. We believe that reaching an agreement with the Company will result in cooperation and good relations between us to the time that the concession agreement expires. There is no doubt that we shall reach (an agreement) that will realize the interests of the Government and protect those of the company, as our Government's motto is protection of the rights of both parties so that no one party will be unfair to the other.

Q. Foreign newspapers report that the agreement which the Government concluded with the Japanese company has aroused clamors in foreign circles. It is also said that this agreement has switched oil policy in the Middle East to a new stage. What are the distinguishing aspects of Japanese agreement which differentiate it from previous oil agreements.

A. What was embodied in this concession agreement is exactly what we want from Aramco. We want the country to participate with the concessionaires in the profits outside and inside the country. We also want the Government to inherit, after the expiration of the concession, all of the company's installations whether inside or outside Saudi Arabia so that the country can have a national industry from which it may benefit.

Q. The concession was originally granted to Aramco or the Arabian Oil Company (sic) as it was previously called. However, circumstances and conditions in the world and the economic value of oil have changed. The purposes for which oil is used have increased. Prices have therefore gone up and profits have increased. Although amendments have been effected in the original agreement, we believe that there is still room to amend the agreement in the interest of the country. Don't you think that this is the proper time to do it?

A. Any agreement between a Government and a foreign country or foreign capital should be based on mutual interest. The owner of the capital should gain and the owner of the natural wealth should exploit his wealth in the interest of the people and the Government. If the agreement becomes at anytime unable to realize mutual interest, then it is no longer suitable for that period of time. Therefore, we find that most of such agreements do not remain stagnant as originally drafted, but evolve and change so as to keep pace with time. This was the case of the original concession agreement ... it does not stand firm but evolves in the interest of the country ... it shall also be amended in the interest of the country with due protection to the owners of the capital. His Majesty's Government is looking after its interests and making every effort it can to gain profit for the country and at the same time protect the rights of the owner of the capital.

Q. We understand from your replies to the previous questions that you believe in the necessity of converting the oil industry in the future into a national one, or to establish within the country national industries based on oil production. What steps have you taken to insure success in this field, and is there an established policy to train Saudi technicians, and do you believe that there is general Arab appreciation of the great importance of the oil industry in the future of the entire Arab World?

A. There is no doubt that we are unable to run the oil industry by ourselves until we are prepared for it. We should promote understanding among citizens, urge them to work in the oil industry, and have them understand the important role of oil in our world. We should also explain to them the advantages and profit that they could personally gain from this field if they pursue this end. Here in the Directorate General of Petroleum and Mineral Affairs, we feel that the oil industry is the most important in the world, and we have realized this fact and are exerting all efforts, with the help and direction of His Majesty's Government, to create a technical class among Saudi nationals and other Arab Brethren. At the present time, we have a considerable number of Saudi Arabs and other Arabs who are working or receiving training in the oil and mineral industry in Saudi Arabia. We also have a number of students who are studying for our account in American Universities. With the help and encouragement of the Government we send four students every year to American Universities to study everything pertaining to the oil and mineral industry. We have great confidence that in the near future we will have considerable number of citizens and subjects of sister Arab countries who will assure a successful industry.

Q. Is there a technical and accurate control over the quantities of oil produced and exported, and are there any oil wells that have been discovered and not put into production?

A. Yes: We do have technical control over the oil produced and exported, and there are such wells not on production, but we hope to do so in the near future.

Q. Is it true that the oil of Venezuela has invaded the markets of Middle East oil, particularly Saudi oil?

A. The contrary is correct. The oil of the Middle East can at present reach Venezuela at less expense than the oil that is produced in Venezuela itself as evidenced by the fact that Middle East oil rather than the oil of Venezuela in being sold in Brazil and Argentina which are Latin American countries and on one continent, namely South America. We should understand from this that the production costs of a barrel of crude oil in Venezuela are many times that of the Arab Gulf, and that the (daily) average production of an oil well in Venezuela is 300 barrels, whereas it is 6,000 barrels in the Arab Gulf. So far, you cannot find any oil in any part of the world that can compete with the oil produced in the Middle East which, if unrestricted, will be able to invade Eastern and Western America, at less cost than the oil of America itself. Therefore, America has taken the necessary action to protect its oil from the invasion of Middle East oil.

Q. The Iraqi Government has taken a new step regarding the oil agreements concluded with foreign companies. It is said that this step aims at automatic amendment in the national interest so that foreign companies will have to take a national form under which they become subject to Iraqi administration. ... Why does not the Saudi Arab Government take the same step or a similar one? Why does not the Government as a first step, prohibit Aramco from importing most of its equipment and materials, and give such right to Saudi companies, with Saudi capital, from whom Aramco could buy the equipment in accordance with outlined specifications and conditions?

A. In August 1953 an agreement was concluded between us and Iraq in Riyadh for the purpose of exchanging information on the oil industry and points of view with regard to policies towards the companies so that the interest of both countries might be guaranteed in face of the oil producing companies since there are common companies between us. This agreement proved to be necessary, since it realizes the purposes for which it was concluded. If sister Iraq has anything to say then it should have an echo in our country. Unless we know officially exactly what has happened in Iraq, we are not in a position to comment on this subject.

But as to the last part of the question, His Majesty's government has actually requested Aramco to buy insofar as practicable, most of its requirements from the country in order to encourage Saudis in importing. To be fair, we should admit that the company has taken some steps in this regard. In general, the

Government appreciates the company's cooperation and wishes it success in order to insure more advantages for Saudi Arabis in this field.

I wanted more information, but I saw Shaikh Abdullah al-Tariki pointing with his stick to the map of oil fields hung beside him on the wall. His magic stick stopped on Ghawar Field, the largest of its kind and the richest in oil reserves in the world. I felt he was asking me if I wanted to enter that field, but I preferred to stop at this point although I wanted more.

Sulaiman al-Qadi

64

Aspects of Economic Change, Foreign Aid and Iranian Development, 1962 *

Economic Development in the Middle East has been facilitated since the 19th century by various types of foreign economic assistance. This assistance has consisted of financial, managerial, and technical aid of various forms. Moreover, assistance has been carried out directly and indirectly by both public and private enterprise agencies. The following selection, however, illustrates the very complex forms that foreign aid operations can assume. The Khuzestan development project is one of the most ambitious irrigation-electricity generating schemes in the Middle East and is matched at present only by the gigantic Soviet-sponsored Aswan High Dam project in Egypt. The regional development parallel between the Khuzestan project and the Tennessee Valley Authority in the United States is obvious. Recently, foreign aid has assumed an inter-regional aspect with oil rich nations such as Kuwayt providing capital for imaginative participation with Iran and with us of World Bank irrigation experts in the planning and loan process.

*   *   *

FINANCIAL BREAKDOWN OF COSTS FOR IRAN's 7-YEAR PLAN

The Khuzestan program, as it is known in Iran, is a high-priority part of the current second 7-year plan of Iran—now in its final year. The financial scope of

* "Activities of the Development and Resources Corporation in Iran," *Hearing before the Committee on Foreign Relations United States Senate, Eighty-seventh Congress, March 20, 1962* (Washington: Government Printing Office, 1962), 5-12.

the 7-year program is estimated to be in the order of $1,200 million. The Khuzestan program for which we are responsible in our agreements with Plan Organization and the Khuzestan Water and Power Authority will total some $155 million when Dez Dam is completed next winter.

Of this total of $155 million, Dez Dam and the initial irrigation program, together with power installations and transmission lines from Dez Dam to Ahwaz and on to Abadan on the gulf, will account for well over one-half this amount—some $95 million. Iran has financed this portion of the program with its own oil revenues plus a $42 million, long-term, interest-bearing loan from the World Bank. The 12,000-acre sugarcane plantation and mill and refinery account for some $31 million financed by Plan Organization oil revenue funds.

From this operation, this sugar operation, Iran will obtain in a few seasons some 18 percent of its present sugar consumption—more than half of which is now imported.

The remaining costs of the program cover soil surveys and regional fertilizer tests and demonstrations, the engineering, geology, and economic surveys and investigations from which the first program was formulated and a long-range unified plan was devised. Also included are the costs to complete several small projects and undertakings started before we arrived but turned over to us for resolution; and the costs of administration and general development not allocated to major projects.

Unique Aspects of Development Resources Contract Arrangement with Government of Iran

This program has been brought to its present stage under a contract arrangement proposed to us by Iran that is probably unique and may be of interest to the committee in its study of private operations overseas.

Iran asked us, within the first year of our work, to accept responsibility for carrying out the projects and programs we recommended and which Iran approved and financed. Thereupon our company built up a full-time field organization in Khuzestan working under our supervision and with professional support from our New York staff.

This is an unusual kind and quality of responsibility in several important respects.

First in the breadth of the responsibility delegated by a sovereign nation to a private American company, a company having no official links nor financial dependence upon the U.S. Government, nor upon the United Nations. But neither we nor the contractors we employ acquire any "concession" or proprietary or financial interest in the resources developed; compensation in all cases is limited to payment for the managerial or technical services rendered.

Scope of Responsibility

The scope of this responsibility is carefully defined, by agreement. On the side of Iran, Plan Organization must review and approve specific projects before our company may begin any project such as a water control dam or a sugarcane development.

After that approval, however, it is up to us, up to our company, to get the job done, through our own employees or through organizations with whom we contract and whom we supervise. Similarly, the disbursements of funds in payment for services or equipment under such contracts are made by us out of funds advanced to our company each 3 months by Plan Organization. At least once and frequently several times a year the program budget is reviewed by Plan Organization, and approved or modified. The accounts are audited by a firm of independent international accountants whose report each 6 months is submitted to Plan Organization. Finally, each party may terminate the entire arrangement upon short notice.

The chief reason advanced by Iran for proposing and continuing this unusual arrangement was Iran's strong sense of urgency, of time urgency that things needed to be done as promptly as possible. The speed of physical and managerial progress thus far attained can be attributed largely to the focusing of responsibility and the flexibility the arrangement provides.

Development Resources Managing Responsibility and International Character of Projects

A second major point about the undertaking is that to achieve the greatest benefits at lowest costs to Iran and in anticipation of Iran's efforts to obtain World Bank financing we brought together, by selection and competitive bidding, an international group of firms and contractors to help carry out the task for which we have over-all managerial responsibility.

Thus, an Italian firm, the successful bidder in international competition, built the transmission line from Abadan to Ahwaz, and another Italian company rebuilt the electric distribution facilities in the city of Ahwaz, as a result of international competitive biddings.

An American firm built a tunnel road down the face of the canyon to the site of the Dez Dam. A Dutch firm of consultants with extensive experience in reclamation and land development made the detailed field study of the first irrigation scheme and is designing the physical facilities. A group of international technicians of the U.N.'s Food and Agriculture Organization worked on soil-fertility studies and related field investigations.

An American foundation trained village workers in the use of fertilizers. Planning of housing was a task contracted to an American firm with worldwide experience.

The initial electrical equipment for the Dez Dam is coming from West Germany, Japan, Canada, and the United States. Aerial mapping for Khuzestan was carried out by a British firm. Under our general supervision, the sugarcane plantation project was put in the joint charge of a Los Angeles engineering firm and a Hawaiian cane sugar company; the sugar mill and refinery were manufactured by a Dutch concern.

In Khuzestan, contractors and consultants working under our supervision comprise a work force in the region from Dez to Abadan of some 4,400 people, including 780 overseas personnel and 3,600 Iranians.

While this list is not exhaustive, it indicates to what extent the undertaking a Kuwayt Fund for Arab Economic Development which is financing development schemes throughout the eastern Arab world.

Khuzestan Development Project in Iran

Now, we should like to describe, in somewhat more detail, the assignment that has occupied most of our time, energy, and attention in the past 6 years, almost exactly 6 years—the Khuzestan development in southwest Iran.

By contract with the Plan Organization of the Government of Iran—to which a year ago was added the Khuzestan Water and Power Authority, an Iranian regional agency established by Iranian law—our company has been responsible to Iran for a substantial overall economic development undertaking.

Southwest Iran is an area of five rivers, fed by the snows of the high Zagros ranges. Its vast desert plains reach south from these mountains some 180 miles to the Persian Gulf. Khuzestan region is the great oil producing area of Iran. Abadan, near the mouth of the Karun River on the Persian Gulf, is the oil city of Iran where the great oil refinery is located.

The five snow-fed rivers of this region—the Karkheh, the Karun and the Dez, the Jarrahi, and the Hindijan—are all within Iranian boundaries. This is a fact of great importance in a part of the world where most rivers of consequence cross international boundaries—a serious complication in the way of development of full beneficial use.

These snow-fed rivers are the greatest single unused natural resource of Iran. Unlike petroleum, this resource is inexhaustible. The plains fed by these rivers were the center of the Persian Empire in its heyday as the world power of ancient times, the first world government. This is the land of Cyrus, Darius, and Shapur the Great. Here many centuries ago, irrigated agriculture, commerce and world trade flourished, but with wars, natural catastrophes, neglect and time, much of the area reverted once more to desert.

In 1956 the then Managing Director of the Plan Organization of Iran, Mr. Abol Hassan Ebtehaj, with the approval of His Imperial Majesty the Shah, invited Mr. Clapp and myself to look at Khuzestan. He wanted our ideas about how its resources might best be developed. We saw a vast desert but we were impressed with the possibilities: mountain-fed rivers, vast uncrowded areas of fertile but arid land, and historic proof of a once flourishing region.

We saw a region where a great potential for hydropower plus irrigation, and flood control plus oil and gas existed in a combination rarely found within a single region within the boundaries of one country.

When we reported our preliminary ideas to Director Ebtehaj he asked us to enter into a contract obligating us to an assignment, not just to study, recommend and advise—but to do with and for Iran what needed to be done in Khuzestan—and to train Iranians in the process. This was to be a part of the first step in the redevelopment of the water and land resources of Khuzestan— for agriculture and land reclamation, and for the diversified industrial and commercial development its vast resources make possible.

Those contractual obligations, we accepted 6 years ago, almost to a day. We accepted the assignment because we believed it could be done and we believed we could do it. We were also influenced in part by an appreciation then of the importance of Iran's future in the free world. This appreciation has deepened and sharpened in these 6 years as we have witnessed at close range the difficulties encountered—and firmly met—by a country trying to make up for lost time in the race for an improved standard of living for its people.

RESULTS OF SECOND 7-YEAR PLAN IN IRAN

Today, the result of the current second 7-year plan, of which our assignment is a part, are visible in many parts of Iran. In Khuzestan, which is the only region with which we are contractually concerned, in what was desert in 1957, we are now conducting the first commercial sugarcane harvest in several centuries near the ancient Biblical city of Shush. Last December, His Imperial Majesty the Shah, accompanied by the Prime Minister and several cabinet ministers, spent a day at the site to inaugurate the mechanized harvest and observe the mill and refinery in operation. The ceremonies, it may be of some interest, began on the banks of the ancient Darius irrigation canal built 2,500 years ago by Roman soldiers, prisoners of the Persians. Sections of this canal, unused for centuries, now form a part of a modern irrigation system drawing water from the snow-fed Dez River, a major tributary of the Karun—Iran's greatest river.

The Dez Dam

The Dez Dam—in a 1,500 foot deep canyon northeast of the city of Dezful—is within a year of completion. It is a multipurpose project for irrigation, flood control and power. It will be one of the highest dams in the world, supplying 130,000 kilowatts of power initially and ultimately 520,000 kilowatts. In October last year, the first bucket of concrete was poured—a ceremony honored by the visit of His Imperial Majesty the Shah and the Prime Minister and his Cabinet.

The city of Ahwaz, the center of the region, where our headquarters in Iran are located, started receiving central station electric service 3 years ago, 1959, over Iran's first high-voltage transmission line, a line we planned and had built bringing power from the thermal electric plants in the Abadan oil refinery.

Since 1959, when reliable electric service became available in Ahwaz, power use has trebled. When the Dez Dam goes into service a year from now its power will flow south to connect at Ahwaz with the line to the Persian Gulf cities.

Regulated waterflow from the Dez Dam, starting in 1963, will make year-round irrigation possible for the first time—initially to the pilot area of 50,000 acres and 57 villages to the north of the sugarcane area; ultimately to an area six times as great. By a new land and water-use policy adopted by Iran in 1960, as an outgrowth of the loan agreement between Iran and the World Bank, water users will pay for the water, adopt new and diversified cropping systems, and landowners will move toward a permanent land tenure system for the cultivators. This irrigation program of increased productivity contains what we believe to be features and advances in Iranian policy and practice of considerable importance to Iran's future; they may also influence other Middle East land practices.

The concepts incorporated in this project gained greatly from the careful and has been made truly international. Of course, Iranians themselves are engaged in every aspect of the enterprise, from technical and managerial posts to the operation of trucks.

Concept of Interrelationship of All Projects

A third characteristic that may be of interest to the committee is that the program is conceived and carried out on the basis of the interaction of each part upon all the other parts, rather than as a miscellaneous collection of separate projects only vaguely related to each other.

Thus, adequate and reliable power and water supply, for example, will stimulate expansion of public and private activities and enterprise in industry and agriculture. Already there are encouraging signs that this is happening. For example, a caustic soda plant, made possible by new dependable power supply, has been established in the region by private Iranian investors within the past 2 years. Municipal power distribution authorities have already been established in two of the principal cities of the region. Managerial and financial assistance administered through the Khuzestan Water and Power Authority, a regional Iranian agency, will help these new local agencies during the first 5 years. The prospects of new uses of the natural gas byproduct of the region's oil wells, which are tremendous, now almost entirely wasted, burned off, appear encouraging once dependable power supply is available.

Technical Training of Iranians Important Feature of Plan

Finally, the creation and staffing of an Iranian organization to take over the operating responsibilities carried by Development & Resources Corp. during the first phase of the program have been a major objective, from the start.

In 1960 in the course of discussions and loan negotiations between Iran and the World Bank, we assisted in the creation of a legally constituted, constituted under Iranian law, regional development agency known as the Khuzestan Water and Power Authority which was established by a law enacted by the Iranian Parliament in 1960.

A year ago this new agency became a coclient with the Plan Organization in the contracts under which we provide our services. Tomorrow, an event of major importance—a milestone in this work—will take place in Iran. The Khuzestan Water and Power Authority, headed by a distinguished Iranian as Managing Director, will take over by formal transfer responsible direction of the power system operations and the central supporting management services from our organization in Iran. The oversea personnel of our organization in Khuzestan who are associated with these operations and services will continue to be employed by us, but will be assigned to the administrative direction of the Khuzestan Water and Power Authority.

Later on a formal transfer of responsibility for the sugarcane project and for the Dez project, when it is completed early next year, will place the whole program in responsible Iranian hands. Our company's original plan to confine ourselves to an advisory and consulting capacity will then have been achieved.

The Khuzestan Water and Power Authority thus will become the repository of experience gained by Iranians in our organization in the past 6 years. It will become the agency of the Iranian Government equipped by training and experience, and with diminishing outside help, to prepare for and carry out the next stages of the long-range development program of which the present projects are the first step.

Future Steps for Iranian Development

The future steps for development—irrigation, flood control, navigation, and power—have been proposed in a unified development report completed by our company in March 1959. There are in the five rivers of the Khuzestan feasible sites for some 13 dams in addition to the Dez Dam. These structures would comprise an integrated multiple-purpose flood control and irrigation water supply system and a low cost power source of 6 million kilowatts. This power system, combined with adequate oil- or gas-fired thermal plants, in due time, could well reach a capacity of 10 million kilowatts. The regulated flow from this system of dams would be more than adequate to supply year-around irrigation to the 2,500,000 acres comprising the best lands of the Khuzestan plains and upland valleys, a vast area of potentially fertile soil-given water. We have proposed to Iran no time schedule for these objectives. We have proposed instead a careful step-by-step approach, the first of which is close to successful completion, including the creation and staffing of an Iranian regional development agency to see it through.

As this region's energy and land resources are put to work, they will stimulate and supply an agricultural and industrial development of great dimensions and wide diversity making great contributions to the stability and strength of Iran— and of the free world.

Mr. Chairman, and members, we appreciate greatly this opportunity to describe our activity and undertakings abroad.

Mr. Clapp and I will be glad to undertake to answer such questions as the committee might have.

The CHAIRMAN. Do you wish to make any statement in addition, Mr. Clapp, or just proceed on questions?

Mr. CLAPP. No, I have no additional statement, Mr. Chairman.

I am sure that covers the picture completely.

POSSIBILITY OF A PUBLIC AUTHORITY AGENCY IN IRAN

The CHAIRMAN. As I understand it, there is a rather unique arrangement by which you have succeeded in creating in a sense a TVA in Iran, is that a correct way to put it?

This new authority is equivalent to the TVA in this country.

Mr. LILIENTHAL. Yes, roughly.

The CHAIRMAN. Does it bear the same relationship to its Government, the Iranian Government, that TVA does to ours?

Mr. LILIENTHAL. Well, as nearly as one can make a comparison between these two countries. I think this is true. It is a semi-autonomous agency created under Iranian law. It is responsible to the Government of Iran, and it is intended to be self-liquidating and self-supporting.

The CHAIRMAN. It has a Board of Directors appointed by the Government?

Mr. CLAPP. No, it has no board at the present writing, Mr. Chairman. The

Managing Director of the Khuzestan Water and Power Authority is appointed by the Prime Minister for a term of 3 years; he reports to the Managing Director, the Deputy Prime Minister in charge of the Plan Organization of Iran.

PLAN ORGANIZATION AND ITS RELATION TO THE GOVERNMENT

The CHAIRMAN. What is the Plan Organization? What is its relationship to the Government?

Mr. CLAPP. The Plan Organization which was set up more than 7 years ago by Iranian law is a separate administrative body reporting to the Prime Minister but not a part of the regular ministries of the Iranian Government.

The CHAIRMAN. Please be a little more precise. You say a separate administrative body; does that mean it has its own board of directors? Is it a separate corporate entity or what? How do you describe it?

Mr. CLAPP. Well, it is difficult to describe it as having a separate corporate entity because those conceptions don't normally apply in Iranian governmental procedures.

The Managing Director of the Plan Organization is the administrative head of the Plan Organization. When we first went there in 1956, the Managing Director was not a member of the Cabinet. He reported directly to the Majlis, the Parliament, and to the Shah.

In recent years the Plan Organization Managing Director has been given the rank or status of a Deputy Prime Minister reporting to the Prime Minister of the Government.

If I may add, Mr. Chairman, they do have a High Council which is a sort of policy board within the structure of the Plan Organization, and they do have a Board of Control within the Plan Organization structure. Each of those bodies has administrative independence from the Managing Director, and are designed to assure the Parliament that the policies of the Plan Organization will be consistent with Iranian governmental policy, and that their financial and fiscal procedures will be carefully reviewed by the Board of Control and the High Council, but separate from the regulatory fiscal functions of the central Government.

RELATION OF KHUZESTAN AUTHORITY TO PLAN ORGANIZATION, AND BOTH TO THE LAW

The CHAIRMAN. The Plan Organization's responsibility is nationwide for development of all of Iran's industries and under it is this Khuzestan authority which is a subsidary of the Plan Organization, is that correct?

Mr. CLAPP. That is correct.

With one important distinction, namely, that the charter of the Khuzestan Water & Power Authority, as authorized by the Parliament, and approved by the Council of Ministers, gives it what you might call perpetual status, whereas the Plan Organization, as presently constituted, expires as a legal body with the expiration of the second 7-year plan within the current year.

The Plan Organization will probably get new life with the adoption of what they refer to as the Third Plan, which presumably will go into effect next autumn.

65

Aspects of Economic and Social Change, The Emergence of a New Economic Managerial Class in Iran, 1963 *

Since beginning in the nineteenth century the realization of modernization schemes have been limited by the scarcity of institutions and men oriented toward fulfilling the needs of a modernizing society. Both of these problems are treated in the address reproduced below. It is interesting to note that even when ostensibly modern business concerns were present often the actual operating procedures utilized by a company were as traditional as they were modern. Also, it is still characteristic of the Middle East to find modern institutions and modern men concentrated overwhelmingly in the capital and other large cities. Iran, unlike some other states in the region, since World War II has encouraged the growth of the private sector of the economy. However, lack of credit and financial resources has hindered this movement as has the rarity of managerial talent. Until recently, those who enjoyed a modern education almost exclusively aimed at careers in the government bureaucracy. Moreover, there has been a great shortage of men with scientific and practical technical training while the talents of women are still virtually unexploited.

*   *   *

In the olden days, and in some quarters even today, when time moved so much more slowly, our ancestors, after a delicious lunch such as the one we have had now, used to leave the affairs of this mundane world to loyal servants and partook of the flights of fancy that only a sweet sleep and daytime dreams can offer. I suspect the honourable chairman has invited me to address you

* Ali Ashgar Pourhomayoun, "Some Observations on Problems of Banking in Iran," *Bulletin* (Teheran: Bank Markazi Iran [Central Bank of Iran], Nov.-Dec. 1963), Vol. II, No. 10, 488-492.

here in the hope of reviving this old, dying tradition which the modern men of affairs can only yearn for but never achieve.

The flood of modern civilization has stolen on our sweet sleep. It crept in in the dying hours of the last Century, but not until the 20's did it burst open our time-worn gates, and descended upon our way of life, challenging, and at times upsetting, the values and institutions which our society had so long taken for granted. Time has not yet sapped the vigour of the flood, and its recent roar makes us pause demanding, as it were, a total and profound reappraisal of those cherished traditions.

The impact of new civilization on our society is a matter of significant interest, particularly in the problems which the institutions of this new civilization face in the light of the peculiarities of the Iranian scene. And here I shall deal with the problems of only one such institution, namely, banking.

Apart from happening to be my profession, and apart from the fact that some people attribute its origin to the Middle East, the subject of banking is in itself also interesting. After all, the hero who invented this most ingenious of machines was probably a mean harsh-looking Shylock of a goldsmith who, motivated by profit through usury, cheated. He not only committed the mortal sin of lending money for interest; but he did it with other people's money. He bought the confidence of the people and made millions.

From this ancestry developed this magnificent money-creating machinery which has come to be a quasi-public institution and a pillar in the economic order of a society, and the banker who, entrusted as he is with this delicate machine, and striving to maintain and foster public confidence, is painted as a conformist.

Generally speaking, banking has developed and can develop only along and in conjunction with other institutions. And like any institution, it reflects the tempo, the character, and the stage of growth of a society. I wish I had more time to stress the point, but I deem it essential to point out that, at best and at worst, like all our problems, we are conditioned and limited by our society.

Many of our problems are the common property of management the world over. More specifically, a bank manager has to consider, on the one hand, his obligations to his shareholders and his staff and, on the other hand, his responsibilities to his customers and to the economy in general. How can the tension between these divergent demands be harmonized to return an adequate profit to the shareholder—even when the shareholder is the State? What form of organization and personnel can best meet these responsibilities?

The problems which a bank management has to encounter in Iran perhaps are best crystallized if we briefly examine the development of banking here; and to that problem I shall direct my attention now.

The first banks which slowly blossomed forth in Iran sowed the seeds of some of the problems with which our banking system has to grapple now.

Modern banking in Iran goes back to the second half of the last century. After an unsuccessful attempt in 1864, the first bank to be established was the New Oriental Bank in 1888. But the Iranian branches of this bank were sold to the Imperial Bank of Iran after the latter was given a concession in 1889.

Though the Imperial Bank of Iran rendered a valuable service to the development of our banking system in the form of popularising the notion of banking and training a number of Iranians, yet it was centred outside of Iran. It remained an alien Bank, and this very element led to its ultimate downfall.

The years 1926-28 have a special meaning to the Iranian banker. Out of the nationalism which marked the inter-war period, emerged the Bank Sepah and the Bank Melli Iran. The latter took over the many functions of the Imperial Bank of Iran and became, among other things, the bank to the government. But in one sense it went overboard. In discharging its functions as the banker to the Government, it followed the latter into every corner of the Country, providing, furthermore, banking services to local merchants. Profit-making was not the dominant thought of those determining the policies of the Bank, specifically, with respect to operating branches.

Necessary as the idea was for administrative, political, economic, and patriotic reasons, yet like the Imperial Bank of Iran, it could not develop a pattern, a tradition, which could be easily emulated by the next wave of banking institutions which followed her.

Following some sixty years of modern banking, and twenty-four years after the establishment of the first State-owned bank, the first private bank was created in Iran in 1949. In later years, particularly after 1953, the movement gathered momentum, and the consequent mushrooming of banks has presented some serious problems.

One of the more serious responsibilities of a management remains that of balancing the concept of profit-making with that of service to a community. To achieve this aim, a banker must conduct a careful study of the many factors which affect the profit potential of a region for the purpose of operating branches.

An important factor which comes to the mind in this respect is the pattern of distribution of population, income and wealth in the country. Since the trend in the movement of wealth seems to favour the towns, the operations of a bank should be easier there. Start operating banks in major cities and towns and you have the bulk of the money supply!

However, the rapid growth of banking has presented the managements of banks with a serious problem of intense competition in towns, and some are turning their attention towards rural areas.

Our rural population is poor, if not impoverished. They not only are unable to earn the income which could allow them a margin of savings, but more often have to dissave in order to meet the elementary requirements of subsistence. But in those very villages, there are the few whose wealth and income far exceed their expenditure, and have consequently much wealth hidden away.

Despite the general poverty of the rural areas, the existence of a hidden supply of wealth as well as a corresponding level of demand should attract the banker. But he must proceed with caution. The geographic distribution of villages, perhaps with the exception of a few provinces in the North, is such as to make establishment of one branch covering several villages impossible. It is, therefore, hoped that with the creation of cooperatives our commercial banking system can have an opportunity to mobilize the hidden savings as well as to provide a service to the community through this cooperation in the form of investing their wealth in the same areas.

A similar trend is the movement of population from towns to cities and from cities to the Capital. A man who has made good in a provincial town tends to emigrate from his native land and seek his fortune most often in Tehran, bringing all he has with him. So that today the population of Tehran stands in the region of some two million. It is safe, however, to predict that, specially after the heavy investments that the Government and other public institutions have undertaken in the provinces, the rate of growth of population in Tehran will slow down, but this factor need not mean that the movement of population would stabilize. In the next few decades we must expect heavy shifts in the pattern of that movement toward areas which provide better opportunities for employment. Therefore, shifts in population and wealth must be a matter of great concern to banking (and specially those in branch banking).

To arrive at a proper assessment of the profitability of operating banks in a given locality, we need proper statistics, which can tell not only of the financial state of a town at any given time, but also of the constant fluctuations which our society is undergoing.

Bank Markazi Iran is shortly to be engaged in another study of the consumer income and expenditure in major towns and cities. But this is only a first step, and there is need for regular collection and analysis of data in order to guide the necessary adjustments in banking pattern. Research in those fields must be encouraged and if need be, subsidised by Bankers, perhaps in a joint enterprise.

The problem of balancing the obligation to the shareholder with that of providing the public with adequate and efficient services presents itself again in the case of operating more than one branch in one city.

Here, the problem is one of organization. Though a vast network of branches cover Tehran yet in some cases the net result has been a decrease in the margin of profit. And the task of the head office management has been by no means simplified. The distribution of branches in our banking system need a thorough reappraisal. It needs to be rationalised so that branch banking will in general become a paying proposition.

A properly located branch, with only a few hundred customers and with a small staff, can afford the manager an opportunity to establish the two-way contact with his customers and his staff which is essential to proper banking.

Apart from a proper distribution of branches, we must consider a proper distribution of authority among the branches and the head office and a clear line of responsibility need be established. At the moment, in some cases the branch manager must depend on the central office for almost every decision of any significance. For example, a central office is expected to decide upon applications for credit by people in the remote parts of the country, about whom they can know little and have to depend, in turn, on the information provided them by the branch manager in that locality. This situation does not in fact make the control of branches any more efficient; it only slows down the communication between the bank and the cusctomer.

A proper distribution of authority must go hand in hand with a proper system of control. And here, too, there is much room for improvement. First of all, an internal system of checking is essential. Even in the most minor branch there must be the means of control to avoid both errors and risk of dishonest operations. (How can you have a one-man branch?)

The external system of control also can be improved. At present, a two-way channel of communication provides the substance of the control exercised by a central office over her branches: first, through perusal and checking of returns made to the central office at regular intervals, and second by the inspections made of local branches by central office inspections. Under this system, we have a central office domiciled in Tehran trying to exercise control over a mass of branches spread over a vast area. How could this system be effective? We may hope that in the near future a system of auditing by independent firms will help to soothe any fears that the public and shareholders may entertain in this respect.

But, for the sake of better organization and control, a more rational and orderly system must replace the present one. Perhaps a system of regional grouping of branches under the supervision of a resident director or simply an inspector, could go a long way in putting the house in order. This form of organization and control, I understand, has already been undertaken with fruitful results. A resident regional director will have a unique opportunity to gain a first-hand knowledge of the conditions and the problems of a given region, to exercise direct control, and to provide personal advice and supervision to any particular branch when the need to do so arises. He will, furthermore, be the vitally needed channel of communication between the branches in his region and the central office.

But control, ultimately, could only be negative. It could restrain the management of a branch from taking up certain measures which the head office would consider detrimental to her interests, but could never induce them to take positive steps.

In the last analysis, there is no substitute for good management. And in this respect, there is a considerable shortage of staff. Along with other attempts, we, the community of bankers, must take positive measures to improve the quantity of the reserve pool of the qualified staff available to us now, and the quality of our management.

Quantitiwise, the only trained corps of personnel that were available to us at the outburst of banking in 1953 were those who had spent a life time in the Imperial Bank or Bank Melli Iran. They were either retired, or indispensable to the Bank Melli herself. On this handful of devoted men, we have thrust an added burden at a time when our banking system has undergone a revolution; when we are trying to understand the problems and methods of banking in a complex world and trying harder to avoid the experiences that the west had to learn so bitterly. Indeed, Bank Markazi Iran, is in a way, the fruit of that endeavour.

This attempt to increase our supply of trained and educated managers, needless to say, takes time and shall tax every grain of our patience. But certain immediate measures can and must be taken. First of all, we must emulate our counterparts in the West and start combing the universities here and abroad for the youth with potential ability for leadership, bring them here, and put them under the grinding mill of experience. With sympathetic supervision they could give surprisingly good results.

Secondly we must make our organization and the present staff mobile. The members of the staff need to be rotated in various departments of a bank, and infused with various experience of banking and with a sense of responsibility. Only then can the potential leader be detected and attended to.

Thirdly, refresher courses must be designed for branch managers before they are assigned to higher responsibilities, and regular seminars and conferences arranged whereby the managers of various levels and even regions can discuss and become articulate about their problems.

The staff themselves must, furthermore, be encouraged to look for ways and means of improving the institutions in which they work. This will provide some means of measuring the initiative and the intellectual agility of the individual member of the staff.

Fourthly, and in connection with what I just said, the recently established Institute for Banking Studies must be strengthened and supported. Full use must be made of its facilities. Bank Melli, Bank Sepah and Bank Markazi who sponsored this Institute welcome the cooperation of other banks in its further development.

In respect to what I have been saying, I need not emphasize the great need to strengthen the Bankers Association. A fully effective Association can do much for the member banks in the form of mutual exchange of information, providing training facility for their staffs, collecting essential economic data, as well as helping to set up an independent centre for pooling information about customers. It could, at the same time, be helpful in the smooth operation of the monetary policy in the country.

Going to a more general field while there is perhaps need for some consolidation of the present banking structure, there is also, I feel, a growing need for specialised credit institutions taking risks which ordinary commercial banks should avoid. Furthermore, a specialised bank can gain extensive knowledge in a given field and, therefore, provide a much better service to a customer operating in that field. It is too much to expect a general commercial bank to be able to provide expert services in every field. What is more, specialised bank can exercise a better control over what happens to the loans and credits which it extends to the borrower. Once a happy working relationship is established between general commercial banks and the specialised institutions, then we can look forward to making an effective and helpful service available to the community.

Here, I should like, for further consideration, to air one or two suggestions. Think for a moment of how much simpler the task of a banker and his clients would be if say the existing banks created a specialised credit institution for providing working capital to industry. Another line for further study would be the savings and loan Association or Building Societies. In this way, considerable savings would be mobilized and the thirst for home ownership better satisfied. Another feature of the recent years has been the development of installment purchase on the so called never-never basis, and there may be room for institutions in the form of hire-purchase or sales finance companies.

Earlier in this talk I made a remark to the effect that we all can be only the products of our environment. I must add, however, that each society, in its urge for survival, always produces a few heretics who cannot accept their immediate conditions and occasionally a rare one among them heralds a wave of the future. Let the banker know that he is somewhat of a heretic and his very habit of thought today is out of tune with the more traditional attitudes of this society.

Not only our very concept of time differs—every minute counts for us—but we realize, perhaps more deeply than any other section of population, that it is profitable to invest in the future. This we have learned and taken for granted in our profession. It must be learnt by our society.

66

Israel's Drive for Social Integration, Observations by Prime Minister Levi Eshkol, 1964 *

Prime Minister Eshkol identifies the integration of Israel's disparate population as "perhaps the most serious domestic problem the State has to tackle." The Jewish population is split into the Sabras (native-born Israelis), immigrants from various parts of Europe, and immigrants from various sections of the Arab Middle East. The conflict of values and customs between the modern, Western-oriented community and the traditional, Oriental communities is deep and is reflected in the significantly lower living standard and opportunities available to the Orientals; indeed, de facto segregation exists in some localities. The government is relying mainly upon education—both junior and adult—to grapple with the problem. Moreover, the large Arab minority that existed before the June 1967 war was reinforced by the hundrds of thousands of Arab inhabitants that came under Israeli rule in the West bank of Jordan, the Gaza strip, and Syria after that conflict. The socio-political and economic problems presented by Israel's Arab minority challenge the ingenuity of Israeli political imagination. The context within which Israel's social development is taking place is determined in large part by the opportunities made available through continued economic progress. Although Israel is a more modern country than its Arab neighbors it is still a transitional state that has yet to achieve full national integration and, as in the rest of the Middle East, religion plays an important unifying (and occasionally a disruptive) role.

*   *   *

Next year will mark an historic occurrence: by aliya [i.e., immigration] and natural increase our population will pass 2.5 million and begin to move toward its third million. This means a fresh effort for us all, but it will make it possible to settle unpopulated and undeveloped areas.

New agricultural settlement will be guided mainly to the north—to Galilee. In the heart of Galilee, barren areas must be redeemed. A long-term plan of development is envisaged, establishing new settlements, enlarging Nazareth, Ma'alot and Carmiel, all on a foundation of fruit orchards and export crops, crafts and manu-

* *Israel Government Year Book 5724* (1963-64) (Jerusalem: Central Office of Information, 1964), 12-14.

facturing, vacation resorts, and services to the Arab and Jewish inhabitants of the area.

Here stony fields must be cleared, terraces laid out, the soil prepared and roads built to make outlying areas accessible. New ways of cultivation suited to local conditions must be found.

There is more to it than economic planning. There is a social and ideological significance. Perhaps it is no accident that we begin just when the "Year of the Pioneers" ends, the eighty-fifth anniversary of the founding of Petach Tikva. In those days, in that colony and its sister-colonies, the cry was heard: "To Galilee!" The response charted the map of the State. Today we renew the call. The development of Galilee, the founding of co-operative settlements there, is a challenge to our youth, from town and countryside. Let them take the task upon themselves!

If we can make the North bloom again, we shall do much to better the lives of all who dwell in it. They will enjoy the finest of services the State can offer its citizens, in education and health, in water, electricity and communications, in employment and in economic development. The new settlers will break down barriers and promote inter-communal understanding among Jews, Arabs, Druzes and Circassians, newcomers and veterans.

Indeed, the plan as a whole is a link in the chain of our measures to integrate our minorities absolutely into every sphere of the State's life and activity.

The minorities are also, indeed primarily, involved in all we do, but they cannot simply make demands upon the State. They—particularly their intelligentsia and their youth—must come to a far-reaching and irrevocable decision of the spirit, to identify themselves with the State, to link their lives and future with it. If they so decide in sincerity, the people, the Government and its policy will be radiantly and finally influenced. Arab youth and intellectuals must strive to elevate the standard and status of their fellows. They can be a bridge between the two peoples. That is what we expect of them.

A growing aliya has begun from the New World, especially Latin America, and other strong, living links between Jews in the West and ourselves were forged. Congresses, conferences and reunions, mounting tourism, bring tens of thousands of overseas Jews into intimate contact with the State. Our needs, on the one hand, and the situation of Diaspora Jewry, on the other, justify a supreme endeavour to make the rapport more intense, to bring to Israel, in their thousands, enlightened young Jews who will be willing and able to settle here and share in the rebuilding. The Zionist and other bodies connected with Israel must be fortified with a spirit of personal pioneering and all its obligations. We must spread a knowledge of Hebrew and Jewish history, educating a generation of newcomers, builders and settlers. The Jewish Agency must widen the scope of its activities in this area, and the Government will stand by it to help it.

We have travelled part of the way towards integration of aliya and the Ingathering of Exiles, but not far enough. There is still a wide gap, the legacy of time, dividing territorial origins. The Government and the public must concentrate their energies upon closing the gap.

It cannot be done in a year or so, but we can and must hasten the process. Education is the most effective instrument for fostering true equality. In recent years, our investments in advancing the education of groups in need of special attention have been multiplied. About a quarter of the country's elementary school pupils, more than a hundred thousand, go to schools where they are given preferential treatment to bring them up to the level of knowledge of other pupils. Teacher training his been intensified: about two thousand teachers in these schools are advised and helped by educational experts. The Ministry of Education has drawn up a plan to apply parallel methods of teaching in all underprivileged classes, and this should even up all the pupils educationally. This year, about twenty thousand children will have a 'long school day', twelve extra hours of teaching and guidance a week; and a 'long school year' with an additional month of studies is contemplated. Thirty thousand pupils get free auxiliary lessons, and the number will increase. All the schools have been assisted to abolish classes whose enrollment is above the national norm, to provide teaching aids for pupils and classes, and to form culture and study groups.

More than fourteen thousand children of three and four years of age go to free kindergartens. The standards of secondary schooling are being developed by teacher training, extra hours of study, rooms for study, libraries and laboratories. A secondary boarding-school exists for gifted children of the Oriental communities, so that they can develop their talents to the utmost.

The Government intends to expand its efforts to close the cultural gap between the communities, and afford equal opportunities to every child.

Education in school, however, is not the whole answer. We must unify all social elements and bring oldtimers into harmony with new arrivals, our sabras with immigrants from Europe and Africa, from Asia and America. To contrive communal schisms, or to heighten contrasts, slows down and obstructs the process of fusion and endangers national unity and solidarity. I think people have begun to see the truth of that, as local government elections in many places have shown, with an overwhelming majority of voters giving their allegiance to national parties and not to the factions that try to exploit communal separatism. But the problem has not been solved; it is perhaps the most serious domestic problem the State has to tackle, and we shall do all that we can to speed a solution.

67

A Summary of Change, a Contemporary Study of a Turkish Village *

It is fitting to close this work with the following selection, for the mass of Middle Easterners are still agricultural villagers. Change, although nowhere near so dramatic as that which has altered the urban scene, has begun to affect village life in the Middle East. The main reason for this is the fact that the walls of isolation and ignorance that traditionally shut off and, to some extent protected, the village from the outside world have been breached. Often, market roads now lead to the local provincial seat. Radio broadcasts from the capital and beyond—and in a few instances, television—disturbs the calm of the evening and brings news of the outside. Also, the state educational system is beginning to spread its tentacles into the rural countryside. Moreover, many young men are pulled out of the village for a time when they are conscripted; often, they receive literacy training in service too. Indeed, the article which appears below is itself a measure of village change for it was based upon a survey conducted in large part by secondary students from areas adjacent to the central Anatolian village being described. Still, the distance that the average Middle Easterner has yet to travel to become an essentially modern person, rather than one animated by an amalgam of new and old attitudes, is clearly drawn.

*　　　　*　　　　*

1. LOCATION OF THE VILLAGE

Keçiller is a village in the northwest, 22.7 kilometers from Dumlupinar Station on the Afyon and Usak railway. From the administrative standpoint it is in the boundaries of Kutahya and the town of Altıntaş. It is 28 kilometers from the Yildirim Kemal Station, with which it is in close touch as we shall explain later.

2. BACKGROUND

There is no precise information on the history of the village. It has been said that it dates back 500 or 600 years. The village was burned by Greek troops during the Wars of Independence [1920] and was then rebuilt.

* Cavit Orhan Tütengil, "A Study of the Village of Keçiller," *Sosyoloji Dergisi 1955-1956* (Sociological Journal) (Istanbul: The Faculty Press, 1956), translated from the Turkish by Sevgi Alkar, Hoover Institution, under auspices of the Center for Near Eastern and North African Studies, University of Michigan, Ann Arbor.

The name "Keçiller" has no meaning today. According to village elders it was the name of a tribe, and probably it was "Keçililer" [meaning "owner of goats"]. The suffix "ler" at the end of the name of the village strengthens the assumption that the first settlers of the village were a tribe.

The village is located between the Kiziltas [Redstone] River, and the slope of the hills north of the river. . . .

The soil around the village is sandy towards the river bed, and limsetone on the hill slopes. Most of the fields are in the eastern direction. Around the river bank there are vegetable fields, fruit orchards, and mills.

Keçiller is in the administrative boundaries of the town of Altintas 38 kilometers away. The villages close to it are Oysu, in the west; and Allioren and Çalkoy in the east. (The Dumlupinar memorial is located near this [last] village.) In the north there is Abya, in the south Yűglűk, in the southeast are the Kűçűk Aslihan villages.

It is estimated that the village of Keçiller is about 1500 meters above sea level. [4950 feet].

3. BUILDINGS

There are three different types of buildings in the village: earthen-roofed, wood, and adobe. All the houses are two stories high and look towards the south. The earthen-roofed houses seem to be steadily decreasing; at present most of the houses are of wood, but now stone and adobe are used in building. The proximity of the forests (1-5 kilometers) increases the use of wood in the building of village homes. There are no galvanized tin-covered houses in the village. The first floor of the house is used for keeping animals, or as storage space. Some houses have separate stables.

The village mosque is built completely of stone and covered with a tile roof. Next to it is a tall minaret and a small cemetery. This was the only building left standing when the village was burned down at the time of enemy invasion.

The other buildings that serve the village generally are the village school and the laundry. The laundry is located on the banks of the river and is used collectively by the villagers. There are no coffee houses in the village. Instead, the village "guest houses" and the grocery stores take the place of coffee houses. The villagers explain the lack of coffee houses by saying that: a) coffee houses cause laziness, b) they are morally harmful to village youths for they encourage them to play and gamble, and c) coffee and tea are unnecessary expenses for the villagers.

The guest houses are rooms which belong to the well-to-do families of the village. Out of town visitors are welcomed as guests in the guest rooms, as well as some of the peasants who gather there by invitation. The guest rooms are passed from father to son. Here coffee and tea are served without charge by the owner of the guest house to the people present in the room. The council of village elders meets in one of these rooms.

In addition the police guard and the regional forestry directorate have established headquarters in the village.

4. Population

According to the 1950 census the population of the village of Keçiller was 725. At that time there were 123 buildings in the village. Today [1956] the number of houses has increased to 131. It is estimated that the population has likewise increased.

5. Non-Agricultural Occupations

There are four mills located on the Kiziltas River. Three of these mills belong the agas [chiefs] of Kűtahya, and one to a villager. The mills owned by the agas are leased for the year. Neither the rent of the mills nor the charges for grinding are paid in money, rather they are paid in grain. The annual rent for one of these mills is 350 ayar [175 bushels]. (An ayar of grain is measured with a big gasoline can.) The miller receives "hakla" for his service, which is one-twentieth of the grain to be ground. Each peasant gives "hakla" to the miller.

The number of permanent grocery stores in the village has increased from two to three this year. In the village grocery stores, there is everything from elastic shoes to dyes, mint candy to salt—all of which is needed by the peasants. Along with money, eggs and grains are used as a medium of exchange.

The village has in it a tailor, a tinker, a cobbler, and an ironsmith. There are also public servants who are paid collectively by all the villagers. These are the imam [the religious teacher], the property-guard, the shepherd, and the village barber. Besides his religious services, the village imam teaches a Kur'an course and theology to the village children. [He directs all religious ceremonies, fetes, deaths, and marriages. Religious marriage is not recognized according to the civil law.] We were interested to note that the services performed by the village barber are enjoyed by all the members of the village free of charge. His fees are paid annually by all the village residents in an amount of grain previously decided upon by all the peasants.

Those who serve the rich villagers for money are called *"bekâr."* In other parts of Turkey, they are called under the names of *hizmetkar, uşak, tutma, irgat* ... etc. The wages of *"bekâr"* are paid annually.

About ten families in the village earn their living by making charcoal and preparing furniture wood. They also have land, but it does not provide for their needs.

The most important occupation of the village men, outside of agriculture, is work in the nearby mines. The mining camp called Bozsivri Lignyit Coal Mines, is located about 14.3 kilometers northwest of the village of Keçiller.

The daily wage of a worker in this mine averages between three to six Turkish liras. In these mines the quality of coal is very good. Not one of the peasants works at the mines as a permanent employee. During harvest time, the mine operators find it difficult to get workers. But sometimes in winter months the mines work on three shifts, three 8-hour work shifts. In summer, by contrast, the mines are operated with fewer workers and one shift.

Bozsivri Lignyit Coal Mines produces three to five thousand tons of coal every year. Workers work under bad working conditions. The mines utilize outdated machinery. During summer and autumn when the roads are good for truck transportation, coal is transported by truck through Keçiller to Yildirim Kemal station and from there it is distributed to large cities by train.

Last year very good quality lignyit coal veins were discovered near the village of Oysu and mining operations have been started.

6. AGRICULTURAL OCCUPATIONS

The principal activity in the village is farming. Although there are no landless families in the village, there are some families whose land will not provide enough for their living expenses. Wheat and barley are the principal grains grown. Every year half of the land is left fallow to prepare it for sowing the next year. Which lands will be left fallow is decided according to long-established traditions. Oxen are used to pull the plow. There are no tractors in the village. The light plow is slowly losing its place to the heavy plow. At the end of the harvesting season, the harvested grain is carried to the threshing area. The threshing places are not decided at random, but according to the established traditions of three groups in the village. A system of collaboration [imece] is used in threshing the grain. It is worth investigation whether this system brought the threshing areas closer, or whether the system was born because the threshing areas were already close. There are three distinct cooperative threshing groups in the village. The system of imece is not found among all the peasants as a whole, but among the members of these three groups.

Oxen are usually used for plowing and threshing. Women work as much as the men in farming. Very few people use horses in agriculture. There are no motorized vehicles in the village, and ox-carts are used for every sort of work. There are only five horse-drawn carriages in the village and women are frequently seen helping push the heavily loaded ox-carts carrying the grain to the threshing areas at harvest time.

Very few families in the village of Keçiller make their living by raising livestock. The shortage of grazing land and the long winters make livestock raising difficult. As a result, the number of goats and sheep is decreasing each year.

Oxen, mules and horses are kept in the village. Ducks, geese, turkeys, and chickens are among the most popular poultry animals. Hunting is decreasing. Moreover, it is argued that the dust and smog caused by the coal transporting trucks has decreased the number of bees and has therefore contributed to further spoiling of the grazing land.

There are no vineyards in the village. Fruit and vegetable production is minor —the early winter frost retards the full ripening of these crops. After grain, beans are the most plentiful crop and they play a very important part in the economic life of the village. The beans of this region are famous, and although they are not used much by the villagers, they are sold as dried beans in surrounding towns and cities.

7. Developments in the Economic Life of the Village

We mentioned above that there were no coffee houses—"loafer institutions" as they are called in sociological language—in the village. We also mentioned that the barber was hired collectively for the year, and that the silversmith and tinker were travelling artisans. Since there is no butcher in the village, no animal is butchered just to provide meat to eat. After recalling that the sales in the grocery stores are made by barter, let us explain the conditions that brought about this system:

A. From an economic point of view, the village is what one might call "introverted," since it is unable to transport goods or to maintain communication over its roads with the surrounding territories throughout the entire year. Furthermore, it does not produce many goods which bring money into the village.

B. Economic institutions first appear as itinerant institutions [the travelling tradesmen]. Here, the exchange value of goods and services usually return in the form of goods and not money. Traditions weigh heavy in the organization of economic relations; for this reason the same economy tends to persist in the village.

C. On the other hand, the wages of the laborers working at the coal mines are paid in money. This tends to create a money economy alongside the barter economy, and is helped along by the passage of coal-carrying trucks through the village on the way to the Yildirim Kemal Station, thus connecting the village with other markets.

D. Tending to delay transformation to the money economy from the barter economy are the established customs (such as the non-payment of money for tea and coffee, and the payment of the barber's services annually in the form of goods). In the snack shop of the Lignyit Coal Company many things can be bought for money. However, no coffee and tea are available, and probably there has been no need felt for them.

The increase in the number of grocery stores in the past year, the existence of a variety of goods in the grocery store, and the existence of some kinds of artisans, even though they are travelling, should be counted as signs of economic development in the village economic life.

8. The Problems of Health

Until a few years ago the village was in a syphilis-fighting region, but at present there are no persons with this disease left in the village. There are toilets in the village houses but they are not connected with a closed sewage pool [cesspool], and run in the open and mix with the fertilizers. Since wood is obtainable for heating and burning, dung is not used frequently for that purpose, but it is used as fertilizer. This is responsible for the increase of black flies which are numerous and make life uncomfortable, and no preventive measures are taken against them.

Village roads are dirty and dusty and have a miserable appearance filled with domestic fowls, dogs and children. Water accumulations by the river cause malaria. We learned as a result of our investigation that health officers have never visited the village. Fortunately there has been no epidemic other than a few seasonal illnesses. The water used in the village is provided by the river. In addition there are four water fountains in the village. It does not seem strange to the people that while the clothes are being washed and animals drink upstream, people drink water from the lower stream.

9. Education in the Village

The first school in Keçiller was opened in 1941, with one rural school instructor. In 1943 a teacher was appointed and the school building which is still in use was built. Now the education in the village continues with five grades and one teacher.

The villagers are not very interested in the school for several reasons. Graduation from this elementary school does not have social prestige and the old system of religious education still continues. Girls are kept away from the school because of conservatism. Many families expect their children to help them in all sorts of ways, and keep their children at home on this ground.

In the year 1952-53 the number of children registered in school was 88, of which 57 were male and 31 were female. In the following year, there were 176 children of school age (7-14) in the village; of these 89 were male and 87 female. Not counting three of the girls who were married, and one disabled child, 172 were expected to attend the school. Only 68 of these registered in school, 39 boys and 29 girls.

The following table shows their distribution according to their grades in school:

Grades	Boys	Girls	Total
I	18	20	38
II	12	5	17
III	4	2	6
IV	5	2	7
V	—	—	—

The village of Keçiller does not have telephone communications with the sur-rounding villages, and with Dumlupinar, Yildirim Kemal Station, Sahinkaya Fire Tower, and the town of Altintas, and through it to the cities of Afyon and Kütahya. The regional establishment of the police station and the forest ranger's office provide these facilities.

Record players and radios (4 of them battery operated) are not unknown to the peasants. Nobody, including the teacher, regularly reads a newspaper.

10. RELIGIOUS LIFE

Along with the mosque, religious instruction and theology are the focal point of village life. However, it is understood that the village youths do not patronize the mosque. During the time of heavy work the *imam* frequently performs the divine service all by himself.

In the village the practice of religion has taken on the form of mere outward piety. Religion has now become little more than a dead and rigid form. It does not influence the spirit of the people, and thus lacks the force to form moral and ethical qualities in human relations. Relations between men and women are com-plicated and obscure, and are difficult to equate with the practice of morality. At present there does not seem to be much polygamy. However, a form of adulter-ous life, screened behind religious marriage, is widespread.

One hodja [religious teacher] who collaborated with the Greeks during the [Turkish] Wars of Independence has made a pilgrimage to Mecca. The teaching of the Koran courses has been continued in spite of the elementary public educa-tion. However, there is a lack of continued interest, and the number of those who learn to recite the Koran is very small.

11. POLITICAL PARTY CONFLICTS

It is interesting to note that the multiparty system, a sign of political democracy, has encouraged the existing village interest groups or opposing factions to take sides in different parties without serious reason.

For a stranger to the village, the difference between the three factions are hard to understand. At present these three factions are shielded behind the political party flags: C.H.P. (Peoples' Republican Party), C.M.P. (People's Nationalist Party), and D.P (Democratic Party) which are in constant conflict. The strange thing is that not one of the three parties has established any organization in the village. In spite of this, each of the parties has leaders and advisers in the village. In our opinion, the results of the general elections [for the members of the Turkish Grand National Assembly] on May 2, 1954, did not give a true picture of the relative strength of these parties in the village. But it is a fact that those under the flag of D.P. are quite strong, those behind C.H.P. should not be underestimated, and although the muhtar left D.P. in favor of C.M.P., those behind the latter are still in the minority.

There were 321 people who voted. Of these D.P. received 226, C.H.P. received 61 and C.M.P. received 31, making a total of 318. (Two of the ballots bore signatures and one envelope had ballots of all three parties; therefore these were not counted.)

The fact that the conflict which appears as a political party conflict conceals the real sources of dispute between the village factions is one of the sobering aspects in considering multiparty life in Turkey. Fortunately, it appears that this relationship in the village of Keçiller is not too unfriendly and not too rigid.

12. Human Relations

To understand this subject it is necessary first to study the relations between men and women, between the same sexes, existing groups and social classes.

In men-women relationships, women are subordinate to men. They have no outdoor activities in common except harvesting. After the harvest is done, men sit in the grocery store or the guest room and women do the house work. Outside of harvesting, men and women do not collaborate. The relations among women are normal, neighborly relationships.

In the village, weddings, collaboration at harvesting, and the celebration of *bayram* (national or religious fetes) are generally held separately by different groups. On holidays the different groups, represented by the different guest rooms, gather to eat the morning meal. Not everyone in the village can enter these guest rooms; one has to be "in"; one must attain a certain status to be accepted by a group; and one must be a member of the group of the owner of the guest house.

Social classes are divided according to wealth and social functions in the village. The groups in the village conform to this division. For example, the group (X) of agas relies on wealth. The muhtar's group is based on administrative authority. The third and most numerous group is that of the *Efe* (braves) and *Kabaday* (braggarts or bullies). The relationship between these groups is not open friendliness but subtle hostility. Thus, damage to an enemy is not to his person, but to his property (his crops, harvest, animals, vegetable gardens, fruit trees, etc.). Cutting the tendons of the rear legs of an ox, stepping on sown fields, destroying fruit orchards, and the like are among daily occurrences in the village. During a night in August of 1954, while we were doing this research, one of the mills in the village was set on fire by the enemies of the miller. The fire was detected in time and extinguished, but it can be said that property owners in the village are perpetually uneasy.

The relations of strangers with the villagers differ with the different groups in the village. The members of the groups with whom the guest is staying [do their best to make the visitor welcome], pay the most attention, and try to help.

One other form of enmity of the groups appears in informing the regional forest ranger in case of illegal lumber smuggling by other groups. Usually these informings follow each other.

In general, men get married before they leave for military service. Those who attempt to get married after they return from military service are considered old and have difficulty finding a girl to marry.

Except for old women, all the young girls and married women of the village conceal themselves from men. Avoiding strangers is a carefully observed mode of behavior.

Young men, old men, and boys wear a hat which they call a "silindir." City people would call it a felt hat. They wear wool knee-length shorts and knee-high stockings. They are a talkative people. They do not hide the fact that they live disturbed lives; but they do not seem to be complaining very much about their conditions.